SCIENCE LEARNING AND INSTRUCTION

Everyone can learn science. How can science courses help learners refine their understanding of science topics by making science relevant to their lives? This book describes the knowledge integration approach to science teaching and learning and contrasts it with typical instruction that implements the absorption approach.

Science Learning and Instruction

- Synthesizes a large body of literature on knowledge integration patterns
- Illustrates the advantages of knowledge integration for lectures, experiments, dynamic and interactive visualizations, collaborative learning, and professional development
- Explains how students learn science and why their ideas are important
- Clarifies how teachers can guide students to become independent learners
- Shows curriculum developers and designers how to take advantage of technology to promote inquiry and understanding of science

Readers of this book will discover ways to improve science teaching as well as their own science learning. By viewing the many intuitive ideas that students develop to explain the natural world as a starting point, this book illustrates how science activities can lead to coherent understanding. The book shows how conducting hands-on and virtual experiments, interrogating scientific simulations, and collaborating with peers can contribute to lifelong learning. Instruction aimed at knowledge integration can empower everyone to take advantage of their natural curiosity about the world and explore the wonder of science.

Marcia C. Linn is a professor of development and cognition specializing in education in mathematics, science, and technology in the Graduate School of Education at the University of California, Berkeley.

Bat–Sheva Eylon is a professor at the Science Teaching Department at the Weizmann Institute of Science, Israel. She specializes in learning, instruction, and professional development of physics and science teachers. She holds the Chief Justice Bora Laskin Chair of Science Teaching.

SCIENCE LEARNING AND INSTRUCTION

Taking Advantage of Technology to Promote Knowledge Integration

Marcia C. Linn and Bat-Sheva Eylon

Routledge
Taylor & Francis Group

NEW YORK AND LONDON

First published 2011
by Routledge
711 Third Avenue, New York, NY 10017

Simultaneously published in the UK
by Routledge
2 Park Square, Milton Park, Abingdon, Oxon OX14 4RN

Routledge is an imprint of the Taylor & Francis Group, an informa business

© 2011 Taylor & Francis

The right of Marcia C. Linn and Bat-Sheva Eylon to be identified as authors of this work has been asserted by them in accordance with sections 77 and 78 of the Copyright, Designs and Patents Act 1988.

All rights reserved. No part of this book may be reprinted or reproduced or utilised in any form or by any electronic, mechanical, or other means, now known or hereafter invented, including photocopying and recording, or in any information storage or retrieval system, without permission in writing from the publishers.

Trademark Notice: Product or corporate names may be trademarks or registered trademarks, and are used only for identification and explanation without intent to infringe.

Library of Congress Cataloging-in-Publication Data
Linn, Marcia C.
  Science learning and instruction : taking advantage of technology to
  promote knowledge integration / Marcia C. Linn & Bat-Sheva Eylon.
  p. cm.
  1. Science—Study and teaching (Elementary) 2. Science—Study and teaching
  (Middle school) I. Eylon, Bat-Sheva. II. Title.
  LB1585.L54 2011
  372.35'044—dc22
  2010044380

ISBN13: 978–0–8058–6054–2 (hbk)
ISBN13: 978–0–8058–6055–9 (pbk)
ISBN13: 978–1–4106–1508–4 (ebk)

Typeset in Bembo by Swales & Willis Ltd, Exeter, Devon
Printed and bound in the United States of America on
acid-free paper by Sheridan Books, Inc.

To our parents:

George William Cyrog (1909–2007) and Frances Vanderhoof Cyrog (1914–1999), lifelong learners who inspired others to follow their example.

Joseph Grünfeld (1916–1985) and Sara Grünfeld (1922–1994) who survived the holocaust and continued to believe in the essential role of education in carving a better future for humankind.

CONTENTS

PREFACE

Everyone can learn science. Young children explore such complex tasks as redirecting streams or building bridges and towers. They observe and predict the behavior of butterflies and cats. They collect and organize twigs, stones, and shells. They test ideas about how best to combine vinegar and baking soda to blow the cap off a plastic container and compare techniques for throwing a ball into a basket or balancing on a beam. Science teachers are reminded of this natural curiosity when students ask why a topic is relevant or complain that they will never use anything they are learning again in their lives. Children desire to make sense of the world. Science courses can capitalize on this enthusiasm by making science relevant to the lives of students.

Evidence of efforts to understand scientific phenomena include the many intuitive ideas that students develop to explain the natural world. Based on the way metal objects feel in a typical classroom, many argue that metals are naturally cold—so they can keep things cold for a picnic. Others explain that twins are children who look like each other. Historically, people believed that the Earth was flat and that the Sun rotated around the Earth. These beliefs all stem from legitimate observations of the natural world. Students can refine their ideas by interrogating the situations where they arise or by using more sophisticated equipment. This process of forming intuitions and gathering evidence to refine them is essential for understanding science—and everyone does it. Science courses can capitalize on this kind of reasoning—and help learners refine their understanding of instructed topics.

In *Science Learning and Instruction* we describe the knowledge integration approach to science teaching and learning and contrast it with typical instruction that implements the absorption approach. This book is designed for classroom teachers, pre-service science methods courses, curriculum designers, software designers, research seminars, learning scientists, evaluators, and individuals who want to become lifelong science learners. The authors come from the United States and Israel and seek to place advances in the field in a broad context.

Users of the book will discover ways to improve teaching as well as their own science learning. Our goal is to empower everyone to take advantage of their natural curiosity about the world and explore the wonder of science.

The knowledge integration approach takes advantage of the desire of everyone to understand personally relevant scientific dilemmas such as how to make energy efficient choices, interpret persuasive messages about health decisions, or research alternatives for their own health care. It capitalizes on the abilities of everyone to gather and interpret evidence about scientific phenomena. The goal of knowledge integration instruction is to increase the coherence and accuracy of scientific understanding.

How Knowledge Integration Works

To illustrate the process of knowledge integration we discuss the idea held by many students that metals are naturally cold. A first step towards developing coherent understanding is to elicit the ideas students hold. These are the ideas that need to be integrated.

Periodically in this book, we insert questions in italics for readers to consider. These questions are designed to engage the reader in integrating ideas.

Take a few moments to think about heat and temperature in general and specifically about the temperature of metals. Jot down some of your ideas. Are heat and temperature the same? Are they different? Can you give some examples that help you answer the question?

When students explore the natural world they develop many ideas about science. For any science topic, learners have multiple ideas. They may think that heat and temperature are the same—because the terms can be used interchangeably in many sentences. They may also think they are different, explaining that you have a temperature when you are sick and use a thermometer to measure heat. They may believe that, for the thermometer, only the higher degrees represent heat. All of these ideas form what we call a repertoire of ideas.

Knowledge integration builds on the repertoire of ideas that learners develop to explain their observations. This approach takes advantage of all the diverse views held by students. Often ideas that reflect unique cultural or personal experiences help other class members think about a topic. For example, students who have wilderness experience might describe ways they have learned to protect themselves from frostbite. Students might demonstrate family cooking practices used to keep foods hot. The knowledge integration approach to science instruction respects all the ideas students bring to science class while at the same time motivating every student to really analyze the meaning of their observations and experiences.

All students can develop an identity of themselves as a science learner when they build on their own ideas. Knowledge integration strengthens students confidence in their ability to learn science by ensuring continuity between the ideas they have already constructed and the new ideas presented in science class. To promote a coherent account of the topic, instruction based on knowledge integration adds new ideas and encourages students to integrate the new ideas with their existing ideas.

Think about the example where the student remarked that metal is naturally cold. How could a teacher help the student understand their observation that metals feel cold? Should the teacher give a lecture? Do an experiment? Give students an idea to explore?

Designing ideas to add to the repertoire is complicated. If the new ideas are confusing or obscure they may be ignored—or memorized for the next test. But they will not become part of coherent understanding of the topic. Instructors need to add ideas that students can link and connect to their own ideas. Ultimately students need to distinguish among their ideas and the new ones added to the mix.

New ideas that help students make sense of their own varied ideas often come from the testing of potential ideas with students or from observing talented teachers. In this book we report on ways we have tested ideas to determine which ones really help students form more coherent views of science.

For example, for those students who think that metal is naturally cold, we ask them to consider their experiences with metal on a hot day at the beach or in the summer on the slide at the playground. Adding the notion that metal feels really hot under these circumstances often helps students refine their view that metals are naturally cold. For example, they might notice that metals are sometimes surprisingly cold and on other occasions quite hot. This idea might stimulate students to wonder why metal feels different from other materials.

To extend the example, teachers have often found it successful to encourage students to compare the way metal and wood feel on a hot day and in a cool room. Students can also test their ideas by using a thermometer to measure the temperature of objects in the same room. Comparing alternative ideas can spur students to reinterpret their observation that metals feel cold. This approach has the potential to help students coalesce some of their ideas about heat and temperature.

In many classes, instead of introducing the example about metal and wood on a hot day at the playground and in the classroom, the instructor might give a lecture about thermal equilibrium. Distinguish between these two approaches. What is the difference between them? How do instructors who lecture view learners? How do those who ask students to make sense of a new idea view learners?

Helping students distinguish between their scientific ideas requires adding new ideas but this is only the beginning. Students need to distinguish among the new ideas, their ideas, and perhaps other ideas that occur to them. To make sound decisions they need to use scientific evidence. In the case of metal and wood, students might explore a visualization showing the rate of heat flow in different materials. They might conduct experiments to measure the temperature of objects that feel differently.

Reflect on the process of knowledge integration. How did you distinguish among your original ideas and the ones that you added while reading this? How might students distinguish among their ideas? How would you know that the ideas have become more coherent?

When students gather evidence to make sense of the ideas in their repertoire and distinguish ideas they add links and connections among their views. To consolidate these ideas students need to reflect on their experiences and come up with a synthesis. They might write a coherent argument, make a poster to explain the situation, or write a persuasive letter to someone who thinks metals are naturally cold.

Assessments of knowledge integration capture this progress. Assessments ask students questions like, *What is the difference between heat and temperature?* They require students to give evidence to support their answer. High scores on knowledge integration assessments indicate that students can support the links among their ideas with evidence and express coherent ideas.

How Absorption Works

This book compares the knowledge integration approach to science learning to the absorption approach. Rather than building on the curiosity and intuitions of learners, much of science instruction involves reading textbooks, listening to lectures, and conducting investigations by following a set of steps. These activities are based on a view of the learner absorbing the information transmitted. This view short circuits the knowledge integration process.

In *Science Learning and Instruction* we show that the absorption view motivates many designers, often based on the reasonable intuition that it took hundreds of years for scientists to develop current ideas, so they need to speed up the process. This book provides evidence that the absorption approach informs the design of textbooks, lectures, experiments, visualizations, and collaborative learning. The book shows that this approach generally fails—students learn very little from materials designed to transmit information.

When absorption fails, designers often hypothesize that students need more motivation to learn. This leads designers to add exciting elements to motivate learners such as startling photographs of man-eating plants, surprising explosions, or humorous anecdotes. These motivating elements often attract the attention of the learner—and may motivate students to come to class. We show that they can interfere with coherent understanding and do not help students learn science.

Instructors also often build on their intuition that students benefit from active learning. They add interactive features to science instruction to both motivate students and engage them in the scientific method. Interactive features may or may not contribute to coherent understanding. They could distract learners from reasoning about conundrums. Some experiments involve actively following a set of steps but do not add useful ideas to the repertoire.

The absorption view of the learner privileges information over coherence. It is consistent with the packing of the science standards with far too many topics. It is often used to justify multiple-choice tests that primarily measure recall.

Goals of Science Learning and Instruction

In *Science Learning and Instruction* we distinguish between absorption and knowledge integration. We offer evidence for the knowledge integration pattern. We show how it plays out in many aspects of instruction including lectures, experiments, visualizations, and collaborative learning. We show how knowledge integration can inform the design of professional development. We summarize the knowledge integration pattern in four processes and illustrate how these processes can be implemented in varied disciplines.

We illustrate these distinctions by comparing classroom activities, teacher roles, and assessment practices. We describe specific solutions for many science topics. Most of the science curricula that are used in this research are free and available as Web-based Inquiry Science Environment (WISE) units (see WISE. berkeley.edu).

Technology and Knowledge Integration

The knowledge integration approach to science learning emerged from decades of research conducted by both the authors. These programs benefitted from innovative uses of technology. The WISE learning environment allows researchers to vary the use of experiments, visualizations, collaborative activities, and assessments to investigate the most effective practices. WISE offers teachers and researchers continuous assessment information and multiple ways to interact with learners. In this research we identify promising uses of technology but also highlight insights that apply to all of science instruction.

In this book we illustrate some of the exciting opportunities technology offers. Consistent with the recent call for Cyberlearning from the National Science Foundation, we show ways that new networking and communication technologies can enhance science outcomes.

Lifelong Science Learning

It is disheartening to hear adults claim they have forgotten all they learned in science classes. The authors of this book find it particularly frustrating when they meet someone new who, upon learning that they are speaking with a science educator, quickly find a reason to escape. Sometimes, they first comment, *don't ask me anything*, and then vanish. We developed the knowledge integration approach to science learning to enable everyone to become a lifelong science learner—and enjoy conversations with science educators.

To promote lifelong learning we end each chapter with a *reflection activity*. These activities are intended to encourage individual reflection or to be discussion starters for classes and seminars using the book to improve science teaching and learning.

Using knowledge integration practices everyone can learn science—even from materials that are designed based on the absorption approach. We show how science instruction can prepare students to become lifelong science learners. We wish to inspire everyone to explore the fascinating and remarkable ideas of science. Our goal is to help everyone enjoy satisfying lives informed by scientific ideas.

ACKNOWLEDGMENTS

We could not have completed this book or the research it synthesizes without the invaluable help of many individuals and groups. Words are not sufficient to capture the many contributions and supports that made this book possible.

We benefitted from the stunning contribution of Suparna Kudesia who coordinated the production of the manuscript, provided thoughtful hints to keep us on track, constantly encouraged us, and subtly guided our work. We appreciate help with figures, boxes, and text from Jon Breitbart and David Crowell.

We are grateful to Naomi Silverman, our editor at Routledge (and before that at Lawrence Erlbaum Associates), who has supported this project over many substantial revisions and reformulations. Naomi's unwavering enthusiasm and encouragement was essential to the success of the book.

National Science Foundation

We want to especially thank our program officers at the National Science Foundation for their guidance, support, and encouragement. Much of the work reported here was conducted by the Technology-Enhanced Learning in Science (TELS) Center for Learning and Teaching. We have benefitted from the insights of our recent program officers including John "Spud" Bradley, John Cherniavsky, Janice Earle, Michael Haney, and Gerhard Salinger. Barbara Olds and Nora Sabelli shaped the projects leading up to TELS. We especially want to thank our first program officers Ray Hannapal and Andrew Molnar who cared greatly about how technology could impact on science learning and motivated us to seek more and better ways to use technology to address educational challenges.

This work was partially supported by the following NSF grants: DRL-0334199, The Educational Accelerator: Technology Enhanced Learning in Science (TELS);

ESI-0455877, Mentored and Online Development of Educational Leaders for Science (MODELS); ESI-708778, Logging Opportunities in Online Programs for Science (LOOPS); DRL-0822388, Cumulative Learning Using Embedded Assessment Results (CLEAR); and DRL-0918743, Visualizing to Integrate Science Understanding for All Learners (VISUAL). Any opinions, findings, and conclusions or recommendations expressed in this material are those of the author(s) and do not necessarily reflect the views of the National Science Foundation.

Bellagio Center

We are very grateful to the Rockefeller Foundation for funding our residency at the Bellagio Center. We were able to establish the structure and main argument for this book while in residence there. We also thank the other residents for insightful conversations, stimulating presentations, and marvelous musical performances.

Center for Advanced Study in the Behavioral Sciences

Linn did initial work leading to this book while on sabbatical at the Center for Advanced Study in the Behavioral Sciences. Linn especially thanks the center leaders including director Doug McAdam and associate director Bob Scott. Colleagues in the Memory Group inspired and sustained thinking about learning and instruction. Linn is also grateful for the opportunity to finalize the manuscript at CASBS and to benefit from the encouragement and leadership of Iris Litt.

Teachers, Administrators, and Students

We especially thank the many administrators, teachers, and students from our participating schools. Over 40,000 students, 400 teachers, and 50 principals have collaborated to improve science learning. By participating in knowledge integration curriculum design, teaching, and learning they shaped the knowledge integration framework and ensured its widespread applicability.

TELS Participants

TELS succeeded because of the fabulous participants who collaborated to create curriculum, assessments, professional development, classroom investigations, methodologies, research reports, and theoretical insights. We appreciate the contributions of the post-doctoral scholars including Stephanie Corliss, Libby Gerard, Hee Sun Lee, Kevin McElhaney, Jacquie Madhok, Kihyun Kelly Ryoo, Ji Shen, Vanessa Svihla, Keisha Varma, and Michelle Williams. We are grateful to the doctoral students for their fresh insights, informative investigations, and willingness to analyze complex evidence from investigations. Graduate students included Andy Carle, Janet Casperson, Jennie Chiu, Paul Daubenmeir,

Tamar Fuhrmann, Tara Higgins, Jennifer King Chen, Colleen Lewis, Lydia Liu, Cheryl Madeira, Kevin McElhaney, David Miller, Elissa Sato, Michelle Shaver Sinapuelas, Stephanie Sisk-Hilton, Beat Schwendimann, Hillary Swanson, Erika Tate, Tammie Visintainer, and Helen Zhang. We benefitted from outstanding students from the masters and credential program including Mandy Bliss, Patty Holman, Alton Lee, Paul Mazzei, Elissa Stone, and Lindsay Wells.

We appreciate the creative designs from the technology group who imagined, prototyped, tested, and refined WISE, often with vague and confusing guidance from the other partners. Technology group members include Jonathan Lim-Breitbart, Geoffrey Kwan, Patrick Lawler, Tony Perritano, and Hiroki Terashima.

The TELS project was managed by the incredible Freda Husic who established practices that immeasurably enhanced our work. She ensured that participating teachers and schools could succeed and that all the participants had a voice in the decision making. Subsequent projects were managed by the amazing Kathy Benemann who coordinated with new schools and teachers and streamlined project communication.

The Science Teaching Department at Weizmann

Over the years, members of the science teaching department at the Weizmann Institute of Science have contributed substantially to Eylon's research and development activities investigating knowledge integration in science. Esther Bagno, a life-long friend and collaborator, made invaluable contributions to conceptualizing and designing knowledge integration activities for students and teachers in high school physics. Uri Ganiel provided continued support and contributions. The fruitful collaboration with Miki Ronen enabled research and development on knowledge integration in technology enhanced environments both in the area of optics learning and in the use of such environments to enhance collaboration in learning. Some of the first studies concerning micro-macro relationships in chemistry were initiated in the early eighties by Ruth Ben-Zvi and Judith Silberstein from the chemistry group, and paved the way to many research and development activities both in Israel and abroad. The contribution of Zahava Scherz in extending the work on knowledge integration to junior high school has been invaluable. All this work was carried out with very able doctoral students of the department: Hanna Berger, Liora Bialer, Osnat Eldar, Yael Kali, Shulamit Kapon, Dorothy Langley, Hannah Margel, Roni Mualem, Ornit Spector-Levy and Edith Yerushalmi. All are now accomplished professionals in different institutions in Israel who continue to contribute to this work.

Springer Science and Business Media

Data for a portion of Figure 10.3 (year 1) was used with kind permission from Springer Science and Business Media: *Journal of Science Education and Technology* (volume 17, issue 4, 2008), Targeted Support for Using Technology-Enhanced Science Inquiry Modules, Table 3, page 349, by Keisha Varma, Freda Husic, and Marcia C. Linn.

Reviewers

We very much appreciate the excellent comments on earlier drafts of the chapters that we received from a wide range of colleagues and collaborators. The reviewers of the chapters included: Joe Campione, Hsin-Yi Chang, Jennie Chiu, Mike Clancy, Doug Clark, Libby Gerard, Sherry Hsi, Jennifer King Chen, Doug Kirkpatrick, Camillia Matuk, Kevin McElhaney, Kihyun Kelly Ryoo, Elissa Sato, Jim Slotta, Vanessa Svihla, Keisha Varma, and Helen Zhang. We especially thank Jim Slotta who helped us shape our message.

Colleagues

We both thank Fred Reif, a pioneer in the study of knowledge integration; A study that turned into a life-long journey for both of us.

In developing the ideas in this book we interviewed many colleagues and friends. We especially thank Robert Bjork, Allan Collins, Andy diSessa, Rick Duschl, John Gilbert, Jim Greeno, Jon Osborne, Roy Pea, Fred Reif, Lauren Resnick, and Alan Schoenfeld for discussing the trajectory of the field with us.

We appreciate the many insightful and thoughtful comments and contributions from all of the TELS partners. The participating institutions and leaders were Jane Bowyer, Mills College; Raj Chaudhary, Auburn University; Doug Clark, Arizona State University; Chris Hoadley, New York University; Beverly Jones, North Carolina Central University; Yael Kali, the Technion; Robert Tinker, Concord Consortium.

We appreciate the comments critiques, and supports provided by the advisory boards that guided TELS and related research. Advisors included Jane Bowyer, Mills College; Derek Briggs, University of Colorado, Boulder; Michelene Chi, Arizona State University; Doug Clark, Vanderbilt; Marilyn Decker, Boston Public Schools; Susan Goldman, University of Illinois, Chicago; Louis Gomez, Northwestern; Mary Hegarty, UC, Santa Barbara; Paul Holland, ETS; Sherry Hsi, Lawrence Hall of Science, UC Berkeley; Yael Kali, Technion, Israel Institute of Technology; Eammon Kelly, George Washington; Rich Lehrer, Peabody College, Vanderbilt University; Min Li, University of Washington, Seattle; Xiaodong Lin, Teachers College, Columbia; Jim Minstrell, Facet Innovations; Trish Morse, University of Washington; Nora Newcombe, Temple; Roy Pea, Stanford; Jim Pellegrino, University of Illinois, Chicago; Senta Raizen, WestEd; Brian Reiser, Northwestern; Mitch Resnick, MIT; Nora Sabelli, SRI; Nancy Songer, University of Michigan; Elisa Stone, UC Berkeley; Barbara Tversky,

Stanford; David Uttal, Northwestern; Uri Wilensky, Northwestern. We especially thank Roy Pea who served as the Chair of the TELS board.

Family

Last, but not least, we are grateful to our loving families who encouraged and supported us in the various stages of working on this book.

1

INTRODUCTION AND OVERVIEW

Make a prediction about some everyday science phenomenon. Think about how you learn best. Jot down the methods of instruction that you think have had the greatest impact on your understanding of science. Note any approaches to learning or instruction that have been particularly unsuccessful or inefficient for you.

Recently we found that two-thirds of students in a local middle school reported that they preferred learning science by doing virtual experiments with dynamic, interactive visualizations of global climate change compared to learning from textbooks, teachers, or peers (Corliss & Spitulnik, 2008). Only 5% selected learning by reading or studying and 3% selected learning from the teacher. Most students report that inquiry activities such as doing projects (often with peers), testing ideas (often in science museums), and exploring conundrums (often with encouragement from their teachers) have been their most effective means of learning. Students tend to believe that activities with uncertain outcomes, involving collaboration, and personal initiative lead to more learning than do more traditional school activities.

How Children Learn

In this book, we argue that children develop promising conjectures, beliefs, ideas, and views about scientific phenomena from observing, interacting, and probing the natural world. They often use colloquial language to communicate complex ideas in ways that amuse adults yet reflect their observational and reasoning skills. For example, 4-year-old Ben was fascinated by dinosaurs and curious about why they died. His favorite dinosaur was Pachycephalosaurus. After reading a book about habitat destruction, Ben realized that the habitat of the dinosaurs became colder. He speculated about dinosaur extinction, concluding that the Pachycephalosaurus died because, "they did not know how to put on their sweaters."

Ben constructed a causal account of dinosaur extinction based on available information. Taking into account the linguistic and conceptual affordances at the command of a 4-year-old, such reasoning could be seen as a legitimate effort to make sense of the available information. We argue that science instruction can build on the ideas that students construct and sustain the enthusiasm and intellectual skills that children use naturally to explore the world.

Students develop a repertoire of ideas such as Ben's from their efforts to make sense of the natural world. Ben has other explanations for the fate of the dinosaurs and will add new ones as he learns more about their habitat and habits.

Rather than having a single idea about a topic like insulation, density, or force, students have multiple ideas (see Box 1.1). These ideas are often connected to a specific context. Thus ideas about insulation may be connected to a practice (like going outside in the cold) or a technology (like a thermos). When students attempt to integrate their ideas they use complex reasoning processes (like applying a successful practice, such as putting on a sweater, that works in one context

---

BOX 1.1 REPERTOIRE OF IDEAS
Repertoire of ideas held by students for selected science topics

Students hold a repertoire of ideas about each science topic.

Howe (1998) found that upper elementary age students generated over 200 ideas relevant to buoyancy.

These included ideas about:

- Shape (round, square)
- Orientation (balanced, stuck to the top)
- Surface (smooth, prickly)
- Material (metal, wood)
- Contents (holes, points)
- Temperature (hotter or colder than the liquid)
- Movement (still, pushed) of the object

Metz (2000) identified ideas held by 2nd and 4th graders about behavior of organisms such as crickets. Students had many ideas about:

- Frequency of chirping explained by temperature, light, both.
- Choice of destination based on:
  - Location (natural habitat, asphalt, sand, shade)
  - Proximity to others (crickets, kids, insects)
  - Weather (heat, cold, dampness)

Ryoo (2010) identified ideas about photosynthesis among 6th graders:

Plant use the heat energy from the Sun to grow. Plants need sunlight, water, and fresh soil to grow. Energy is involved in the plant's growing because the Sun gives off heat energy and it helps all kinds of plants grow to help us survive.

Plants gets energy from the soil. The energy is transformed into nutrients. The energy in the plants is made into cells which are used in the plant. The energy ends up making the plant grow.

The plants use the sunlight so it can grow and become healthy. the plants also use the sunlight energy to get vitamin D.

The energy comes the Sun, the energy is transformed into photosynthesis.

The plants get energy from the Sun and when they get watered. The energy is transformed into a living organism after it grows. The energy in the plants make it grow very big. he energy from the original plant gets transferred over to the fruit or vegetable that grows from it.

Plants get their energy from the Sun and when the Sun shines on the plant it grows from energy. When the energy ends it goes into the soil.

Plant use sunlight to grow. But How? Plants get energy to grow, from the Sun. The energy is transformed by the chloroplast. The energy in the plants use it s food. Where the energy ends up is in the air.

Plants get energy from chloroplasts in their cells. The chloroplasts make sunlight into food and food makes energy. Then the energy in the plants are released and It turns into oxygen that humans breathe in to live. The "energy" (oxygen) ends up turning into carbon dioxide as we breathe it out. The plants take the carbon dioxide into their systems and turn it into energy.

to solve a problem in a new context), draw on evidence (such as evidence that sweaters keep you warm), and make links (like linking the habits of dinosaurs and children). Students also need opportunities to gather new information and modify their ideas (like distinguishing between domesticated animals who wear sweaters and wild animals who lack sweaters). This process is crucial for success in school, in life, and even in science classes.

Curiosity about scientific events motivates children to explore, observe, connect, and question their ideas. The goal of discovery learning (Dewey, 1901), constructivist instruction (Piaget, 1970b; Vygotsky, 1978), and inquiry learning (e.g., Linn, Davis, & Bell, 2004) is to sustain this process of investigation in science courses. Yet, this approach is frequently abandoned because decision makers believe it takes too long, costs too much, or does not work.

Absorption versus Knowledge Integration

In spite of these examples and testimonials, most science instruction implements the absorption approach: Instruction transmits information in lectures, textbooks, and cookbook-like science activities. Students are expected to "absorb the information." When absorption fails, it is common to argue that (a) students are not sufficiently motivated or do not work hard enough, (b) students need to develop a larger vocabulary, master some set of facts or details, or develop more powerful reasoning skills before they can understand the material, or (c) students are inhibited by misconceptions or naïve ideas that interfere with their ability to absorb the new knowledge. The absorption approach guides the design of most textbooks, lectures, and even laboratory experiences. In this book we argue that instruction should be designed using a *knowledge integration* (KI)★ approach that involves building on personal ideas, using evidence to distinguish alternatives, and reflecting on alternative accounts of scientific phenomena. We document the widespread use of the absorption approach and provide evidence to support the KI view.

The absorption approach aligns with many beliefs people have about science learning. Scientists require years of research to discover the complex and coherent insights about science concepts. In order to bring learners up to speed, instructors reasonably argue that it is efficient to simply tell their students about all the prior research and findings within a domain. Once they have laid out an elegant explanation, instructors and authors generally assume that their students have understood the material.

However, assessments of many courses refute this assumption. For example, in physics the Force Concept Inventory (FCI, Hestenes, Wells, & Swackhamer, 1992) and the Force and Motion Conceptual Evaluation (FMCE, Thornton & Sokoloff, 1998) show that most students cannot reason with the ideas their instructors transmitted in physics courses. These tests use student explanations of everyday examples of force and motion such as the trajectories of baseballs to construct multiple-choice items. Instructors are surprised when these assessments show that most of their students lack understanding of Newtonian laws of motion. Often the students are successful on textbook questions involving the applications of formulas but cannot extend classroom ideas to typical situations. At first, instructors might conclude that their students are unmotivated, confused by complex vocabulary, or beguiled by misconceptions. However, an intensive research program has convinced instructors that new course activities based on inquiry learning and peer exchange can improve outcomes (Crouch & Mazur, 2001; Hake, 1998; Thornton & Sokoloff, 1998). These new approaches engage students in using their physics ideas in complex, everyday situations and challenge students to interpret observations of the natural world using physics principles.

Similar findings have been reported for other important science topics such as students' epistemological views about the nature and role of empirical investigations. Developing and refining new scientific methods and gaining insight into scientific advance in a specific discipline typically takes years of study. Instructors and most science standards argue that students need to learn the scientific method and appreciate the nature of science. Following the absorption approach, textbooks explain the scientific method in generalities and often highlight the main steps scientists follow. Students often practice the steps in classroom experiments. Even when exercises specifically address the logic of science, they generally present the logic in a narrow context such as a puzzle or game. As a result, students do not experience the complexity of science and are not prepared to analyze unintended consequences or side effects of experiments.

Assessments such as the Maryland Physics Expectations (MPEX, Redish, Saul, & Steinberg, 1998) and the Views About Science Survey (VASS, Halloun, 1996), constructed in a similar manner to the Force Concept Inventory, show that students generally have a superficial understanding of the nature of research in mathematics, physics, biology, and chemistry. Rather than gaining an appreciation of the foundations of scientific inference and evidentiary discourse, students in typical courses are often convinced that science is a mechanical process that proceeds smoothly and formulaically. They do not appreciate the controversy and uncertainty surrounding most empirical work (Kuhn, 1970; Latour, 1987; Longino, 1990; Thagard, 1992). Students who see science as unfolding rather than emerging from inquiry are unlikely to question information from authorities or to become fascinated by science.

An unintended consequence of instruction based on transmitting information is that students often add new ideas but do not distinguish them from their existing ideas. The new ideas are added to the repertoire of ideas held by students but isolated from other ideas. Furthermore, analyses of science textbooks in many countries shows that science is presented as a fragmented and fractured set of facts (see Chapter 2). Students may not even appreciate that scientists aspire to a coherent body of knowledge.

As a result, when an opportunity to apply a scientific idea arises, students tend to use the ideas they already have rather than the new, fragmented ideas they have encountered. Since students have many more opportunities to revisit their personally developed ideas, they tend to remember those but forget the ideas from science class. It is no wonder that adults regularly assert that they have forgotten everything they learned in science class.

Instructors often seek to transmit elegant, well organized accounts of science rather than illustrating the dilemmas they faced or the wrong paths they followed in reaching the insights. Often these elegant solutions are captured in formulas, symbolic representations like the periodic table, or complex sequences of rules.

Such an approach makes it difficult for students to figure out how the science in the classroom connects to their everyday experiences. The frustration of students often manifests itself in constant complaints that they will never need the information they are learning.

Instructors often respond to this concern by arguing that students have not developed the logical capacities necessary to understand the material. This view is often buttressed by evidence from research of developmental psychologists such as Piaget (1970a). Yet, as Bruner (1962) so compellingly argued, much research shows that students can learn complex ideas when they are presented in such a way that they connect to the ideas students have developed by observing the natural world. In this book, we illustrate how this process might work.

Thus, the goal of transmitting complex information to students is appealing to textbook designers, lecturers, and curriculum authors. Sometimes the transmitted information is elegant and inaccessible. At other times it is fragmented and disconnected. In this book, we argue that science learning would be far more effective if students had the opportunity to integrate new information with their many, contradictory ideas. We suggest that students need, as a goal, the view that science ideas can be coherent. When students seek coherence, they use evidence to sort out the conflicting ideas. They seek to apply the abstract ideas to personally relevant situations. And, they appreciate the beauty and excitement of science.

The absorption approach does succeed for a few learners, but probably not because they have absorbed the information. Those who succeed in conventional approaches to instruction most likely act like experts, in that they evaluate what they hear, seek to clarify the ideas they learn for themselves, and test the new ideas against their existing views (Slotta, Chi, & Joram, 1995). These students frequently ask questions and interact with instructors. Not surprisingly, such students provide their teachers with convincing success stories in support of the absorption approach, which may serve to reinforce its primacy in the classroom.

Our goal in this book is to make it feasible for all students to become autonomous learners who view scientific evidence critically and endeavor to develop a coherent view of scientific phenomena. We also seek to help teachers adopt a role of intelligent facilitator of discourse and inquiry, rather than all-knowing disseminator of facts. Clearly, this will amount to a transformation of teaching and learning in science classrooms. But many have called for such a radical reform (Collins & Halverson, 2009), and indeed there is a wealth of evidence from the research literature in education and the broader learning sciences that the absorption model is antiquated and insufficient for the task demands placed upon science education in the 21st century. We hope that this book will lead the reader into his or her own inquiries about learning and instruction, inspiring deeper insights about KI and a wealth of new approaches for inquiry in the science classroom.

Review the predictions that you made above. Did you include activities that involved absorbing new science content? Were they successful or unsuccessful?

Implications of Absorption

The absorption approach fails to meet the needs of students or their teachers. Expecting students to absorb information implies that their pre-existing ideas are of limited value. Furthermore, most students are cognitive economists, seeking to use their cognitive resources economically (Linn & Hsi, 2000). When instruction emphasizes absorption, it sends the message that students do not need to evaluate evidence critically or attempt to reconcile apparent contradictions. Indeed, the absorption approach may convince students to avoid making sense of science at all.

We have found that many middle school students believe it is better to memorize rather than understand science (Madhok, 2006; Songer & Linn, 1991). They often justify their response by saying they tried understanding and were less successful on the test than when they memorized the information presented. Courses that convince students to memorize rather than understand miss an important opportunity to engage students in evaluating new ideas. They may deter students from critiquing persuasive messages about drugs, the environment, or evolution.

The absorption approach leads teachers to tell their students about science rather than guiding students to interact with materials in order to develop their own understanding. It results in textbooks designed to transmit information. When students fail to learn, the absorption model may make teachers feel powerless to improve learning outcomes. To maintain attention, textbook writers often add enticing photographs or sidebars about oddities such as reports of raining frogs or fish rather than guiding students to interpret new material. Teachers often resort to adding attention-getting and crowd-pleasing elements such as demonstrations involving explosions or videotapes of rare animals, rather than engaging students in exploring complex ideas about science.

The absorption approach is consistent with policies that require learners to master mindless details or memorize vocabulary words before proceeding to interesting science topics. Such policies are based on the assumption that the absorption approach fails only because students lack some details or facts, do not pay attention, or lack proper guidance. However, research in the learning sciences shows that children and adults learn vocabulary in the context of use. Memorizing isolated definitions is much less successful than reading text and inferring meaning (Bransford, Brown, & Cocking, 1999). Many studies show that engaging students in complex science or literature results in vocabulary acquisition but that direct teaching of vocabulary is unsuccessful (Gildea, Miller, & Wurtenberg, 1990; Lee, 1997).

The wide appeal of the absorption approach has been used as a basis for administrative policies that justify the fleeting coverage of numerous topics found in most science standards in the United States (Linn, Lewis, Tsuchida, & Songer, 2000; Mullis et al., 1999). Such policies typically require students to repeat the same course when they fail to learn rather than diagnosing the factors that led to failure.

Assumptions about the success of college courses that generally depend on transmission and the importance of the disciplinary knowledge teachers gain in those courses has been used to justify policies that require reassigning teachers to the discipline of their original undergraduate degree—even when they have years of successful and creative experience teaching in a related discipline. We have seen many award-winning and effective teachers moved by their school boards from physics to mathematics or from earth science to biology because their original degree was in mathematics or biology. Although these teachers have always made every effort to succeed in the new assignment, it is disheartening to see them struggle to develop equally creative approaches for the new topic. It takes years of listening to students and testing alternative responses to develop powerful approaches for teaching complex science topics. Teachers need time working with varied students to appreciate the many intuitive and culturally-relevant ideas that they bring to science class. Developing strategies to respond to student ideas generally requires some experimenting. When teachers are reassigned based only on their disciplinary background, schools and students lose the pedagogical content knowledge they have developed while teaching and education becomes less—rather than more—successful.

In summary, the absorption approach to science instruction has intuitive appeal as an efficient and practical solution to a complex challenge of imparting all the knowledge held by experts. Even when the ideas seem to make sense at the time they are encountered, if the new ideas are not connected to related information they will be isolated and forgotten rather quickly (Bransford et al., 1999; Vygotsky, 1978). Furthermore, absorption reinforces a passive approach to science learning and does not capture either the ways in which children learn on their own or the methods that experts use to explore new phenomena. The absorption approach is thus unlikely to help students extend their knowledge to new topics or to resolve conundrums. It leads to institutional policies that deter learners from building on their own ideas and using their own judgment.

Pick a few science insights you have had and consider how you learned about them. Did you learn about them by absorbing information or by integrating ideas? Did you test and refine your ideas?

Knowledge Integration

We offer the KI perspective on instruction as an alternative to the absorption approach and illustrate how it can succeed to transform science learning. The KI perspective builds on extensive evidence that students have a repertoire of ideas about any science topic. It takes advantage of research demonstrating the value of guiding students to engage in inquiry. When students engage in inquiry they compare and contrast the ideas in their repertoire as well as new ideas introduced in classes. With guidance, students learn to sort out their views and select promising ideas. Developing skill in integrating ideas prepares students to become good citizens, good scientists, or good knowledge workers in the 21st century society (Collins & Halverson, 2009).

In this book we discuss how the KI perspective empowers both teachers and students. We analyze research on instruction to show how science classes can help learners build on their repertoire of ideas, evaluate new ideas, use evidence to make sense of competing views, select the most viable alternatives, and continue this process throughout their lives.

We use the lens of an *instructional pattern* to analyze research on science teaching and learning. We define an instructional pattern as a sequence of activities performed by teachers or students such as informing, assessing, motivating, guiding, planning, listening, reading, discussing, debating, reflecting, predicting, questioning, experimenting, designing, and distinguishing viewpoints. We explore the sequence of activities in multiple instructional settings and for diverse science topics. We contrast the typical patterns that govern the design of science instructional materials following the absorption approach with patterns following the KI approach. The KI pattern is informed by recent research focused on how students develop ideas about the natural world and how they sort them out.

In our earlier work, we identified a general pattern as well as a set of specific patterns for common instructional features such as collaboration or experimenting (Linn & Eylon, 2006). In this book, we focus on the general pattern and discuss how it applies to specific settings. Thus, we synthesize the KI approach into one general pattern that includes four processes: elicit ideas, add ideas, distinguish ideas, and reflect on ideas. We refer to this as the KI pattern in this book. We discuss how these processes play out in a series of contexts including lectures, experiments, visualizations, collaboration, and professional development.

Prior work has identified curriculum design principles for KI that have succeeded in empirical investigations (Linn, Davis, & Bell, 2004). These principles are available in a Design Principles Database (Kali, 2006). The principles have been useful to designers who seek a solution to a problem similar to the problem addressed in the research study or who wish to refine an existing inquiry unit. However, it is not evident, from these principles, how to design a larger unit or course (Kali, Linn, & Roseman, 2008).

This book describes the general KI pattern and synthesizes research on typical science contexts such as lectures and experiments to show how the general pattern can inform design. The book contrasts the KI pattern with the absorption pattern to clarify the advantages of instruction focused on helping learners integrate their ideas.

Taking Advantage of Inquiry

KI takes advantage of research in science education showing that students can learn important science concepts earlier and more deeply through guided interaction with inquiry-based models and tools rather than from absorption-based lectures and textbooks (see Bransford et al., 1999; Krajcik et al., 1998; Linn & Eylon, 2006; Linn, Lee, Tinker, Husic, & Chiu, 2006; Taylor, 1980; White & Frederiksen, 1998). A distinguishing feature of this perspective is its reliance upon student-initiated inquiry. Students actively explore with tools and models by trying different parameters, arrangements, and initial conditions, then running experiments to see the results of their selections (Blumenfeld, Fishman, Krajcik, Marx, & Soloway, 2000; NRC, 2000; Slotta, 2004; Tinker, 2008). Giving students some control over their own learning provides invaluable feedback about their own understanding. This is particularly true if students systematically investigate each variable and look for interactions. Students benefit from opportunities to isolate the effects of variables and identify rules (Klahr & Nigam, 2004). They learn from exploring varied interactions among variables, including relationships based on thresholds and contingencies (McElhaney & Linn, 2010; Schauble & Glaser, 1996).

Effective and extensive use of inquiry learning is rare in American classrooms (Becker, 1999; O'Sullivan, Lauko, Grigg, Qian, & Zhang, 2003; Schmidt, Raizen, Britton, Bianchi, & Wolfe, 1997) and in most other countries (Roth et al., 2006). We define inquiry as the intentional process of diagnosing problems, critiquing experiments, distinguishing alternatives, planning investigations, researching conjectures, searching for information, constructing explanations, debating with peers, and forming coherent arguments. This book seeks to clarify the conditions under which an inquiry-oriented approach can succeed, and to offer guidelines to those wishing to promote inquiry that leads to integrated understanding.

KI is a way to organize and take advantage of the extensive research on inquiry learning (Linn & Eylon, 2006; Slotta & Linn, 2000, 2009). KI emphasizes the central importance of engaging learners in guided inquiry through a broad range of experiences. It depends on ample opportunities for students to integrate their observations and link them with prior knowledge through various forms of reflection and communication.

Respecting and Building on Student Ideas

The KI approach to science instruction emphasizes respecting rather than ignoring the ideas and reasoning processes that students develop on their own. Many studies (see Box 1.1) document the varied and creative ideas that students develop about scientific phenomena (Cooke & Breedin, 1994; Driver, Leach, Millar, & Scott, 1996; Howe, 1998; Linn & Hsi, 2000; Metz, 2000; Pfundt & Duit, 1991). KI takes advantage of this repertoire of rich, confusing, and intriguing ideas that students bring to science class by encouraging students to compare ideas, analyze evidence for ideas, and distinguish among ideas.

One reason that students develop a repertoire of ideas is that they create explanations for each perplexing phenomenon they encounter. This same process typifies much of the historical work in science—researchers created Phlogiston to explain what was lost when materials burned (Thagard, 1992). Students develop ideas to solve personally-relevant problems such as keeping food safe for a picnic, throwing a ball far, keeping warm on a cold day, or kicking a moving ball towards a target. They are intrigued by conundrums they encounter in movies, on television, in books, or at museums such as dinosaur extinction or volcano eruptions. They wonder about observable phenomena such as sunsets, mountains, and valleys. They seek explanations for dilemmas such as keeping warm while swimming or avoiding the flu. KI respects this process of reasoning while also encouraging students to broaden their perspective by combining similar ideas into a more coherent view and testing their ideas more broadly.

When ideas are elicited then teachers and curriculum designers can guide students to distinguish them from other ideas (Petrosino, Martin, & Svihla, 2007). Predicting outcomes of experiments or observations is a successful way to elicit ideas and often improves learning outcomes (White & Gunstone, 1992). For example, asking students to draw a sequence of images depicting a chemical reaction revealed many ideas that surprised teachers (Ben-Zvi, Eylon, & Silberstein, 1987; Zhang & Linn, 2008). Some students represented reactions as involving an instantaneous change from one form to another without any images of bond breaking or bond formation. Other students drew the reaction as starting with several molecules but ending up with one big molecule. Some students drew all the molecules breaking into atoms and then reforming. These drawings clarify how students interpret the textbook and other sources of information. Curriculum designers and instructors need to consider all the ideas students are likely to hold when they plan instruction.

Many researchers have documented the ideas students develop in science (Eylon & Linn 1988; Pfundt & Duit, 1994). DiSessa (1988) identified what he called *phenomenological primitives* as a set of ideas held by students that have emerged from their perceptual and physical experiences.

Others have referred to the various ideas that students hold (see Figure 1.1) as alternative views, misconceptions, or preconceptions (Reiner, Slotta, Chi, & Resnick, 2000). The KI approach argues that calling students' ideas *misconceptions* is itself misconceived. These ideas, while certainly not consistent with scientific norms, are nevertheless grounded in observations and experience (Smith, diSessa, & Roschelle, 1993). Building on these ideas ensures that students seek coherence.

Adding Ideas to the Repertoire—Pivotal Cases

To help students sort out their varied ideas, the KI approach calls for adding scientifically normative ideas. In this sense, KI is consistent with absorption. However, to promote KI, the new ideas are added to help students sort out their views.

Range Of Ideas Expressed By Students About Topics In Energy
• *I think the metal spoon will be hotter than the wood or plastic spoons because... metal attracts heat when either on a heated surface, in heat, or below heat.* • *I think wood would feel the hottest because wood attracts heat.*
• *You can burn your feet on the street, because the heat energy from the sun's rays heat the asfalt. The energy goes to the asfalt then when you step on it the heat energy moves to your feet. The heat energy changes by being less hot on your feet if you stand there, because your feet are blocking the sun's rays.*
• *Because the heat from the Sun goes to the ground. The energy moves to the ground to your feet. Through your body in your system then transfers out cold.*
• *Because the ground is hot from the Sun. it goes to your feet the rays make the heat that goes to the ground the energy changes at night cause it is colder at night.*
• *The energy changes by it moves to the feet and becomes more hot.*
• *The energy comes from the Sun to the street. The energy goes for the street to your feet. The street has high thermal conductivity. The energy changes by new energy comes the old energy goes away until it is time for it to work again.*
• *The energy comes from windmills. The energy goes to the power lines. Energy moves by circulation. Energy changes by the area.*

FIGURE 1.1   Diverse ideas about energy held by middle school students

For KI, designing the best ideas to add is a design challenge. For example, as we discuss in Chapter 3, what ideas should be added to help students understand why metal and wood feel differently at room temperature? Students in science classes often measure the temperature of wood and metal with a thermometer, find they have the same temperature, and are told that is because of thermal equilibrium. Adding thermal equilibrium is relevant but often makes no sense to students. After all, the metal and wood do not feel as if they are the same temperature.

Students need to combine understanding of thermal equilibrium with the idea that heat flows at different rates depending on the material. The KI approach has identified pivotal cases as promising new ideas that help students make these kinds of links.

Visualizations are one valuable means of adding pivotal cases about dynamic phenomena such as heat flow. We define visualizations as *interactive*, computer-based animations of scientific phenomena including models and simulations. We focus in this chapter on visualizations designed to add ideas that cannot be directly observed such as atomic interactions (chemical reactions, electrostatics), cellular processes (mitosis, meiosis), and astronomical phenomena (solar system, seasons). By interactive, we mean visualizations that allow users to change parameters, select views, contrast conditions, and analyze alternatives.

A pivotal case that involves a visualization of rate of heat flow can dramatically change learning outcomes as Lewis (1996) demonstrated in her dissertation research (see Chapter 3). Another pivotal case to help students understand thermal equilibrium and heat flow asks students to compare how metal and wood objects feel on the playground on a cold day and on a hot summer day. Students can accurately predict that metal objects will feel hotter than wooden objects on a hot day and that the reverse is true on a cold day. We then encourage them to use this information to sort out their observations. They may benefit from a third pivotal case involving rate of conduction. In this case, students consider whether using a wooden stick or a metal stick would be better for roasting marshmallows. Students have excellent intuitions about the advantages of a wooden rather than a metal stick. They can elaborate the differences between these conditions and convert their ideas into a narrative. Adding pivotal cases to the repertoire and encouraging students to sort out their ideas fosters coherent understanding. We have begun to describe criteria for pivotal cases (Figure 1.2).

Guiding Students to Distinguish Ideas

Adding ideas to the repertoire is not sufficient to ensure coherent understanding. This is a weakness of the absorption approach as discussed above: Students can add new ideas but isolate them. KI emphasizes guiding students to gather evidence and distinguish alternatives.

We identify many ways that successful courses can help students distinguish among their ideas and construct a coherent argument (e.g., Clark & Sampson, 2008). Many times, students have enough information to reach a valid conclusion but they need guidance to distinguish among potentially competing ideas. For example, students regularly select aluminum foil over a wool sweater to wrap a beverage to keep it cold (Lewis & Linn, 1994). Yet, students generally have relevant information. They know that some materials are better than others for maintaining temperature: Styrofoam cups maintain the temperature of drinks longer than metal cups. But they may think that both Styrofoam and metal coolers

PIVOTAL CASE CRITERIA			
Create compelling comparisons	Place inquiry in accessible, culturally relevant contexts	Provide feedback to support pro-normative self-monitoring	Enable narrative accounts of science

FIGURE 1.2 Criteria for pivotal cases

keep drinks cold (since some coolers have metal on the exterior and insulators inside). They also know that their body maintains its temperature while the drink does not. But most students also report that wool sweaters warm them up, and conclude that wool might warm a cold drink. They need guidance to sort out the insulating properties of a sweater from the role of their body as a heat source.

In this book we analyze successful and unsuccessful ways to provide guidance that enables students to distinguish ideas. We identify promising approaches in the context of experiments, lectures, and collaborative learning.

Encouraging Reflection

To develop coherent understanding even distinguishing ideas is often not sufficient. Students also need to consolidate the results of their investigations into a coherent account of the situation. Students benefit from opportunities to compare the soundness of the ideas in their repertoire. Often these ideas arise in distinct contexts, were gathered using varied methodologies, and rely on different technologies. For example, students might compare results from virtual experiments in a simulated environment and results from empirical tests to get a complete picture of the forces on an airplane. The simulations might use sophisticated instruments while the empirical tests might use model airplanes. Integrating these varied forms of evidence is part of knowledge integration. In this book, we analyze instruction that leads to coherent ideas and characterize the conditions that enable students to integrate their knowledge.

In summary, this book describes the KI approach to instruction and offers evidence to distinguish it from the absorption approach. The KI perspective on science learning and instruction represents a consolidation of the experiences of many researchers, classroom teachers, technology designers, and assessment specialists. It has emerged from reflection on a broad range of empirical evidence.

KI is consistent with the ways that scientists advance their understanding. Scientists have many sophisticated ideas that students lack but they too often have a repertoire of ideas that needs consolidation. Scientists have complex ways to combine and compare ideas and methods of analysis that are not available to students. Nevertheless, scientists, like students, build on their repertoire of ideas. Scientists gather evidence by observing, interacting, and probing the natural world. They face the same challenges as students when they analyze the validity of experimental methods and select promising reasoning strategies.

We show how the KI perspective can improve student science learning and how technology-enhanced instruction makes this efficient and effective. We demonstrate that new technologies that support the design of interactive visualizations and virtual experiments combined with online learning environments make implementing a KI perspective to instruction both feasible and successful.

Roles of Teachers, Students, and Technology

Teachers play an important role in guiding the KI process. They structure activities to promote inquiry. For example, they monitor student progress and determine when to interrupt the class to provide examples or clarify activities. They offer hints and encouragement when students get stuck. They identify students with expertise in an aspect of the inquiry and find ways to take advantage of the distributed expertise in the classroom. They summarize progress at the beginning of each lesson and set expectations for students.

Students participating in KI instruction have many opportunities to begin to monitor their own progress and to guide their own learning. They have the opportunity to develop lifelong skills that will serve them well in dealing with scientific dilemmas in the future. KI instruction motivates students to recognize gaps in their knowledge and to seek ways to fill those gaps. If students can learn to guide their own inquiry, they can continue to build understanding even after science class is over.

Technologies also contribute to the success of KI by providing learning environments that guide inquiry, scaffold student reflections, and present timely evidence. The embedded assessments in such learning environments can capture student progress so teachers can use the information to plan their next activities.

Assessing Science Learning

To determine the benefits of instruction, assessments need to measure consequential accomplishments aligned with the goals of instruction (Pellegrino, Chudowsky, & Glaser, 2001). National assessments call for inquiry instruction that promotes coherent understanding of science (NRC, 1996). Yet, many assessments emphasize recall rather than reasoning and can even be insensitive to inquiry instruction (Clark & Linn, 2003). To measure inquiry, researchers have explored a variety of approaches (Briggs, Alonzo, Schwab, & Wilson, 2006; Hunt & Minstrell, 1994).

Assessments that require students to explain their reasoning and engage in KI by using evidence to link ideas have consistently been shown to tap the accomplishments students achieve in inquiry courses (Lee, Linn, Varma, & Liu, 2009; Linn et al., 2006). Research shows that published multiple-choice items and even constructed response items that have dichotomous scoring rubrics can obscure sophisticated reasoning about inquiry (Lee, Liu, & Linn, in press).

The recent increase in high stakes testing associated with the No Child Left Behind legislation in the United States has drawn attention to the unintended consequences of assessment (Heubert & Hauser, 1999; Shepard, 2000). Using tests that are poor indicators of performance for students who are learning English and insensitive to instruction in science (Lee, Liu, & Linn, in press), these tests can lead to loss of talented teachers and principals (*NYTimes*, Winerip, July 18, 2010).

Schools are forced to implement policies that require closing schools when performance fails to meet arbitrary levels. Many teachers and principals, faced with these policies, have left teaching or moved to schools with affluent students who perform well on the current tests.

Assessments that measure KI can demonstrate the advantages of instruction that is designed to promote inquiry (Kali, Linn, & Roseman, 2008; Liu, Lee, Hofstetter, & Linn, 2008; Liu, Lee, & Linn, 2010a; Pellegrino, Chudowsky, & Glaser, 2001). To measure KI, an item typically asks students to select an alternative and defend the choice using evidence (see Box 1.2). KI items and rubrics are sensitive to instructional variations (e.g., Clark & Linn, 2003) and useful for guiding refinement of instruction (see Chapter 3). The levels of KI describe a progression

---

BOX 1.2 KI ASSESSMENT ELECTRICITY

KI assessment item and rubric for responses to a question about electricity

> i) You are watching TV and microwaving popcorn. Your parent starts the dishwasher. Suddenly, all the electricity goes out because they've blown a fuse. Which of the following can cause the fuse to blow? (Circle One)
>
> (a) Too much current in the circuit
> (b) Too much voltage in the circuit
> (c) Too much resistance in the circuit
>
> ii) **Explain** your choice.

Score	Level	Description	Examples
0	**No answer**		
1	**No KI** Students have isolated ideas, either normative or non-normative, in a given context.	Have relevant ideas but make incorrect links between them. Have both relevant and irrelevant ideas separately. Have irrelevant ideas.	The current is constant for the given circuit. By starting the dishwasher, the only thing that is changing is the amount of voltage in the circuit. Thus this must be the cause of the blown fuse.

2	**Partial KI** Students possible connections between concepts/ ideas in a given context, but cannot elaborate the nature of connections	Have relevant ideas and attempt to connect them, but cannot fully elaborate connections between them.	Voltage and resistance are both constant in those situations. Only current changes with the addition of multi-appliances.
3	**Limited KI** Students have an understanding of how two scientific concepts/ideas interact in a given context	Elaborate one scientifically valid link between two relevant ideas.	When there is too much current the wires heat up and eventually the fuse will blow.
4	**Complex KI** Students have an understanding of how more than two science concepts/ideas interact in a given context	Elaborate two or more scientifically valid links between relevant ideas.	More devices on one parallel circuit (which is the kind in houses) causes the amperage to go up. Too many high amperage devices can cause the current to go above what the fuse/circuit breaker is rated for blowing it.
5	**Systemic KI** Students have a systemic understanding of science concepts	Compare similarities and differences between contexts, and apply concepts relevant to each context.	

of student ability that rewards coherence of ideas and use of evidence to support conjectures. Students at the top level often demonstrate ability to approach a science problem based on multi-faceted understanding and can coordinate pieces of empirical evidence with theory.

International assessments starting with TIMSS (Hiebert et al., 2003; Stigler, Gonzales, Kawanaka, Knoll, & Serrano, 1999) have included classroom video studies to highlight the variation in instructional practices across countries (see Chapter 2). These studies help validate assessment and connect teaching practices to student learning. Aligning instruction and assessment is a first step towards ensuring that inquiry learning is valued in education.

Reflect on the absorption and KI approaches to learning. Why do both of these approaches often remain in the repertoire of ideas held by instructional designers? What is your experience with assessment and student learning? What evidence is needed to help designers select optimal instructional activities?

Shifts and Convergences

This book builds on our prior syntheses of research in science education. We described the research on teaching and learning science as following a sequence of shifts and convergences. We argued that these shifts and convergences resulted from the broadening backgrounds, commitments, and research methods of those who participate (Eylon & Linn, 1988; Linn & Eylon, 1996; Linn & Eylon, 2006). The community of scholars who study science learning has broadened to include experts in the science disciplines, assessment, classroom teaching, pedagogy, cultural studies, linguistics, technology, and software design. Research partnerships have shifted from hierarchical organizations led by one discipline (like physics) or specialization (such as logical reasoning) to groups that come together in the context of mutual respect (Linn & Eylon, 1996). Further, the research contexts have expanded beyond narrow, decontextualized problems to complex, realistic science activities, dilemmas, and socioscientific issues. Researchers have gone beyond interviews and surveys to embrace a broad range of research methods including instructional comparisons, video studies, and curriculum design research.

In 1988, we called for more collaboration and connections across research programs (Eylon & Linn, 1988). We identified somewhat divergent research traditions focused on science misconceptions, problem solving ability, individual differences, and development.

In 1996, we noted that researchers from these research traditions were now joining forces and converging on a view of the learner as formulating intuitive ideas (Linn & Eylon, 1996). The many studies of students' misconceptions or intuitive beliefs suggested that these ideas had merit and represented the efforts of learners to construct understanding of science (diSessa, 1983; Pfundt & Duit, 1994). Researchers argued that these diverse and often non-normative ideas were based on experience with the natural world (diSessa, 1988), developmental constraints (Inhelder & Piaget, 1958/72; 1969), or lack of motivation to learn in school (Eccles, 2009). Evidence for the repertoire of ideas students develop remained controversial (Linn, 1995). For example, researchers informed by the work of Piaget (1970a) generally assigned students to a single stage rather than acknowledging that students had a cacophony of contradictory and incomplete notions that they brought to science class. Piaget's work led to the idea that student ideas develop in a sequence. But, a large body of work highlighted the importance of varied, culturally-motivated ideas, clarified the importance of equity, and emphasized the need to respect diversity (Lee, 2009; Linn, Bell, & Davis, 2004).

In 2006, we emphasized that the participants in science education research now come from a surprising range of fields and recognize the importance of incorporating each other's perspectives (Linn & Eylon, 2006). For example, researchers have documented the repertoire of ideas in a broad range of scientific fields and contexts. They have studied the ideas held by learners of varied ages (e.g., Howe, 1998; McDermott, 2001; Metz, 2000). They have studied teachers (Davis, 2003; Shepard, 2000; van Zee, Iwasyk, Kurose, Simpson, & Wild, 2001), participants in science laboratories (Dunbar, 1995; Latour & Woolgar, 1986), and those aspiring to a wide range of careers such as medical students (Crouch, Fagen, Callan, & Mazur, 2004). Researchers have expanded the contexts that they study to include science learning in museums (Allen, 2002; Leinhardt et al., 2002), family conversations (Bricker & Bell, 2008; Ochs & Capps, 2000), online chat (Barron, 2000; Hsi, 1997) and classrooms (Edelson, Gordin, & Pea, 1999; Krajcik et al., 1998).

In 2006, Linn participated in a community that included expertise in a wide range of fields to integrate the theoretical and empirical work of the Technology-Enhanced Learning in Science (TELS) center and the Center for Curriculum Materials in Science (CCMS). These centers, funded by the National Science Foundation, both sought to offer a comprehensive view of topics such as learning, curriculum design, and equity to the field. The two centers merged their views in a book called *Designing Coherent Science Education: Implications for Curriculum, Instruction, and Policy* (Technology, Education-Connections Series) edited by Yael Kali, Marcia C. Linn, and Jo Ellen Roseman (Teacher's College Press, 2008). This book shows how the KI framework connects to research from many diverse communities. It illustrates how research is converging on a view of instruction that integrates research from a broad range of science topics and focuses on KI.

Emerging Focus on Learning Sciences

As the sequence of shifts and convergences progresses, educational theories are becoming more and more powerful and useful. Essentially, the field is integrating theoretical frameworks based on evidence from student learning. Although theories are still fragmented and often too vague to be applied to educational decisions, the emerging field of the learning sciences is engaged in its own process of KI that has already yielded powerful insights. This book contributes to that process.

The KI perspective integrates two powerful frameworks for learning. First, there is constructivism, as originally articulated by Piaget (1964) and Vygotsky (1978). This view grows out of the work of Dewey (1901) and has been elaborated by many including Bruner (1962), Papert (1968), and Wertsch (1985).

Constructivism emphasizes supporting learners as they make sense of the world. The degree of support that students need or benefit from is a contentious issue. Strict constructivists eschew guidance. The design of guidance that leads to coherent ideas and lifelong learning is the focus of this book.

Second, the book draws on cognitive theory including work on desirable difficulties (Bjork, 1994) that extend research on memory and on skill acquisition to more complex learning tasks. Research in the cognitive tradition has focused on learning more than on instruction. Many early studies investigated on how to guide learning to minimize forgetting or to avoid errors (Anderson, 1983; Estes, 1960; Hilgard & Bower, 1966). Instructional studies often targeting simple tasks like recall of lists were of short duration. This work is often seen as compatible with the absorption approach, but actually offers a far richer account of learning.

For example, cognitive tutors were originally created to guide students while minimizing errors. This was based on the idea that when students make errors they practice erroneous ideas. Research on the Algebra Tutor showed that students were frustrated by what they perceived as micro-management from the tutor (Schofield, 1995). The emphasis on correct responses rather than on distinguishing ideas sometimes motivated learners to assume that the tutor had one approach but that others were also possible. Thus, the instruction neglected some of ideas in the repertoire of the students. As a result, students sometimes assumed that their answers were also acceptable but not as good as those of the tutor. By ensuring that students made few errors, the Algebra Tutor did not fully address all the ideas in the repertoire of the student. Recent research on tutoring has added important ideas about how to guide students to achieve deep understanding of complex topics. By integrating findings from these instructional studies with results from studies of more open-ended inquiry we gain a more complete understanding of effective instruction (VanLehn, 2006; Van-Lehn et al., 2005, 2007).

In collaboration with Robert Bjork, we have integrated the KI perspective and the desirable difficulties framework (Linn et al., 2010; Richland, Linn, & Bjork, 2007). Adding desirable difficulties actually increases the likelihood of errors during learning but has demonstrated benefits for performance on end-of-unit assessments. Thus, instructional activities like generating explanations, distinguishing among alternatives, and embedded assessments increase errors but also lead to better learning outcomes. Integrating this research with other instructional studies illustrates the value of guiding students so that they learn from their errors.

In this book we seek to advance understanding of instruction in science education by integrating multiple theoretical traditions. We synthesize these research studies in design principles and instructional patterns. We draw on studies of the effectiveness of instruction in laboratory, classroom, and informal research contexts.

Integrating Research Methods

The ideas presented in this book draw on multiple research methods, often motivated by very different assumptions. We contrast investigations with varied theoretical ideas, empirical methods, and practical examples. We show how combining these resources and methodological traditions can guide instructional design (see chapters on experiments, lectures, and visualization). We describe how our own curriculum design process takes advantage of the theoretical frameworks, research evidence, and expertise of experienced users and designers of materials.

Combining these traditions allows us to draw on research that uses diverse methods. Constructivist studies pay attention to the systemic nature of education, involve a wide range of educational topics and materials, and consider the intentional, cultural, and deliberate nature of the individual. They often use design research, cases studies, and quasi-experimental methods. The duration of instruction is generally days, weeks, or months. Outcome measures often capture cumulative understanding. While these studies frequently yield successful instruction the causes of success are not always clear.

Research on memory and forgetting is commonly conducted in laboratories using decontextualized materials. These studies generally attempt to isolate a factor such as *spaced practice* or *tests as learning events* that could have widespread impact. The vast majority of these studies take advantage of the psychology course subject pool. They involve undergraduates and last a total of one or two hours. They use experimental designs with various control groups. Often control groups are included even when they are not expected to benefit learners. Although these conditions cannot be implemented in classrooms because they are known to be ineffective, the findings from laboratory studies can enhance understanding by isolating promising instructional practices.

For example, to integrate research on the role of visualization in science we draw on widely varied theoretical and research traditions (see Chapter 8). We distinguished laboratory studies from classroom studies to signal the distinct research methods they use and to show how these methods contributed to the findings (see Chapter 9).

In summary, the shifts and convergences in research on science education can be described as following a KI trajectory, and appear to be converging on an increasingly coherent account of learning and instruction. This book combines work from multiple traditions. These traditions use different research methods and investigate rather different questions but can inform each other. We show how the combination of these views has potential to increase understanding of instructional design.

Technology and instructional Research

Technological breakthroughs spur as well as enable many advances in science (e.g., Cloud Chamber, transistor, computer, PET scanner). Recent research has shown the benefit of learning environments (Ashburn & Floden, 2006; Linn, Lee, Tinker, Husic & Chiu, 2006), design technologies (Kafai, Peppler, & Chapman, 2009), collaboration (Falk & Drayton, 2009), and games (Slator, 2006; Steinkuehler, 2008), These technologies along with advances in design of programming

---

BOX 1.3 COMPUTATIONAL THINKING
Exploring the benefits of computational thinking

Virtually everyone sees substance in the notion of computational thinking, but there are more views of computational thinking than there are individuals (NRC, 2010).

Computational thinking is important for everyone

Computational thinking allows for:

- Succeeding in a technological society
- Increasing interest in the information technology (IT) professions
- Maintaining and enhancing U.S. economic competitiveness
- Supporting inquiry in other disciplines
- Enabling personal empowerment

Computational thinking is key to new specialties that integrate disciplinary knowledge and computational algorithms.

Two examples are:

Human Genome Sequencing
- *Computational thinking*
    ◦ Algorithm is repeatedly applied precisely formulated unambiguous procedure
    ◦ Search, pattern matching, and iterative refinement
    ◦ Randomization as an asset in repeated fragmentation

- *Disciplinary knowledge*
    ◦ DNA as a long string of base pairs

Modeling of Economic or Sociological Systems
- *Computational thinking*
    ◦ Aggregation of multiple independently specified rule-based agents
    ◦ Sensitivity to initial conditions

- *Disciplinary knowledge*
    ◦ Knowledge of community as collection of independent decision makers

environments have led to the identification of new goals for science learning. These new goals were first referred to as fluency with information technology (Snyder et al., 1999). More recently computer scientists defined computational thinking (see Box 1.3; NRC, 2010).

Technologies can also inhibit progress and reinforce unproductive practices. Everyone has a favorite example of technologies that just implement the pages of a textbook or drill on minutiae. Valuable research has begun to clarify how technology can contribute to coherent understanding and KI (Kali, Linn, & Roseman, 2008).

Advances in using technology have benefitted from cognitive tutors and technology-enhanced learning environments that allow researchers to contrast powerful patterns. Tutors often directly address unproductive views and guide practice on preferred approaches (Anderson, Corbett, Koedinger, & Pelletier, 1995). Emerging environments gather nuanced and sophisticated understanding of the students' repertoire of ideas, use creative representations, and can introduce new ideas aligned with the students' views (Anderson, Corbett, Koedinger, & Pelletier, 1995; Linn, Clark, & Slotta, 2003; Slotta & Linn, 2009; VanLehn, 2006; VanLehn et al., 2005, 2007; Zucker, 2008).

Technology-enhanced learning environments, such as the Web-based Inquiry Science Environment (WISE, Slotta & Linn, 2009) enable learners to carry out relatively open-ended investigations and to get guidance as they conduct their explorations (Figure 1.3). These environments can use technology to scaffold or support complex investigations (Krajcik, Blumenfeld, Marx, & Soloway, 2000; Lee & Songer, 2003; Quintana et al., 2004). Using carefully designed technology tools to guide students through inquiry activities and scaffold their reflections WISE (Figure 1.3), these environments can elicit student ideas, offer alternatives, and encourage investigation of the choices.

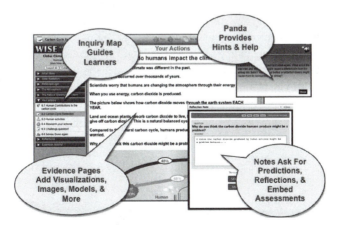

FIGURE 1.3   Web-based Inquiry Science Environment (WISE) features

Environments like WISE and the Cognitive Tutor can incorporate interactive visualizations to illustrate new ideas. For example, the Geometry Tutor uses a unique and powerful means ends representation for geometry proofs (Anderson et al., 1995). WISE can incorporate visualizations from Molecular Workbench (Pallant & Tinker, 2004), Biologica (Horwitz & Christie, 1999; Horwitz & Tinker, 2001), and NetLogo. Research shows that these environments can guide inquiry activities and help students understand the nature of scientific reasoning as well as learn complex science topics (Linn, Davis, & Bell, 2004; Linn, Lee, Tinker, Husic, & Chiu, 2006).

Klahr and his collaborators have compared laboratory instruction and hands-on experimentation to understand how hands-on activities contribute to effective understanding (e.g., Triona & Klahr, 2003). These researchers show that hands-on experiences are no more beneficial than computer simulated experiences. They show that well-designed experiments include opportunities for making predictions (to elicit student ideas), opportunities to reflect, and opportunities to critique. These activities build on student ideas and take advantage of the mix of ideas available in the classroom.

New technologies have the potential to strengthen the research on instruction. They enable new activities using visualizations and virtual experiments. They gather detailed accounts of science learning. They allow tests of precise alternatives. The research in this book benefits from technological advances and informs the design of instruction using technology.

Overview and Chapter Summaries

The chapters in this book illustrate the advantages of KI over absorption in a variety of instructional contexts including lectures, experiments, dynamic and interactive visualizations, and collaborative learning. Two case studies (Chapters 3 and 4) provide the foundation for KI and illustrate how the ideas in the framework emerged. All the chapters feature research demonstrating promising practices to provide a comprehensive and nuanced understanding of the constructivist view of the learner. The concluding chapter highlights the themes that emerge within the book and discusses the open questions and next steps needed to strengthen science teaching and learning.

Several themes permeate the book. First, each chapter discusses the importance of aligning assessment with instruction. We discuss how typical assessments such as multiple-choice tests that emphasize recall of isolated ideas are not sensitive to instruction (see Clark & Linn, 2003). These assessments do not measure the complex understanding that students need to succeed in their lives and send the wrong message to designers and classroom teachers. These assessments may cause designers to emphasize recall rather than understanding, in spite of extensive research showing that isolated ideas are quickly forgotten. Both teachers and textbooks often feel compelled by the nature of the assessments to emphasize isolated ideas or to communicate science in ways that prevent deep understanding. This book draws attention to the limitations of this approach and suggests that deeper understanding of fewer topics is likely to improve lifelong science learning.

Second, all the chapters illustrate the advantages of new technologies for promoting KI. Many of the results reported in the book are possible because of the features of technology-enhanced learning. For example the powerful visualizations and virtual experiments depend on technology. In addition, embedded assessments and logging of student activities provide more nuanced outcome measures for both research and teaching.

Third, all the chapters highlight the role of the teacher in promoting KI. In the chapter on teaching (Chapter 10), we contrast absorption and KI as features of professional development. We identify professional development practices that lead to lifelong teacher learning. We emphasize that the transition from absorption to KI involves building on teacher views that include beliefs compatible with absorption.

To orient the reader, we provide short synopses of each chapter. We describe the focus of the chapter, definitions of terms that are introduced, the role of KI, the use of technology, and the connections to other chapters.

Chapter 1: Overview

The goal of *Science Learning and Instruction: Taking Advantage of Technology to Promote Knowledge Integration* is to illustrate the knowledge integration (KI) approach to instruction by contrasting it with the absorption approach. The book describes the advantages of KI over absorption for lectures, experiments, dynamic and interactive visualizations, collaborative learning, and professional development. The opportunity to leverage new technologies to promote KI permeates the book. For example, powerful visualizations and virtual experiments depend on technology. In addition, embedded assessments and logging of student activities provide nuanced outcome measures for both research and teaching.

Chapter 2: Typical Instructional Patterns

The typical patterns that students encounter in science textbooks, lectures, laboratories, and online materials view the learner as absorbing information. We define a pattern as the sequence of activities that characterize instruction for a topic or unit. Patterns such as *motivate, inform, and assess* are based on the belief that students learn by absorbing information. Since transmission does not often succeed, instructors often add inducements intended to provide external motivation. Furthermore, when assessments identify student misconceptions instruction often admonishes students to abandon these ideas rather than building on them. We contrast the absorption approach with the Ikatura method and discuss how instruction could help students understand the seasons.

Chapter 3: Transforming Science Instruction with Technology: A Thermodynamics Case Study

Research conducted over a 15-year period explores design of curriculum materials to help middle school students (age 12–14) develop coherent understanding of thermodynamics. Designed by a partnership involving classroom teachers, discipline specialists, technologists, and educational researchers, the research incorporates recent research on learning and instruction. The research benefitted from KI assessments that documented improvement as the curriculum was refined. The research identified ways to take advantage of technology starting with Apple II computers and culminating in the Web-based Inquiry Science Environment (WISE). It documented successful ways to guide inquiry, document student work, incorporate visualizations, take advantage of real-time data collection, and use embedded assessments to provide feedback to both students and teachers.

Chapter 4: Particulate Structure of Matter

Research on curriculum reform in Israel resulted in a new program for the country. A partnership designed and tested multiple versions of a high school physical science curriculum. Working with teachers in a wide variety of schools, the researchers aligned instruction and assessments. The research illustrates the difficulties of teaching the structure of matter and shows the benefit of using visualizations and incorporating practical examples. A unit on textiles allowed students to connect ideas about structure of matter to familiar materials. Effective professional development built on the ideas held by the teachers and guided them to distinguish alternatives and use evidence to inform their practice.

Chapter 5: Knowledge Integration Principles and Patterns

The KI principles and patterns emerged from extensive classroom research. The KI principles guide designers in making science accessible, making thinking visible, encouraging students to learn from others, and promoting autonomy. The KI general pattern describes four processes that are essential for learners to develop coherent views: eliciting ideas, adding new ideas, distinguishing these ideas, and reflecting to sort out the ideas. The term *idea* refers to each distinct view held by the learner. Ideas include observational, intuitive, mathematical, visual, and analogical views. By eliciting ideas instruction takes advantage of the diverse, culturally-determined views students develop and ensures that all students can build on their views.

Chapter 6: Lectures and Technology

Lectures were necessary when monks read rare and fragile manuscripts to students. We define lectures as scheduled presentations to a group by one or a few speakers who plan their remarks. Today lectures typically transmit information in universities, religious gatherings (sermons), business meetings, and public venues with limited success. Lecturers have consistently sought to incorporate new technologies to improve transmission or motivate learners. Informed by the KI pattern, lecturers have shortened lectures, incorporated ways for students to make predictions, included peer-to-peer collaboration, and added opportunities to reflect. For example, in physics, classes have shorter and shorter lectures and more and more audience interaction and involvement.

Chapter 7: Experimentation and Knowledge Integration

Experimentation is viewed by many as vital to science education for communicating new, empirically validated ideas, introducing scientific methods, and motivating students to participate in science. We define experimentation broadly to include any form of inquiry that is guided by the student. In spite of the promise most experiments add little value because they follow the absorption pattern of: *motivate, interact, and assess.* Using the KI pattern and new technologies that support virtual experiments and guide students to explore contemporary issues such as global climate change, airbag safety, or recycling improves outcomes. The KI pattern supports new goals for science such as the Partnership for 21st Century Skills, computational thinking, and fluency with information technology.

Chapter 8: Making Visualizations Valuable

Interactive visualizations enable learners to explore phenomena that are too small (such as molecules), fast (such as explosions), or massive (such as the solar system) in scale to observe directly. Many visualizations are used to motivate learners in conjunction with the absorption pattern. Using the KI pattern and new technologies to design instruction using visualizations takes advantage of rapid prototyping, iterative refinement, user customization, embedded assessment, and logging of student interactions. Visualizations add value when they align with the knowledge of the learner, focus on difficult ideas that are hard to express in other formats, take advantage of interactivity, and support self-directed exploration for science topics that are fundamentally dynamic (such as chemical reactions or mitosis).

Chapter 9: Collaboration for Knowledge Integration

The KI pattern can strengthen collaborative activities by guiding students in eliciting ideas, adding ideas, distinguishing ideas, and reflecting. We define collaboration as occurring when two or more individuals are engaged in a learning activity. Online tools such as brainstorms and gated discussions can support collaboration.

Collaboration succeeds when participants jointly approach a dilemma, respect each other, communicate with each other, seek feedback from each other, offer help to others, and resolve differences. Teachers need to establish norms, monitor progress, and develop ways to evaluate individual contributions to group projects. Technologies and the KI Pattern have improved collaborative activities but outcomes across individuals remain uneven.

Chapter 10: Professional Development for Knowledge Integration

Using technology-enhanced units for KI can improve student learning as the chapters on experimentation, lecturing, collaboration, and visualization suggest. However, teachers believe their students benefit from the absorption approach and find KI challenging, especially when combined with new technologies. Effective teaching requires guiding individuals, small groups, and the whole class to explore questions and develop explanations of the outcomes. Two recent multiyear technology-enhanced projects that link professional development to student learning outcomes illustrate promising approaches. These and other projects show that multiyear support, analysis of evidence from student work, and support for evidence-based customization contribute to success.

Chapter 11: The Case for Knowledge Integration

This book makes the case for KI and shows why absorption not only fails but, in addition, hampers the development of lifelong learning skills. We need curriculum materials that guide students to reconsider their ideas, question their observations, and seek coherence across problems and contexts. We need teachers who promote coherent understanding and policies for curriculum and assessment that value KI. With sufficient opportunities to develop a commitment to KI, students will become autonomous integrators of ideas and succeed even when instruction does not make it easy. In addition, an emphasis on KI will prepare students who can use 21st century skills and engage in computational thinking.

In summary this book is designed to support teachers, curriculum designers, researchers, policy makers, and learners who wish to improve science learning outcomes. Readers are encouraged to take advantage of distributed expertise and form partnerships to build on the findings in the book to advance understanding of learning and instruction.

Reflection Activity

Select a KI assessment item from this chapter or another chapter. Either (a) use the item with a group of students or (b) write down five different responses you think students might give. Be creative. Use the KI rubric in the chapter to assess the responses. Compare this rubric to the rubric used for typical classroom assessments.

Note

*   Knowledge integration will be referred to as KI throughout the rest of the book

2

TYPICAL INSTRUCTIONAL PATTERNS

Introduction

In this chapter we analyze typical instruction and show how the absorption approach dictates the experiences that most students encounter. As mentioned in Chapter 1, we define an instructional pattern as a sequence of student activity structures, including: generating ideas, predicting, adding ideas, listening to lectures, reading, distinguishing ideas, reflecting, sorting out ideas, interacting, performing assessments, discussing, debating, questioning, experimenting, designing, and distinguishing viewpoints and teacher activity structures including: planning, motivating, informing, assessing, questioning, responding, guiding, and reflecting. We analyze four contexts for typical instruction: textbooks, whole class lectures and discussions, laboratories, and online materials.

To illustrate our ideas we analyze instruction on the topic of seasons and contrast American and Japanese instructional patterns. We describe a common Japanese practice, known as the Ikatura method that is consistent with the KI approach (see Box 2.1). We discuss results of a Third International Mathematics and Science Study (TIMSS, Roth et al., 2006) that compared videotaped science lessons in the United States (where students scored 18th out of 38 countries in science achievement), to videotapes of lessons in four high scoring countries (including Japan). This study provides evidence for the emphasis on absorption in American curriculum materials and the emphasis on KI in Japan.

The reliance on the absorption approach deters students from developing a coherent understanding of science and building on their science ideas in their everyday lives. Students could learn more, understand science better, and develop more coherent ideas if the typical absorption patterns were replaced by KI patterns.

BOX 2.1 IKATURA METHOD

Classroom activity common in Japan that supports knowledge integration

Japanese science teachers frequently use what is referred to as the Ikatura method to conduct class discussions (Hatano & Inagaki, 1991). In the Ikatura method, students' ideas are respected and tested. A similar approach, called a Benchmark Lesson, has been described by diSessa and Minstrell (1998). In the Ikatura method teachers:

- Pose a problem and ask students to make predictions.
- Engage students in small group discussions of the predictions.
- Elicit student predictions and list all the alternatives on the board.
- Ask students to vote on the alternatives. Students typically disagree.
- Perform an experiment showing result for the problem.
- Ask students to interpret the evidence in small groups and explain their ideas.
- Hold class discussion about alternative views. Students explain their views and show how they connect to the experiment.
- Identify evidence needed to resolve any remaining disagreement. Students might identify another experiment that would help.
- Repeat the process of predicting and explaining.

Ikatura method: an example

While discussing the experiment shown here before the objects were added to the water, students:

- *Discussed* the mass of a beaker filled with water plus a wood or metal object of similar mass.
- *Predicted* whether the beaker with the wood object floating on the water would have the same mass as the beaker with the metal object sinking in the water (see Figure 2.1.1).

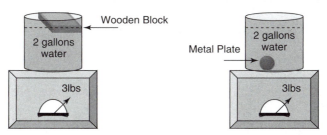

FIGURE 2.1.1 Beaker on scale

- *Compared* the mass of the water plus the floating object to the mass of the water plus the sinking object.
- Made *predictions* about what would happen and watched the *experiment*.
- *Discussed* how the experiment supported or refuted their ideas in their small groups.
- *Reported* their group consensus to the class.

In this example, one student was convinced that *the beaker would weigh less when the object was floating*, although the experimental results contradicted this finding.

- He suggested *another experiment* that he believed would support his point.
- This experiment also *contradicted his predictions*, but he was not convinced.
- The students *designed another experiment* to distinguish among the views represented in the class.
- The teacher *conducted the experiment* and repeated this cycle until the class *reached consensus*.
- Students then *recorded their ideas* in a report.

In this approach, teachers followed this sequence of activities:

1. *Elicited* student ideas
2. Asked students to *select* their most compelling idea
3. Conducted an experiment to *add ideas*
4. To *distinguish ideas*, asked students use the results of the experiment to support or refute their prediction, discuss their ideas in small groups, and *reach consensus*
5. Repeated steps 1 to 4 to achieve class consensus
6. Asked students to *reflect* individually in their reports

Thus, this approach implements *elicit ideas, add ideas, distinguish ideas, and reflect*.

Textbooks

Textbooks articulate current scientific knowledge as described in standards. Authors of precollege textbooks rely on standards and review panels rather than evidence from student learning to determine content and format in many countries. The opinions of review panels in a few populous states (California, Texas, and New York) have the most power in the United States. Evidently textbook reviewers commonly use what has been called the *thumb* test (reviewers thumb through the book rather than reading sections) to make decisions. Thus, publishers are motivated to create attractive pages and address each topic to increase appeal to reviewers rather than conducting research to identify effective ways to illustrate complex concepts (Chall & Squire, 1991; Lee, 2010; Tyson-Bernstein & Woodward, 1991). Political constraints also matter (Skoog, 1979). For example, in 2003 only three states had standards that included evolution (Skoog, 2005).

To cover the large number of topics mandated by state standards, contemporary American precollege textbooks are packed and grow longer every year. As textbooks have continued to grow in length, the California Board of Education has found it necessary to limit the weight of textbooks but has not found any method for limiting the number of topics in textbooks. The Board justified the weight limitations by pointing to injuries children have sustained by carrying heavy backpacks. Backpacks on wheels have only complicated this situation. It is common to see middle school children who weigh less than 80 pounds pulling 40 pound backpacks. Imagine the consequences if textbooks are distributed electronically and the weight of the backpack is no longer an issue!

Heavy Books, Light on Learning

Research analyzing the ability of textbooks to communicate coherent understanding of science has reported that textbooks may be heavy but they are not effective (Roth, 1991; Roth et al., 2006; Stern & Roseman, 2004). For example, the Project 2061 science textbook analysis evaluated the coherence of the information textbooks provided about science topics and found them to be incoherent (Kesidou & Roseman, 2002; Stern & Roseman 2004). They analyzed whether textbooks address key ideas identified in national and state standards, develop an evidence-based argument in support of the key ideas, organize the content coherently by making connections among the key ideas, include information appropriate for the grade, do not include information that extends beyond the grade level, and provide accurate information that avoids reinforcing student misconceptions (AAAS, 2002). They concluded that textbook authors often include information that goes beyond the standards and requires more sophisticated ideas than students could reasonably be expected to have.

In addition, they found that it was often impossible for students to make realistic connections among ideas because important information was left out. Many texts include boxes, photos, and other motivational materials that are disconnected from the text and too sophisticated for students to grasp. Specific examples of the analysis can be found at the website (http://Project2061.org). Project 2061 concluded that textbooks, in general, are incoherent and fail even in the goal of informing students about the information needed to gain standards-based understanding of science. They summarize this research by complaining that Americans have heavy books that are light on learning.

Science Assessments

Science assessments reinforce the emphasis on details rather than coherence found in textbooks. Analysis of state and national tests such as those used for the National Assessment of Educational Progress (NAEP) show that they primarily measure recall of information (Hyde, Lindberg, Linn, Ellis, & Williams, 2008). These assessments suggest to students and their teachers that the goal is to memorize science facts.

Publishers typically provide multiple-choice items that emphasize recall of isolated ideas in teacher's guides, in machine chapter tests, for classroom response systems such as clickers, and in boxes alongside the text. Boxes in textbooks often feature multiple-choice items released from state tests that reinforce the emphasis on details.

Impact of Textbooks

Although the importance of textbooks for communicating science knowledge is widely acknowledged (Ball & Fieman-Nemser, 1988; National Educational Goals Panel, 1998; Tyson 1997) few studies have tested the impact of textbooks, diagrams, or illustrations (Lee, 2010a, b). Comparison of textbooks across countries by TIMSS concluded that the fleeting coverage of far too many topics in American textbooks may contribute to the low performance of students on international comparison tests (Schmidt, McKnight, & Raizen, 1996). The report commented that American textbooks provided students with a curriculum that is, "a mile wide and an inch deep" (Schmidt et al., 1996, p. 68). Consistent with this report, several studies have compared classes that did not study a science topic to classes using the textbook and found no differences in performance (Graesser, McNamara, & VanLehn, 2005; Linn, Songer, & Eylon, 1996).

Textbooks are the most common instructional experience in science, according to a survey of student practices (Braun, Coley, Jia, & Trapani, 2009; Figure 2.1). Braun et al. (2009) investigated correlations between student-reported science activities and school outcomes on the NAEP. Using textbooks was the most common activity reported. Since American textbooks cover more topics than textbooks in other countries, these results suggest that most students experience the fleeting coverage of science topics described by Schmidt et al. (2001). The study authors concluded, "These data suggest that it is reasonable to recommend that science teachers should make some use of science textbooks in their teaching" (Braun et al., 2009, p. 4).

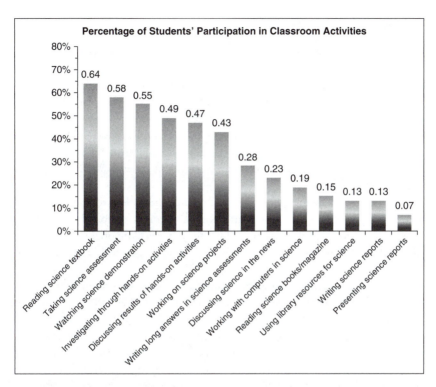

FIGURE 2.1 Percentage of eighth-grade students reporting their participation in class-room activities related to science almost daily or once/twice a week

Source: Braun, H., Coley, R., Jia, Y., & Trapani, C. (2009, May). *Exploring What Works in Science Instruction: A Look at the Eight-Grade Science Classroom (Policy Information Report)*. Princeton, NJ: Educational Testing Services (ETS).

It appears that students who use textbooks extensively learn more of the details assessed by NAEP and might also spend more time on science altogether. It is reassuring to note that students who reported doing hands-on activities in science, writing long answers to science tests and assignments, as well as talking about measurements and results from hands-on activities were also more successful than those who reported less frequency of these activities. Taken together, the constellation of successful activities is more consistent with inquiry learning (discussed below) than with the absorption model.

The study found that 64% of students reported using textbooks regularly while only 28% reported writing long answers to science questions at least once a week. Since textbooks are already in widespread use, augmenting textbooks with activities that explore topics in depth could have an across-the-board benefit for student learning.

Inquiry and Textbooks

Current textbooks spend little time on inquiry or on the controversies in science that might require inquiry for resolution. We define inquiry as the intentional process of diagnosing problems, critiquing experiments, distinguishing alternatives, planning investigations, researching conjectures, searching for information, constructing explanations, debating with peers, and forming coherent arguments. One analysis reports that controversies are mentioned less frequently than once every 100 pages of science textbooks. Even in the lengthy California texts, this would mean that controversy occurs less than eight times in the book (Champagne, 1988).

Rather than engaging students in comparing their ideas to those of others and developing criteria to distinguish among them, textbooks move directly to assessing student understanding. Thus, they neglect important activities that might allow students to compare the ideas presented in the textbook to their own ideas.

Many textbooks address inquiry standards by including one or two pages at the end of each chapter that list inquiry activities teachers could organize on their own (Roth, 1991). These activities typically require extensive teacher preparation such as ordering from biology supply houses or amassing experimental apparatus. Simply their placement at the end of the chapter in an isolated section shows that these activities are not informed by the extensive findings from research on inquiry (see Figure 2.2). As a result, textbook companies may identify inquiry possibilities but students rarely experience inquiry.

Textbook Patterns

Overall, analysis of textbooks suggests that they lack coherence, downplay inquiry, neglect student ideas, and include assessments that emphasize recall of details. Textbooks offer students little opportunity to test their ideas, develop evidence to support alternative ideas, reflect on their views, or integrate their ideas. Texts seek to motivate students (and appeal to reviewers) with eye-catching visuals. These include photographs, boxes with surprising facts, and other features that the 2061 study notes, are not well connected to the main goals of the unit. While the purpose of the text is to inform students, the 2061 study (AAAS, 2002) suggests that they often neglect connections among ideas.

Textbooks include assessments that ask students to recall or repeat information they previously studied, consistent with the absorption approach. They rarely reward students for interpreting scientific material and making inferences. Teachers' guides typically feature multiple-choice items taken from standardized tests that teachers can use for practice. As the Braun et al. (2009) study shows, frequent use of these tests could lead to decreased success in science while writing long answers could be of considerable benefit.

LATITUDE AND ANGLE OF THE SUN

Inquiry: What is the relationship between the angle of sunlight and latitude?

Time for inquiry activity: 25 minutes

Materials needed:

1. Flashlight   2. Globe

Activity:

Step 1: With the globe on a flat surface, point the flashlight directly at the equator, ensuring that the flashlight is parallel to the ground. Write your observations about the path of the light.

Step 2: Repeat the process, but point the flashlight between 35°–40° N latitude. Write your observations about the path of light.

Step 3: Repeat the same process again, but point the flashlight between 35°–40° S latitude. Again, note your observations.

Refection:

> What did you observe between the different ways that the light hit the globe?
> What affect to do you think these differences could have on the climate of geographical location?

FIGURE 2.2   Sample inquiry activities found at end of each chapter in typical science textbooks

Source: National Geographic Society (U.S.). (2007). *Focus on Earth Science California, Grade 6*. Princeton, NJ: Glencoe/McGraw-Hill School Pub Co.

We define the pattern in typical textbooks in most countries as: *motivate, inform, and assess*. This approach to the design of science instruction contributes to the low regard students have for science. Students want to connect what they learn to their lives but textbook accounts of science make it difficult (Madhok, 2006). Consistent with survey reports from NAEP (Grigg, Lauko, & Brockway, 2006) and other sources, students using textbooks in current science courses report dissatisfaction with science as a topic and a disinclination to persist in the field. Sadly, this trend seems to be intensifying as schools and even teachers are rewarded for the performance of students on tests that reinforce unproductive memorization-based learning practices by assessing recall of isolated details.

In summary, textbook publishers are burdened by the overwhelming number of standards, the likelihood that students have not learned prerequisite information, and, in some states, limits on textbook weight. Textbook selection committees compound the problem by relying on examination of the books rather than asking for evidence of efficacy. As a result, most textbooks implement an intuitive view of the learner as absorbing information. When textbooks call for inquiry, they provide little support for teachers who might implement such activities (Duschl, Schweingruber, & Shouse, 2007; NRC, 2006).

Textbook Accounts of the Seasons

To show how iterative refinement might improve the design of textbooks, we look at textbook accounts of the seasons. The Private Universe project (Schneps & Sadler, 1989) conducts interviews on graduation day at universities like Harvard and MIT. One common question concerns the causes of the seasons (Dussault et al., 2005; Sadler, 1992).

Jot down your own ideas about what causes the seasons. Predict what you think students might say.

These researchers have found that few students explain the seasons using scientifically normative ideas. Most graduates say that, in summer, the Sun is closer to the Earth than in winter. These responses reflect everyday experiences such as the experience of getting closer to a heat source and feeling hotter. Although American students cover the topic of the seasons, analysis of typical textbooks suggests that the absorption approach to instruction and lack of user testing makes it unlikely that students would benefit. Intriguingly, the only student on a recent film who could explain the seasons attended high school in Israel. In Israel, textbooks are designed and tested by research partnerships rather than being composed by publishers. In addition, several Israeli researchers have investigated effective ways to teach about the seasons (Nussbaum, 1985).

Examination of American textbooks shows that descriptions and illustrations of the causes of the seasons are confusing. For example, an Earth science textbook (Tarbuck & Lutgens, 2008) explains that a shift in the angle of the Sun can affect the amount of solar radiation reaching the surface of the Earth but does not connect this to related ideas. Students are encouraged to notice that one unit of solar energy striking at a 30° angle spreads over twice as much area as it does when striking over a 90° angle. The authors evidently expect students to absorb this information but the explanation requires extensive unpacking. An illustration shows the angle of incidence and reflection for a 30° and a 90° angle but makes it hard to understand why this is important.

Most textbooks fail when they attempt to represent the three-dimensional relationship between the orbit of the Earth, the tilt of the Earth, and the Sun using two dimensions. Most illustrations display the orbit of the Earth from a 45° angle, making it look like the Earth is closer to the Sun during some months than others. They also make the Sun far too small relative to the size of Earth, giving the idea that the Earth is much closer to the Sun than it is. For example, in the Tarbuck and Lutgens (2008) book the illustration shows the Sun closer to the Earth in September and March than in December and June because the

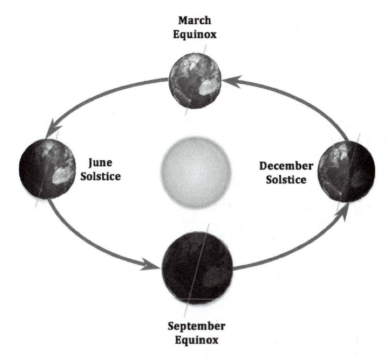

FIGURE 2.3 A view of the Sun-Earth system from a 45° angle found in most text-books. This view reinforces the idea that the distance between the Earth and Sun varies by season

Source: National Geographic Society (U.S.). (2007). *Focus on Earth Science California, Grade 6.* Princeton, NJ: Glencoe/McGraw-Hill School Pub Co.

ellipse illustrating the orbit of the Earth is depicted at a 45^0 angle (p. 458). This depiction elongates the orbit of the Earth, reinforcing the idea that the Earth might be farther from the Sun during some seasons than during other seasons and reinforces a common misconception (see Figure 2.3).

Finding an effective illustration is difficult. Looking down on the plane of the orbit would show the true shape of the orbit (almost a perfect circle) but obscure the angle of the axis of the Earth. Looking along the plane of the orbit would show the angle of the axis of the Earth very clearly but the orbit shape would become a straight line. So, the commonly used drawing is a compromise between two perspectives. In addition, representing the distance between the Earth and the Sun accurately would also help learners understand the seasons.

Compare the representation in Figure 2.3 to your predictions. Does the drawing help you think about the causes of the seasons?

Designers have tried various solutions to this dilemma. For example, the Private Universe teacher's guide introduces a distinction between indirect and direct rays of Sun. This seems to introduce new confusions since all rays are the same but that they hit the Earth at different angles. Specifically, to explain an illustration, they say, "First, in summer, the Sun shines higher in the sky and its rays beat more directly down, warming the surfaces they contact. In the winter, when the Sun is lower in the sky, light reaches the ground at a lower angle, spreading out its warming ability. This is the phenomenon sometimes referred to as 'indirect rays'" (Schneps & Sadler, 1989, p. 18). These materials make it hard for teachers to find effective ways to help students make sense of the abstract and complex ideas in the textbook.

In addition, most text depictions fail to connect to the views of learners. Students come to science class with extensive experience about moving closer and further from heat sources (Bell & Linn, 2000; diSessa, 1988). They know that the closer you move to a hot object, the hotter you will feel. They see this idea as relevant to the seasons. Although learners may have used flashlights to vary the angle with which light hits a surface, they also commonly believe that (a) light needs to come out of your eyes for you to see and (b) light is everywhere, objects are immersed in a bath of light (Bell, 2004a; Driver, Asoko, Leach, Mortimer, & Scott, 1994; Kali, Linn, & Roseman, 2008; Linn & Hsi, 2000). The textbook authors are not helping students distinguish between the ideas in their repertoire and the novel ideas about the nature of the seasons offered in the textbook. Instead they appear to assume that students will absorb the new information and somehow abandon their other ideas. Since students have extensive evidence for their intuitive ideas and are offered no evidence for the ideas presented in the textbook, they are not compelled to reconcile their ideas with the sophisticated new ideas presented in the textbook (Smith & diSessa, 1993).

Iterative Refinement of Illustrations and Instruction

Researchers such as Nussbaum (1985) have shown that there are effective ways to illustrate the relationship between the Earth, the Sun, and the direction of the rays from the Sun. Nussbaum conducted extensive user testing and found that although the formal explanation of the changing seasons includes only two major ideas: the changes in the angle between the Sun's rays and the ground, and the period of time the Sun appears in the sky during daytime, it is extremely difficult to comprehend the 3D positions of the Earth and Sun. Israeli educators succeeded in building on the ideas held by students by introducing additional basic concepts and using diagrams that were refined in studies with young students (see Figure 2.4).

Try out the ideas in Figure 2.4. Do they help you refine your predictions?

Nussbaum constructed illustrations that focus on each concept described in Figure 2.4. The illustrations encourage the students to use a 3D model (such as a ball). By using these illustrations students can understand the importance of the angle of light rays coming to the Earth and connect that to the length of the day

Building on Student Ideas about Seasons

No.	Concept/Idea	Visual Representation
1	We live on an infinite plane (horizon plane) that is tangent to the spherical Earth.	
2	Rays that come from the Sun (and other far away objects) are almost parallel.	
3	The angle between the rays of the Sun and the horizon plane determine the amount of heat that is transferred to the Earth.	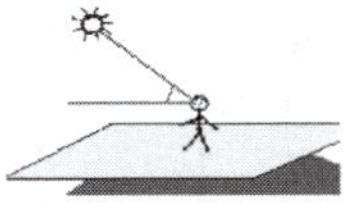
4	Based on ideas 1–3, the relationship between the Sun and the angle of the Earth on its axis determines the amount of heat that is transferred to the ground.	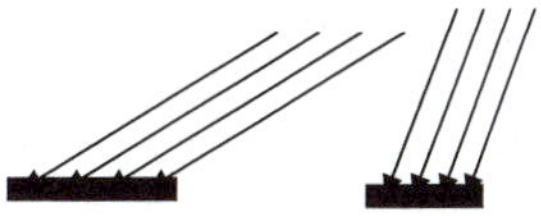
5	The connection between the Earths' axis and the amount of time that the Sun appears in the sky (daytime length).	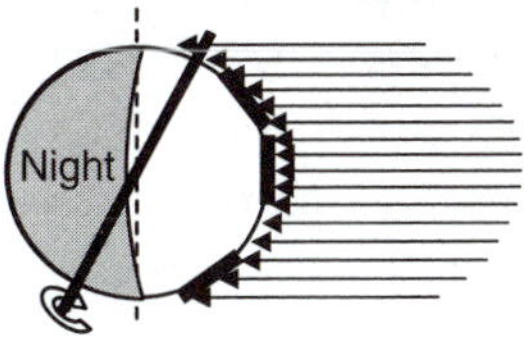
6	The true shape of the Earth's orbit (almost a circular path instead of an ellipse).	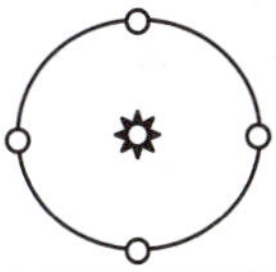

FIGURE 2.4 Factors that contribute to understanding the cause of the seasons

during the different seasons. Contrasting the illustrations developed by Nussbaum with those used in textbooks, shows how important it is to design, test, and refine scientific representations (see Figure 2.3).

Reflect on the causes of the seasons. Did you consider how the angle of the Sun impacts the temperature of the Earth in the morning, at noon, and in the evening on a sunny day? Does your view explain why it is summer in Australia when it is winter in North America? Does it explain why days are longer in summer than in winter?

This topic seems well suited to a powerful visualization and some designers have recently created intriguing options (see EduTube (2008), What causes the different seasons? (animation) http://www.edutube.org/en/video/what-causes-different-seasons-animation). Finding ways to build on the ideas held by students rather than just telling them the right answer, could strengthen understanding. For example, students could connect to the common advice to bring a sweater on a warm day because it will be colder in the afternoon.

In summary, with no requirement to show that textbooks impact coherent science understanding or cumulative learning, textbook designers neglect advances in understanding of the learner. They transmit ideas rather than helping students connect the science topics to their everyday life.

This approach is illustrated in the example of the seasons. Even if students learn to repeat information about the angle at which rays from the Sun hit the Earth, this information is not necessary or sufficient for them to understand the actual causes of the seasons. And, because the new information does not connect to other ideas, it is rapidly forgotten, as reflected in the interviews of high school students as well as graduates at Ivy League colleges (Dussault et al., 2005; Sadler, 1992).

Lecture and Discussion

Besides textbook assignments, the most common instructional activity for both pre-college and college courses is the lecture. Typically, a lecture includes both teacher presentations and teacher-led discussions. Both pre-college and college instructors rely heavily on lecture classes for transmitting information. A study by NCES (http://nces.ed.gov/, 2002; Chen, 1998) reports that, in higher education, 83% of instructional faculty use lectures as the primary instructional method for undergraduate classes.

Historical Antecedents

Prior to widespread access to books, lecturers read (often quite fragile) books to disseminate information to a large audience and participants took notes. In fact the word *lecture* has as its root the verb *to read* consistent with this practice. With the advent of the printing press books became more available, and lecturers often read annotations of the books, which led to the notion of lecture notes.

Lectures also played an important historical role in announcing scientific advances or debating alternatives at scientific meetings or public lectures. This is somewhat consistent with the news conferences on breakthroughs that occur today. Advances in physics and engineering were often demonstrated at academic meetings. The famous lecturers of Marconi, Fleming, and Maskelyne illustrated controversies about wireless communication. Marconi, an inventor of wireless telegraphy and a talented advocate for his approach as well as an entrepreneur, attempted to win converts in lectures at the Royal Institution. In one particular lecture in 1903, Marconi's opponent, Maskelyne, interfered with the public demonstration of his system by sending messages from his own transmitter. This famous lecture had the desired intent of raising awareness about wireless communication and confusing potential commercial vendors concerning the best approach to developing wireless devices (Larson, 2006).

Lecturers have embraced new technologies to transmit their information. Lecturers took advantage of diagrams, photographs, and artistic works. They adopted slide projectors to add images to inform the audience. Art history and architecture were major innovators in using such presentation technologies. For example, art lecturers took advantage of lantern slides starting in the 1800s. Magic lanterns were able to animate a sequence of slides and to provide comparisons between different works (Leighton, 1984). The availability of electricity and advances in photography brought 35mm slides, silent films, and eventually full motion and sound films. These were soon followed by overhead projectors, computer projected images, various forms of movies, and interactive visualizations.

Starting in the 1980s, software for creating overhead transparencies and eventually computer presented images (e.g., PowerPoint) became extremely popular. Recently the *New York Times* reported that PowerPoint has permeated all aspects of communication in the military, motivating some young officers to report that they spend most of their time making PowerPoint slides (Bumiller, 2010). Lecturers go to great lengths to incorporate slides into their presentations (see Box 2.2).

BOX 2.2 THE LECTURER'S DILEMMA
Challenges of using visual materials in lectures

In spite of dangers and faulty equipment, lecturers persist in using *slide technology*.

- Early versions of the slide projector became available in the 1600s.
- For example, the **Magic Lantern** used candles or oil lamps as a light source and a concave mirror to enlarge the image (Miyahara, 2007). Slides were initially painted on glass and eventually prepared using photographic techniques.

To achieve a brighter image, before electricity became useful, some projectors used *limelight*.

- Limelight involved directing a combination of hydrogen and oxygen at a cylinder of quicklime (calcium oxide) (Reid, 2001).
- This is the source of the phrase, *in the limelight* but also a possible source of a *dangerous fire* if the combination of gases is not carefully controlled.

The challenges of projecting images are endless.

- For example, one author (Linn) tells the story of preparing overhead projector transparencies (translated into Chinese) for talks in China in the 1980s.

  - Of the six talks, only one succeeded somewhat.
  - For the others the problems were:

    - No overhead projector available
    - Burned out bulb
    - Electricity off for the day
    - Electrical plug not compatible with the outlet
    - Blown fuse.

Numerous lecturers injured their arms and backs carrying bulky computers, computer projectors, and even backup transparencies to scientific meetings in the 1990s.

The first "portable" Apple computer—dubbed the "luggable" by its supporters—was released in 1989*. It weighed 16 pounds and had a 40 MB hard drive.

* http://oldcomputers.net/macportable.html

In science, lecturers have used research tools to illustrate lectures. For example, geologists use GIS systems, physicists use modeling and simulation tools, and biologists often show microscopic images. We discuss how these images can go beyond transmission to support KI in Chapter 6.

Impact of Lectures

Compared to laboratory activities, personalized instruction systems, and self-paced systems, lectures are generally less effective (Kulik & Kulik, 1979; Kulik, Kulik & Cohen, 1980; Odubunmi, & Balogun, 1991). Light (2001) reports that students generally value lectures less than other forms of learning and studying. Many studies have documented the limited benefits of lectures (Lewis & Lewis, 2008). Lectures often fail to prepare students for practical work or future instruction (e.g., Van Dijk, Van Der Berg, & Van Keulen, 2001). Many studies show that instructors overestimate the ideas their students hold (Hake, 1998; Halloun & Hestenes, 1985a). Using outcome measures such as the Force Concept Inventory (Hestenes & Halloun, 1995b), researchers have shown that lecture courses are often unsuccessful at helping students develop conceptual understandings (King, 1992). The Force Concept Inventory was designed to assess whether students could apply physics ideas to typical situations. Large numbers of the faculty were shocked to see how poorly their students understood basic physics concepts.

At first, many instructors responded to this evidence by arguing that students were not paying attention (add adding more exciting demonstrations). Over time, the physics research community has identified more successful practices (McDermott, 2006), often involving fewer lectures and more inquiry activities (computer-based visualizations; peer tutoring; laboratory-based projects). Indeed, partly in response to results of their students' performance on the Force Concept inventory, MIT has completely re-formatted their introductory physics course (previously one of the most famous lecture courses of all) to be more focused on student inquiry and small group exchanges (Pinker, 2010).

Many students vote with their feet and skip lectures altogether. Others fall asleep, often while trying to concentrate. In universities where lectures are available on video, the attendance in some courses has declined precipitously. Yet few students view such videos and video viewing declines over the course (e.g., Billings-Gagliardi & Mazor, 2007). In a study of medical students who were expected to attend lectures (Cardall, Krupat, & Ulrich, 2008), over 80% of students reported making decisions about whether to attend lectures on a case-by-case basis. In one study, about 60% reported attending the lectures and about 15% reported viewing the videos (Billings-Gagliardi & Mazor, 2007). In another study, most students reported attending lectures out of professional responsibility or desire to interact with friends. Few students (less than 5% in one study) indicated that they attended the lecture to ask questions or interact with the lecturer (Cardall, Krupat, & Ulrich, 2008).

Lectures and Motivation

A broad array of research on lecture classes illustrates the challenge of engaging students in lectures (Bjork, 1999; King, 1992; Van Heuvelen, 1991). In general, students have difficulty capturing the ideas presented in lectures and often lack techniques for elaborating or clarifying the information they do process (King, 1992; Bransford, Brown, & Cocking, 1999).

This occurs, in part, because student attention lapses for longer and longer time periods as the lecture progresses (Johnstone & Percival, 1976). Studies show that students recall more information from the beginning of the lecture than from the end (Hartley & Davies, 1978).

Lectures also fail because they are often poorly aligned with the needs of students. Students sometimes complain that instructors read directly from the textbook (Linn & Kessel, 1996), which may have been a good idea in medieval times when only the monk or nun had a copy of the book but is not as compelling today. In addition, students complain about lecturers who mumble to the blackboard rather than addressing the class or plow ahead even when the entire class is not able to follow the discussion (Linn & Kessel, 1996).

Some instructors give highly engaging and exciting lectures that motivate students to come to class. Lectures that please students often include demonstrations, humorous anecdotes, and, recently, audience participation. Activities such as the one-minute reflection (Light, 2001), clickers (Crouch & Mazur, 2001), and tablet computers (Anderson et al., 2004) increase student satisfaction with lectures and benefit learners under certain conditions (see Chapter 6).

Lecturers often seek to motivate students to enter science or choose a specific specialty, For example to illustrate the excitement and mystery of chemistry, Bassam Shakhashiri, when he was the assistant director of the National Science Foundation (1984–1990), regularly gave a lecture entitled, *Science is Fun,* which included a large number of rather exciting chemistry demonstrations that often included explosions and color change reactions (Shakhashiri, 1985).

Bjork (1999) argues that many student-pleasing activities such as audience response systems (i.e., "clickers") may actually be counter productive because they lull students and instructors into thinking they understand (see also Brown, 1992). This research suggests that lecture courses often implement the same, *motivate, inform, assess* pattern that was discussed above for textbooks.

Lectures and Note-Taking

In medieval universities instructors read their notes to students who copied them down and studied from them. With the advent of blackboards, lecturers often wrote out notes, proofs, or other information. The availability of the overhead projector motivated lecturers to project their notes instead of writing notes on the blackboard. This allowed instructors to face their audience rather than turning their backs to the audience.

With the availability of mimeograph and copy machines, instructors sometimes made copies of their notes in hopes that this would increase the ability of the lecture to inform students by freeing students to listen more closely to their lectures. The practice of distributing lecture notes and the availability of notes taken by professional note-takers has varied consequences. When students have copies of the notes they sometimes do as their instructors suggest and pay more attention to the lecture, but at other times students may not really know how best to take advantage of the notes plus the lecture. At worst, the notes just make the lecture more complicated and difficult to process. Students who believe they already have the notes may actually not pay as much attention to the lecture as they would if they were worried about recording the information so they could use it in the future.

Presentation technologies such as PowerPoint encouraged the practice of displaying notes while speaking about them. This technology has led some to believe that everyone now thinks in bullet points (Pinker, 2010) and others to condemn PowerPoint (Tufte, 2001).

Real-time note-taking emerged when word processing programs could be immediately displayed on a computer screen. In this approach a scribe captured notes for a group discussion. Individuals participating in the discussion could monitor the accuracy of the transcription of their remarks into the notes in real time while the discussion progressed. This practice had a short history primarily because displaying the notes while the discussion was ongoing interfered with the natural flow of the discussion. It motivated participants to complain that their remarks had not been accurately captured and distracted others from processing the verbal contributions.

In summary, note-taking technologies primarily increase the amount of information and the format of information communicated to the audience. Although most students take notes, providing notes for the audience is a complex issue. Notes have the potential of focusing the audience on the lecture. They can also lull the audience into complacency or confuse the audience by requiring them to decode the notes along with the lecture. Note-taking technologies do not generally contribute to the interaction between the presenter and the audience.

Class Discussion

Studies of class discussion show that instructors commonly implement patterns such as *initiate, respond, evaluate* (IRE, Mehan, 1979). In this pattern, the instructor initiates the discussion with a question and expects a certain form of response. Students respond to the question, and each response is evaluated. Through such exchanges, instructors either reinforce normative ideas or criticize non-normative views rather than seeking ways to build on student ideas. The instructor may accompany the question and response sequence with a lecture to inform the class. Instructors could get more information about students' ideas by incorporating exchanges such as those used in the Ikatura approach (see Box 2.1) than they can from class discussion using the *initiate, respond, evaluate* pattern.

Implications for Lectures

The limitations of lectures and class discussions discussed here reflect the difficulties that individuals have in learning from such instruction, the limited opportunities for students and instructors to exchange information, and the focus of lectures on transmitting information. Lectures cover topics consistent with the course goals, but do not necessarily connect with the views of students. Noting student disinterest, instructors add demonstrations, jokes, and other motivating elements. This approach can attract an audience but does not necessarily improve learning. Discussions offer instructors a way to gather information but are used primarily to reinforce correct ideas, consistent with the *initiate, respond, evaluate* pattern.

Typical assessments used in large lectures compound the problem. Most instructors rely on multiple-choice tests that are supplied by textbook publishers (and automatically scored). These items fail to encourage students to articulate their ideas and do not require students to extend their knowledge to new problems or deal with complex dilemmas (Hake, 1998). As a result, most instructors have limited opportunities to learn about student ideas. When assessments like the Force Concept Inventory (Hestenes & Halloun, 1995) that reveal student ideas were introduced instructors were shocked to discover the limitations of their students' understanding.

In Chapter 6 we discuss alternatives such as classroom response systems (like clickers) that can reveal the understanding of all the students attending the lecture and tablet PCs have can be used to administer complex assignments to small groups and then to transmit the answers to the instructor. These approaches reveal the places where students falter. Of course, instructors also need to respond to students by promoting KI rather than saying which ideas are correct.

In summary, typical lecture classes, like the textbook, reflect a view of the learner as absorbing information from instructors who transmit information to students. While many lectures include time for class discussions, instructors typically seek correct answers rather than building on student ideas. To evaluate progress—and sometimes to motivate students—courses include quizzes, midterms, and finals based on materials from textbook publishers. There are few opportunities for students to reconsider their ideas and limited information to help the instructor understand the ideas held by their students. These experiences reflect the *motivate, inform, assess* pattern and the *initiate, respond, evaluate* pattern.

In spite of their limitations, lectures are here to stay, in large measure because they are an inexpensive way to provide contact between faculty and students. Students who persist to advanced degrees often learn how to listen critically to lectures and to distinguish their own ideas from those of the lecturer. Unfortunately, students often emulate their professors when they become instructors themselves. To take advantage of lectures, research suggests that instructors should elicit student ideas and engage students in analyzing their own views (as discussed in Chapter 6). Shortening or eliminating lectures, adding elements such as those in the Ikatura method (see Box 2.1), or implementing strategies such as peer discussion can replace the *motivate, inform, assess* pattern and the *initiate, respond, evaluate* pattern with more promising patterns.

Science Laboratory Experiments

Science laboratories are the third major component of science instruction and also reflect the absorption approach. As the NCES survey (Grigg et al., 2006) reveals, 60% of science courses in college require lab assignments and about half of those courses include group projects. Laboratory activities are also fairly frequent in precollege courses (see Figure 2.1). The Braun et al. (2009) report found that doing hands-on activities, talking about measurements and results, writing long answers to assignments, and working with others were all associated with improved outcomes but were quite rare. A recent National Academy of Science report entitled America's Lab Report (NRC, 2006; Singer, Hilton, & Schweingruber, 2005) indicated that most precollege laboratories reflect the absorption approach to student learning. Furthermore, comparing reviews of research on laboratories separated by 20 years, Hofstein and Lunetta (1982, 2004) point out that little has changed. Typical laboratories can be seen as implementing a variation of the *motivate, inform, assess* pattern.

Goals of Laboratory Activities

To engage students in inquiry, the laboratory activity is often selected based on a belief that active learning is preferable to passive learning. Active learning is an imprecisely defined term. It can include students using scientific equipment, responding to questions, talking to peers, or manipulating materials. Active learning is often justified on the basis of motivation rather than on developing understanding. Like the pictures and boxes in textbooks, laboratories can be exciting. Active engagement can be motivating but does not necessarily lead to inquiry learning.

Laboratories often have goals of informing students about the scientific process of experimentation. They may inform students about research practices or the scientific method by engaging them in following an experimental protocol (see Figure 2.5). They may inform students about techniques such as using a pipette

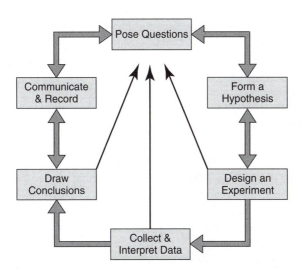

FIGURE 2.5   Typical depiction of the scientific method in precollege courses

or pan balance or operating a complex instrument such as a mass spectrometer. In many cases, students see laboratories as akin to following a recipe, they may not even interpret their results but rather fill in the answers they know are expected (NRC, 2006).

These goals likely benefit some audiences of students and not others. Most students would benefit from a better understanding of the nature of science such as appreciating how scientists negotiate meaning. Students who hope to become bench scientists may benefit from learning techniques, but since laboratory technologies change rapidly, few schools can keep up to date. Developing the ability to learn new techniques may be an even more important or relevant goal for such students.

Evidence for the goals of laboratories can be gleaned from the assessments and grading practices. When laboratories reward students for correctly identifying a reagent or accurately weighing a substance, they communicate that following procedures is the goal. Often students feel that their laboratory reports are graded more on whether they achieved the correct solution than on creative interpretation of anomalies (Hofstein & Lunetta, 2004).

Piagetian Theory and Laboratories

Designers often justify recipe-like laboratory activities based on a misguided interpretation of developmental psychology. Piagetian developmental theory is interpreted by some as implying that students younger than age 12 or 13 cannot reason abstractly and, therefore, need laboratories that are well specified in order to be able to interact with the materials and carry out the expected activities (Duschl et al., 2007; NRC, 2006). Although this view has been discredited and many researchers have demonstrated that students starting in first grade can reason abstractly under the right instructional conditions (Case, 1978, 1985; Chi & Koeske, 1983; Metz, 2004), typical laboratory activities often reflect a view of the learner as capable of concrete but not abstract thought. Laboratories designed to align with a view of the learner as concrete frequently neglect opportunities for independent exploration, reflection, and design of new investigations. This can be seen as consistent with the absorption approach because students are informed of scientific advance but not engaged in authentic science investigations.

Research reviews (Hofstein & Lunetta, 1982, 2004; NRC, 2006) substantiate the shortcomings of laboratory experiences and the limited progress on this agenda. To convert a laboratory from an active experience to an opportunity to develop coherent or linked understanding of the science topic requires redesign and a process of iterative refinement (Kali, Bos, Linn, Underwood, & Hewitt, 2002; Linn, Bell, & Davis, 2004). Laboratories can support inquiry learning as found in the TIMSS comparison study (Roth et al., 2006), but this goal is infrequently achieved (Kali, Linn, & Roseman, 2008).

In summary, research shows that instructors often justify laboratories as implementing active learning and motivating learners. Recipe-like laboratories reflect a view of the learner as benefiting from motivation to learn science and lacking ability to work abstractly. These laboratories inform students about scientific methods and procedures. Typically laboratories assess students by requiring laboratory reports that follow a clearly delineated format. In addition, typical classes incorporate the content into exam questions that might ask for recall of scientific procedures. As the research above suggests, these experiences rarely succeed (Hofstein & Lunetta, 2004; Linn & Hsi, 2000). These laboratories follow the same *motivate, inform, and assess* pattern identified for textbooks and lectures. In this pattern, the motivate steps refers to active, hands-on activities.

As discussed in Chapter 7, the National Academy report on laboratories (NRC, 2006) calls for *integrated instructional units*. It emphasizes opportunities for using laboratories to engage students in inquiry and to increase coherent understanding. In this view, laboratory experiences should be linked with other types of activities, such as lectures, reading, and discussion, to achieve the goals of helping students develop inquiry capabilities, as well as a coherent understanding of the science topic.

In summary, typical recipe-like laboratories can motivate and inform students but fail to take advantage of the capabilities of the learner. Implementing the *motivate, inform, and assess* pattern in the laboratory neglects the important goal of inquiry learning and inhibits the ability of students to develop autonomous investigative skills.

Online Courses and Materials

The potential of technology for science learning is stunning (e.g., Borgman et al., 2008; Collins & Halverson, 2009; Pea et al., 2003) but has not yet been achieved. The most common online uses of technology in science education are for multimedia lectures, drill and practice, and distance learning (Becker, 1999; Rainie & Hitlin, 2005). Today, many states are considering online science textbooks and universities offer distance-learning options for many introductory science courses. Consistent with the absorption approach, most online materials are designed to increase the total amount of information transmitted, provide immediate feedback rather than encourage inquiry, and increase motivation.

Multimedia Lectures and Distance Learning

Initial distance learning solutions sought to implement activities found in large lecture classes such as lectures and demonstrations but found that students often dropped out. To increase interest and take advantage of the format, lecturers have experimented with movies and special effects, online question and answer sessions, and peer-to-peer discussions. Adding more innovative features such as game-like elements or online feedback has increased motivation but not reduced the high rate of attrition. In both face-to-face and online formats, multimedia lectures reflect the view of the learner as benefitting from motivation to absorb information. A quick search of YouTube videos shows that science lectures are available but their popularity is low, especially compared to other videos (e.g., World of Warcraft gaming sessions). Multimedia lectures generally follow the *motivate, inform, assess* pattern used in typical classroom lectures.

Research shows that video lectures are even less effective in helping students learn than live lectures (Figlio, Rush, & Yin, 2010). When students select online learning opportunities, however, those who complete the online course are often as successful as those in the face-to-face lecture (Dolan, 2008).

When combined with predictions and opportunities to reflect, some uses of visualizations in lectures have been effective (Yang, Andre, & Greenbowe, 2003). As discussed in Chapter 6, adding audience participation can improve lectures. In general, the actual lecture is getting shorter and is often being replaced by labs or audience participation.

Drill, Games, and Online Learning Environments

Initially drill was perhaps the most popular use of online learning. Online drill and practice on science facts and multiple choice test items often accompanies textbooks. These activities are designed to determine whether information from the textbook has been absorbed. Drill is not nearly as successful in supporting long-term recall of information as more complex activities such as generation of explanations, consistent with extensive research in psychology laboratories (Bjork, 1994). In addition, Bjork & Bjork (2011) report that the frequency of errors during instruction can be a poor indicator of long-term learning. When designing exercises, authors often focus on responses that are readily scored rather than more complex accomplishments, reminiscent of the *initiate, respond, evaluate* pattern discussed in conjunction with lectures.

Designers have explored many ways to take advantage of the power of games to sustain interest of users. Educational programs that emulate games and incorporate similar reward structures (such as rewards for rapid responses, competition among classmates, and opportunities to earn points by solving puzzles) motivate learners but may not lead to integrated understanding (Lepper, 1985). These uses of gaming implement the *motivate and assess* pattern.

Today designers are exploring novel uses of online opportunities often delivered in one-on-one or small group self-paced learning environments (e.g., Slotta & Linn, 2009). Study of complex games such as Whyville and design environments such as Scratch offer promise for education (e.g., Kafai et al., 2009; Richland et al., 2007; Slator, 2006). Technologies can provide scaffolds to enable students to explore visualizations, conduct open-ended experiments, construct knowledge, collaborate, or engage in design (Eylon, Ronen, & Ganiel, 1996; Linn, 2003; NRC, 2006; Quintana et al., 2004).

We discuss how these complex environments can support KI in subsequent chapters.

Impact of Typical Patterns

The patterns of instruction that students encounter in current textbooks, laboratory experiences, lectures, and online activities incorporate a view of the learner as absorbing information. They reinforce a view of science learning as memorizing details. And they reflect a view of development as constraining reasoning capabilities. They frequently seem guided by an idea that science itself is not interesting, so that extrinsic rewards (in game-like activities) or sensational ideas (in textbook boxes or lecture-demonstrations) are needed to motivate students. Textbooks often focus on covering the many standards rather than offering coherent accounts of science. These patterns may inhibit students' inclinations to understand science, lead them to expect extrinsic rewards for studying science rather than deriving intrinsic benefits from this endeavor, and send the message that reasoning about science is complicated and difficult rather than accessible and essential for success in our society.

In contrast, successful programs take advantage of the views of the learner (Bransford, Brown, & Cocking, 2000; Bruer, 1993; diSessa, 1988; Eylon & Linn, 1988). They guide interactions to enable students to distinguish their ideas (Hatano & Inagaki, 1991, 2003; Slotta & Linn, 2009). They engage students in activities that help them develop the ability to guide their own learning (Brown, 1992; Linn & Hsi, 2000).

Cross-National Research

Confirmation of the absorption-based nature of instruction in American classrooms comes from a recent comprehensive study of classroom science practices in five countries conducted by the Third International Mathematics and Science Study (TIMSS). The study compared the United States, which was placed 18th out of 38 countries, to four (Australia, the Czech Republic, Japan, the Netherlands) of the highest scoring countries (Roth et al., 2006). For the study, one hundred schools were identified in each country. In each participating school, one 8th grade class was chosen randomly. The class was videotaped for one complete period or lesson. In order to get a sense of the instruction that takes place throughout an entire school year, videotapes were collected at different times in the 100 participating schools in each country. In addition, a questionnaire was administered to students and teachers concerning the videotaped lesson. Response rates ranged from 81–100% across the populations.

To analyze the videotapes, categories of activities were identified and used to code the videos. There were many similarities across the lessons, as well as substantial differences. All of the usual class activities discussed in this chapter were observed: textbook use, lecture–discussion, laboratory activities, and some online activities. However, very few examples of technology-enhanced learning were observed, consistent with international surveys showing limited use of technology for science.

Coherence

Looking at the coherence of science content in the lessons from each of the five countries, the TIMSS video study found the United States to lag behind other countries. The Japanese classes were the most focused on emphasizing strong conceptual links, consistent with the example of the Ikatura method (see Box 2.1) used widely in Japanese classrooms. In the United States, students learned content with strong conceptual links 30% of the time, whereas Japanese classes featured strong conceptual links 70% of the time. Australia and the Czech Republic each had over 50% of class activities with strong conceptual links. Research shows that students who develop coherent understanding in introductory courses develop lifelong interest in science and are more likely to choose science careers than students who do not develop this coherent understanding (Tai, Liu, Maltese, & Fan, 2006).

The United States was way ahead of other countries in doing activities with no conceptual links. Remarkably, 20% of the time, the United States classrooms featured science activities with no conceptual links, whereas the other four countries averaged less than 10% of the time doing activities with no conceptual links.

Further support for these findings comes from in-depth analysis of the classroom videotapes. Researchers computed the proportion of science lessons that focused on acquiring facts, definitions, and algorithms versus those making connections. In Japan, 72% of the time was spent making connections, consistent with the emphasis on coherence. In the United States, 66% of the lessons involved acquiring facts, definitions, or algorithms. This complete reversal of emphasis is reported in other studies comparing science instruction in Japan and the United States (Lewis & Tsuchida, 1997, 1998; Linn, Lewis, Tsuchida, & Songer, 2000).

These results reinforce the analysis of teacher-led discussions and textbooks in the United States as following the *inform, assess* pattern and lacking connections to student ideas or to other parts of the curriculum. These findings also resonate with the analysis of textbooks in America conducted by Project 2061 (Roseman, Kesidou, Stern, & Caldwell, 1999; Roseman, Linn, & Koppal, 2008).

Representations

Another way that the United States curriculum diverged from the curriculum of the highest scoring countries was in using multiple representations to communicate about science. Most countries supported introduction of science disciplinary content with firsthand data, visual representations, and multiple forms of evidence more frequently than the United States. Instruction in the Czech Republic, Japan, and Australia paid considerable attention to student ideas by emphasizing first-hand data, illustrating ideas with more than one phenomenon, and using more than one visual representation well over half of the time. In contrast, in the United States, all three of these indicators were low.

Motivation

Consistent with the *motivate, inform, assess* pattern described above, the United States leads in frequency of using motivating activities such as games, puzzles, surprising and dramatic demonstrations, competitive activities, and role play. In the United States 63% of science lessons include these potentially motivating activities and more instructional time is allocated to these motivating activities than in all the other countries except Australia. This finding aligns with the observation that teachers in America frequently introduce science lessons with demonstrations but do not necessarily connect these activities to the topics under investigation. The finding also resonates with the Braun et al. (2009) result that moderate use of demonstrations is more effective than extensive use of demonstrations.

Inquiry

Analysis of inquiry activities in the five countries suggests that the *motivate, inform, and assess* pattern is more common in the United States than in the other countries. The Japanese use inquiry in ways consistent with the description of the Ikatura method (see Box 2.1), following a pattern such as *elicit ideas, predict, observe, explain, reflect*. Japanese students make predictions almost a quarter of the time, whereas all of the other countries spend about 10% or less time on making predictions. Another area where there are large differences in inquiry activities concerns observing, collecting, and recording data. In Japan 59% of the lessons include such activities compared to 31% in the United States. Furthermore, in Japan, 37% of the time students go on to organize and manipulate the collected data compared to 19% of the time in the United States. This emphasis also resonates with the Braun et al. (2009) results showing that in the small number of classes where students manipulate data, there are benefits on NAEP assessments.

Implications of TIMSS Study

The authors of the video study summarize the approaches to science teaching in each of the five countries. They argue that, in the Czech Republic, science content is judged to be difficult and science lessons typically focus on developing normative science knowledge and using techniques such as review and public oral assessment of students. The balance of strong conceptual links in half the lessons, combined with frequent goal and summary statements, contributes to content coherence. Content coherence is also supported in the Czech Republic by the use of multiple visual representations.

In contrast, in the Netherlands, students are assigned independent practical activities and report on their work using written reports. Students work independently, initiating their own content-related questions, and summarizing their findings. This is successful, in part, because it is a constant practice and students develop skill in working independently over years of doing projects.

Japanese lessons emphasize making connections between ideas and evidence and developing coherence using inquiry-oriented inductive activities. Teachers typically ask students to make predictions, help students organize results into graphs and charts, and conduct activities that enable students to interpret their data. Japanese science lessons enable students to jointly determine a main idea from their activities. The video study authors conclude that only a small number of ideas were developed in Japanese science lessons, but each idea was treated in depth and that multiple sources of supporting evidence were utilized, consistent with other analyses of Japanese instruction (Lewis, 2002; Lewis & Tsuchida, 1997, 1998; Linn, Lewis, Tsuchida, & Songer, 2000). The efficacy of this approach is made possible by the consistency of implementation over multiple years of schooling.

Australian science classes, according to the video study authors, are similar to Japanese lessons in that they focused on a limited number of ideas, drew on multiple forms of evidence, and emphasized coherence and connections between ideas and evidence. Similar to Japanese instruction, Australian students were guided by their teachers to collect, manipulate, and organize data and worked in groups to interpret their results. In contrast to all the other countries, Australian science lessons used real-life issues and independent practical activities very frequently. Although Australian lessons do add what could be seen as motivating activities as often as American lessons, it appears that these activities are directly integrated into the lesson and contribute to student understanding of the relevance of science for their lives.

The authors of the video study were somewhat at a loss to characterize 8th grade science lessons in the United States. They conclude that the main feature of these lessons is their emphasis on implementing a variety of activities. They say that there is a balance between independent practical activities, independent study activities, and whole class discussions, suggesting that activities in United States classes are heterogeneous. Compared to all of the other countries, United States teachers spent far more time attempting to engage students' interests and involvement, using both real-life issues and motivating activities such as games, puzzles and role play. This approach in the United States appears to be troublesome from the standpoint of coherence. Although many motivating activities and visual representations are used in these classes, they are not frequently linked to the science ideas in the curriculum and therefore it is difficult for students to create coherent connected understanding of science. The authors report that observations of the videotaped lessons suggest that content is typically organized around isolated ideas rather than coherent arguments.

This analysis of science lessons reinforces the typical patterns described in this chapter. It suggests that American instruction neglects coherence far more than instruction in the high scoring countries. Students in high scoring countries experience more instruction aimed at achieving coherence than do students in the United States. In the Netherlands, students are motivated to work independently. In Australia and Japan, students are guided by their teachers to go through an inquiry process that leads to coherent understanding. In the Czech Republic, teachers require students to achieve coherence across multiple topics.

Although international comparison tests may be a rather blunt instrument for distinguishing among accomplishments in science courses, these findings resonate with the general argument that coherence is a more central goal of instruction in Australia, the Czech Republic, Japan, and the Netherlands than it is in the United States. In this book, we argue that patterns used in American textbooks, lectures, and laboratory materials available to teachers contribute to the incoherence reported in the TIMSS video analysis by focusing on absorption of information. We employ the KI framework because it emphasizes respect for student ideas and calls for deliberate effort on the part of students and teachers to achieve coherence. The KI processes and patterns we will discuss subsequently in the book address the lack of coherence and are likely to strengthen student understanding.

Conclusions

A variety of evidence suggests that the instructional patterns that underlie typical textbooks, lectures, and laboratories in the United States reflect an outdated view of the learner as absorbing information. As a result, they fail to build on student ideas, to respect the intellectual efforts of the learner, and to enable learners to use their full reasoning processes to monitor and advance their own understanding.

We argue in this book that students need to integrate rather than absorb knowledge and offer instructional patterns for aligning curriculum, classroom instruction, and assessment that will ensure that such opportunities arise (see example in Box 2.1). These new patterns are particularly appropriate to guide design of activities using technology-enhanced materials.

Reflection Activity

Locate a science textbook that presents a topic of interest to you. Identify the pattern implemented in the textbook. Discuss whether the textbook primarily implements absorption or KI.

3

TRANSFORMING SCIENCE INSTRUCTION WITH TECHNOLOGY

A Thermodynamics Case Study[1]

Introduction

In a series of research studies, the Computer as Learning Partner project has transformed middle school instruction in thermodynamics by incorporating new technologies and refining instruction based on evidence from student work. The curriculum addressed direction of heat flow, heat, temperature, insulation, conduction, thermal equilibrium, and related topics appropriate for middle school. During most of the studies reported here, Eylon was an adviser to the project. The research on thermodynamics has been carried out over a 20-year period and is described in a series of papers and books (Lewis & Linn, 1994; Linn, 1995; Linn & Hsi, 2000; Linn, Davis, & Bell, 2004; Linn, Songer, & Eylon, 1996; Slotta & Linn, 2009).

This research featured iterative refinement of a semester-long middle school science curriculum that:

- guides student inquiry and provides feedback with a learning environment.
- documents student work using embedded assessments and logging of activities.
- provides a teacher interface for monitoring classroom activities, grading student work, sending comments to students, and customizing the curriculum.
- takes advantage of powerful, interactive visualizations and virtual experiments.
- incorporates real-time data collection using temperature-sensitive probes.
- aligns assessment, curriculum, instruction, and professional development using the KI framework.

The iterative refinement of the Computer as Learning Partner curriculum was guided by a partnership of teachers, researchers, technologists, designers, evaluators, and discipline experts. The partnership agreed on the goal of promoting integrated, coherent understanding.

As the partnership investigated student learning they were struck by the numerous ideas about each science topic that students bring to class. Using interviews, observations, and insights from the classroom teacher, the partnership documented the many ideas that students hold about thermodynamics as well as the careful reasoning that led to the ideas (Linn & Hsi, 2000). They recognized that this repertoire of ideas was a fabulous resource for science instruction (see Figure 1.1, Chapter 1 and Box 3.1). Although the ideas held by students were often inaccurate, the reasoning processes generally drew on evidence from observations or experiences and involved inferences based on this information. The partnership

---

BOX 3.1 PIVOTAL CASE THERMODYNAMICS
A pivotal case illustrating scientific basis for thermal equilibrium

A **pivotal case** is an example that teachers add to help students shift or pivot their thinking from a *less productive idea to a more productive idea*.

For example, many students have the intuitive idea that *metals are naturally cold*. Students gain support for this view by noticing that in the classroom the table leg (or other metal object) feels cold to the touch compared to other materials, like wood. A WISE activity in thermodynamics guides students to measure the temperature of the objects in the room and to note that they all have the same temperature, except objects that have heat sources such as computers or people.

Teachers can introduce a pivotal case to help students sort out these views.

A pivotal case contrasts two alternatives. For thermodynamics this might be the *classroom experience* and either the *playground* or *the beach example* (*see Figure examples*).

The **playground** example asks students, "Have you ever been playing outside in the summer time and gone down the metal slide? If metals are naturally cold, then why does a metal slide feel so hot during the summer? How does the slide feel compared to a wooden bench?"

The **beach** example, asks students, "Have you been at the beach on a hot day and touched a metal car. If metals are naturally cold, then why does the car feel so hot? How does the metal on the car feel compared to a wooden table at the beach?"

Examples

These **examples** often help students realize that there must be some other explanation for how metals act than being "naturally cold."

Criteria for pivotal cases	Example of thermodynamics case
Create compelling comparisons that highlight the confusions of students and control for the relevant variable.	The examples compare a hot and typical environment: classroom and playground on a hot day.
Select culturally and personally relevant examples where students can accurately predict the outcome although they may not be able to explain the reason.	Students know that the metal slide feels warmer than the bench on a hot day. Both classrooms and playgrounds are personally relevant.
Select examples that provide feedback to support pro-normative ideas.	The examples provide feedback on the idea that metals are naturally cold.
Select examples that are easy to convert into a narrative that links the relevant information.	Students can create narratives that link their experiences to beliefs such as the idea that metals can impart cold to objects.

Successful hypothetical dialogue

Excerpts from a possible teacher, student dialogue:

S: Metals are naturally cold; that's why the table leg feels cooler than the wooden table top.

T: Have you ever been playing outside in the summer time and gone down the metal slide?

S: Yes.

T: How does it feel?

S: It's really hot!

T: If metals are naturally cold, then why does the metal slide feel so hot during the summer?

S: Good question!

T: How does that fit into what we've been learning in class? For example, in the equilibrium lab?

S: There we learned that everything comes to the same temperature.

T: What about heat bars?

S: There we learned that heat flows through metals faster than it flows through stuff like wood.

T: So where is the heat flowing in the case of the table leg?

S: Um, well, from hot things to cooler things—so from me into the table leg.

T: And is it flowing quickly or slowly?

S: Quickly.

T: How about in the case of the slide—where is the heat flowing there?

S: From the slide into me.

T: And is it flowing quickly or slowly?

S: Quickly. Oh! I get it. So it's the same temperature, it just feels different because the heat is flowing into it or out of it really quickly! That's cool!

sought to guide students to use these reasoning processes to gain more coherent and accurate ideas.

The partnership realized that the repertoire of ideas often lacked some of the accurate ideas needed to understand topics such as the difference between heat and temperature. The designers came up with creative ways to add new ideas using hands-on experiments with the temperature-sensitive probes, virtual experiments, and visualizations.

The partnership realized that adding ideas is not sufficient to promote integrated, coherent understanding. The ideas students develop on their own have a long history and multiple arguments in their favor. Yet, as discussed in Chapter 2, instruction often informs students of new ideas and neglects the process of sorting out, prioritizing, distinguishing, and integrating new and existing ideas. The partnership focused on ways to help students distinguish ideas using scientific evidence, make links across observable, atomic, and symbolic representations, and sort out incoherent views.

Since many ideas in the repertoire held by students emerged in everyday personally-relevant situations, the partnership sought to engage students in analyzing familiar problems. The partnership created virtual experiments to test ideas about topics such as home insulation, keeping drinks cold for lunch, and determining the most efficient way to heat a large volume of water. Progress occurred when students not only learned new ideas but also linked and connected these ideas to solve dilemmas such as:

- how to keep a picnic cold on a warm day,
- why metal feels colder than wood on a cool day but hotter than wood on a hot day,
- how a thermos keeps hot things hot and cold things cold.

From this work emerged the KI framework that summarizes promising techniques for promoting robust, generative understanding of science.

The partnership conducted *design research*, testing alternative designs in classrooms and using evidence from student embedded assessments to guide decisions. Results from design research were synthesized into design principles and the KI pattern. The principles and the pattern had the goal of giving designers a head start on creating new materials that promote KI. To illustrate the impact of design research and the insights emerging from current curriculum investigations, this chapter highlights the leadership of many of the members of the Computer as Learning Partner partnership.

This research program has benefitted from grant support from the National Science Foundation, Apple Computer, the United States Department of Education, and the Spencer Foundation. The community-building efforts of the National Science Foundation have enabled researchers involved in design research and curriculum innovation to interact with each other, critique developments in each other's research programs, and jointly develop insights into effective science instruction. The principles, patterns, and processes emerging from this research could not have occurred without the extensive support and energy gained from this community.

Methodologies

The research involved iterative design studies inspired by work in engineering, architecture, and computer science (Alexander, Ishikawa, & Silverstein, 1977; Bell, Hoadley, & Linn, 2004). In this approach, the partnership of designers with the relevant expertise uses classroom observations, analysis of student responses to embedded questions, pretests and posttests, new technologies, as well as analysis of the discipline to diagnose weaknesses and plan a curricular project. The partnership revises the curriculum and compares the performance on the new version to performance on the prior version. Based on specific comparisons of embedded assessments as well as overall comparisons using pretests and posttests, the partnership identifies factors that contribute to improved performance.

To evaluate the effectiveness of the innovative curriculum projects the research program used KI assessments. The research has benefitted from continuity of outcome measures. From the very beginning, the research partnership focused on the difference between heat and temperature and included, as an outcome measure, a combination question. In the multiple-choice part of the combination, students indicate whether heat and temperature are the same or different. In the explanation part students explain their answer and include several examples (see selected responses and scoring rubric in Figure 3.1). This item has proven to be sensitive to instruction designed to help students distinguish between heat and temperature (Clark & Linn, 2003) and robust in multiple research studies (Linn & Hsi, 2000).

i) In general, are heat energy and temperature the same or different?
CircleOne: <u>Same</u> <u>Different</u>
[Rubric Coding: Same (1), Different (2), Multiple answers (9), Blank(0)]

ii) What is the **main reason for their similarity or difference**?
Include an **example** that helps to explain your answer

Score	Level	Description	Examples
0	**No answer**		
1	**Off-Task**	Response is irrelevant or "I don't know." Student writes some text, but it does not answer the question being asked.	
2	**Irrelevant ideas or links** Scientifically irrelevant ideas (misconceptions). OR Scientifically invalid connections between ideas.	Scientifically-invalid statements such as the following: • Temperature is certain degrees Temperature is warm or cold or hot. • Energy is warm, cold or hot. • Heat is temperature.	• Heat is a force. • Temperature is usually from the Sun or how you feel. • They are usually similar but not the same. There can be a low, let's say 20 degrees heat energy, the temperature could be 10. • I think there same because heat is a force of energy and it has a temperature. For example heat produce a energy when you heat some thing up like thermometer it raises the liquid in side and it gives the temperature of the heat.
3	**Partial link** Unelaborated connections using relevant features. OR Scientifically valid connections that are not sufficient to solve the problem.	Scientifically correct statements that do not address what the question is asking. For example: • Heat is a form of energy. • Heat energy can be added, transferred, and lost. • Heat energy is a form of energy caused by heat. • Heat energy is produced by heat energy sources such as sun. • Temperature is how hot/cold something is.	• Temp. is how hot something is, heat energy is energy caused by heat. • Because heat energy is the energy the created heat gives off, and temperature is the measurement of the energy that is created.
4	**Single link** One scientifically complete and valid connection.	One of the following: Difference 1: • Temperature is a measure (measurement) of the average molecular motions in a system. • Heat: the amount of energy in the system. Difference 2: • Temperature is measured in For C, while he energy is measures in J. Difference 3: • Heat energy can transfer in radiation, conduction, or convection.Temperature is not transferable. • Temperature of a closed system can change by the influx of heat energy. Difference 4: • Use everyday examples of how objects with the same temperature can have different amounts of energy.	• Temperature is the measure of heat energy. As an object heats up or gains heat energy, its temperature rises. • Because temperature is just how hot it is, heat energy is actually giving off heat; like the Sun compared to how hot the Sun makes it. • Because temperature is a measure of thermal energy while the energy is something else. if it is a hot day you feel the energy not the temperature because that is just a measurement.

FIGURE 3.1 Knowledge Integration thermodynamics assessment and scoring rubric

The researchers also used numerous other items to measure student progress in thermodynamics (Liu, Lee, Hofstetter, & Linn, 2008). Recently we developed several new item types. To facilitate scoring of responses we have experimented with two-tier items involving a sequence of multiple-choice questions (see Box 3.2). Two-tier items can extend the topic coverage but are not as sensitive as constructed response items (Lee, Liu, & Linn, in press). We discuss new item types designed to capture the development of coherent understanding including MySystem and Energy Stories in Chapter 8 (see Box 8.3). Reusing the same items regularly in research studies allows direct comparisons across many versions of the curriculum.

BOX 3.2 TWO-TIER ASSESSMENTS

For large classes, multiple-choice assessment is improved with two-tier items that ask students to select an explanation in the second tier (Lee, Liu, & Linn, in press).

Typical two-tier item (Odom & Barrow, 1995)

Multiple-choice tier (scored 0 or 1)

If a small amount of salt (1 tsp) is added to a large container of water (4 liters or 1 gal) and allowed to set for several days without stirring, the salt molecules will:

- a. be more concentrated on the bottom of the water. (0)
- b. be evenly distributed throughout the container. (1)

Explanation tier (scored 0 or 1)

The reason for my answer is because

- a. salt is heavier than water and will sink. (0)
- b. salt dissolves poorly or not at all in water. (0)
- c. there will be more time for settling. (0)
- d. there is movement of particles from a high to low concentration. (1)

KI two-tier item

We tested two-tier items for KI assessment and found that they could distinguish among levels 1, 2 and 3 but were difficult to create for levels 4 and 5 (Lee, Liu, & Linn, in press). The multiple-choice tier is scored 0 or 1. The explanation tier uses KI scoring: 0 for incorrect or irrelevant answer, 1 for some general evidence, and 2 for linking evidence to choice (Lee, Liu, & Linn, in press). For example:

Multiple-choice tier (scored 0 or 1)

1. Keisha is pushing her bicycle up a hill. Where does Keisha get the energy to push her bicycle?

   (a) From the food she has eaten. (1)
   (b) From the exercise she did earlier. (0)
   (c) From the ground she is walking on. (0)
   (d) From the bicycle she is pushing. (0)

Explanation multiple-choice tier (scored 0, 1, 2)

Which of the following explains your choice?

   (a) Exercise gives her strong energy. (0)
   (b) The ground gives her support to push the bike. (0)
   (c) The food is broken down to sugars muscles can use. (2)
   (d) The bike gives energy back to her. (0)
   (e) Chemical energy is stored in food. (1)
   (f) Energy is created when she eats food. (1)

Most of the Computer as Learning Partner design research used cohort comparisons or classroom comparisons to determine effective practices. In a cohort comparison a teacher delivers instruction about a topic, participates in redesigning the instruction, and tries the curriculum again with his or her next group of students. Cohort comparisons control for teacher effects and have comparable student populations, as long as no major change in participants occur from one implementation to the next. Of course, teachers become more proficient in delivering the instruction even without changes to the curriculum, so that proficiency is part of the impact on success.

In classroom comparisons two versions of curriculum materials are delivered to classes randomly assigned to conditions. Sometimes, the same teacher delivers two alternative approaches. In other cases, teachers are randomly assigned to instructional alternatives. These studies also afford relatively good control over initial conditions, although class-to-class comparisons are always limited by the variability of students within classes and the culture that has developed in the class.

Some studies use a within-class comparison by taking advantage of a learning environment like WISE. In this approach, students are randomly assigned to one of two, or sometimes more, variations of the curriculum. Although curriculum variations are randomly assigned, because the two approaches occur at the same time in the classroom, contamination can occur if students collaborate across groups and encounter a different version of the curriculum.

In summary, design research has greatly enhanced the possibilities of studying curricular innovations and understanding their effectiveness. In general, design research is aimed at improving curriculum designs. Design research studies also have the goal of identifying principles, patterns, theoretical views of learning, or recommendations that can inform future designers. Design research has the potential of giving future designers a head start on creating materials for new topics.

To summarize this research program this chapter associates the advances with the teachers, graduate students, and post-doctoral scholars who participated in the research partnership. The chapter describes how the researchers summarize their findings in descriptive instructional principles. These instructional principles form the basis of a Design Principles Database discussed in Chapter 5.

Robert Tinker: Innovative Technologies

The Computer as Learning Partner project was spurred by the work of Robert Tinker, the founder of TERC and later of the Concord Consortium. Tinker and his colleagues designed tools for real-time data collection using temperature-sensitive probes and other devices connected to Apple II computers starting in about 1983. The probes play an important role by permitting students to concentrate on their experiments while the technology takes care of the details (Mokros & Tinker, 1987; Pallant & Tinker, 2004). The temperature-sensitive probes support experimentation on heating and cooling by gathering and graphing changes in temperature in real time.

In addition, to help students distinguish heat and temperature, Tinker developed a device to deliver a dollop of heat (using an immersion heater) and to graph changes in temperature when a dollop is added to a large and small quantity of water. Tinker has continued to design innovations with modern technologies, identifying effective uses for simulated experiments, new learning environments, and, recently, dynamic, interactive visualizations of unobservable processes such as molecular interactions (Tinker & Xie, 2008).

Nancy Songer: Predictions and Probeware

Nancy Songer joined the partnership as a graduate student at the University of California, Berkeley, and identified ways to take advantage of the real-time data collected with temperature-sensitive probes. She designed activities to help students understand the difference between heat and temperature, as well as the direction of heat flow, insulation and conduction, and thermal equilibrium.

In designing instruction, Songer was struck by the difficulty that students have interpreting the results of their experiments. Often, students interpreted the experiments in the direction they expected the results to come out, rather than paying close attention to their investigations. For example, when students were looking at cooling curves for water in a Styrofoam cup and a metal cup, if they thought the metal would keep the water warm, they would ignore the labels on the graphs and assert their expectation.

Building on the discussion of the Ikatura method in Chapter 2 and other research (e.g., Gunstone & Champagne, 1990), Songer incorporated a pattern called *predict, observe, explain* that had proved successful in hands-on experiments. She asked students to first make predictions, then test their prediction, and finally reflect on whether the prediction was supported by the experiment. The partnership designed instruction that allowed students to draw lines in a graph showing their predictions concerning the outcomes of their experiments. Students wrote justifications for their predictions. They then conducted the experiments and reconciled their predictions with the outcomes. The use of predictions was much more effective than the version of the curriculum that involved observation but not predictions (Songer & Linn, 1991).

Convincing students that their experiment contradicted their prediction was not trivial. Often students seemed comfortable with both their prediction and the outcome. They did not necessarily compare the two views to see which was more compatible with the simulated experiments.

In addition, some students had difficulty conducting consequential experiments. They might change several variables at once. Or they might make the starting temperature of their experiment too close to room temperature and be unable to observe any changes. To help students evaluate their experiments, the research team added a critique activity where groups of students commented on the experiment of their peers. The first efforts were unsuccessful because students lacked criteria for distinguishing among good and bad experiments. Often critiques were focused on grammar or spelling rather than on the nature of the investigation. The designers added activities to help students identify criteria for evaluating experiments.

The classroom teacher, in discussing these results with the research team, suggested using a group critique activity. In the group critique, students review a composite experiment attributed to students from another class. The composite experiment illustrated many of the confusions found in class investigations. The classroom teacher, Doug Kirkpatrick, or "Mr. K." as he is known to his students, presented this experiment to the class and asked students to identify weaknesses in the experiment. Mr. K. guided the group to formulate a set of questions they could ask to determine whether the experiment was valid. This list was revised several times and ultimately posted in the classroom. A cohort comparison study demonstrated that students who participated in the critique activity were better at evaluating experiments and more successful in understanding thermodynamics concepts than students studying the previous version of the curriculum who did not experience the critique activity (Linn & Hsi, 2000).

This series of investigations established the importance of eliciting ideas and developing criteria. The success of eliciting student ideas, by using techniques such as making predictions, prior to introducing new ideas is consistent with the constructivist recommendation to build on student ideas. Eliciting ideas prepares learners to consider their existing ideas as they interpret new information.

However, eliciting ideas is not sufficient to improve understanding. It is possible for learners to add new ideas without distinguishing them from the elicited ideas. Students often add new ideas but limit their use to school examinations. The findings for the critique activity show the importance of distinguishing between ideas by using scientific criteria. By encouraging students to distinguish elicited and new ideas, instruction helps students develop the ability to use criteria to select the best scientific ideas.

Mr. K.: Heat Flow or Molecular Kinetic Theory

The partnership conducted several studies to identify the most effective way to add new ideas to the repertoire held by students. In reading students' predictions and reflections, the classroom teacher, Mr. K., became convinced that the textbook was not communicating the molecular kinetic model for thermodynamics to the students (students studied this topic in the textbook before doing experiments). He noted that students could not interpret their experiments at the atomic level. Students needed a more normative idea about heat propagation than they had but molecular kinetic theory was too abstract (see also Wiser & Carey, 1983).

The partnership consulted expert engineers, chemists, and physicists and asked them questions such as: which is better for keeping a drink cold, a sweater or aluminum foil? Experts often found these questions challenging (Linn & Hsi, 2000). Many tried to explain using molecular kinetic theory but became confused. Practicing engineers often used a heat flow model to explain the phenomena students encounter in their lives such as why Styrofoam is better than a metal cup for keeping a drink warm or why some jackets are better than others for keeping people warm (Linn & Hsi, 2000). In this model, heat flows from warmer to colder objects and the rate of flow depends on the conductivity of the material where it is flowing (Linn & Muilenburg, 1996). The research team decided that if heat flow helped engineers think about everyday problems, it might also be excellent for students.

The decision to feature heat flow rather than molecular kinetic theory was rather unprecedented. Experts warned the partners that they were reinforcing a view of heat as a substance. Chi (1992; Chi & Slotta, 1993) argued that heat flow and molecular kinetic theory were based on distinct ontologies and predicted that emphasis on heat flow would prevent students from developing sophisticated ideas.

The team persisted with heat flow, based on extensive evidence that molecular kinetic theory was inaccessible. Robert Tinker appreciated the dilemma and many years later, as discussed below, created the Molecular Workbench software that makes atomic level phenomena visible and accessible.

Cohort comparison studies of classes using heat flow and those using the molecular kinetic model demonstrated that heat flow was more accessible and interpretable—but not straightforward (Linn & Hsi, 2000; Songer & Linn, 1991). These studies helped the partnership refine their ideas about how best to add ideas concerning thermodynamics.

Eileen Lewis: Visualizing Heat Flow

Eileen Lewis, a graduate student and post-doctoral scholar participating in the thermodynamics research, analyzed end of semester assessments and concluded that the heat flow approach was more effective than the molecular kinetic model but quite difficult nevertheless. Lewis began this research by reviewing the repertoire of ideas that arose when students were asked to explain why metal and wood feel differently at room temperature. She confirmed that adding molecular kinetic theory did not help students improve their understanding—this theory does not connect to the beliefs of students or convince them to question their views. She realized that the heat flow model was more likely to help students understand but needed clarification. She found that students often reported that heat flowed at the same rate in all materials except air where they thought it flowed faster (Lewis, 1996; Lewis & Linn, 1994). Since an important aspect of insulation and conduction concerns the rate at which heat flows through materials, Lewis sought a way to communicate this idea.

Based on this evidence, Lewis designed the heat flow visualization and conducted research to show that adding this idea to the mix of views held by students could help them realize that the rate of heat flow depends on the material. Lewis realized students needed opportunities to investigate whether heat flows at different rates depending on the material. In collaboration with the technology team, Lewis designed a visualization of the rate of heat flow, shown in Figure 3.2. Using this visualization, students could change the material and observe how fast heat flows depending on the material selected.

Lewis pilot tested the heat flow visualization with students and found that it was helpful to encourage students to explain what their predictions were, as well as what they learned from interacting with the visualization. Lewis encouraged students to use the heat flow visualization in conjunction with their observations of the world. In a classroom comparison study, Lewis compared students using the heat flow visualization to those who did not use the heat flow visualization and found a substantial increase in performance (Lewis & Linn, 1994). This study underscores the importance of making sure that new ideas will help students improve their understanding.

Lewis found that even the heat flow model was not sufficient to help students understand why metal feels colder than wood at room temperature. Many students explained this situation by saying that metals had the property of imparting cold. They even extended this reasoning to argue that metals were good for

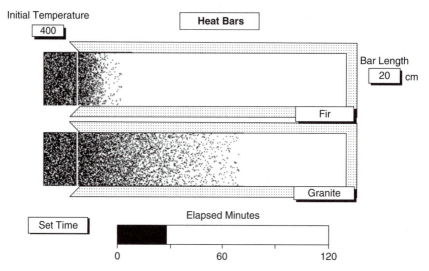

FIGURE 3.2 Screenshot from the heat bars software showing rate of heat flow in two materials

keeping drinks cold in a lunch. Lewis wanted to help students realize that heat was flowing faster out of their hands when they touched the metal, rather than that metal had the property of cooling their hand.

To understand this phenomenon students need to combine their understanding of the rate of heat flow with understanding of the direction of heat flow. To address this challenge, Doug Clark created a visualization showing both direction and rate of heat flow between a human hand and various materials. He extended the virtual experiment to consideration of wood and metal on hot and cold days. On cold days, the hand is warmer than the metal and the wood. So, heat is flowing from the warm hand to the cooler wood or metal. Since it flows faster into the metal, the metal feels colder. On hot days, the hand could be cooler than the wood and metal. *Predict which feels warmer, the wood or the metal?* This comparison of hot and cold days forms a pivotal case. In a classroom comparison study, Clark showed the impact of this visualization on student learning (Clark & Jorde, 2004).

Taken together these studies document how difficult it is to design ways to add new ideas. Some ideas like molecular kinetic theory are inaccessible because they are too abstract. Others, like heat flow, succeed best when accompanied by visualizations that target commonly misunderstood ideas but may need elaboration to connect to related phenomena such as the relative temperature of the hand and the object. Computers offer new opportunities for adding ideas in virtual experiments and visualizations. These technologies allowed the group to make unobservable and abstract ideas more understandable.

Nancy Songer: Viewing Science as Coherent

Nancy Songer reviewed student responses to pretests and posttests and conducted exploratory interviews. This evidence led her to wonder whether students were inhibited in developing coherent understanding of thermodynamics because they relied on memorizing facts rather than integrating ideas as called for in the KI pattern. She devised a number of ways to measure students' views about the nature of science and examined the relationship between these views and learning outcomes (Linn & Songer, 1993).

The research team devised a survey asking questions about science learning and about the nature of science. Questions asked about memorizing versus understanding, about whether scientific ideas change, about why scientists disagree, and about how science progresses. Students frequently indicated that memorization was better than understanding because they had done better on tests when they memorized.

When asked about whether everything in the textbook is true, students often thought this was a trick question. They commented that everything except the false questions on true-false items is true.

When asked about how scientists learn new things, students frequently said that they conducted experiments, rather than memorizing. Thus, students advocated for memorizing themselves but thought scientists relied on experiments.

When asked about why scientists sometimes disagree with each other, students made rather revealing comments. Some said that scientists were perverse and liked to argue. Others said that scientists disagree because they do not all have the latest information. A few students took a more dynamic view of the enterprise, saying that scientists might disagree for legitimate reasons because they had different conjectures about how best to resolve open questions. Many students articulated a relativistic view of science, saying that there were many alternatives and you really could not work out which one was the most likely to be correct.

Although most students held a diverse set of ideas, Songer characterized students as preferring one of three main views of science. First, a view of science as unfolding in an orderly manner as scientists gather more facts. Second, a view of science as relativistic, changing depending on who does the experiment or which technique is used. Third, a view of science as progressing by fits and starts, as research methodologies and results develop. She found that students who held the view that science progresses by fits and starts not only profited more from the thermodynamics instruction, but also remembered far more of the things they had learned than students holding the other views (Linn & Songer, 1993). This finding has subsequently been replicated by others (e.g., Linn & Eylon, 2000).

The Songer research made clear that science instruction aimed at coherent understanding could fail because students did not share that goal. Guiding students to integrate rich ideas about how to learn science and the experimental nature of science might help them make sense of the discipline itself. A series of experiments showed that students benefit from an appreciation of the complexity of scientific advance.

Philip Bell: Scientific Controversy

Phil Bell, a graduate student, extended this theme of making the nature of science understandable by introducing scientific controversies. When he first suggested debate projects to participating teachers they were skeptical, arguing that the topics they teach are not really an area of active debate. Bell respectfully disagreed, showing that students held conflicting views gained from experience with the natural world. He started with a project focused on light propagation. This project contrasts views based on visual acuity (light dies out further from the source) with the scientifically normative view of light propagation (light goes forever). Teachers were surprised by the success of this approach. Bell went on to collaborate with the teachers to design a series of debate projects on topics such as causes of increasing frog deformities or remedies for the worldwide threat of malaria to help students appreciate the nature of science. Bell reported that exploring debates in science enabled students to gain more insight into the nature of science (Bell & Linn, 2002).

Initially, Bell studied the advantage of assigning students to research one side of the debate, letting students chose which side of the debate to take, or asking students to prepare for both sides of the debate. Bell found that assigning students to a debate topic was more effective than letting students choose. He found that when students prepared for both sides of the debate they were more successful in distinguishing among ideas than when they prepared for only one side of the debate (Bell, 2004a; Bell & Linn, 2000).

Careful analysis of the impact of the debate project revealed that students were learning to distinguish ideas, but were not reconciling all of their ideas at the end of the project. To improve on this situation, Bell added a final report after the debate. Comparing instruction with and without the final report, Bell found that the final report strengthened student understanding of the topic as well as the coherence of student ideas (Bell, 2004). This combination of distinguishing ideas in the debate and reflecting to achieve coherence helped clarify the nature of KI.

Jacquie Madhok: Relevance of Science

Jacquie Madhok, a graduate student and former high school teacher, extended the investigation of the role of beliefs about science learning and achievement. She studied the relationship between student beliefs about the relevance of science and course achievement in both semester-long and longitudinal investigations. National and international studies show that student interest in careers in science, technology, engineering, and mathematics (STEM) is declining. Science courses that emphasize memorization and neglect connections to personally relevant examples are a potential contributor to this decline in interest (Joseph, 2004; Pintrich, 2003; Stipek et al., 1998).

Students in the CLP curriculum studied many personally relevant contexts such as (a) using insulation to design coolers to keep picnics safe, drinks warm or cold, (b) designing wilderness clothing to protect individuals from the elements, (c) making energy-efficient decisions about house design, and (d) evaluating tips for energy conservation. Madhok (2006) asked students questions such as: Has the science I learn in school got little in common with my life outside school? She asked students to give examples to explain their answers. In the semester-long studies, Madhok analyzed responses of 1,320 students from 12 semesters of the CLP curriculum. She found that experience with the curriculum led to increased beliefs that science was relevant to life. In addition, students who reported more relevance for science also achieved more. These results are consistent with Eccles' (1994; Eccles, Wigfield, & Schiefele, 1998) expectancy-value model in that students who value science and believe they can succeed are likely to persist in science. The results reflect the elements of the CLP curriculum that are designed to make science accessible.

In her longitudinal study, Madhok followed a subset of students from middle school to high school. She found that beliefs about the relevance of science persisted into ninth grade but declined in eleventh grade. In interviews, students often mentioned that the chemistry course they studied in eleventh grade was more about mathematics than science and did not seem relevant. These findings suggest the importance and fragility of beliefs about the relevance of science.

Judy Stern: The Checklist

Judy Stern, a graduate student and member of the technology team involved in the thermodynamics project, drew on her classroom observations to design ways that the technology could support the teacher. Stern observed that Mr. K., the classroom teacher, spent a great deal of time helping students figure out what to do next when they were using real-time data collection and probes to conduct experiments. She created a technology support for students called the checklist. The checklist guided students through their experiments and provided hints on difficult questions (Lewis, Stern, & Linn, 1993; Stern & Kirkpatrick, 1991).

Taking advantage of the checklist allowed Mr. K. to investigate ways to interact with individuals or small groups. He spent more and more time exploring how students made sense of their explorations. In moving from group to group, Mr. K. often identified disciplinary challenges or confusions that many students faced. At these points he interrupted the class to draw attention to obstacles that many groups faced and to showcase insights that different groups had achieved.

Mr. K.: Pivotal Cases

Mr. K. reported that being free to talk to students greatly enhanced his appreciation of the problems that students were facing and some of the reasons why the curriculum needed revision. These conversations combined with results from interviews conducted by researchers including Lewis, Songer, Madhok, and Bell motivated him to find better ways to communicate new ideas to students. He frequently came up with clever examples to respond to student difficulties.

Judy Stern, recognizing the benefit of these examples, rigged a tape recorder to Mr. K.'s lapel so that he could record the conversations he was having with individual groups. Mr. K. and Judy Stern jointly reflected on these videotapes and tape recordings and realized that Mr. K. was adding compelling examples that reflected his understanding of the disciplinary content. We synthesized the characteristics of effective examples and referred to them as pivotal cases (Linn, 2005).

For example, to help students understand the rate of heat flow Mr. K. frequently asked students to contrast how wood and metal felt in the classroom and how they remembered wood and metal objects feeling when they were at the beach on a hot day. Students typically responded to this question by noting that, at the beach, metal feels hot and wood feels cooler, while the classroom, metal feels cooler and wood feels warmer. Mr. K. would then encourage students to think about this case in making sense of their ideas about insulation and conduction. Many of the pivotal cases that Mr. K. introduced were incorporated into the curriculum as illustrated in the heat flow visualization discussed above and developed by Clark (Clark & Jorde, 2004).

From these studies criteria for pivotal cases emerged. They include:

- creating compelling comparisons (such as comparing hot and cool surroundings).
- placing inquiry in accessible, culturally relevant contexts (such as familiar settings).
- providing feedback to support student reasoning (such as tactile information about how metal and wood feel in hot or cool surroundings).
- enabling narrative accounts of science (such as by selecting problems that are personally relevant).

The hot and cool surroundings example and the heat flow visualization mentioned above both meet the criteria for pivotal cases. The heat flow visualization offers very compelling comparisons of different materials. The visualization involves heating the end of the material, an idea that is familiar to students. The visualization provides clear feedback. In addition, students engaged in exciting conversations as they conducted virtual experiments (Linn, 2005). In addition, both of these pivotal cases helped students clarify their ideas.

In summary, the work of Judy Stern and Mr. K. revealed the importance of pivotal cases for introducing new ideas. Successful cases need to respond specifically to the repertoire of ideas held by students. Design of effective cases requires careful analysis of student ideas as well as substantial disciplinary understanding of the curriculum topic.

Sherry Hsi: Adding Collaboration

Sherry Hsi, a graduate student, noted that many students articulated incoherent ideas and were prompted by peers to revise their ideas. She reasoned that if students were to collaborate and contrast their ideas, they might gain more coherent understanding. Hsi thought that students might benefit by hearing ideas articulated by others and possibly could reformulate their own ideas in light of hearing explanations that other students had figured out even when these ideas were inaccurate. In addition, she thought that students might develop their critiquing skill if they had the opportunity to respond to the ideas that other students presented.

Hsi's design for collaborative activities took advantage of two insights from previous work on the thermodynamics curriculum. First, from the *predict, observe, explain* work of Songer, it was clear that eliciting ideas from students before they engage in collaboration was helpful. Therefore, Hsi designed a collaborative environment that required students to first generate their ideas before they started discussing ideas with their peers. In addition, Hsi took advantage of research showing that driving questions placed in personally relevant contexts were very effective for motivating students to learn science. Hsi created driving questions such as, "Is it better to bake brownies in a metal pan or a glass pan if you want them to cook faster?"

Sherry Hsi created multimedia discussion starters that illustrated the personally relevant problems, presenting alternative designs for picnic baskets or other topics. Students first generated their own ideas in response to the driving question and then carried out a discussion about the driving question.

Hsi conducted a research study where she compared a class discussion to an online multimedia discussion. She found that students made more progress in the multimedia discussion and that participation was more equitable. Only 15% of the students participated in the class discussion compared to 100% in the online discussion. The greater progress in the online discussion seemed to stem from the finding that students used more evidence to support their claims when they wrote online explanations and critiques than when they contributed to class discussion. In addition, in the online discussion students were able to make anonymous comments. This option probably contributed to the increased number of comments. Hsi concluded that the collaboration activity elicited ideas, added ideas from other students, helped students distinguish among the views they had in their repertoire, and encouraged students to develop shared criteria for evaluating conjectures about thermodynamics. To encourage reflection, students were asked to summarize their solution to the driving question after the discussion.

In summary, Sherry Hsi's work sought to improve the coherence of student ideas by taking advantage of the varied views held by all the students in the class. Hsi also capitalized on prior research showing the advantage of eliciting ideas before engaging in a discussion and placing collaborative activities in the context of personally relevant problems. Hsi found that activities designed with these guidelines in mind engaged students in actively critiquing each other's ideas and that, under these circumstances, students used more evidence to warrant their assertions than they did in face-to-face class activities.

Betsy Davis: Adding Reflection

Inspired by work on reflection (Bransford, Brown, & Cocking, 1999), self-explanation (Slotta & Chi, 2006), and embedded explanation questions (Linn & Clancy, 1992), Betsy Davis, a graduate student, set out to study the effects and effectiveness of prompts for reflection in the curriculum. In the context of a critique project, Davis contrasted various approaches to reflection. She studied generic prompts that ask students to reflect on their current thinking and more specific prompts that directed students to reflect on specific aspects of the topic. Her results revealed that generic prompts were more successful than specific prompts for students with relatively high prior knowledge. She also found that about one-third of the students failed to take advantage of the reflection prompts to actually sort out ideas. Her findings encouraged the research team to pay more attention to reflection activities, ensuring that they were accessible to students and likely to promote the sorting out of ideas that is needed in order to develop coherent understanding.

In summary, Nancy Songer, Eileen Lewis, Doug Clark, Philip Bell, Mr. K., Judy Stern, Sherry Hsi, and Betsy Davis all came up with techniques for increasing the coherence of student ideas and contributed to the support of the KI pattern. As a result of these changes, the curriculum was more effective and students gained more coherent understanding than they did before these changes where made. Overall, from the first version to the last version reported here, there was a 400% increase in the coherence and effectiveness of student ideas (Linn & Hsi, 2000).

Jim Slotta: The WISE Learning Environment

Up until this point, the thermodynamics curriculum had typically lasted from 10 to 14 weeks, but new state standards and pressures called for creating a more concentrated version of the thermodynamics activities as well as adding new topics to the curriculum. In addition, the results from research suggested that a powerful learning environment could go beyond the checklist to strengthen student outcomes. The technology team, led by Jim Slotta, a former post-doctoral scholar and now a faculty member, built a new learning environment that supported many more activities than were possible with the checklist, and integrated visualizations, as well as collaborative activities.

Using first the KI environment (Bell, Davis, & Linn, 1995) and then the Web-based Inquiry Science Environment (Linn, Clark, & Slotta, 2003), the designers took advantage of the features that current technologies made possible for science instruction (see Figure 1.3 and Figure 3.3). Designers could sequence activities using the inquiry map, embed powerful assessments, and make all student work accessible to the teacher. Because WISE was served from a central computer, all student work was stored on the server. Furthermore, the WISE environment allowed the researchers to embed instructional patterns into each activity. It was possible to elicit ideas, request predictions, include pivotal cases, such as visualizations, prompt for explanations, support online discussion, and elicit reflections. The units developed by the team are free and available at http://wise.berkeley.edu.

Based on the research in the field, the designers created four types of projects that could be used for any scientific topic. They created a critique project based on Mr. K.'s activity, showing the benefit of having students critique

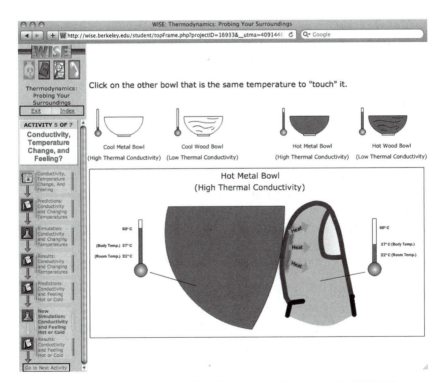

FIGURE 3.3   Screenshot of a thermal equilbrium visualization in the WISE Thermodynamics unit

experiments in order to build coherent understanding. In addition, they created an experiment project based on the success of the *predict, observe, distinguish, explain* research. They also created a debate project based on research showing the benefit of having students debate scientific topics and contrast alternatives (Linn & Hsi, 2000). Finally, the team created a design project that allowed students to design solutions to problems, such as creating an energy-efficient house (Hoadley & Linn, 2000). Each of these projects incorporated lessons learned from prior research and made it easy for designers to create disciplinary-specific activities that involved either critique, debate, experiment, or design (Linn, Clark, & Slotta, 2003).

Research with WISE revealed additional ways to promote coherent understanding (Linn, Davis, & Bell, 2004). In addition, a longitudinal study of the impact of the thermodynamics instruction revealed insights into the long-term impact of technology-enhanced learning (Linn & Hsi, 2000).

Doug Clark: Molecular Workbench

Doug Clark, a former graduate student and now a faculty member in science education, revised the thermal equilibrium project when new powerful visualizations of molecular interactions were developed by Robert Tinker and the Concord Consortium. Clark redesigned the thermal equilibrium unit, incorporating Molecular Workbench visualizations (Figure 3.4). Clark included both the heat flow model and the molecular model and designed a module for the TELS center that linked these two approaches. The module, delivered over a five-day period, has proven to be very effective in helping students gain coherent understanding of thermal equilibrium. In addition, the module demonstrates that, with appropriate visualizations, it is possible to use the molecular kinetic model effectively. Although Songer found initially that molecular kinetic theory was too abstract for students to incorporate into their thinking, given current resources and visualizations, Clark demonstrated that using the Molecular Workbench visualization can give students insight into molecular kinetic theory, especially when combined with the heat flow model. This finding was replicated by Hsin-Yi Chang, a postdoctoral scholar, in a project that encouraged students to critique accounts of thermal equilibrium (submitted to Chang et al., 2008).

Doug Clark and Eileen Lewis: Longitudinal Studies

Eileen Lewis conducted a longitudinal study of student learning (Lewis, 1996) that was extended by the research group (Linn & Hsi, 2000). These data were also analyzed by Jacquie Madhok as noted above and by Doug Clark. In several studies, the researchers found that students maintained a large repertoire of ideas about thermodynamics during the semester-long course (Lewis & Linn, 1994; Linn &

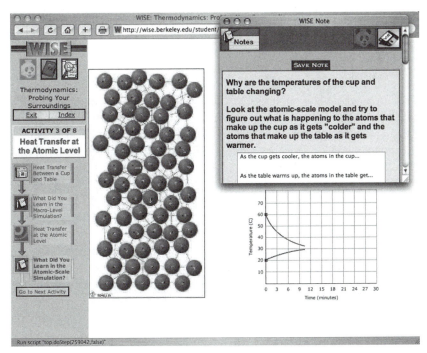

FIGURE 3.4 Screenshot of a Molecular Workbench activity embedded in a WISE Thermodynamics unit

Eylon, 1996). Over time students tend to promote ideas that are supported by the evidence they gather (Clark, 2006; Clark & Linn, 2003). These studies confirmed that the curriculum was enabling students to add ideas to their repertoire and to sort these ideas out.

The findings of Davis on reflection, Bell on debate, Lewis on longitudinal progressions, and Clark on longitudinal repertoires convinced the research partnership that students engage in a complex process of generating, sorting out, prioritizing, promoting, distinguishing, and selecting ideas as they learn a complex topic like thermodynamics. Activities that support this process lead to more normative and coherent ideas about science. Overall, these research studies reinforced the emphasis on the integration of ideas in design of instruction and supported the value of KI.

These studies also drew attention to the importance of the specific ideas that students develop as they seek to make sense of the topic. When students make an effort to sort out ideas, even if the view they formulate is not supported by all the empirical data, they are engaging in the sort of reasoning that leads to understanding. Thus when students conclude that materials with holes in them are poor insulators they are using evidence that heat can flow through openings like doors. Over time, these students often come to realize that holes like those in sweaters may have a different role. These holes may trap air and thus offer insulation potential.

Discussion

This series of design studies of the thermodynamics curriculum reveals the advantages of an iterative refinement approach to instruction, the benefits of carrying out this instruction in a technology-enhanced format, and the value of selecting a common assessment measure that allows for easy comparison from one version to the next. The results of the studies led to the development of the KI pattern as well as specific design principles. These patterns and principles summarize the effective elements of the learning environment. They also offer future designers insight into successful instructional solutions (Kali & Ronen-Fuhrmann, 2007).

Design research offers enormous potential for improving instructional materials and strengthening our understanding of how students learn science. Too often, instructional materials are deployed without appropriate testing and revised without serious reliance on evidence from student learning.

Design Principles and Patterns

The case study reported here, and other design research, has spurred science educators to seek new ways to synthesize findings such that the complexities and insights gained from design research can inform future designs. One approach involves identifying design principles. Linn and Hsi (2000) summarized the thermodynamics case study experiences in four general principles and fourteen more specific principles. More recently Kali developed a Design Principles Database to capture principles emerging in many research projects (Kali, 2006).

In the thermodynamics case study, the researchers were able to consolidate their insights in the KI pattern. These studies support the set of four KI processes (see Chapter 5). They call for specific activity sequencing and guidance for students. These sequences can be delivered using the WISE learning environment.

Role of Technology

By itself, technology is like a pencil, book, or film—it can be effective or ineffective. The results in this case study show that a process of iterative refinement resulting in the WISE learning environment along with real time data collection using probeware, and powerful visualizations such as Molecular Workbench software can transform thermodynamics instruction. Together these technologies allow designers to create inquiry activities that students can study in small groups, gather evidence concerning the most effective practices, and refine the instruction to make it more and more successful.

The thermodynamics case study illustrates the value of learning environments combined with KI patterns. The WISE environment guides students through specific activities that are selected based on the KI pattern. For example, in the collaboration activity students first generate their own ideas and then participate in a discussion. The WISE environment also can provide help and hints, as students need them. Finally, the learning environment gathers embedded assessments just-in-time, so that it is possible to get a detailed record of how students are responding to instructional materials.

The thermodynamics teams' experience with the WISE learning environment shows its value for supporting comparison studies. Researchers can reliably compare versions of common activities including collaboration, experimentation, or interacting with visualizations. The learning environment also offers exciting opportunities for teachers who can turn the more routine classroom management activities over to the technology and spend their time guiding students interactions with complex variables.

By making unseen processes visible, Molecular Workbench changed our perspective on using the molecular kinetic model for middle school science. Initially the team concluded that available approaches for communicating a molecular account of thermodynamics were inadequate to the task. The researchers interviewed experts from a broad range of backgrounds and developed a heat flow model and appropriate visualizations that proved highly effective in helping students understand complex ideas about thermodynamics and distinguish among heat flow, thermal equilibrium, insulation and conduction, and the difference between heat and temperature. Eventually the availability of the Molecular Workbench software enabled the developers to incorporate a molecular model into instruction about heat flow and thermal equilibrium. This software has proven successful in several studies (Casperson & Linn, 2006; submitted to Chang et al., 2008; Chiu & Linn, 2008; Linn et al., 2006).

The thermodynamics team has considered using additional technology resources to engage students in designing their own representations. The Chemation software is one technique for incorporating the opportunity for students to design chemical reactions. As Chang et al. (2008) show, using Chemation allows students to test their ideas by designing a sequence (sort of a flipbook) of molecular interactions to show how molecules might combine and recombine to form new reagents. Chemation is particularly appealing because it runs on a handheld computer and, therefore, could be utilized in a variety of different learning environments. One finding from the Chemation research concerns how students deal with remainders when building models of chemical interactions. Students often accurately combine atoms and molecules to form new compounds, but simply erase extra molecules that do not combine in the planned interaction. By erasing these extra molecules, students are violating principles of conservation of matter and, also in the case of examples concerning greenhouse gases, missing the point about remainder reactions. The goal of the activity is to show that certain chemical reactions produce as remainders gases that are harmful if they get out of balance in the environment.

In summary, modern technologies are an enormous benefit to science education research. They allow researchers to compare approaches to activities such as interacting with visualizations and find the most promising alternatives. They can deliver interactive experiences to augment hands-on experimentation. They can also make hands-on activities such as experiments with probeware more successful.

As described at the beginning, several features of technology are important. Specifically, a technology-enhanced environment:

- takes advantage of powerful, interactive visualizations and virtual experiments. In separate investigations the Heat Flow and Molecular Workbench visualizations improved student understanding of heat flow.
- incorporates real-time data collection using probeware. In the case study, students learned to interpret graphs as a result of using probeware to generate heating and cooling curves.
- uses a learning environment that guides inquiry, documents student work, and provides feedback to both students and teachers. In the case study the WISE environment, which is free and available to everyone, was very successful (see http://wise.berkeley.edu).
- implements the KI pattern to ensure that students develop coherent ideas. As illustrated in the examples above, features such as visualizations and experiments need to be embedded in the KI pattern to succeed.
- aligns assessment, curriculum, instruction, and professional development using the KI framework. This case study shows the benefit of alignment of assessment and curriculum to demonstrate the impact of innovations and help discern effective from ineffective practices. Results of professional development aligned with the framework are also very successful (Slotta & Linn, 2009).

Research on technology-enhanced learning is also enhanced by these features. The WISE environment can deliver well-controlled alternative forms of instruction, use embedded assessments to capture student progress in the moment, implement innovations such as modeling or collaborative learning, scaffold complex activities such as inquiry or design, gather long-term progress of learners, record teacher–student interactions, and offer comprehensive supports for teachers. This evidence ensures that researchers identify the most promising uses of technology.

Emerging research practices such as case studies and design studies capture the interplay of multiple factors in specific contexts, emphasize iterative refinement of instruction, and document the trajectories of students and teachers. This detailed documentation of learning allows researchers to use evidence to improve promising innovations so they succeed in multiple contexts.

Reflection Activity

Visit the WISE website (http://wise.berkeley.edu), register as a teacher/researcher, and select a WISE project to review. Identify features of the unit that you think would be effective for students.

Notes

1 An earlier version of this chapter appeared in *A school day in 2020 (2010)*—Proceedings of the Fondazione per la Scuola della Compagnia di San Paolo held in 2008, Turin, Italy.

4

PARTICULATE STRUCTURE OF MATTER

A Case Study

Introduction

In this chapter we discuss a case study of curriculum reform that revealed some promising patterns for high school physical science. The case study involves helping students understand the structure of matter and was conducted by Eylon and her colleagues in Israel (Ben-Zvi, Eylon, & Silberstein, 1986a, 1988; Linn, Songer, & Eylon, 1996; Margel, Eylon, & Scherz, 2008).

Structure of Matter

Materials has always been a central topic in junior high school science studies and usually includes the following topics: the particulate nature of matter; states of matter; changes in the state of matter; atoms and molecules; elements, compounds, and mixtures; the structure of the atom; and the relationship between the structure and properties of materials. Many of the traditional curriculum approaches (Dory et al., 1989; Zilag et al., 1980) are based on declarative definitions of the scientific concepts and on confirmatory experiments. In particular, in many textbooks the ideas about the particulate nature of matter are presented as postulates: that matter consists of particles that are too small to be seen; that particles are in intrinsic motion; that there is empty space between the particles. The structure of matter is one of the most fundamental topics in science. A meaningful understanding of this topic is essential for developing a solid basis for further scientific studies. It is revisited in high school chemistry courses but not all students take these courses so middle school physical science is often the first and last time that students encounter this topic.

In the last two decades, studies have consistently shown that many middle school (and high school) students have difficulty understanding the particulate nature of matter, despite considerable effort spent on this topic in school (e.g., Andersson, 1990; Brook, Briggs, Bell, & Driver, 1984; Johnstone, 1991; Krajcik, 1991; Millar, 1990; Nakhleh, Samarapungavan, & Saglam, 2005; Novick & Nussbaum, 1978). For example, Brook showed that only 20% of the 15-year-old students in Britain understood the structure of matter (Brook et al., 1984).

Researchers have suggested several possible causes for students' difficulties in understanding the particulate nature of matter. One possible reason is that, in science, materials are described in three ways: macroscopic, microscopic (unobservable), and symbolic (Johnstone, 1991). Research into improving the Israeli curriculum revealed some of the gaps and misunderstandings in student knowledge that seem to come from the typical instruction on the particulate nature of matter, as even at the end of Grade 10 many still lacked a satisfactory understanding of the micro–macroscopic relationships (Ben-Zvi, Eylon, & Silberstein, 1988). These studies have shown that many students have problems understanding the meaning of the three ways of representing materials, and that they do not easily relate to and shift from one way to the other. Krajcik (1991) found that some Grade 9 students refer only to macroscopic features when they have to describe materials. For example, students drew wavy lines and clouds when they had to represent air. Another major problem is that students have difficulty distinguishing images of single atoms from discussions that refer to behavior of the aggregate. Ben-Zvi et al. (1988) report on students from 11 tenth-grade classes who had studied chemistry for eight months and were asked to describe O_2, $O_{2(g)}$, N_2O_4, and NO_2 in drawings and explanations. Most students knew how to represent one diatomic molecule of an element as two connected atoms but had difficulty with compounds. About one-third of the sample drew N_2O_4 as two connected or disconnected fragments—an additive view of structure. Only 30% of the students could accurately represent a compound in the gaseous state. In another study (Ben-Zvi, Eylon, & Silberstein, 1986a) of 10 classes conducted at the end of 10th grade chemistry, students responded to questions such as:

A metallic wire has the following properties:
(a) Conducts electricity (b) has brown color (c) is malleable.
The wire is heated in an evacuated vessel until it evaporates. The resulting gas has the following properties:
(d) Pungent odor (e) yellow color (f) attacks plastics.
Question.
(1) Suppose that you could isolate one single atom from the metallic wire, which of the six properties would this atom have?
(2) Suppose that you could isolate one single atom from the gas. Which of the six properties would this atom have?

The results indicated that 40% of the students believed that a single atom had the properties of the aggregate that formed the solid or the gas. Only 15% explained that an atom could not be regarded as a small piece of material with all the properties of the aggregate. Johnson (1998) found that some students creatively construct what might be called hybrid views where they argue that molecules interact to create solids but atoms alone have specific properties such as color. Some students describe materials as being continuous, containing particles of the substances (Novick & Nussbaum, 1978). These results imply that, in addition to students' difficulties in understanding the basic ideas of the particulate nature of matter, they have difficulty applying these ideas in describing the unobservable structure of actual materials.

Johnson (1998) suggests inadequate instructional methods as another possible reason for the observed difficulties. For example, Andersson (1990) reports that the emphasis on single molecules in textbooks reinforces a single atom view and discourages reasoning about aggregates of particles. Another example reported by Ben–Zvi et al. (1986b) is concerned with students' interpretations of the textbook statement that in the gaseous state the distance between the particles is much larger than in the liquid state. In an interview study several students said, *"atoms in molecules of gaseous materials are farther apart than atoms in molecules of the same materials in the liquid state."* That is, students construed this argument to apply to atoms rather than molecules.

Other researchers have suggested teachers' lack of a sound scientific background as an additional reason for the observed difficulties (del Pozo, 2001; Kokkotas, Vlachos, & Koulaidis, 1998).

The issue has been raised whether it is possible to learn the particulate nature of matter in lower high school. Some educators (e.g., Fensham, 1994) suggest postponing the teaching to upper high school, others (e.g., Skamp, 1999) present evidence that it is possible to teach the topic to upper elementary school children. It is agreed that frontal, formal traditional teaching (definitions, visual aids) cannot bring about the necessary conceptual change. A major challenge is to examine what type of instruction leads to meaningful understanding (Gabel, 1999; Laverty & McGarvey, 1991; Ridgeway, 1971). For example, Kozma, Chinn, Russell, and Marx (2000) suggested that the material sciences curricula should guide students to use multiple representations of materials, visual and verbal, in conjunction with associated phenomena discussed in the classroom. Recent work, has been concerned with the ways to take advantage of computerized visualizations to support the learning of this complex topic (e.g., Frailich, Kesner, & Hofstein, 2009)

First Reform: Improving High School Curriculum

To remedy the limitations in student reasoning, a new curriculum for 10th grade, *Chemistry: A Challenge* (Ben–Zvi & Silberstein, 1986) was designed. *Chemistry: A Challenge* uses an historical approach. The designers of the curriculum claimed that the difficulties students have in adopting the particulate view of matter are not surprising since it took mankind about 2000 years to develop them. The intuitive views held by students are similar to ideas of scientists in the Greek period. The curriculum helped students distinguish this view from the particulate view. The atom was therefore presented as an ever developing idea, the characteristics of which change in accordance with new facts that have to be explained. The curriculum featured representations involving multitudes of particles rather than single particles. The instructional patterns used in this curriculum considered students' prior knowledge, but followed the typical patterns described in Chapter 1 and did not allow students to genuinely grapple with their ideas.

In a comparison study involving 1,078 students, half studied the traditional curriculum and half studied the new curriculum. The new curriculum helped the middle and lower achievers understand aggregates while the high achievers were successful in both instructional programs (Ben-Zvi, Eylon, & Silberstein, 1986b, 1987). Follow up research showed that about 30% of the students still lacked a satisfactory understanding of structural aspects of matter at the end of 10th grade (Ben-Zvi, Eylon, & Silberstein, 1988). Remnants of these difficulties were found two years later at the end of the 12th grade in the matriculation examination performance of students who opted to specialize in chemistry (Ben-Zvi & Hofstein, 1996).

Another Reform: Strengthening Middle School Science

In the mid-1990s the *Tomorrow 98* (Committee on Science and Technology Education, 1992) report recommended a reform in Israeli science and mathematics teaching. The Weizmann group was able to design new science curricula for middle school. The resulting Weizmann Institute of Science 2009 MATMON curriculum (http://stwww.weizmann.ac.il/menu/groups/index.html) for middle school had one strand addressing materials science. This strand was designed for 105 hours in grades 7–9. The materials strand had the following learning goals:

1. Developing a fundamental understanding of central topics and concepts such as the particulate nature of matter and the atomic view of materials.

2. Forming the relationships between structure, properties, and applications of materials, as a means of understanding numerous phenomena in the world around us. This entails integrating the macroscopic view with the unobservable view, providing particulate and molecular explanations.

3. Learning about the process of modeling and using a variety of strategies to explain the structure of matter. (e.g., building blocks, computer simulations, and theoretical representations).

4. Connecting the scientific world with the world of technology and exploring how technology influences everyday life and affects the society in which they live.

5. Developing learning and inquiry skills as an integral part of learning scientific content.

The design was based on previous research on the repertoire of students' ideas about the particulate nature of matter. It took advantage of prior research on ways to build on these ideas in constructing the normative particulate model (e.g., del Pozo, 2001; Kokkotas et al., 1998; Novick & Nussbaum, 1978; Nussbaum & Novick, 1982). The curriculum emphasizes knowledge construction and KI, which are consolidated by exploring the same ideas in several contexts, thus reinforcing and further developing them (Margel, Eylon & Scherz, 2004, 2006). The curriculum, taught in grades 7–9, consists of several learning units that implement this constructivist approach.

Structure of Matter Unit

The particulate model of matter is studied, usually in 7th grade, in the first unit, The Structure of Matter: Vacuum and Particles (Nussbaum, 2000). The unit uses debates to elicit student ideas (see Box 4.1, showing an exemplary task), demonstrations and laboratory experiments to illustrate ideas about matter, critique activities to develop ability to distinguish ideas, and reflection opportunities to help students sort out their ideas. The demonstrations, experiments, and debates focus on relevant everyday phenomena such as smell, properties of soap bubbles, and characteristics of adhesives.

BOX 4.1 EXEMPLARY DEBATE

An exemplary debate activity in the unit *Vacuum and Particles*

Demonstration

The class watched an experiment where a plastic soda bottle was flattened, filled with a few milliliters of pure acetone, and capped. The flattened bottle was put into boiling water. The liquid acetone disappeared and the bottle returned to its unflattened state.

The class was asked:

1. What happened to the particles of the liquid acetone that were in the plastic bottle when the bottle was heated?
2. How does the heating cause the acetone particles (liquid phase) to be distributed (gaseous phase)?
3. How do the particles of the gaseous acetone cause the bottle to expand?

Example student discussion

Rafi: The liquid acetone spread around, because they were warm, crowded, and stuffy, and they felt uncomfortable. They tried not to get close to each other. They tried to move apart. Then they pushed against the sides of the bottle, in order to give themselves more room and so that it would be less crowded and stuffy inside.

Efrat: I disagree with Rafi. How can you say that particles feel warm? Do they have feelings? That would be like saying that a frying pan on the stove feels hot and that it wants to run away.

Shlomit: I agree with Efrat that particles of acetone don't have feelings or desires or opinions! Particles of matter are not alive!

Shilo: Let us assume that particles of liquid acetone (which are very crowded like any other liquid) move around all the time in straight lines. But since the are so crowded, they bump into each other all the time, They push each other and finally they also push the bottle's wall outside.

Tirza: Then, how, according to Shilo, does the liquid acetone disappear when we warm it up? How warming it up turn it from a liquid to a gas? I still think that the acetone particles attempt to escape from the heat and they want to burst out of the bottle.

The open debates lead to an intellectual "Give and Take" about the structure of materials, contrasting the continuous model of matter versus the particulate model. Sequences of predict-observe-explain activities allow students to test their initial models. For example: one key debate centers around the meaning and plausibility of vacuum as an important part of physical reality. Students' intuitions, especially about materials in the solid state, are that they are packed with matter. Nevertheless, accepting the idea of vacuum is basic to comprehending the structure and properties of materials and the differences between the three states of matter. Guided by the historical development of the ideas in this domain (Nussbaum, 1998) the unit starts with the gaseous state. An investigation of the properties of air allows students to speculate and debate about the structure of matter. After seeing that air is compressible, the students debate about what actually makes air compressible. Specifically, there is a discussion of the different states of matter, emphasizing the construction of the concepts of vacuum and particles and distinguishing them from the continuous model of matter. After looking at the gaseous state, the unit uses the same methods—give and take and experimentation, investigations of students' ideas concerning the liquid and solid states of matter—leading to the relevant differentiation in the particulate model for the different states of matter.

From Elementary to Complex Structure Unit

The second unit, From Elementary to Complex Structure (Yayon, Margel, & Scherz, 2001) develops the basics of the atomic/molecular models, usually taught in the eighth grade. The particulate structure of matter is extended in this unit by introducing students to different types of particles (atoms, molecules, and ions), to the molecular structure of some elements, compounds, and mixtures and to explanations of observed (macroscopic) phenomena in molecular or particulate terms. The students are encouraged to use a variety of models (e.g., building blocks, computer simulations, and symbolic representations) to illustrate the structure of matter.

This unit engages students in predicting unobservable phenomena. A special activity called the black box demonstrates how modeling helps students understand unobservable phenomena. In this activity students have to guess what is inside a sealed box using indirect tests (Yayon & Scherz, 2008). By guessing what is inside, students are making predictions and interpreting the evidence.

Fibers Unit

The particulate structure of matter is elaborated in the *About Fibers* unit (Margel, 1999). This multidisciplinary unit uses molecular structure of polymers to illustrate scientific and technological concepts. It consolidates the relationship between the structure, properties, and applications of materials, as implemented in fabrics, threads, fibers, polymers, and composites (see Box 4.2).

This unit also employs several KI strategies that allow students to investigate their own ideas, evaluate them in light of new information, and sort them out. For example, students explain how the structure of materials such as wool, rayon, and wood explains their properties. They connect explanations about the material to ideas about atoms and particles using both visual and verbal explanations (Kozma, Chin, Russell, & Marx, 2000). In particular, they represent the relationship between materials, giant molecules, and atoms or particles using both visual and verbal explanations. The students are introduced to safety textiles (e.g., bulletproof vests, medical textiles, fire fighter uniforms, and astronaut suits), they carry out inquiry projects on topics such as textile design (e.g., designing a diaper) and conduct debates on issues such as: Should we design materials that will not wear out? They revisit the ideas later in a unit about industrial programs that create dye colors.

In all activities the particulate model of matter is emphasized, revisited, and extended. Throughout the program students get the opportunity to learn about the relationship between the structure of materials, their properties, and their applications using a variety of organization tools such as concept mapping (Margel, Eylon, & Scherz, 2006).

BOX 4.2 CONCEPT MAP

A concept map representing the structure of the unit About Fibers (Margel, 1999)

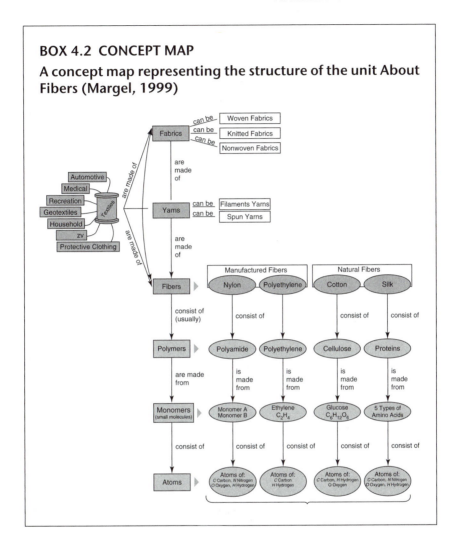

Longitudinal Findings

A longitudinal study (Margel, Eylon, & Scherz, 2007) investigated the progression in students' conceptions of the structure of matter. Students studied the subject of Materials using the MATMON curriculum for three years. The study investigated: conceptual understanding: progression from macroscopic to particulate conceptions and from particulate conceptions to molecular conceptions; and applications: applying the ideas to familiar and unfamiliar materials and making the transition from using everyday language to scientific language. A delayed test on applications was administered six months after completion of the unit. The study investigated how the curriculum units influenced conceptual understanding and applications to unfamiliar materials.

The sample consisted of an experimental group of 1,082 junior high school students who studied the units as part of the new curriculum, and a comparison group of 218 junior high school students who studied this topic following the traditional curriculum. Progress was assessed using assessments that asked students to represent the structure of several materials five times during the 3-year period: Before starting the curriculum (pretest), after each of the three units, and in the 9th grade half a year after finishing the curriculum (see example task in Figure 4.1). At the pretest many students were not able to distinguish between structure, properties, and the uses of materials. These distinctions are essential for full understanding of chemistry. When asked about the structure, the students would mainly give descriptive answers, referring to observable (macroscopic) properties, applications, or origin of the materials. The repeated testing after each instructional unit provided an opportunity to investigate the progress of the students both in terms of the conceptual model, and in the context of application, and relate the progress to the nature of the various units.

The following briefly summarizes the results:

The Conceptual Model

Overall the curriculum advanced students' conceptual understanding towards particulate conceptions. When averaged on all materials, in the final retention test

---

Consider the following materials:

Iron, Water, Air, Nylon, Juice, Wool, Oxygen, and Paper

Describe in words and draw the structure of these materials as if you were using a very powerful magnifying instrument.

**EXPLANATIONS
DRAWINGS**

Iron _____

Water _____

FIGURE 4.1   Assessment of the structure of matter

in the 9th grade about 83% of the students from the experimental group included a particulate representation in their responses compared to 28% in the comparison group. The curriculum was less effective concerning the molecular conception. About 23% of the experimental group included a molecular representation compared to 1% of the students in the comparison group. Figure 4.2 shows how the different representations (observable-macroscopic, particulate, and molecular) for water changed from the 7th to the 9th grade in the experimental and comparison groups. The first learning unit which constructively develops the ideas of the particulate model (Nussbaum, 2000) led to very significant advancement in students' use of particulate representations in the 2nd test. In the 3rd test, given after the second unit, which dealt with the molecular model, there was a further increase in particulate representations. Moreover, about 40% of the students drew a molecular representation for water. The findings for the particulate and molecular representations were retained also in the 4th test given after the third unit (About Fibers) in which students had additional opportunities to use particulate and molecular representations. As mentioned above, in the 5th retention test, given half a year after instruction ended, the particulate representations were retained, but there was a decrease in the occurrence of the molecular representations.

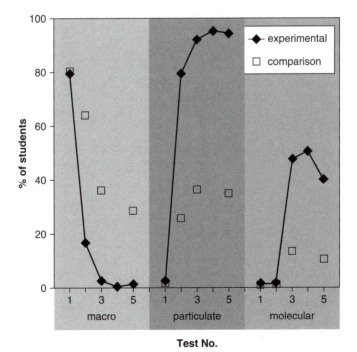

FIGURE 4.2 Frequency of student responses to questions about the representation for water in the five tests; N(experimental) = 1078, N(comparison) = 278

Context of Application

On the second test, given after the unit Vacuum and Particles, about 60% of the students correctly used this idea to describe the structure of materials that were not discussed in class at that time, such as nylon, wool, and paper (transfer). The second unit, which developed the links to molecular notions, led students to start using scientific terms from class in their verbal descriptions on the third test. The contribution of the third unit, About Fibers (Margel, 1999), where students studied textiles, fibers and polymers, was substantial. There was an increase in the number of students who drew and described in words the structure of all materials, including those that were not mentioned in class, according to their molecular structure.

To illustrate the changes both in the conceptual model and in the context of application, Figure 4.3 shows examples of three students' drawings of nylon, a material that was not studied in class. Students made macroscopic-observable, particulate and molecular drawings. The first student used a particulate representation after the third unit, while the third student included an aggregate representation of particles after the first unit, started to use molecular representations by the second unit, and used a model of the fiber after the study of the third unit. This student maintained these ideas in the delayed test administered half a year after completing the unit. In summary, the results show that students added ideas to their repertoire subsequent to instruction in a manner consistent with the goals of the curriculum.

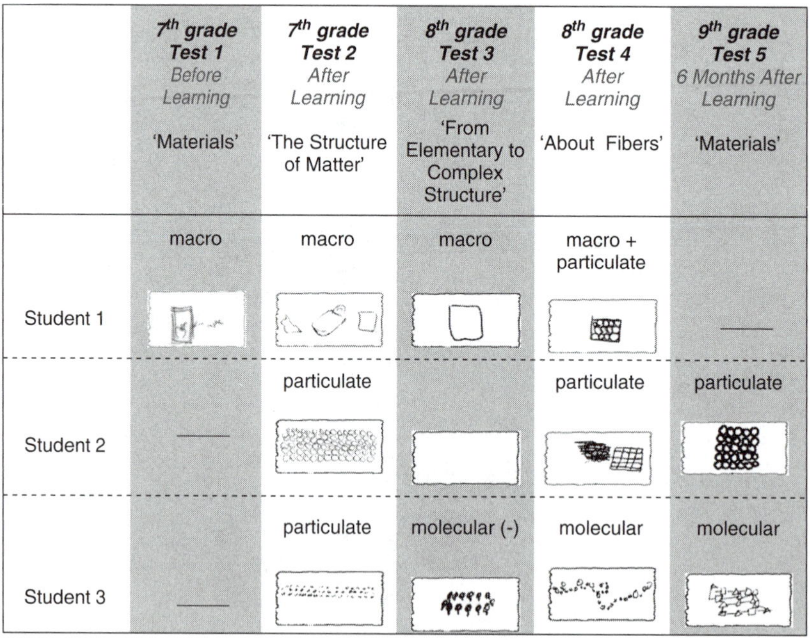

	7th grade **Test 1** *Before Learning* 'Materials'	*7th grade* **Test 2** *After Learning* 'The Structure of Matter'	*8th grade* **Test 3** *After Learning* 'From Elementary to Complex Structure'	*8th grade* **Test 4** *After Learning* 'About Fibers'	*9th grade* **Test 5** *6 Months After Learning* 'Materials'
Student 1	macro	macro	macro	macro + particulate	———
Student 2	———	particulate		particulate	particulate
Student 3	———	particulate	molecular (-)	molecular	molecular

FIGURE 4.3 Examples of three students' drawings of nylon in the five tests

Retention

The results show that during instruction, students were most likely to use a molecular representation but after the course was over, they often preferred a particulate representation. Some students always preferred the molecular representations. Some used a descriptive model based on observation of surface features for all tests. Student performance was summarized in five frequency profiles (see Figure 4.4). These profiles illustrate students' learning trajectories. Students who studied Materials according to the new instructional approach were most likely to add the particulate model to their repertoire. When students did add the molecular model, they often dropped it in response to subsequent assessments. The results suggest that most students added the particulate model and continued to connect it in new contexts. Some students did connect the molecular model to their other ideas, often as a result of the textile unit. The textile context offers many pivotal cases that enable students to distinguish the molecular and particulate models (see Box 4.2). The designers were disappointed because only 50% of the students were able to use a molecular model during instruction and fewer than 25% of the students could use the molecular model in interpreting properties of new materials.

These results suggest that one way to strengthen understanding of the molecular model is to explore it in multiple compelling contexts. Students should encounter such opportunities in secondary school.

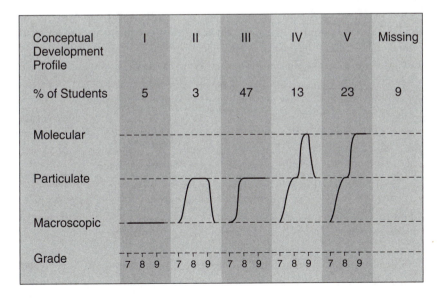

FIGURE 4.4 Conceptual development profiles of selected students in junior high school

Professional Development

A multi-year professional development program to promote inquiry teaching accompanied the reform. Junior high school teachers participated in extensive professional development to develop an understanding of inquiry learning and teaching and to appreciate its benefits. For example, teaching the unit Vacuum and Particles involved a change in the teacher's role from that of presenting information to her/his students, to guiding give and take discussions of ideas. In the unit About Fibers, involving project-based learning, teachers guided students in science and technology projects. This involved a variety of inquiry skills (e.g., helping students frame questions) that were not part of most teachers' traditional practice. Many questions arose from teachers during the professional development activities. *Why should we spend all this time on building the particulate model of matter? Why can't we just tell them and convince them with several experiments?* The teachers had difficulty distinguishing between the *motivate, inform, assess* pattern using demonstrations (Chapter 2) and the *elicit ideas, add ideas, distinguish ideas, reflect* pattern implemented in the curriculum.

The professional development helped teachers distinguish these patterns and appreciate the strengths of the KI approach. This approach resonates with Leithwood's (Leithwood & Steinbach, 1991) recommendation to guide teachers to distinguish their own practices from the innovation. We observed how teachers who initially just followed the procedures provided often integrated the new practices over time. Similar findings have been reported by Slotta (2004) and Gerard, Spitulnik, and Linn (2010) for teachers who were followed over several years (see Chapter 10).

Teachers initially found the new, inquiry-oriented practices awkward but became more and more keen on allowing students to discuss their ideas and compare alternatives. They were less inclined to shortcut discussions and give students the right answers even when they asked for them. In the classroom they responded to student ideas and were willing to focus the investigation on personally relevant topics. However, many teachers endorsed inquiry but only adapted pieces of the curriculum such as one of the experiments, without enabling students to explore their own ideas or encouraging students to consolidate their ideas. The researchers found that when teachers add parts of inquiry to their practice it is less successful than when they add the whole pattern.

In both the TELS project (Chapter 3) and MATMON, teachers helped design their own professional development. They asked for help and support as they debated, compared, and negotiated their ideas. Teachers became more adept at knowing when to add a pivotal case and when to allow students to flounder a bit longer.

This atomic model case study illustrates how a partnership of developers who recognized that students lacked understanding of the particulate nature of matter, utilized powerful research to create an activity that would enable most middle school students to make progress. They first helped students gain insight into the particulate nature of matter. Having instilled this insight, the research team then sought to help students understand the molecular basis of matter. This second step proved quite difficult and is only partially achieved in the research reported in the case study.

The Role of Technology

How can technology advance the learning in this domain? The use of visualizations has potential as it enables students to visualize processes they cannot directly observe. In the case study, students were encouraged to use various software programs to support the learning process. One of the programs involved visualizations of particle motion under different conditions (e.g., heating, diffusion, etc.). Another program used a 3D visualization tool to examine the structure of molecules using a variety of representations. The use of these programs was not mandatory and only a few students had a chance to use them.

One subsequent study by Margel, Eylon and Scherz (2004) explored the possibility to use the Scanning Tunneling Microscope (STM) as a method to help students visualize the unseen chemical structure of materials. The study was carried out with a group of 60 eighth grade students. After the students studied the particulate model of matter they carried out a 1.5 hour activity with the STM in a research laboratory. The activity followed the *predict, observe, explain, critique* instructional pattern (see Figure 4.5): students made predictions, prepared a sample of graphite, observed the sample using the STM, matched objects to pictures, and discussed issues such as orders of magnitude. To introduce the STM, Margel et al. (2004) worked closely with the teachers who were worried that the technology would break or not function when needed. Teachers predicted that students would have more trouble carrying out the activities than they actually did. Student familiarity with technology enabled them to approach this new resource more comfortably than teachers predicted. Today, STM machines are available and affordable by many schools making this approach potentially valuable.

The study investigated how the activity contributed to the students' knowledge and convictions concerning the particulate model of matter, and how these contributions depended on the students' initial conceptions. Figure 4.5 shows typical explanations by the students. The activity increased student confidence in the particulate model. Students who demonstrated a particulate conception of matter before the activity could relate their predictions to the observations and improve their account of the phenomena. Students who did not demonstrate understanding of the particulate conception of matter were initially unable to make sense of their observations (see explanations of students 8 and 9 in Figure 4.5). This study shows the promise of the STM as well as the importance of disciplinary knowledge for interpreting complex visualizations. In summary, the STM technology enriched understanding for those with a particulate view of matter.

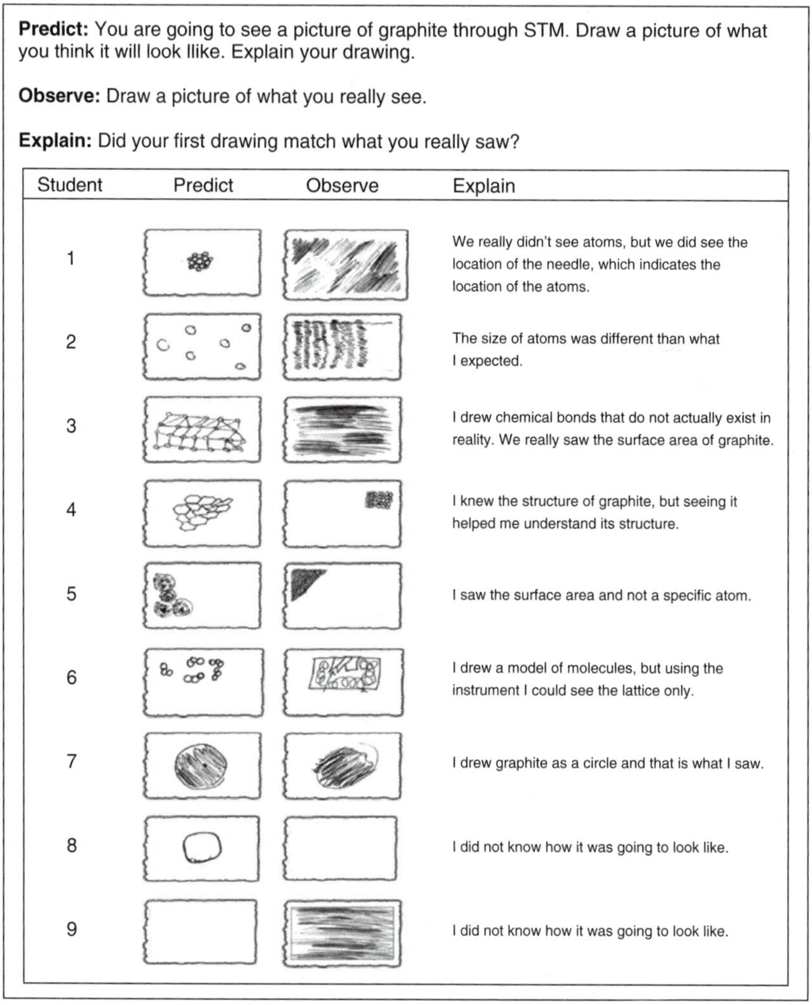

Predict: You are going to see a picture of graphite through STM. Draw a picture of what you think it will look llike. Explain your drawing.

Observe: Draw a picture of what you really see.

Explain: Did your first drawing match what you really saw?

Student	Predict	Observe	Explain
1			We really didn't see atoms, but we did see the location of the needle, which indicates the location of the atoms.
2			The size of atoms was different than what I expected.
3			I drew chemical bonds that do not actually exist in reality. We really saw the surface area of graphite.
4			I knew the structure of graphite, but seeing it helped me understand its structure.
5			I saw the surface area and not a specific atom.
6			I drew a model of molecules, but using the instrument I could see the lattice only.
7			I drew graphite as a circle and that is what I saw.
8			I did not know how it was going to look like.
9			I did not know how it was going to look like.

FIGURE 4.5 Typical answers of students to the *predict, observe, explain* (POE) assessment for the Scanning Tunneling Microscope (STM)

As described above, after completing their studies in junior high school, many students could not accurately represent the molecular structure of many substances. These students revisited the ideas in 10th grade. Another study introduced web-based interactive animations in 10th grade. These proved to be effective in improving achievement and in changing the learning environment from teacher-directed to collaborative learning with guidance from the teacher (Frailich et al., 2009).

These results are congruent with results summarized by Kozma and Russell (2005) who found that web-based interactive animations helped students understand chemical bonding as well as other difficult and abstract concepts associated with equilibrium, electrochemistry, and chemical solutions. Similarly, Barak and Dori (2005) found that the use of computer-based models helped promote students' understanding of chemistry at four levels: the macroscopic, microscopic (unobservable), symbolic, and chemical process levels. Ardac and Akaygun (2005) found that students who learned with the aid of dynamic computer-based models outperformed their peers (who had no such experience) regarding molecular representations. Further discussion of computer visualizations can be found in Chapter 8.

Discussion

The particulate case and the thermodynamics case (Chapter 3) both illustrate the advantages of using visualizations and other technologies to illustrate unobservable processes. Both also highlight the importance of iterative refinement studies in investigating these relationships in order to understand their impact.

In the area of professional development, both case study partnerships were able to develop techniques that enable teachers to use complex, powerful materials effectively. The research teams in Berkeley and Israel have found that teachers benefit from similar kinds of professional development for using inquiry materials. Typically, teachers need to learn how to interact with small groups of students, what questions to ask, and how to guide students to think on their own.

Both research programs reveal the advantages of instruction that includes a sequence of activities. Unlike the typical patterns reported in Chapter 2, these successful materials used more elaborate patterns that stressed coherence of ideas. We explore these ideas further in Chapter 10.

Design Research

The case studies of thermodynamics (Chapter 3) and the particulate model of matter use three methodologies consistent with design research. First, they build on past curriculum innovations to create powerful visualizations. Second, they use comparison studies to investigate specific curricular features. Third, they use cohort comparison and longitudinal investigations to investigate long-term impact.

Both case studies include a series of iterative refinements of the instruction in thermodynamics, and in the atomic view of materials, that reflect similar analysis of student thinking. In both projects the designers initially struggled in their attempts to impart a molecular or molecular kinetic model of materials. The solution to this program came through the development of visualizations.

Both research programs also used a broad array of assessment techniques, including surveys, pretests and posttests, interviews, observations, embedded assessments, and longitudinal studies. These varied outcome measures helped the partnerships in both programs to identify the repertoire of ideas held by students and to identify ways to promote and measure integrated understanding. In all cases, the authors sought measures that required students to connect ideas that had been presented in class to those they had developed in their everyday experience. Both projects also asked students to make connections between atomic or molecular representations and descriptive and observational representations of scientific phenomena.

The longitudinal investigations reported in both studies shed light on the importance of studying how students grapple with their varied ideas over time. In both cases, students articulated non-normative ideas, but ideas that were consistent with their observations. In the thermodynamics case study, students reported on how materials that were at thermal equilibrium felt as if they were different temperatures. Their challenge was to reconcile how objects felt with what they knew of their internal temperatures.

Similarly, in the atomic case study, students grappled with the difficulty of reconciling their observations that the world is made of solid objects with the scientifically normative view that objects are composed of a variety of atoms that constantly interact with each other. A common view aligned with students' observations, was that materials are made of tiny particles that are all the same and that stick together, rather than being composed of molecules that interact.

In addition, the longitudinal studies provided compelling evidence that students continued to grapple with their ideas throughout the entire science course, maintaining most of their ideas and looking for evidence that would allow them to reconcile, sort out, promote, or re-conceptualize their views. The longitudinal studies also revealed the difficulties that students have in achieving coherence. They showed that students turn to alternative views, depending on the context of the application, when they have difficulty explaining their ideas. In the thermodynamics case study, students often used quite different accounts of heat and temperature for thermal equilibrium, heating and cooling, heat flow, and insulation and conduction—often without considering that these phenomena stemmed from a common explanatory model.

Both projects made progress in assessing student learning by asking students to make drawings of their ideas. These drawings were particularly helpful when students made predictions about visualizations before using them in their classes.

The atomic model group in Israel had a somewhat unique opportunity to iteratively refine curriculum materials because they have been selected by the government to improve instruction over a period of years. Because Israel is a relatively small country, they were able to work with all of the teachers using the curriculum. They could assemble all the teachers to participate in the design and testing of the curriculum.

In summary, new design methods involving iterative refinements, longitudinal studies, and innovative assessments strengthen understanding of instruction and offer researchers in science education a robust way to investigate curriculum materials. The opportunity to use evidence from student learning, diagnose weaknesses in student understanding, and redesign the curriculum based on that diagnosis has proven to be an extremely valuable approach for curriculum research. These iterative refinement studies have largely involved curriculum materials that are less than a whole course long. Many studies have been enhanced by the availability of technology.

Reflection Activity

Reflect on you own ideas about the particulate nature of matter. Explain how solids and liquids differ in their molecular structure. Discuss how the activities in the Materials unit could help students distinguish among ideas.

5

KNOWLEDGE INTEGRATION PRINCIPLES AND PATTERNS

The case studies in the last two chapters offer new, promising ways to improve science instruction. The cases implement instructional patterns that differ from those in typical instruction. These cases draw on a wider range of student ideas, including views about numerous naturally-occurring problems, than typical instruction. They take advantage of the diverse ideas students generate.

In this chapter, we use patterns and principles to capture the growing body of knowledge concerning ways to promote KI (Kali, 2006; Linn & Eylon, 2006). We show how collating design knowledge from successful instruction in the form of KI patterns and principles can guide curriculum designers wishing to capitalize on our improved understanding of the way people learn. The KI patterns and principles contrast with the patterns in Chapter 2 that described materials designed following the absorption approach.

Initially researchers identified principles to describe the features of instructional materials that promoted KI (Linn & Hsi, 2000; Linn, Davis, & Bell, 2004). The KI principles emerged from design studies aimed at improving college computer science courses and middle school science courses (Linn, 1995). Linn and Hsi (2000) described principles to elaborate four main design goals: Make Science Accessible; Make Thinking Visible; Help Students Learn from Others; and Promote Autonomy. Subsequent research clarified each of the design goals by describing specific principles (Table 5.1; Linn, Bell, & Davis, 2004). Kali (2006) brought the principles to life by creating a design principles database that links the specific principles to features of curriculum materials. Features include visualizations, reflection activities, collaborative activities, novel representations for evidence, and games.

Kali (2006) led a community wide effort to create the design principles database. She organized workshops and online forums where researchers identified effective features of instructional programs and associated each feature with a

Table 5.1 Metaprinciples and Specific Design Principles for Knowledge Integration

Making Science Accessible to All Students	Making Thinking Visible	Helping Students Learn From Each Other	Promoting Autonomy for Lifelong Science Learning
Encourage students to build on their ideas and develop powerful scientific principles	Model the process of considering alternatives	Encourage students to listen and learn from each other	Engage students in reflecting on progress and ideas
Encourage students to investigate personally relevant problems	Scaffold students to explain their thinking	Design social interactions to promote productive and respectful discussion	Engage students as critics
Scaffold science activities so students understand the inquiry process	Use multiple visual representations from varied media	Scaffold groups to design shared criteria and standards	Engage students in varied science projects
		Use multiple social activity structures	Establish an inquiry process

principle and one of the KI design goals. The community contributed the features to a publically accessible database (http://www.edu-design-principles.org). The database has been helpful as a resource in designing courses and refining curriculum materials (Ronen-Fuhrmann & Kali, 2009).

Linn and Eylon (2006) noted that the principles were not sufficient to guide designers to create instruction that led to coherent understanding. To clarify when features succeed, they analyzed the processes students follow to integrate their ideas and identified instructional patterns that improve the impact of the features. They identified four general processes that, in combination, can promote KI: Elicit Ideas, Add New Ideas, Distinguish Among Ideas, and Reflect and Sort Out Ideas. They argued that combining these four processes can enhance instruction for lectures, classroom experiments, scientific visualizations, collaborative learning, professional development, and other activities (Table 5.2). These principles and patterns give designers a starting point for new curriculum materials. Tests of new materials, using design study methods can, in turn, refine these features, principles, and patterns.

In this chapter, we distinguish:

- KI principles. Specific guidelines that promote coherent understanding.
- KI features. Instructional designs that implement a KI principle.
- KI patterns. Sequences of processes that reinforce each other to help learners create coherent views of instructed topics.

Table 5.2 Examples of Specific Knowledge Integration Patterns

SPECIFIC PATTERN	DESCRIPTION
Orient, Diagnose, and Guide	Recursively defines the scope of a topic, connects the topic to personally relevant problems, links the new topic to prior instruction, identifies student entering ideas, and adds ideas to stimulate knowledge integration.
Experiment	Involves a recursive process of framing a question, generating methods for investigating the question, carrying out an investigation, evaluating the results, and using the findings to sort out the repertoire of ideas.
Collaborate	Students generate their own ideas, respond to group ideas, support their views, and reach consensus. Negotiating meaning is central to student understanding.
Reflect	Encourages learners to analyze the connections they make between their ideas and monitor their understanding. Varying prompts reveals which approaches succeed (Linn, Davis, & Bell, 2004).

	PROCESS			
SPECIFIC PATTERN	*Elicit or generate ideas from repertoire of ideas.*	*Add new ideas to help distinguish or link ideas.*	*Distinguish ideas.*	*Sort out ideas by promoting, demoting, merging, and reorganizing.*
Orient, Diagnose, and Guide	Generate alternative ideas about a topic or phenomena.	Orient learners to a topic with a mini-lecture, video, or demonstration.	Diagnose weaknesses and offer analogies, pivotal cases, or examples.	Reconsider ideas based on alternatives, evidence, and criteria.
Experiment	Elicit questions and frame the investigation	Generate or use methods to gather evidence.	Evaluate results using criteria consistent with the methods.	Connect results of experiment to repertoire of ideas.
Collaborate	Generate ideas for a class or online discussion.	Review the ideas of other contributors.	Evaluate ideas using personal or group criteria.	Create group consensus about connections.
Reflect	Identify question or conundrum.	Generate, read, listen, or observe ideas.	Identify personally valid, uncertain, or invalid ideas.	Revise ideas and seek needed information.

KI Image of the Learner

The KI principles and patterns reflect a new image of the learner that is compatible with the findings of the TIMSS video study (see Chapter 2), the *How People Learn* book (Bransford et al., 1999), and the case studies described in Chapters 3 and 4. In this view, learners hold a repertoire of ideas rather than a single view of a scientific topic. Furthermore, learners intentionally generate and reformulate ideas to make sense of the world. However, although learners develop these ideas they often fail to link ideas from one situation to ideas generated in another situation governed by the same principles. To promote KI, instruction can guide learners to distinguish their varied ideas, add new ideas to help sort out the alternatives, and reflect on the process.

Since learners develop many of their ideas while exploring personally-relevant scientific topics, the KI approach capitalizes on the reasoning that students use in these situations. By introducing new ideas in the context of contemporary problems and helping students make sense of these situations, science instruction can prepare students to develop an increasingly sophisticated understanding of science across the lifespan.

This image of the learner differs from the view of the learner as absorbing information, constrained by developmental limitations, and in need of extrinsic motivation, that permeates the typical patterns reported in Chapter 2. In this chapter we synthesize the findings reported in the case studies as well as other research to support the KI approach.

Repertoire of Ideas

The case studies in Chapters 3 and 4 show how learners develop a repertoire of ideas about scientific phenomena. The ideas in the repertoire come from a plethora of experiences including culturally specific activities (Bell, Lewenstein, Shouse, Feder, & National Research Council, 2009; Lee, 2009), personal initiative, museum visits (planetariums, aquariums, science museums), hobbies (chemistry sets), compelling observations (metal feels cold), language conventions (turn up the heat), and textbooks (atom is smallest piece of matter).

In this book, we use the term *idea* to refer to each distinct view held by the learner. We include observational, intuitive, mathematical, visual, and analogical views. The repertoire includes ideas that might be held by a number of students, or even most students, as well as unique ideas that are often tied to a context of application. Students can develop separate ideas in contexts such as school or home or sports.

The realization that students generate a repertoire of ideas, as noted in Chapter 1, is one of the important advances in understanding of science learning (diSessa, 1983; NRC, 2006; Siegler, 2000). Piaget first drew attention to the alternative ideas about science that students hold (Inhelder & Piaget, 1958/1972; Piaget,

1970b). Today we see that this repertoire can drive rather than limit learning opportunities (Linn, Songer & Eylon, 1996).

Considerable research, building on Piaget's studies, identifies the many ideas students develop in science (Bransford, Brown, & Cocking, 1999; diSessa, 1983; diSessa & Minstrell, 1998; Eylon & Linn, 1988; Pfundt & Duit, 1994). These studies demonstrate that students may hold many contradictory ideas about the same topic.

Researchers argue about how and when students change their ideas (e.g., Smith et al., 1993; Vosniadou, 2008). Many developmental psychologists have argued that young children cannot use scientific reasoning (Klahr, 2000; Kuhn et al., 1988). Others have shown that young students can use scientific reasoning to explore scientific problems (Case, 1980, 1985; Linn, Clement, Pulos & Sullivan, 1989; Metz, 2000). Recently, the value of cultivating scientific reasoning early has been supported in several synthesis reports (Duschl, 2005; Bransford et al., 1999). The KI approach capitalizes on this repertoire and encourages students to distinguish among their ideas using scientific evidence.

Sources of Ideas

The repertoire of ideas takes advantage of the diversity of learners. Learners generate ideas as they interact with the environment, peers, family, many forms of media, and various forms of science instruction. Some ideas come from *deliberate* efforts of students to interrogate the world such as when they plant tomatoes in sun or shade, break open a rock, test whether objects sink. Others come from students' *cultural* experiences such as legends and beliefs held in their communities, family hobbies, dinner table conversations, and interactions with relatives. Some ideas are based on students' *interpretations* of the phenomena they encounter such as when they argue that a fire is alive because it moves or consumes plants (Linn, Davis, & Eylon, 2004).

The repertoire includes distinct varieties of ideas. It includes ideas about the discipline (concepts such as force or photosynthesis), the nature of investigation (such as what makes a good experiment), the role of science in society (such as whether science is authoritative or constraining), and the nature of science learning (such as whether to memorize or understand).

The repertoire also includes different types of evidence and explanations. Students draw on observations, anecdotes, films, books, and experts. Students link their ideas using descriptive, symbolic, visual, analogical and causal explanations among others.

These combined sources generate a rich assortment of ideas, including many inaccurate or partially correct ideas that reflect the efforts of students to make sense of the world. Students benefit when they compare, distinguish, and evaluate their repertoire of ideas.

The repertoire of ideas can be viewed as a pool of ideas with each having a chance to explain new phenomena. As students interact with the world they promote some ideas and demote others. They also develop criteria that they use to distinguish among the ideas.

Building on the Repertoire

Effective instruction takes advantage of the capability of the learner to generate a repertoire of ideas. Rather than telling students which ideas are accurate, as is common with the typical patterns described in Chapter 1, evidence from successful practices shows the importance of supporting students so they inspect, critique, test, and reformulate their repertoire themselves. This form of instruction is often referred to as inquiry learning. It encourages distinguishing among the ideas in the repertoire and conducting independent investigations to sort them out. Many successful instructional programs encourage students to sort out, compare, contrast, promote, demote, and in other ways identify the most promising ideas in their repertoire.

The instructional patterns utilized in typical science materials neglect variability in student ideas, both within and across individuals and fail to take advantage of this variability. Researchers and philosophers, using metaphors such as survival of the fittest ideas (Toulmin, 1961), or the value of multiple perspectives (Holyoak & Thagard, 1995; Thagard, 2000), point out the significance of alternative views of scientific phenomena.

This image of learning takes advantage of the diverse ideas students bring to science class because these ideas reflect efforts to make sense of personal experiences. This view promotes equity because it confers respect on culturally-motivated views of science. It also stresses the importance of the social context of instruction by encouraging students to pool their ideas and critique the ideas of others. When students jointly explore scientific phenomena each idea held by a individual can be considered and evaluated by others. By capturing the unique, personally-motivated, and culturally-relevant ideas held by students, the KI approach gives learners some insight into the ways that scientists generate alternatives for novel problems.

Learners regularly compare and reconsider their ideas for topics that they find interesting and relevant. For example, students compare their ideas about music, sports teams, movies, books, friends, and travel destinations. In these areas, as in science, a big issue concerns the criteria students use and the evidence they have for their decisions.

In science, students need to compare ideas and consider new ones. This is most successful when the topics are relevant and compelling. Topics can be relevant to learners for many reasons. Students might learn chemistry to prepare for a career in medicine, master mechanics because they are curious about how things work, or study genetics because a family member has cystic fibrosis. Often everyday scientific events such as new sources of energy, efforts to find a vaccine against malaria, or new ways to recycle tires can be used to spark interest in science. Scientific controversies such as the pace of global climate change, the best policy for eradicating malaria, or ways to clean up an oil spill, can inspire students.

To promote KI, assessments need to be aligned with instruction (Chapter 3). KI items help students practice generating ideas and connecting ideas using evidence (see Box 5.1).

BOX 5.1 KI ITEM AND RUBRIC
An Energy Story from the WISE Thermodynamics unit

Energy Story Assignment: Write a story using scientific evidence that explains why you can burn your feet when walking barefooted down the street on a summer day. Where does the energy come from? Where does the energy go? How does the energy move? How does the energy change?

Knowledge Integration Rubric:

Score	Level	Description	Examples
1	No answer, off task or I do not know. Student does not answer the question being asked.		
2	Non-normative ideas or links: Scientifically non-normative ideas, vague ideas, or scientifically invalid connections between ideas, or repeating the question as an answer.		The energy comes from the wind. The energy moves because you are walking. The energy changes its temperature.
3	Partial link: Unelaborated connections using relevant features OR scientifically valid connections that are not sufficient to solve the problem.	Student answer presents ideas from one category in a normative way.	Light from the Sun heats up the ground, which heats up your feet.

| 4 | Full link: One scientifically complete and valid connection. | Student answer connects ideas from 2 categories in a normative way. | The heat conducts from the ground to the feet. Heat flows from the ground to your foot because the ground is warm and your foot is cold. Heat flows from the ground to your foot until they are at the same temperature. |
| 5 | Complex links: Two or more scientifically complete and valid connections. | Student answer connects ideas from 3 or more categories in a normative way. | Energy travels as radiation from the Sun to the ground and is transformed into heat. |

Science instruction can support students in gaining awareness of their repertoire and monitor their progress. Developing a lifelong habit for evaluating ideas can lead to a more and more coherent account of scientific phenomena.

KI Principles and Features

The case studies in Chapters 2 and 3 reveal aspects of instruction that promote KI. Successful instruction motivates learners to bridge between the ideas they have developed on their own and new, more sophisticated ideas. The case studies reported in Chapters 3 and 4 and prior research (Linn & Hsi, 2000) identify principles and features of instruction that promote KI. We have identified four categories of design goals reflected in the principles: make science accessible, make thinking visible, help students learn from others, promote autonomy.

Make Science Accessible

The first category of KI principles articulated by Linn and Hsi (2000) concerns making science accessible (see Table 5.1). To make science accessible designers consider the interests that students have about the topic and introduce the instruction in personally relevant contexts. Designers choose contexts that are likely to arise in the future so learners will have the chance to use their new ideas again. By making science accessible, designers show that science applies to everyday life.

Making science accessible motivates students to participate, makes science relevant to students, and connects science instruction to a topic that students might encounter after science class is over. An example from the WISE Global Climate Change project illustrates this category (see Figure 5.1).

The thermodynamics case study illustrated the many personally relevant contexts that involve thermodynamics. The research emphasized contexts such as (a) using insulation to design coolers to keep picnics safe, drinks warm or cold, (b) designing wilderness clothing to protect individuals from the elements, (c) making energy-efficient decisions about house design, and (d) evaluating tips for energy conservation.

Many of the ideas elicited in the thermodynamics case study never arise in typical instruction. This is because typical materials present science in a narrow range of contexts. In fact, most typical thermodynamics instruction emphasizes, at best, experiments involving the heating and cooling of water, possibly in Styrofoam cups or glass beakers.

The atomic case study team identified similar interesting contexts that contributed to the eliciting of student ideas and also convinced students about the importance of the molecular model. For example, in the *Fiber* unit students explore atomic structure by analyzing a variety of textiles and their properties.

In summary, to make science accessible, designers often broaden the focus of a topic, compared to the treatment in textbooks. For example, adding additional insulators to the study of thermodynamics or multiple textiles to the study of atomic structure. They draw on authentic student experiences and culturally-relevant ideas. These examples increase the relevance of science by including applications that students encounter in their lives. They have the potential of con-

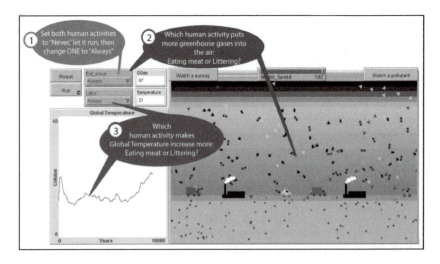

FIGURE 5.1   Screenshot of a NetLogo simulation in the WISE Global Climate Change unit

vincing students to think about their own ideas and to enable students to revisit their ideas when they encounter the topic in the future.

Making Thinking Visible

The second category of KI principles that Linn and Hsi (2000) identified concerns making thinking visible in two ways (see Figure 5.2). First, it includes making scientific events like molecular interactions visible for students, in scientific visualizations. Basically, students have to take on faith that materials are made out of atoms and molecules. A visualization can give students a way to think about the particulate nature of matter. Students might be able to use the images in the visualization to make sense of observations about the natural world.

Second, making thinking visible also includes motivating students to articulate their ideas, making their ideas visible for teachers and for collaborators. Both the case studies show the benefit of making student ideas visible in relevant contexts. When students predict the temperature of objects or the trajectory of a projectile, they make their ideas visible. These student predictions help teachers understand their students' beliefs and reasoning processes. Teachers can use this information for assessment as well as to customize instruction.

Both the thermodynamics and atomic cases also reveal the benefit of combining scientific visualizations and student drawings to articulate ideas. The scientific visualizations illustrate normative ideas. The drawings often show views that students cannot articulate, but are part of their repertoire (Chiu, 2010; Edelson, 2001; Zhang, 2008). When students draw their ideas, they give teachers insight

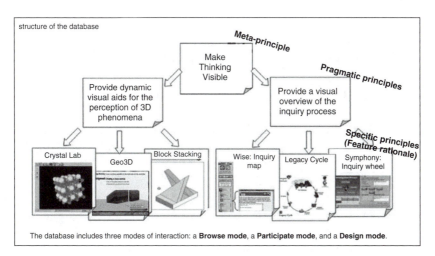

FIGURE 5.2   Screenshot from the Design Principles database for the principle Making Thinking Visible, http://www.edu-design-principles.org/dp/designHome.php

into the images that they bring to science class. In the atomic case, repeated drawing reveals the developing ideas held by the student. This helps teachers guide students to take advantage of the visualizations.

Predictions that students make in the thermodynamics curriculum when using temperature-sensitive probes also make thinking visible. By asking students to draw the curve that they expect the temperature sensitive probe to produce, the researchers engage students in connecting their own ideas to the experimental outcomes. It was intriguing to observe students cheering as the probe data appeared, encouraging the curve to align with their predictions and apparently thinking that cheering might help!

In summary, the case studies illustrate important features that contribute to the design goal of making science visible. Ideas are represented in molecular visualizations, student explanations, student drawings, modeling environments like NetLogo, and real-time data collection. They can also arise when using new technologies that provide a window on scientific processes such as STM, nanotechnology, and genetic engineering. The design goal of making ideas visible is an important feature of science instruction that is exciting today as more powerful simulations and models become available.

Help Students Learn from Others

The third category of KI principles identified by Linn and Hsi (2000) concerns features that help students learn from each other. This category refers to features of instruction that allow students to collaborate, cooperate, or interact. See example in Box 5.2.

BOX 5.2 LEARNING FROM OTHERS

Screenshot of a gated collaboration supporting collaborative learning

The gated collaboration activity was developed at part of the University of California Web-based Inquiry Science Environment (UC-WISE, see: http://www.cs.berkeley.edu/~clancy/web/ucwise.html)

Gated collaboration example

- A question is posed to the students: Which solution do you prefer for temperature conversion? Explain your reasoning.
- After responding online, a student is able to view the answers provided by their classmates. Thus students are required to engage with the content before reading possible answers from others.

- Students comment on solutions of others. For example, one student says, "I prefer the recursive method because it is simple to understand and implement even if it does involve more steps."

Gated collaborations typically use questions that lend themselves to multiple solutions where viewing other students' answers shows a diversity of answers and provides students with experience evaluating alternative responses.

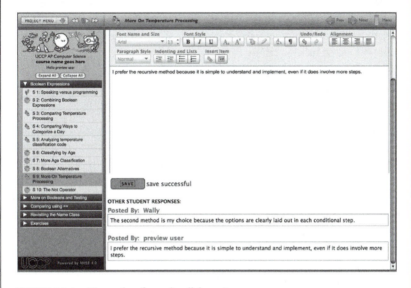

FIGURE 5.2.1   Example of gated collaboration

Several factors make peer collaboration valuable. First, students might encounter ideas articulated by their peers that resonate with their own ideas. Second, a peer might critique an idea held by the learner in a way that either motivates the learner to reconsider their perspective or clarifies the topic.

Designers face challenges when seeking to help students learn from others. When students learn from each other they could reinforce non-normative ideas or waste time trying to explain complex ideas (Linn & Hsi, 2000). Many point out that stereotypes about who can succeed in science can impede effective communication (Burbules & Linn, 1988; see Chapter 9).

The thermodynamics case study illustrates ways to address the challenge of helping students learn from others. It includes online activities that engage peers in productive discourse. One approach to strengthening opportunities to learn from others is a gated discussion (Box 5.2). In this approach students articulate their own ideas before participating in the discussion and then are required to go back and resolve differences between new views and the ones that they articulated previously. A gated discussion also enables teachers to get insight into the kinds of learning students achieve from interacting with their peers.

The atomic case study reveals some valuable features to promote learning from others. In the atomic case study, while learning about the molecular model, students make drawings of their ideas and post them around the classroom. Then other students have the opportunity to critique these drawings and the class develops criteria to distinguish ideas. Eventually, the class reaches some consensus concerning the molecular model.

In summary, features that allow students to learn from others contribute to KI. They require careful design to ensure that students respect the views of others and use evidence to decide which are more valid. Gated discussions and the Ikatura method described in Box 2.1 are successful examples.

Promote Autonomy

The fourth category of KI principles identified by Linn and Hsi (2000) concerns promoting autonomy. As both case studies reveal, instructional features can engage students in sorting out their ideas, but instilling a lifelong practice of reconsidering their ideas about the discipline and about the nature of science is more difficult. Reflection prompts can help students identify links among ideas. These activities engage students in activities that they could perform autonomously but do not guarantee that students will develop a sense of themselves as scientists or even as individuals who can make progress in understanding science. Developing an identity as someone who can explore a science topic and a feeling of agency about science is the ultimate goal. Using science to solve everyday problems is a good starting point (see Figure 5.3).

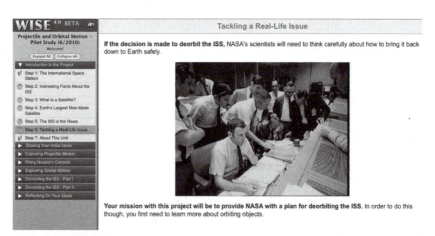

FIGURE 5.3   A reflection prompt in the WISE Thermodynamics unit (included picture is from NASA's JSC Digital Image Collection, http://images.jsc. nasa.gov)

In the case studies, students practice activities they could perform autonomously. For example, reflection prompts in the thermodynamics case study ask students to explain how they would wrap a drink to keep it cold and to use evidence from experiments to defend their choice. In thermodynamics, students write letters to the editor of a fictitious newspaper to critique a news article about keeping cool in the summer and use evidence from their experiments to recommend to policymakers more effective use of insulation in houses. Projects in the atomic case study also engage students in potentially autonomous activities by posing challenges such as, designing clothing that never wears out.

In summary, by taking advantage of opportunities to combine and refine ideas in naturally occurring contexts, students get experience in using their ideas for problems they might encounter outside of science class. They practice autonomous reasoning about accessible problems. Focusing on these two principles strengthens the probability that students will gain lifelong understanding of the topics that they encounter.

Design Principles Database

The KI principles specify instructional features that can promote coherent understanding. Kali (2006) has encouraged a large group of designers to link the most promising features of their instructional materials to the design principles (see Figure 5.2). These principles and related features are available in a database (http://design-principles.org) of materials that have promoted KI in research studies. These include brainstorms and gated discussions (see Box 5.2), visualizations of chemical reactions to make thinking visible (see Figure 5.2 and Figure 5.4), and reflection prompts (see Figure 5.5). Researchers have used the database in courses and workshops (Kali & Linn, 2009; Ronen-Fuhrmann & Kali, 2008).

In summary, the design principles identify features that can help designers improve KI instruction. They reflect the combined wisdom of many research teams. To combine the features in ways that help students integrate their ideas we have synthesized successful sequences of instructional activities and identified KI patterns.

KI Patterns

While helpful, the KI principles and features can definitely be combined in unsuccessful instructional patterns. For example, if instruction only made thinking visible, students would not make much progress. In addition, the principles are not sufficient to ensure KI because the coordination of learner activities is not delineated. This is a common shortcoming of principles. They do not specify exactly how they should be combined (Brown & Campione, 1996)

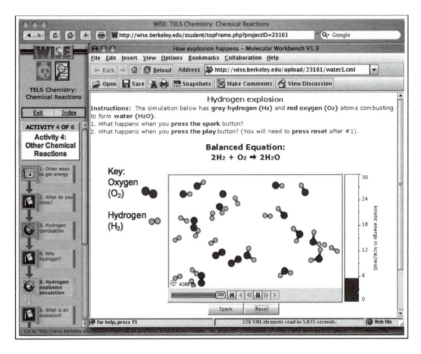

FIGURE 5.4   Screenshot of the WISE Molecular Workbench visualization for chemical reactions

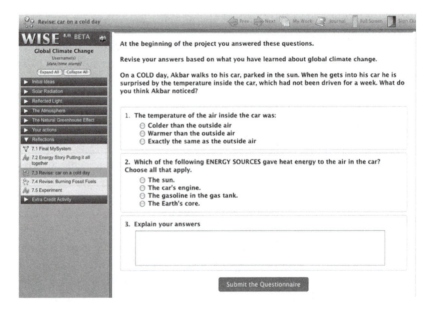

FIGURE 5.5   Screenshot of the WISE Global Climate Change unit showcasing reflection prompts

Patterns identify the combination of processes that students need to integrate their ideas. The need for patterns is evident in the description of the principles themselves. Many of the KI principles include suggestions for combining activities effectively. For example, experiments are improved by predictions, collaboration is improved by first articulating personal ideas, and visualizations are enhanced by reflections. The discussion of principles, underscores the need for guidance in combining activities. Patterns show how these opportunities can be embedded in instruction.

In this chapter, we describe the KI pattern. In Chapters 6–10, we articulate how this pattern applies to specific instructional activities including lectures, classroom experiments, visualizations, and collaboration. Patterns take advantage of the principles but go beyond the principles to synergistically encourage KI.

The KI pattern identifies the combination of processes that lead to coherent ideas. The KI pattern resulted from synthesizing research on instruction. It captures promising ways to stimulate learners to build a coherent perspective on a science topic.

Research suggests four KI processes that, when combined, promote KI. These four processes make up the general KI pattern. The basic pattern can be customized for a wide range of activities.

Elicit the Repertoire of Ideas

The first process involves eliciting the diverse ideas that students bring to science class by encouraging students to articulate their ideas in the many contexts they typically encounter. By asking students to articulate ideas about a scientific phenomenon in a broad range of contexts, rich culturally-motivated ideas can be captured. Often, when students collaborate with each other, they describe ideas in their repertoire that might have been difficult for them to articulate without a conversation.

This KI process is important because, when instruction fails to elicit the range of ideas that students hold, it is common for learners to isolate their school ideas and retain their other ideas for use in everyday situations (Linn & Hsi, 2000). For example, students sometimes comment that heat and temperature are the same at home but different at school or that objects remain in motion in science class but come to rest in the playground.

Being receptive to student ideas requires respecting the ideas that students bring to science class. Research conducted by Piaget (Inhelder & Piaget, 1958/1972; Piaget, 1970a) identified the kinds of ideas that students develop when interacting with scientific phenomena. Many interpreted this work to mean that instruction needed to eradicate bad ideas. By the 1980s, researchers had begun to realize that the ideas students develop have merit and deserve respect (Smith et al., 1993). As we discussed (Eylon & Linn, 1988) at the time, students bring a wealth of useful, diverse, and culturally-motivated ideas to science class. Instructional materials that respect and build on these ideas have more impact on student learning than curriculum materials designed without consideration of student ideas (Vosniadou, 2008).

Examples of Eliciting Ideas

As shown in the case studies, researchers have found ways to respect and elicit student ideas in predictions, brainstorms, and gated discussions. The brainstorm discussion used by the thermodynamics team illustrates how diverse ideas could help contribute to effective learning (see Figure 1.1). In addition, both the thermodynamics and atomic design teams identified ideas that students hold in the specific topic area that might persist unless addressed as part of instruction (e.g., for thermodynamics, distinguishing ideas about how objects feel from ideas about the temperature of objects as shown on a thermometer).

Both the case studies also illustrated how technology can contribute new contexts for eliciting scientific ideas. Both case studies allowed students to explore simulations, conduct virtual experiments, and use real-time data collection. For example, in Thermodynamics, students conduct virtual experiments about insulation and conduction to test a variety of materials to wrap items such as potatoes hot from the oven, soft drinks cold from the refrigerator, and ice cream from the freezer. These virtual experiments extend the contexts for exploration. Because they featured predictions, they elicited ideas and enabled learners to use the results of their experiments to build on their ideas.

In summary, the case studies illustrate techniques for eliciting student ideas. They also demonstrate the value of eliciting student ideas from a broad range of contexts, in order to ensure that diverse, culturally-motivated ideas are respected and explored in science instruction. Several studies show that when ideas are not elicited, students fail to consider them in interpreting new views. (e.g., Crouch & Mazur, 2001; Linn & Hsi, 2000; Petrosino et al., 2007).

Add New Normative Ideas

The second KI process is adding new normative ideas that get integrated with existing ideas. Designing ideas that have the potential of stimulating KI is difficult. Ideas are often too abstract (Driver, 1985). Often new ideas stifle consideration of alternative views. It takes less mental effort to isolate ideas than it does to distinguish and compare ideas. Research on the design of effective examples illustrates the difficulties students have with many textbook accounts (Clement, 1993). Clement noted that explaining friction using examples of cars driving on icy roads only reached a small number of students who had actually driven on such roads. When textbooks attempt to explain the seasons (Chapter 2), the drawings may reinforce the idea that the Sun is closer to the Earth in some seasons and farther away in others.

Research in the 1980s compared introducing rules or examples (Hiebert, 1986), contrasting historical with contemporary accounts of scientific phenomena (Holton, 2003), and comparing drawings to text accounts of material (Larkin & Simon, 1987). This research resulted in the appreciation of the importance of multiple representations of scientific ideas. These findings have encouraged researchers to experiment with a variety of formats for introducing new ideas (White & Frederiksen, 1998).

Rather than seeking contradictions or even determining whether ideas are similar or different, students are prone to add the new ideas they encounter in instruction and use them for the next test. This is especially problematic if tests emphasize recall and if courses do not include cumulative measures of progress.

If ideas remain isolated, they will be quickly forgotten as reported for classes that implement the absorption approach (see Chapter 2). Courses may prime students to memorize new ideas rather than considering their meaning. As the TIMSS study and the iterative refinement of instruction in the case studies suggest, designing ideas that make sense to students is a research question. In the typical patterns described in Chapter 2, instructors often rely on the textbook (or representations designed for experts), without determining whether this depiction of scientific phenomenon communicates to students.

Examples of Added Ideas

The process of designing new ideas is enhanced by new technology. Animations, visualizations, virtual experiments, and models can be tested and refined to meet user needs. It is possible to create interactive representations such as molecular workbench visualizations (Figure 5.4).

The case studies illustrate how technology has dramatically expanded the opportunities for selecting appropriate scientific ideas by offering visualizations, animations, and new representations captured in electron microscope photographs or movies and with tools such as the STM. The case studies suggest criteria for new ideas that we refer to as pivotal cases (Linn, 1995; see Figure 1.2).

Similarly, Clement (1993) has argued for bridging analogies to help link the ideas presented in science class to those developed by students. For example, Clement demonstrated that students understood the force of an object on a table better when they compared it to the force of the object on the spring of a bed.

The case studies demonstrate the benefit of trial and refinement to determine which ideas students will find most compelling. For example, the heat bars visualization in Chapter 3 required extensive refinement before it succeeded. To encourage students to convert their observations into a narrative, the designers used familiar materials. Students could contrast the wood and metal by creating a personal story about the materials. Recently, we have explored energy stories to take advantage of narrative for promoting KI (see Box 5.1).

In summary, the importance of testing and refining new ideas so they can be integrated is essential. Design of the ideas to add to the repertoire is important and complex. Adding generative ideas has the potential of coalescing the repertoire. Technology offers new avenues for capturing scientific ideas, including visualizations of unseen processes. We discuss how KI patterns have improved the use of visualizations in Chapter 8.

Distinguish among Ideas Using Scientific Evidence

The third KI instructional process involves motivating students to distinguish among ideas. Students encounter scientific ideas on the Internet, in textbooks, advertisements, experiments, from personal experience, interactions with teachers, interactions with peers and family, and in instructional contexts. In order for students to distinguish among these ideas, they need an understanding of scientific evidence. Helping students learn to evaluate their ideas is, therefore, an important KI process.

Students often report that everything in the science text is true (see Chapter 3). In addition, they often accept bogus results available on the Internet or in popular publications because they are cloaked in scientific jargon. Because science courses neglect the controversies that lead to scientific advances and rarely show the limitations of research methods, they often reinforce uncritical acceptance of scientific claims (Bell & Linn, 2002). In order for students to successfully evaluate ideas and develop criteria for distinguishing among the views in their repertoire, they need experiences that combine methods of investigation with interpretation of the results of experiments. Students need to understand and distinguish among techniques for studying disparate kinds of scientific phenomena and to appreciate the reliability of those methodologies. Importantly, students need to appreciate that scientific knowledge is tenuous and often backed by evidence that can be refuted with subsequent experimentation.

The patterns in Chapter 2, by neglecting student views, fail to emphasize criteria for distinguishing among ideas. When students absorb information, rather than actively comparing ideas and identifying evidence that could be used to distinguish among ideas, they do not learn to evaluate new information. Recall that distinguishing ideas was common in countries where students succeeded on TIMSS (Chapter 2).

Successful inquiry programs emphasize opportunities to test and elaborate ideas (Kali et al., 2009; Tabak, & Reiser, 1997; Vosniadou, 2008) as well as, opportunities to develop criteria and practice evaluating novel information. Distinguishing among the ideas students generate about the natural world take advantage of the evidence that led students to develop the ideas.

To illustrate the benefits of encouraging students to distinguish ideas, it is useful to consider how students develop their ideas. Students might hypothesize that electricity flows out of the wall or that in summer the Sun is closer to the Earth based on observations of electrical cords or of being hotter when closer to a heat source. Students can test these ideas as well as alternatives using virtual experiments. Many researchers show that building on student ideas is more successful than are efforts to eradicate ideas. Eradicating ideas might also discourage the reasoning that led to the ideas in the first place (Carey, 1985; diSessa, 1988; Linn & Eylon, 2006; Slotta & Chi, 2006; Smith et al., 1993). By neglecting the process of distinguishing existing and new ideas, the absorption approach leaves students with few reasons to use instructed ideas outside of school.

Examples of Distinguishing Ideas

Both case studies show how students can use evidence to distinguish among ideas. They show that students develop criteria for distinguishing ideas by engaging in debate activities that draw on scientific evidence, gathered through experimentation and collected from secondary sources.

In both of the case studies, teachers played an important role in helping students find effective ways for using evidence and encouraging students to develop criteria for distinguishing among the available evidence. Teachers encouraged students to ensure that the evidence they used in their arguments was collected using valid and reliable scientific methods.

The case studies also illustrate how technology such as the inquiry map can guide students to conduct scientific research and identify criteria for distinguishing among scientific ideas. Resources like Sense Maker (Bell & Linn, 2000) and activities like letters advocating for a specific view help learners apply criteria and distinguish ideas.

In summary, distinguishing among ideas using evidence is possible even for very young children. It is effective as part of KI. This is perhaps the most important difference between typical and KI patterns. Even inquiry frameworks such as the learning cycle would benefit from strengthening emphasis on the process of distinguishing ideas (see Chapter 7).

Encourage Reflection

The fourth KI process encourages reflection: motivating students to monitor their progress and sort out their ideas. Well-designed reflection activities help students develop cohesive and coherent understanding of science. Students who compare and contrast their views by reflecting can become effective at guiding their own efforts to continuously update and refine their ideas. To build cohesive and effective understanding, students need the ability to distinguish not only among scientific ideas, but also among scientific claims, types of evidence, and scientific methodologies. Reflection activities can help students to identify overlaps and gaps in their knowledge, see connections among their own ideas, and resolve contradictions.

Importantly, reflection involves learning how to allocate limited energy to the most central confusions and to monitor progress. Many students prefer to act like cognitive economists, conducting only the essential activities required in their science classes. These students may ignore important conundrums. Science courses need to help students engage in sustained reasoning, refine their ideas, and deal with ambiguities, to prepare them for future dilemmas.

The absorption approach in Chapter 2 motivates students to respond to the barrage of information in science textbooks and the multiple-choice assessments by memorizing material they expect to encounter on tests. Memorizing does not prepare students for the many everyday problems they will face such as deciding among health care alternatives, choosing energy efficient solutions to problems, or evaluating competing claims for healthy diets.

Students need to sort out the ideas in their repertoire because they will encounter these challenges in many future situations. Designers can encourage students to guide their own learning, help learners develop the skills to distinguish among ideas, and emphasize the value of coherent views. This approach has been called intentional learning (Bereiter & Scardamalia, 1989), self-regulation (Brown, 1987; White, Shimoda, & Frederiksen, 1999), autonomous learning (Linn & Hsi, 2000), and self-explanations (Chi, Bassok, Lewis, Reimann, & Glaser, 1989). In science education, this means enabling students to debug their experiments, critique investigations, and question assertions. Students often follow directions rather than taking responsibility for their own learning. Projects or interactive discussions, where students are responsible for identifying a scientific question and exploring its ramifications, provide opportunities for sustained reasoning that includes sorting out ideas. These activities are usually the first to be eliminated when instructional time is limited.

Examples of Reflection

Both of the case studies show how inquiry activities can guide students to reflect on their ideas and create a coherent argument. Both the thermodynamics and the particulate case study help students to develop the propensity to reflect by requiring them to write reflection notes, summarize arguments, or structure their ideas in charts or posters. Both case studies show that a proportion of students fail to take responsibility for their own science learning. Some students argue that memorizing information, rather than trying to understand it, is a preferable approach for learning science (Linn & Hsi, 2000).

In summary, the case studies illustrate the importance of requiring students to sort out ideas using scientific evidence. They show that students need encouragement to develop criteria to distinguish among the sorts of evidence they encounter and opportunities to synthesize the results of their efforts.

Overall, the four KI processes underlie the kinds of intellectual activities that recent research in science education shows have an impact on student learning.

In contrast, the absorption approach to instruction, reflected in patterns such as *inform, assess* neglects student ideas and encourages memorization. These patterns fail to take advantage of the repertoire of ideas. Students add the ideas they learn, but retain their own ideas as well. If students add the new ideas but get little practice in using them and gain limited experience applying them in out-of-school contexts they are likely to isolate them from the ideas they already have. In contrast, successful instruction in the case studies and other research emphasizes encouraging students to make connections among student ideas. The absorption pattern, even when calling for active learning, does not generally include active integration of ideas. The KI pattern takes advantage of student ideas and promotes coherence by encouraging learners to distinguish among alternatives and prioritize their views.

Conclusions

The case studies as well as a large body of related research characterize students as developing a repertoire of ideas about any scientific phenomenon. These studies show that science instruction is more effective when the repertoire is respected and utilized in curricular activities (Kali, Linn, & Roseman, 2008; Linn, Davis, & Bell, 2004). The KI perspective focuses on how students develop this repertoire and how they build, enhance, and coalesce the repertoire into generative ideas and become lifelong science learners.

Longitudinal investigations reinforce the value of the KI processes. (Chiu, 2010; Clark, 2006; Lewis, 1995). Longitudinal results show that students add and organize their ideas over time. Some ideas introduced in class do not persist beyond science class, are never connected to the ideas that students bring to science class, and are not selected over the students' original ideas. These longitudinal studies underscore the advantages of designing instruction that enables students to revisit their ideas, because then the ideas that they learned in class come up in other settings. For example, the longitudinal investigation in the thermodynamics case study found that most students revisited ideas about insulation and conduction regularly after they left science class. They frequently mentioned thinking about how to keep beverages warm or cold. They considered how sweaters and jackets could keep people warm and ice cream cold. As a result they continued to refine their ideas and build coherent understanding.

Curriculum Design

The case studies illustrate a set of KI principles and an instructional pattern that can be used to improve curriculum design. In this chapter, we characterized four KI principles: Make Science Accessible; Make Thinking Visible; Help Students Learn from Others; Promote Autonomy. We also identified the general processes of the instructional pattern: Elicit Ideas, Add New Ideas, Distinguish Among Ideas, and Reflect on Ideas. In subsequent chapters, we will show how these general processes play out in specific contexts including lectures, classroom experiments, scientific visualizations, collaborative learning, and professional development.

Recent research illustrates how curriculum designers can take advantage of the KI processes to design instruction that leads to coherent understanding. This process starts with eliciting the ideas that students hold and using them to inform the design of instructional activities. Research suggests the importance of designing and testing effective new ideas to add to the repertoire that connect to the ideas students already hold.

Even with well-designed new ideas, students often cannot distinguish the new ideas from their existing ideas. Instruction succeeds when students gather and utilize evidence to distinguish among ideas.

Finally, students need opportunities as well as inclinations to engage in a sustained process of organizing and distinguishing, sorting out and prioritizing, the ideas in their repertoire. Research conducted in both case studies shows the importance and effectiveness of activities that support this process.

Next Steps

The case studies illustrate how the KI processes emerged and were clarified. In interpreting the case studies, we distinguished between the features of the emerging instruction and the underlying processes. In subsequent chapters, we will focus primarily on the processes that comprise the instructional pattern. We will discuss principles when they help characterize the features that have proven successful in recent curriculum innovations.

The case studies illustrate how technological advances have contributed to our understanding of learning and instruction. Both the patterns and principles can help designers take advantage of emerging research. They are particularly well-suited to technology-enhanced instruction.

Reflection Activity

Select a narrow topic that you would like to teach to someone. Use the four KI principles to generate some ideas for teaching the topic. Discuss how the principles helped you think about instruction. Now apply the KI pattern, taking advantage of the ideas you already generated. How does the pattern help you shape your plan for teaching the topic?

6

LECTURES AND TECHNOLOGY

Introduction

Lectures have a long history, probably originating about the time humans developed speech. We define lectures as scheduled, didactic presentations to a group by one or a few speakers who plan their remarks in advance of the presentation. We distinguish lectures from theatrical productions that follow a script and from impromptu comments or tutorials. In preparing their presentations, lecturers typically have some idea about their audience. They may or may not have a set time limit, but most lectures are under two hours in duration.

Lectures are widespread today in universities, religious gatherings (sermons), business meetings, auditoriums (public lectures), and tourist venues. Universities have found lectures to be cost effective since they serve many students and require minimal technology. Some public lectures attract large audiences and charge reasonable fees. Although lectures require little or no technology (maybe an amplification system for a large hall), lectures have historically included demonstrations of scientific phenomena. In addition, lecturers have embraced almost every new technology including slides, overhead projectors, film, video, computer projection, software for slides, and audience response systems. These technologies have met with both success and failure.

Most lectures are designed following the absorption approach. They generally implement the *motivate, inform, assess* pattern of instruction. They seek to transmit information rather than to promote coherent understanding (see Chapter 2). Lectures include features such as demonstrations, videos, or visualizations to enhance transmission of information and also to entice students to attend or pay attention to the presentation. Many studies document the limitations of lectures (Kulik & Kulik, 1979; Kulik, Kulik, & Cohen, 1980;

Odubunmi, & Balogun, 1991), show that instructors overestimate the impact of lectures (Hake, 1998; King, 1992), and find that students value them less than laboratory activities, personalized instruction systems, self-paced learning, and studying with peers (Light, 2001).

In this chapter, we show how the KI approach can improve the impact of lectures, including making use of new technologies for lectures. We also identify some of the autonomous learning capabilities (see Chapter 5) that help students take advantage of lectures.

Assessing Impacts of Lectures

Most instructors would argue that courses teach students both science principles and ability to use these ideas to solve problems in the discipline. They would probably agree that their courses teach for KI. Course assessments vary in the degree to which they measure these goals. Typical multiple-choice items (such as those that often accompany textbooks) feature primarily recall questions. They are less sensitive to the coherence of student ideas than KI assessments (see Box 1.2, Chapter 1; Clark & Linn, 2003; Linn et al., 2006). Even two-tier items are not sensitive to advanced levels of performance (see Box 3.2).

When researchers developed assessments such as the Force Concept Inventory (FCI, see Hestenes, Wells, & Swackhamer, 1992) to distinguish among common misconceptions and normative ideas in physics, many instructors were disappointed in the impact of their lectures (Hake, 1998). Although they saw progress on the typical textbook-provided assessments they found serious gaps in understanding on the Force Concept Inventory. These findings led instructors to redesign courses, including lectures to increase emphasis on coherence.

KI assessments not only distinguish between normative ideas and common intuitive ideas but also ask students to use evidence to construct arguments. KI assessments have the added feature of asking students to explain everyday situations. These assessments are ideal for measuring the impact of instruction designed to promote KI and develop coherent ideas as well as reveal weaknesses of absorption.

Aligning instruction and assessment to achieve KI ensures that students recognize the importance of using evidence to explain scientific events. Engaging students in applying the concepts from the course to everyday examples requires them to distinguish ideas and consolidate their insights. KI assessments can help communicate the goals of science courses, and even demonstrate the importance of science for solving realistic problems. Although KI assessments are more time-consuming to score than multiple-choice items scored with an automated system, KI assessments can help teachers by revealing the reasoning of their students. These assessments also augment the curriculum by requiring students to explain complex situations.

KI Approach to Lectures

We describe research showing that adding the elements of the KI pattern can convert an ineffective effort to transmit information into an effective opportunity to integrate ideas. We highlight two main research trends. First, the relentless enthusiasm for integrating new technologies into lectures. We describe how researchers have refined the transmission of information by creating innovative images and resources. Second, the recent efforts to increase participation in the lecture. Whereas improving transmission with new technologies is not sufficient on its own to improve lecture outcomes, several research programs have identified ways to take advantage of new technologies and incorporate new activities that promote coherent understanding by eliciting ideas, adding new ideas, supporting the process of distinguishing new and existing ideas (often by using collaborative groups), and enabling learners to reflect on their repertoire of ideas.

Implementing the KI pattern has generally succeeded by increasing the participation of the audience. In several universities, computer science instructors have even eliminated lectures in favor of interactive laboratories designed following the KI pattern (Clancy, Titterton, Ryan, Slotta, & Linn, 2003). In physics, researchers have moved towards shorter and shorter lectures and more and more audience interaction and involvement (Beichner, 2000; Crouch & Mazur, 2001; Mazur, 1997). Many instructors use interactive lecture demonstrations (ILD, see Sokoloff & Thornton, 2004) that resemble the Ikatura method (see Chapter 2). In this approach, the lecturer presents a compelling demonstration, then pauses the demonstration to ask the audience to make predictions (with or without an automated audience response system), then forms small groups to discuss alternatives, and then asks students to reach conclusions.

Learning to Learn from Lectures

Most learners are inclined to absorb lectures, often recording details but rarely criticizing the claims in the presentation. To become lifelong learners, students need to develop autonomous or independent learning skills to take advantage of lectures (see Chapter 5). As understanding of the learner has grown, a KI approach to learning from lectures has emerged. Basically, learners who benefit from lectures distinguish their own ideas from those in the lecture, look for gaps in their knowledge, and reflect on what they have learned. They seek to make sense of the material, integrate it with their own beliefs, and reorganize their ideas.

This is a rare occurrence. For example, recent work by Sinapuelas (2010) and others (Bjork, 1994; Bjork & Bjork, 2011) shows that many students in introductory college chemistry courses avoid testing themselves on their understanding and come away with limited understanding. Rather than distinguishing their own ideas from those in the lecture, students, at most, add the new ideas to their repertoire. Researchers report that this approach extends to study skills.

Students underline the textbook—often in multiple colors—rather than trying to explain the concepts to themselves. When reviewing previous exams or studying their lecture notes students rarely solve the problems first and then check their accuracy. Instead, they read the tests and the answers. They are satisfied if they think they understand the responses, but they do not find out whether they could generate accurate responses. Thus, students apply the absorption approach to their own learning, assuming that looking at the material will be sufficient to improve their understanding, rather than using autonomous learning skills to benefit from lectures, textbooks, or other materials.

Improving Lectures Using Technology

Research conducted to improve lectures so they contribute to KI can improve the instructional activities and help learners develop autonomous learning skills for interpreting lectures. Over the years, researchers have developed and tested numerous technologies to improve lectures. All involve taking advantage of technology and adding individual and peer activities. As mentioned above, the major contribution of this research has been to shorten or even eliminate the lecture part of the activity.

Adding Ideas

Based on a belief that demonstrations and new technologies present ideas more effectively than speech alone, instructors have experimented with almost every new approach for transmitting information including real-time observation of medical procedures (e.g., Greene, 2007), demonstrations, animation software, and various types of slides. The limitations of these technologies were discussed in Chapter 2. Here we identify promising directions.

Visualizations

Using technologies to design visualizations of new ideas for students can contribute to the success of a lecture. Some new technologies are ideal for adding ideas to the repertoire held by the student. Images and animations provide an opportunity to inform the audience. In geology, images of geological formations have been valuable (Kali, Orion, & Mazor, 1997). In physics, lecturers use software to demonstrate complex phenomena (Redish, 2003; Sprott, 1991).

A few studies show benefit of using visualizations to demonstrate complex ideas in lectures. For example, Yang, Andre, and Greenbowe (2003) compared dynamic and static visuals to help college students learn electrochemistry in a lecture. Both groups made progress but students with expertise in visual processing learned more from animated visuals than their peers who had limited expertise in visual processing.

Demonstrations

Demonstrations in lectures typically have the goal of informing or motivating students. They fail when students passively listen and do not distinguish the ideas in the lecture from their own views or actively identify gaps in their knowledge (Hake, 1998).

Lecturers have used demonstrations since at least the 1800s. Famous lectures with demonstrations include Faraday's Christmas Lectures and Feynman's Introductory Physics lectures, from the California Institute of Technology (Feynman, Leighton, & Sands, 1963). Faraday designed his Christmas Lectures for a young audience. In his lecture in 1859, Faraday used more than 80 demonstrations (see Box 6.1). In order to illustrate the force of gravity, his demonstration involved

---

BOX 6.1 FARADAY CHRISTMAS LECTURES
Examples of a few of the 86 demonstrations in one of Faraday's Christmas Lectures

Delivered before a juvenile audience at the Royal Institution of Great Britain during the Christmas holidays of 1859–60

For the 1859 lecture, Faraday selected gravitation. He generally discussed gravity in the context of mechanical force, electrostatics, heat, latent heat, center of gravity, magnetism, gravity and falling objects, and related topics. He also conducted numerous demonstrations. His own notes referred to 86 separate demonstrations (Halsall, 1998; The Woodrow Wilson National Fellowship Foundation, 2007).

Examples used in his lecture included the following:

I. **Mechanical Force: (Materials: sheet of paper, stick of shell-lac)**
Suppose I take this sheet of paper, and place it upright on one edge, resting against a support before me (as the roughest possible illustration of something to be disturbed), and suppose I then pull this piece of string, which is attached to it. I pull the paper over. Then, if I give it a push upon the other side, I bring into play a power, but a very different exertion of power from the former.

II. **States of Matter: (Materials: bag to hold air; block of ice; water boiling in a flask; [nearly equipoised scales, one of which contained a half-pint glass vessel]; bar of platinum; bar of aluminum)**
You see what I mean by the term matter—any of these things that I can lay hold of with the hand, or in a bag (for I may take hold of the air by inclosing it in a bag)—they are all portions of matter. For instance, here

is water—it is heavy; but let us examine it with regard to the amount of its heaviness or its gravity. I have before me a little glass vessel and scales, and the glass vessel is at present the lighter of the two; but if I now take some water and pour it in, you see that that side of the scales immediately goes down; that shows you (using common language, which I will not suppose for the present you have hitherto applied very strictly) that it is heavy, and if I put this additional weight into the opposite scale, I should not wonder if this vessel would hold water enough to weigh it down.

III. **Center of gravity: (Materials: toy that stands up when laid down)**
Here is a toy I happened to see the other day. That toy ought to lie something in this manner, and would do so if it were uniform in substance; but you see it does not; it will get up again. And now philosophy comes to our aid, and I am perfectly sure, without looking inside the figure, that there is some arrangement by which the centre of gravity is at the lowest point when the image is standing upright; and we may be certain, when I am tilting it over, that I am lifting up the centre of gravity (a), and raising it from the Earth. All this is affected by putting a piece of lead inside the lower part of the image, and making the base of large curvature, and there you have the whole secret.

Faraday concluded by using the time-honored tradition of listing vocabulary on the board. He remarked:

I am sorry to see our time for parting is drawing so near. As we proceed, I intend to write upon the board behind me certain words, so as to recall to your minds what we have already examined; and I put the word Forces as a heading, and I will then add beneath the names of the special forces according to the order in which we consider them; and although I fear that I have not sufficiently pointed out to you the more important circumstances connected with the force of Gravitation, especially the law which governs its attraction (for which, I think, I must take up a little time at our next meeting), still I will put that word on the board, and hope you will now remember that we have in some degree considered the force of gravitation—that force which causes all bodies to attract each other when they are at sensible distances apart, and tends to draw them together.

both gravity and electrostatics: He uses a charged stick to cause a sheet of paper that is standing up to fall over. In addition, his demonstrations used scales to weigh platinum, aluminum, and water to show the effect of gravity on materials that differ in density. His lecture went on to illustrate latent heat, chemical energy, attraction between objects, and ultimately the center of gravity, as well as showing that objects falling to the Earth in a vacuum fall at the same rate. This single lecture covered about half of an introductory course in physics! The Faraday Christmas Lectures and the Shakhashiri Science is Fun demonstrations (see Chapter 2) can motivate people to wonder about what happens in scientific investigations and potentially increase their interest in becoming scientists.

When lecturers ask the audience to make predictions or to consider alternative explanations for the observations they increase success (see Box 2.1). Kraus (1997) found that adding explanations to demonstrations had limited impact beyond the observation of the demonstration itself. Similar findings were reported by Sokoloff and Thornton (2004). They found limited value for demonstrations alone but big effects for adding predictions.

For example, to distinguish instructor explanations from lectures and demonstrations, a comprehensive study compared four conditions (Crouch et al., 2004):

- Lecture alone
- Lecture and demonstration
- Lecture, demonstration, and instructor explanation
- Predict, observe demonstration, and instructor explanation.

Results for the first three conditions were similar (about 30% success on the Force Concept Inventory). Only the condition with predictions had a substantial impact on students.

These findings suggest that demonstrations are not successful alone. Rather, consistent with other studies showing the value of eliciting ideas (Linn & Hsi, 2000) or asking students to make predictions (McLelland, 2006; White & Gunstone, 1992), they succeed when combined with activities that lead to KI.

In summary, demonstrations can succeed when students are asked to make predictions to help them identify gaps in their knowledge. Some technologies such as visualizations are valuable for illustrating processes that are too expensive, difficult, or awkward for students to perform themselves. Demonstrations need user testing to ensure that they emphasize important aspects of the phenomenon, communicate to the audience, appear authentic rather than magical, and providing observers with insights into the salient scientific processes.

Elicit Ideas

Technologies such as audience response systems make it efficient for instructors to gather information about student ideas. Eliciting ideas contributes to KI by encouraging students to consider all of their ideas as they build coherent accounts of science. When students neglect some of their ideas during learning, they often return to them later.

Designing peer-to-peer technologies to elicit ideas has proven valuable in collaborative learning (see Chapter 9). For example, a gated discussion (see Box 5.2) allows instructors to pose a question, ask students to submit ideas, and allow students to see ideas of others after they enter their ideas. This technique can work in lectures when students are connected by tablet PCs or other devices.

Predictions

Predictions have been shown to be valuable in the discussion of demonstrations above and in the Ikatura method (see Chapter 2). All prediction activities, however, are not equally successful.

Eric Mazur at Harvard has conducted a series of experiments to clarify the role of predictions and demonstrations in lectures. Mazur has compared lectures to interactive lectures (with predictions), and lectures plus demonstrations. These investigations have shown benefits and limitations of the interactive lecture (Mazur, 1997; see Box 6.2). In early studies, students enjoyed the

---

BOX 6.2 MAZUR INTERACTIVE LECTURE
Exploring the benefits and limitations of the interactive lecture

Eric Mazur has been interested in improving lectures since the 1980s. In a series of studies, Mazur and his colleagues refined the introductory calculus-based physics course at Harvard to improve the coherence of student ideas (Crouch, Fagen, Callan, & Mazur, 2004; Lorenzo, Crouch, & Mazur, 2006).

Lecture small group study

In one study, they investigated three versions of the course, adding activities where small groups collaboratively negotiate understanding of course topics. These activities were designed to help students distinguish ideas and develop more coherent understanding:

- *Traditional lecture and section.*
- *Partially interactive mode.* The students read relevant materials before class and the traditional lectures were replaced by peer instruction (Mazur, 1997). Class activities alternated between short (10–15) mini-lectures and conceptual questions that students discussed in small groups. No change in the sections.
- *Fully interactive mode.* In addition to peer instruction in the lectures, the 1.5 hr sections were replaced with 2 hr workshops using proven materi-

als such. For the first hour, groups of 3–4 students followed a set of conceptual, hands-on tutorials developed by McDermott (McDermott & Schaffer, 1998a,b) and Redish (2003). Students conducted the experiments and discussed concepts with each other. Students then carried out cooperative quantitative problem-solving activities (Heller, Keith, & Anderson, 1992).

Results. The Force Concept Inventory was administered before and after instruction. The results show that the more interactive the engagement the higher the gains in understanding. The partially interactive mode approximately doubled the normalized gain in scores and the fully interactive mode approximately tripled it. Gender gaps that existed for the pretest disappeared on the posttest for both of the interactive modes.

Lecture demonstration study

Another study (Crouch, Fagen, Callan, & Mazur, 2004) contrasted four conditions in an introductory physics course with 133 premed students:

- Lecture without a demonstration,
- Demonstration with the instructor's explanation [equivalent time],
- Prediction, demonstration, and explanation [adding 2 minutes per experiment],
- Prediction, demonstration, explanation, peer-to-peer discussion [adding 2 minutes for prediction + 6 minutes for discussion per experiment].

On the final exam, students predicted outcomes and explained the results using physical situations that were identical to the class experiments.
Results. Consistent with the knowledge integration pattern (Chapter 5), the fourth condition was most successful. Students made a prediction, observed the outcome, listened to the instructor's explanation, and sorted out their predictions, the outcome, and their fellow students' ideas in small groups.

Surprisingly, the demonstration added very little value to the lecture alone, consistent with the limited value that lectures intended to inform have on students. Even when the outcome measure essentially asked students to predict the outcome for the exact same demonstration, whether students saw the demonstration or not they were equally likely to succeed. It appears that little learning resulted from the lecture or demonstration.

Adding a prediction had a four-fold impact on the quality of explanations students gave on the final exam. Since the prediction added only two minutes per experiment, the instructional benefit relative to the time cost is substantial. Adding a prediction step to focus attention on the outcome and motivate students to identify gaps in their knowledge, was extremely effective.

The fourth condition was not much more effective than the prediction condition suggesting that discussions with peers did not add very much additional benefit. Since the discussion in the classroom required an additional six minutes, it is less cost effective, but could be beneficial when used judiciously. This finding suggests that in-class discussion may need more refinement to ensure that students distinguish ideas and reflect on the demonstration.

A NEW MISTAKE-CATCHING STATEGY

The president-for-life of all mistake-avoidance strategies

Asked to graph the velocity versus time of a certain motion (not known), a student draws Graph 1 below. Then she draws Graph 2, showing the position versus time *for the same motion.*

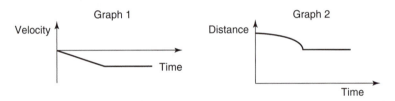

A. For you, which of the graphs is generally easier to draw: Graph 1 or Graph 2. Explain your answer. Then compare your answer with a partner's.

B. The student who drew the above graphs is more confident with position graphs. She's 99% her drawing of Graph 2 is correct. Is there a way that she could use her position graph to check for mistakes in her velocity graph? If yes, try it and explain the process. [Hint: **Think about which feature of a position graph indicates your velocity.**]

C. Many students report that even when they are asked to draw only a velocity graph they draw a position graph also. Why do you think that is?

FIGURE 6.2.1   Example activity used in Lecture Small Group Study (University of Maryland Physics Education Research Group. (Fall 2002). "Class discussion: the president-for-life of mistake-avoidance strategies," available online at: http://www.physics.umd.edu/perg/ILD/ILD_01_Motion_Graphs.pdf.)

interaction but did not learn the material consistent with the *motivate, inform, assess* pattern. Subsequent investigations showed that adding activities where students make predictions and then discuss alternatives is better than predictions alone. In one study, adding predictions and peer interactions not only increased performance, it also eliminated a gender gap that occurred on the pretest (Lorenzo, Crouch, & Mazur, 2006; see Box 6.2).

Subsequent studies compared a general demonstration to demonstrations addressing particular student difficulties (Crouch et al., 2004). They found that demonstrations designed to respond to student predictions, were more effective than generic demonstrations. Similarly, McDermott (2001) showed that enabling students to contrast conditions to investigate their own ideas improved student learning over conducting experiments designed by the instructor. These results show that eliciting ideas is not sufficient alone but increases the value of lectures when students have a chance to observe a demonstration that addresses their prediction and distinguish the results of the demonstration from views of peers who hold different views.

Audience Response Systems

Audience response systems allow instructors to pose problems to the class. They can be used for generating predictions. They are also used for interacting with the class.

From the 1970s, smart classrooms with response pads built into the seats became available. Instructors could pose problems and all the students could respond at once. One of the authors (Linn) had an opportunity to use a smart classroom for a statistics course. Linn found that writing good questions that stimulated reasoning was challenging. It was easy to write recall questions and the questions supplied by the textbook manufacturer were generally recall-oriented. Even a good question was not sufficient to stimulate complex reasoning during class.

Building on the Ikatura method highlighted in Chapter 2, audience responses can be enhanced by asking students to explain why they chose an option. Involving small groups in distinguishing alternative answers and reporting back to the class adds value, consistent with the KI pattern.

Over time the smart classroom has been replaced by mobile response systems. A popular approach which is often referred to as "clickers," is one where individual students are required to buy a handheld device that interfaces with equipment in the classroom. The classroom equipment can combine the responses from all the students in the class and display the distribution. A less high-tech version of this approach is one where students have colored cards and are asked to hold up a different color card for each of the response alternatives.

Audience response technologies including clickers have taken on a life of their own and are widely used in precollege science, mathematics, and computer science courses. One reason that polling students is popular is certainly that it keeps the class awake and engaged in making selections among alternatives. As discussed for smart classrooms, effectiveness depends on the quality of the questions asked as well as the response of the instructor. Developing good questions that allow students to think about the issues and that reveal the kinds of confusions that students hold is difficult.

Often college and precollege textbooks provide sample questions that are quite superficial. Perhaps to make teachers feel successful, these questions generally require recall of details reported in the text rather than reasoning (often the answer is highlighted in the teachers' version of the text). This use of clickers is consistent with the absorption approach to instruction in that it implements an *inform, assess* pattern. Questions that require KI combined with opportunities to distinguish ideas and use evidence to form arguments, have been investigated by many groups. Even with excellent activities, the most documented advantage of audience response systems involves asking for predictions.

Audience Questions

Instructors elicit ideas when they ask questions or entertain audience questions. However, instructors, as illustrated in *Ferris Bueller's Day Off*, often initiate the question, elicit responses, and then evaluate each answer (using the *initiate, respond, evaluate* pattern described in Chapter 2). In this approach, students who give an answer that is different from the one that the teacher expected are criticized, ignored, or prompted until they come up with a more appropriate answer. Tragically, after eliciting a correct response the teacher might assume that the topic is understood by the class rather than realizing that the responses as a whole are indicative of the need to help students distinguish among their repertoire of ideas.

Many lecturers include opportunities for the audience to ask questions. Ostensibly questions support the listener by providing an opportunity to ask for clarification or to reduce a potential conundrum and inform the lecturer about audience confusions. However, some lecturers view questions as a sort of challenge to their expertise or a waste of precious lecture time. They may make those asking questions feel uncomfortable because they missed an obvious point. In these classes, the only students brave enough to ask questions are often those who understand the material the best. If the lecturer assumes that the questions asked by the most vocal members of the class are a cross-section of questions the class holds, the lecturer might assume more sophistication among class members than is realistic. These questions may give the lecturer a false sense of security.

One alternative is to ask students to submit questions in writing. To support large numbers of questions, anonymous questions, and even student responses, lecturers have used techniques such as online submission of questions, written questions submitted to proctors in the lecture hall, and tablet computer interactions between students and instructors. This approach engages students who might otherwise lose interest. It could frustrate students if their questions are never answered.

In summary, eliciting ideas is widely practiced using new technologies. Eliciting ideas is not sufficient to promote KI. When students volunteer ideas in response to questions or ask thoughtful questions they may give the instructor an incomplete image of the ideas held by students.

Distinguish Ideas

The most neglected part of the KI pattern is usually distinguishing ideas. Once lecturers elicit ideas, they have a chance to distinguish among them. Several strategies for modeling the process of distinguishing among alternatives are promising. Lecturers who troubleshoot unanticipated dilemmas, solve unfamiliar problems posed by students, or discuss case studies can model the process of distinguishing among ideas. As discussed, other approaches involve peer interactions during the lecture.

Modeling

One way to model the process of distinguishing ideas is to demonstrate troubleshooting. Lecturers can debug a computer program or describe why they selected wrong paths in a mathematics problem solution. Spontaneous examples arise when lecturers encounter difficulties with performing demonstrations (see Box 2.2). Consistent with the failures of slide technologies, failed demonstrations are widespread and well-documented. Today demonstrations (especially failed ones!) can appear on YouTube practically before the lecture ends. When things go wrong, instructors often engage in a kind of reasoning that students themselves encounter in their own explorations of unfamiliar topics. Furthermore, as lecturers flounder and consider alternatives they can invite the class to contribute ideas and comment on failed solutions.

Debates where two different individuals contrast their views can also model the process of distinguishing ideas. Famous debates occurred around the Marconi work on wireless communication as well as between Darwin and his scientific colleagues when discussing the origin of species. Debates about scientific phenomena have continued to play a role in public lectures and even in theatrical productions such as *Inherit the Wind*. Debates (see Chapter 9), provide an excellent opportunity for learners to see the contrast between alternative viewpoints.

Mike Clancy developed case studies for his computer science lectures to help distinguish among the wrong paths and conundrums that occur when solving computer science problems (Clancy & Linn, 1999; Linn & Clancy, 1992b). Clancy's approach was to assign a particularly complex problem for students and then to identify the various wrong paths and confusions that students encountered. He then incorporated those faulty decisions into his case study narratives, illustrating decisions, choice points, and bugs encountered. He engaged students in making predictions and discussing decisions among themselves. In the course of discussing these decisions, Clancy also provides insights into his own decision-making progress, acknowledging, for example, common but unhelpful habits such as failing to initialize variables. These case studies were eventually published as chapters and implemented in learning environments so students could study them on their own (Clancy & Linn, 1996; Clancy, Titterton, Ryan, Slotta, & Linn, 2003).

A similar approach is taken by Alan Schoenfeld when teaching mathematics. He challenges students to pose complex, difficult, poorly formulated or otherwise perplexing problems. He spends the first few minutes of his lecture talking through his attempt to make sense of the problem. In these mini-lectures, Schoenfeld illustrates his own thinking processes including flaws in his own reasoning as well as mechanisms for catching his own errors.

Pioneered by Julia Child, the cooking demonstration has become a mainstay of network television. Child implemented many of the same approaches found in the Clancy case studies. She described her own failures, discussed alternative solutions, and offered debugging advice when, for example, the mayonnaise refused to thicken. The variety of alternative cooking and home improvement shows that have emerged demonstrate the range of interests of the potential audience. Many cartoons satirize instructions found in some cooking and home improvement shows, suggesting that viewers start by raising their own cattle, harvesting their own wheat, or building their own table saw. These satirical comments reveal an important issue: the need to align the lecture and demonstration with the knowledge of the audience. These demonstrations also vary in their ability to engage the audience in filling in gaps in their knowledge or diagnosing weaknesses in their understanding. Child approached this dilemma by creating cookbooks from her shows that provided basic recipes (along with variations) and described procedures in extraordinary detail (Beck, Bertholle &, Child, 1961).

These approaches to modeling the process of distinguishing ideas illustrate the criteria students might use to select among the alternatives they consider. To appreciate these lectures, students need opportunities to apply the process themselves. Furthermore, following the KI pattern, they need to consolidate their ideas in reflection activities.

Peer Interactions

Peer interactions to distinguish ideas transform the lecture into interactive or collaborative learning. Participation can take the form of critiquing alternatives, generating alternatives, conducting small group demonstrations, or engaging in small group discussions. The instructor could pose a question, use a version of the Ikatura method to generate alternatives, and engage students in discussion of ideas. Technologies, such as computer tablets and handheld computing devices can support peer-to-peer discussion in a blog, threaded discussion, or brainstorm, either during a lecture or immediately after the lecture (Iles, Glaser, Kam, & Canny, 2002; Simon, Anderson, Hoyer, & Su, 2004).

Audience participation demonstrations can take advantage of the diverse characteristics of the students. Angy Stacy, Professor of Chemistry at the University of California, Berkeley, hands out small vials of gels in an introductory chemistry lecture. In one demonstration, students in groups of 4 to 8 smell vials that contain various forms of mint (peppermint, spearmint) and identify the odor. Inevitably students disagree about several of the vials. They speculate on the explanation and generate a list of ideas. Stacy gathers ideas from the audience and then adds ideas about chemical structure to help sort out the data. Students return to their group to discuss the new information and reflect on their own ideas.

Research by Canny and his collaborators extends audience response technologies to interactive class discussions during the lectures. Depending on the design of the lecture and the selection of discussion questions, a software program called LiveNotes can contribute to effective lectures. Tablet PCs are used to elicit ideas and encourage peer-to-peer discussion. In LiveNotes, all of the student comments are displayed for all other students to read (Kam et al., 2005). Today, this process is often replaced by texting and instant messaging during class. Many instructors attempt to ban cell phones or instant messaging because the frequency of messages on the topic of the lecture is often low. LiveNotes is an alternative that harnesses the desire of students to interact and focuses it on class topics.

A study conducted by Nicole and Boyle (2003) compared peer instruction with class-wide discussion and showed the value of peer instruction. In the class-wide discussion, the instructor poses a question and students discuss their responses in small groups. They then respond to a clicker activity to indicate their answers. The instructor displays the choices of the whole class and conducts a class-wide discussion followed by a summary. Although the class-wide discussion is intended to support consensus, students reported that they became confused because many alternatives were put forth and it was not clear which evidence aligned with which alternative. Because students discuss potential answers before they make a prediction, this approach may short-circuit the process of distinguishing ideas. In contrast, the peer instruction approach asks for predictions prior to discussion and uses the discussion to force consensus among students with differing views.

In summary, peer-to-peer discussion during lectures has some promising features for helping students distinguish ideas. Careful design is needed in order for the activities to succeed.

Interactive Engagement

Research in classes featuring interactive engagement shows the importance of helping students distinguish ideas in small groups. These studies (e.g., Mazur,

1997) compare a method of peer instruction to the lecture. The lecturer divides the lecture into mini-presentations of about five to seven minutes. After each presentation, the lecturer poses a challenging multiple-choice question with well-thought out distracters based on previous student responses. Typically, the distracters capture the most common ideas in the students' repertoire of ideas. Students use a colored card or use some kind of a technological device such as a clicker to indicate their selection. The instructor then tabulates the results. The instructor forms heterogeneous groups of 2 to 5 to discuss the alternative responses. Students chat with neighbors who chose different answers and attempt to reach consensus. This approach engages students in considering their own ideas and linking to well-designed examples. This approach combines three of the KI processes (elicit ideas, add ideas, distinguish ideas) to help students develop criteria and distinguish their ideas. Assessments or homework that asks students to construct arguments can implement the last process of KI and lead to coherent understanding. During an average lecture, four to six mini presentations and small group discussions can arise.

Several studies show that for students in a calculus-based introductory physics course mini-lectures interspersed with opportunities to predict outcomes and discuss alternatives achieve Force Concept Inventory (FCI) gains that are twice those of students in the same course taught traditionally (e.g., Crouch & Mazur, 2001). In addition, students' quantitative problem-solving skills improved in spite of the reduced emphasis on specific problems in class (Crouch & Mazur, 2001). This approach, where small groups holding alternative views reach consensus, has also been shown to be beneficial in online instructional environments (Clark et al., 2010).

Mazur's success has motivated instructors in multiple disciplines to develop interactive engagement lectures featuring problems that lend themselves to class discussions (Beichner, 2000; Lundberg, Levin, & Harrington, 1999). Hake (1998) conducted studies of forms of interactive engagement involving 6,000 students learning mechanics in introductory physics courses in high schools, colleges, and universities. Hake's characterization of interactive engagement involves activities like making predictions, discussing alternatives with a neighbor, or responding to quiz questions interspersed in the lecture. To measure impact, these studies used the Force Concept Inventory. Hake reported a strong relationship between interactive engagement and learning. Classes with passive lectures were the least successful in achieving student understanding. Classes that involved interactive engagement in instruction were more successful.

McDermott (1991) has also shown the benefits of interactive engagement. She compared lectures to lectures plus collaborative tutorials. She designed the tutorials to overcome what she perceived to be inadequate instruction in lectures. In the tutorials, students make predictions, engage with the tutor in testing their predictions, and discuss the relationship between their predictions and the outcomes. McDermott reports that collaborative tutorials dramatically improve learning outcomes. These findings show the benefit of both collaboration and individual instruction. The effectiveness of collaboration is consistent with the findings in the Braun et al. (2009) study showing that when students report working with others on a science activity or project they learn more than when they do not have this experience.

Comparison studies refine the value of the various activities that are possible in lectures. In the early Mazur research (1997), peer-to-peer discussion was better than lecture alone. However, in the Crouch et al. (2001) study, peer-to-peer discussion added little value over making predictions and took an added six minutes per experiment.

In summary, the interactive lecture approach is consistent with the KI pattern described in Chapter 5 in that students generate ideas in predictions, add ideas from their peers, engage in group discussion to distinguish ideas, and typically reflect on homework problems. Some studies suggest that only the first two activities fit well into the lecture format. The other activities might be accomplished in laboratories or as homework.

Pivotal Cases

Pivotal cases as discussed in Chapter 3 help students distinguish ideas. They have been used in some of the approaches of Mazur (see Box 6.2). They have several criteria:

First, a pivotal case connects to the ideas held by students by illustrating the phenomena in a personally relevant context. In the Mazur study, students studied an example of distance and time graphs for a car merging onto a freeway. Using examples that are personally relevant is advantageous because they allow students to relate their own ideas to the example and also because the example itself may arise in the future, enabling the learner to revisit the ideas and think about them again.

In addition, personally relevant examples have the benefit of anchoring instruction in a concrete and understandable context. Bransford (Bransford et al., 1999) demonstrated that anchored instruction, where personally relevant ideas were often introduced using video clips, brings the challenges of science to life. Challenges such as "determine the most efficient way to fill a plastic swimming pool" can be illustrated in a short video. Students can use the video to gather information about the challenge. Students who experienced anchored instruction were more successful than students who did not experience anchored presentations in solving new, complex problems.

Second, pivotal cases should contrast alternatives that highlight confusions faced by students. For example, in Mazur's interactive lecture demonstration students compare a velocity and time graph to a distance and time graph for the same phenomena. Specifically they observe a cart that rolls away from a detector slowly and steadily for two seconds, then stops rolling for two seconds, and then starts rolling away from the detector again gradually speeding up like a car merging onto a highway. Students are asked to draw distance and time graphs and velocity and time graphs to represent the situation.

After drawing their predictions, students test their ideas using motion probes. Students discuss the discrepancies between their graphs and the graphs drawn using the probes. In addition, the students compare the velocity and time graphs to the distance and time graph and use the two to test the accuracy of their understanding. Students identify important similarities as well as important differences.

Third, pivotal cases should be easy to convert into a narrative. The example from the Mazur study of slowing to a stop and then merging onto a highway is more appropriate for individuals who drive than for those who are passengers (consistent with its use in a college course).

Fourth, an effective pivotal case allows the learner to use everyday knowledge to test the accuracy of their solution. In the car example students observe the car's motion and compare the distance and time graph to the velocity and time graph.

In summary, helping students distinguish ideas during lectures typically involves activities that go beyond students listening to the instructor. Success usually requires all of the KI processes. To distinguish ideas, they first need to be elicited in brainstorms or possibly with audience response systems. Usually ideas need to be added, often in a way that allows for distinguishing—such as in a pivotal case, debate, or model of contrasting alternatives. Distinguishing can happen in small groups but it is not always the most efficient use of lecture time. To consolidate the process, students need ways to reflect and sort out ideas.

Reflecting and Sorting Out Ideas

When students reflect on the ideas in a lecture and their own ideas they have a chance to connect promising ideas and refine ideas that are contradicted or unhelpful. This process is essential to successful outcomes—without reflection, students may just add new ideas but not determine which are helpful for coherent understanding. Instructors can design homework, laboratory assignments, and projects to promote reflection.

Richard Light (2001) at Harvard University developed a technique called the one-minute paper to get a more accurate account of student response to the lecture. It has the added value of encouraging reflection. Using the one-minute paper approach, instructors ask students to summarize the main point of the lecture, raise questions that they have, and identify murky parts of the presentation. Responses can be anonymous. Instructors can use this information to plan their next lecture. Reviewing the responses provides a more comprehensive image of student progress than relying on questions asked by audience members.

The one-minute paper also advantages students. It asks them to identify gaps in their knowledge and delineate the information they need to resolve the gaps. This starts the reflection process. At the same time, it prompts students to engage in activities that would improve the outcome of the lecture—spontaneously reflecting on the information.

In summary, new technologies can go beyond enhancing the goal of informing students to engage students in looking for gaps or identifying complex aspects of the topic. The interactive lecture demonstration can include all the elements of the KI pattern. It starts with eliciting ideas. Students add ideas in the interactive demonstration. The small group might use evidence or criteria to distinguish ideas although this may only occur in certain circumstances, which could account for the uneven impact of this approach. Reflection and consolidation of information may also be neglected or relegated to subsequent individual review of the materials.

Lecture Trends

Studies of audience response systems, questioning, peer-to-peer activities, mini-lectures, and predictions argue for reducing lectures in favor of other activities. For example, in many cases mini-lectures are as effective as 50-minute lectures, leaving time for other activities.

Many research groups have demonstrated the benefit of short orienting lectures combined with opportunities for students to respond to questions. For example, Beichner (2000) (see Box 6.3) investigated short lectures in courses at MIT and other universities. He found that the short lectures actually lead to improved student learning compared to long lecturers. Using the additional time in the lecture for small group interactions was also beneficial. This finding is consistent with Light's (1990) short lectures and with his one-minute summaries for identifying the difficulties that students faced in interpreting the material in the lecture.

BOX 6.3 SCALE-UP

A Student-Centered Active Learning Environment for Undergraduate Programs

In Student-Centered Active Learning Environment for Undergraduate Programs (SCALE-UP) activities student teams (2 or 3 students) conduct investigations while their instructor provides guidance by asking questions, sending one team to help another, or asking why someone else got a different answer. This approach is possible in a classroom with moveable furniture. A lab is not needed. Rather, each team has a laptop for searching the web. This

---

works best for classes with under 100 students but has succeeded in larger classes. Physics, chemistry, math, biology, astronomy, engineering, and even literature courses have utilized this approach.

Beichner et al. (2008) show that students in SCALE-UP classes gain a better conceptual understanding than their peers in traditional lecture-based classes. At schools where they have a choice, students almost always prefer SCALE-UP based classes compared to lecture courses. In addition, fewer students fail SCALE-UP courses: on average failure rate is around 7% compared to 18% in the typical class (Beichner, 2007).

Sample activities for introductory physics courses [available at: http://www.ncsu.edu/per/scaleup.html]:

Measurement

1. What is the thickness of a single page from your text? (No measuring tools are allowed.) Use this result to find the diameter of a single period at the end of a sentence in the book.
2. When you quickly pull a piece of scotch tape off the table, it wraps itself around your arm because of static electricity. Estimate the number of excess charges on the tape.

Estimation

1. How far does a bowling ball get before it stops skidding and is only rolling?
2. How many candy bars worth of energy does it take to push a shopping cart past the snack aisle?

Source: Beichner, R. J. (2008). *The SCALE-UP Project: A Student-Centered Active Learning Environment for Undergraduate Programs.* Invited white paper for the National Academy of Sciences: The National Academies Press, Washington, D.C.

Clancy (Clancy & Linn, 1999) experimented with mini–lectures but ultimately modified computer science instruction to make it a completely lab–centric course. In the lab–centric course, students were assigned to required lab sections where they took quizzes, listened to online mini lectures, solved problems, discussed alternative solutions with peers, compared their solutions to the solutions of other individuals, critiqued solutions presented to them, and engaged in other activities. Clancy et al. (1999) found that the lab–centric course was not only more effective than the traditional lecture and lab–course but in addition was more efficient, covering more material in the same amount of instructional time.

Subsequently, a number of different universities have instituted lab-centric courses for computer science (Abelson & Sussman, 1985). In general, research and student reports indicate that mini-lectures embedded in lab-centric courses are more effective than class lectures. These universities have found cost-effective ways to implement lab-centric courses. In the lab-centric courses, students participate in closed labs led by a teaching assistant and assisted by an undergraduate who took the course in the past. The undergraduates earn course credit for their participation thus, making the lab-centric course economically feasible.

Several instructors were reluctant to abandon lectures either because they enjoy giving lectures or because they feel that the students enjoy hearing a lecture. Several experiments (Titterton, Lewis, & Clancy, 2010) revealed that one lecture per week combined with lab-centric experiences for the rest of the time was successful for those instructors who find lecturing an appealing activity. Other instructors are pleased to abandon lecturing and instead teach lab-centric courses. Instructors report that designing the course required a reasonable amount of planning and organization but ultimately ran smoothly and resulted in higher student ratings for instructors compared to the lecture approach.

A benefit of lab-centric courses is that fewer students drop the course. Instead of waiting until the first midterm, the lab-centric course begins to diagnose student difficulties with the very first lab. Students get immediate assistance based on their quiz scores and therefore, are more likely to resolve misunderstandings and be able to persist in the course.

In summary, considerable research suggests that lectures designed to inform students have limited value for instruction. Modifying lectures by varying the activities and adding opportunities for the instructor to determine how well students understand the material benefits learners.

Short lectures such as 5 to 10 minute mini-lectures as well as explanations as short as 90 seconds, can be beneficial. Several factors contribute to this finding: First, short lectures are well-designed and targeted specifically to the main points students need to master. Second, short lectures maintain student attention. Third, short lectures rarely use technologies like PowerPoint and may, as a result, focus student attention rather than distracting learners.

Conclusions

Lectures are ubiquitous and historically a primary form of instruction. Yet there are many limitations to lectures and recent research suggests alternatives that might be as cost-effective and considerably more instructionally effective.

Although informing students is a component of instruction, transmitting information is neither necessary nor sufficient to instruct most learners. New approaches to lecturing acknowledge some of the difficulties that students might face in learning the material covered in the lecture, but do not fully engage the student in using appropriate reasoning processes to learn the material. In addition, activities such as lecturing on case studies or asking students to pose problems for solutions that shed light on the processes of making sense of new ideas are rare.

Shortening lectures, ensuring that students can make predictions, engaging students in gap-finding, and helping students resolve the discrepancies between their ideas, those of others, and those they observe in their courses requires an interactive and comprehensive instructional approach. The KI pattern offers guidance in resolving this complex dilemma and in improving instruction in lecture-based courses.

This chapter identifies the technologies that have been used to strengthen, augment, or modify lectures as well as the research conducted to determine effective ways to design lectures. Taken together, these results point towards the benefit of the KI pattern for helping instructors create effective lectures. The pattern resonates with the constructivist perspective on the learner, and also is consistent with frameworks for inquiry instruction put forth by the science education national standards (NRC, 2000).

Lecture designs generally reflect the view that students will learn how to learn from them but the evidence for students developing these skills in large numbers is slim. For some learners, new ideas will motivate them to recognize gaps in their knowledge. If students encounter new ideas but fail to recognize that those ideas differ from their own, they are unlikely to pay attention to them. In addition, if they encounter ideas and simply add them to their repertoire without distinguishing them from other ideas, they also are unlikely to benefit from the instruction. Isolated ideas are quickly forgotten. Students themselves need to learn how to learn from lectures. Using the KI processes during lectures is a first step towards developing autonomous abilities to benefit from lectures.

KI and Lectures

Lectures that use predictions, audience response technologies, or other approaches to elicit ideas are generally more effective than those that delay opportunities to discover student ideas. By eliciting ideas instructors can tailor instruction to the needs of learners.

Designing lectures or demonstrations to effectively add new ideas is essential. As we have seen, mini-lectures are more successful than longer lectures. Also, demonstrations that incorporate visualizations or the features of pivotal cases are effective.

In addition, to be effective, lectures need to add ideas that are personally relevant. It is very common for students to conclude that science is irrelevant to their lives. Since lectures are already potentially uninformative, it is particularly important that lecturers find ways to add ideas to the repertoire that connect to students' own experiences. This point has motivated the design of courses for non-majors that have titles like Physics and Technology for Future Presidents (Muller, 2010).

To succeed, lectures also need to help students distinguish ideas. When students are asked to explain or generate a new explanation after they encounter a demonstration and to reconcile the demonstration with their prediction they can distinguish their own ideas from those in the lecture. Successful methods generally involve peer-to-peer interactions. However, several studies reveal limitations and inefficient use of time when lectures focus on distinguishing ideas and suggest that these processes might best be supported in homework or laboratory activities (e.g., Crouch et al., 2001). This is consistent with many lecture classes becoming more like laboratory sessions.

Laboratory-like sessions can help students develop criteria for distinguishing among ideas using empirical evidence. In the interactive lecture demonstration, students use empirical evidence to distinguish ideas. In the lab-centric computer science courses, students have the opportunity to run their programs and to compare the results of their program to the anticipated results. Thus, students have empirical evidence to distinguish their solution from the desired solution.

In many situations, criteria are more subtle or complex. For example, developing criteria about an effective experiment or how best to define variables in a computer program requires that instructors provide opportunities for students to compare criteria and determine which are most effective. This might be most successful in a laboratory activity. In the lab-centric courses students respond to a brainstorm step where they generate the solution to a problem and, once they have entered their solution, examine the responses of other students. The assignment is to explain the differences between the solutions and to determine which is most effective. This brainstorm activity may be more effective than the small group discussions in the interactive lecture demonstration because of additional instructional time.

When students reflect, they have an opportunity to consider the demonstration, the views of their peers, the lecture, and their existing ideas. By reflecting students identify the gaps in their knowledge and may fill those gaps. Ideally, students over the course of their career will become more and more autonomous at recognizing when they have a knowledge gap and identifying techniques for filling the gap.

Reflection Activity

Describe a lecture you recently attended. Reflect on your own activities while listening to the lecture. Did you frame questions for the speaker? Did you take notes? Did you always agree with the speaker? Discuss how the lecture could have been more effective for you.

7

EXPERIMENTATION AND KNOWLEDGE INTEGRATION

Introduction

Children investigate the natural world by growing plants, building structures, interacting with pets, kicking balls, exploring ponds, and preparing foods. Children formulate conjectures and test them against their experiences or manipulations of their surroundings. These experiments include comparisons of alternatives (for planting, cooking, throwing objects) as well as observations (of plants, rocks, trajectories, ecosystems, household appliances, animals, chemical combinations) and elaborate constructions (of boats, paper airplanes, animal houses, forts, costumes, machines). Many ideas about science that children have in their repertoire come from these explorations. To promote KI we seek to build on these autonomous and self-guided experiences and encourage lifelong exploration of science.

Individuals face a multitude of claims and persuasive messages. Drug advertisements can convince healthy people they need treatments. Political messages can advocate policies that benefit those who paid for the advertisement. Activities that emphasize debate or critique can help students appreciate ways that scientific information is used to advance specific agendas (Linn, Davis, & Bell, 2004; Shear, Bell, & Linn, 2004). This emphasis places responsibility for developing a coherent account of science on the learner. Typical cookbook experiments or opportunities to learn scientific techniques such as following a protocol are not sufficient to develop autonomous science learners. We need to prepare students to make decisions about personal heath, energy conservation, and public policy.

Experiments are often implemented using the absorption approach rather than capitalizing on the natural curiosity of children to explore the world (see Chapter 2). This means that many adults learn to avoid science. One author (Linn) notes that at social gatherings if she mentions her field is science education, it is common for people to remark "don't ask me anything," and head for the nearest bar.

The KI approach to experimentation is designed to motivate learners to revisit their science ideas and build on them as well as to learn to interrogate the natural world and to continue that process all during their lives. Students learn to read and they continue to need to read everyday. They learn math and use these skills to estimate costs and make decisions about purchases. Yet, many students learn science but never find ways to use science in their daily lives.

The KI approach implements the principle of making science accessible to increase the relevance of science. KI units feature inquiry around problems such as earthquake prediction, energy decision making, or genetic inheritance that are likely to come up in students' lives in the future. When students learn experimentation by following the KI pattern they are prepared to solve new problems.

The KI approach builds on the experiences of children. Children usually start experimenting by making conjectures (such as expecting a metal boat to sink). Children add new ideas by conducting experiments (often in a rather haphazard fashion). They might drop the metal boat into the water bow first and see that it does sink but then accidently place it horizontally and see that it floats. Children often react to unpredicted results by engaging in more experiments—testing other objects to see if they float, testing the boat many times. They may use criteria to distinguish their experiences that lead to inaccurate conclusions (such as treating each trial equally and concluding that metal sometimes floats). Children often summarize the ideas they gain from interacting with the natural world in incorrect views. This helps explain the many alternative ideas that researchers have identified (e.g., Eylon & Linn, 1988). For floating and sinking, researchers have identified numerous ideas that students have in their repertoire (see Box 1.1). These ideas represent efforts to make sense of science.

Thus, from the KI perspective, experimentation is vital to lifelong science learning. Learners can resolve conundrums, test their own ideas, and evaluate scientific assertions by conducting experiments. Students can develop empirically-validated ideas and use scientific methods. Experiments can motivate students to participate in science, promote autonomous learning, and increase equitable outcomes from science courses (Feldon, Timmerman, Stowe, & Showman, 2010). People need these skills to solve scientific dilemmas all during their lives. Yet, research suggests that experiments often fail to achieve these goals (see Chapter 2; Hofstein & Lunetta, 1982, 2004). For example, survey findings suggest that as they continue in school, students abandon their idea that science is relevant to everyday situations and view science as primarily associated with the formal topics in school (Baram-Tsabari & Yarden, 2009; Madhok, 2006).

Implementation of experiments often follows the absorption approach to learning. Experiments transmit procedures, implement active learning, or are used to motivate students to study textbooks or listen to lectures (Palmer, 2009). Students generally rate opportunities to interact or experiment highly (Hofstein & Lunetta,

2004; Light, 2001). Experiments often follow patterns such as *interact, assess* or *motivate, interact, assess* because students carry out experiments and write reports that are graded. From the KI perspective, this pattern does not help students add new ideas and is unlikely to promote coherent reasoning.

In this chapter we discuss how experimentation succeeds when all the elements of the KI pattern are included in classroom activities. The KI approach to science learning emphasizes the goal of coherent understanding. The processes of KI contribute to the development of lifelong science learning skills.

This approach to experimentation is consistent with science standards that generally call for inquiry learning. We define inquiry as the intentional process of generating predictions, diagnosing problems, critiquing experiments, distinguishing alternatives, planning investigations, researching conjectures, searching for information, constructing explanations, debating with peers, and forming coherent arguments.

In this chapter we review the goals for classroom experimentation, discuss recent literature showing promising ways to implement the KI pattern, and distinguish the pattern from the numerous other guidelines for experimentation. We conclude with recommendations for designing effective experiments in science courses.

Goals for Experimentation

To promote KI, experiments need to go beyond active learning and beyond motivating, informing, and assessing to promote coherent understanding. The importance of improving classroom experimentation was articulated in the National Research Council report, *America's Lab Report* (Singer et al., 2005). This report documents limitations of the current role of experimentation in science courses and offers a contemporary image of experimentation. It lists the following goals for experiments:

- Learning subject matter
- Developing scientific reasoning
- Understanding the complexity and ambiguity of empirical work
- Developing practical skills
- Understanding of the nature of science
- Stimulating interest in science and science learning
- Developing teamwork abilities.

The report warrants these goals by reviewing research on the complexity of scientific investigation in the natural sciences. Studies of the nature of empirical investigations reveal that the actual implementation of the experiment is a small part of the intellectual effort that leads to new scientific knowledge (Keller, 1985; Kuhn, 1970; Latour, 1987; Thagard, 1992; Tweney, 1991). Most agree that the knowledge of the social context of experimentation, including how power is distributed, is central to scientific advancement (e.g., Keller, 1985; Latour, 1987; Longino, 1990). Communicating these ideas in science courses has proven difficult (Carey & Smith, 1993; Klahr & Dunbar, 1989).

America's Lab Report (Singer et al., 2005) calls for "integrated instructional units" that combine labs, lecture, discussion, and reading to achieve understanding of the discipline. The report argues that unlike typical labs, such integrated instructional units advance student success on the goals for laboratories identified in the report. Results of the case studies (Chapter 3 and 4) resonate with this claim. In addition to improving understanding of complex science concepts, there is evidence that integrated units help students learn about the nature of science and increase interest in science (Sadler, Chambers, & Zeidler, 2004).

As the report suggests, the field needs a better understanding of how students learn about the complexity and ambiguity of empirical work and develop practical and teamwork skills. The goals identified in *America's Lab Report* (Singer et al., 2005) are reflected in many state and national standards. Most science standards (e.g. AAUW, 2000; American Association for the Advancement of Science, 1994; Department for Education and Employment, 2000; National Research Council, 1999, 2000; Israeli Ministry of Education, 1996) mandates teaching science as inquiry.

Experimentation activities have the potential to help students develop inquiry skills, form robust, realistic images of science, develop understanding of advances in technology, expand their ability to critique persuasive messages, and become lifelong science learners. To achieve the vision of experimentation as presented in *America's Lab Report*, instruction needs to be refocused. We draw attention to several key ways to refocus experimentation.

Illustrate the Nature of Experimentation

Science proceeds in fits and starts. Researchers take wrong paths, and use invalid methods. Those in power influence scientific experimentation by controlling resources or censoring specific viewpoints (Keller, 1985; Latour, 1987; Longino, 1990). Yet, the nature of experimentation is often neglected in experimentation activities.

Many studies show that students have simplistic or unrealistic images of scientific experimentation (Abell, Martini, & George, 2001; Baram-Tsabari & Yarden, 2009; Bell & Linn, 2002; Linn & Hsi, 2000; Songer & Linn, 1991). For example, textbooks often list the steps of the scientific method implying that experimentation is straightforward and linear (see Figure 2.5). Reducing experimentation to a series of steps obscures the dilemmas experimental scientists face. Emphasizing the nature of science can increase understanding of these issues (Mazzei, 2008; Yacoubian & BouJaoude, 2010).

Students often have very limited understanding of the social context of scientific research (e.g., Carey & Smith, 1993; Leach, Hind, & Ryder, 2003; Sadler, Chambers,

& Zeidler, 2004). The practice of science can be made more accessible by featuring diverse science role models in STEM fields (Else-Quest, Hyde, & Linn, 2010).

To improve this situation, inquiry projects can feature controversial, confusing, or unresolved dilemmas. The success of debate projects on topics such as dinosaur extinction (Linn & Hsi, 2000), causes of frog deformities (Shear et al., 2004), policies for curing malaria (Slotta, 2004), and explanations for light propagation (Bell, 2004a) illustrate the advantages of this approach. For example, Mazzei (2008) demonstrated that a project contrasting Lamarck and Darwin could impact both the understanding of the survival of the fittest and the understanding of the way science progresses (see Box 7.1).

BOX 7.1 NATURE OF SCIENCE

Knowledge integration instruction designed to distinguish the positions of Lamarck and Darwin and illustrate how science progresses

Mazzei (2008) developed an instructional intervention to help students understand the nature of science called "Did Birds Evolve from Dinosaurs?" that contrasted views of Darwin and Lamarck. He engaged students in exploring that science is (a) tentative and subject to revision, (b) influenced by human interpretation, and (c) based on empirical evidence.

Knowledge integration pattern

To elicit ideas, students agreed or disagreed with the statement: when scientists are interpreting evidence there is only one way to interpret this evidence. Then they explained their answer.

To add new ideas, students reviewed evidence supporting Lamarck and Darwin, conducted experiments using a simulation that illustrated evolution, and decided which evidence led scientists to accept Darwin's views. They also speculated about why it took 30 years for Darwin to publish his findings.

To distinguish ideas, students revisited their initial ideas and responded to explanation prompts that asked them to (a) speculate about how Darwin might use experiments using current technology that supports research on bacteria to strengthen his theory, and (b) explain why evidence from the fossil record is more convincing today than it was in Darwin's time.

To add more ideas, students studied evidence for the discovery of the Gigantoraptor. Then they responded to explanation prompts that asked them to discuss the impact of this discovery.

To sort out ideas, students responded to explanation prompts that asked them to reflect on the role of evidence in reaching scientific conclusions and to explain how evidence from the fossil record shows that science is tentative and subject to revision.

Assessments

Sample questions and scoring rubrics for pretest and posttest questions are shown in Figures 7.1.1 and 7.1.2.

Score	Level	Criteria	Examples
0	**No answer**		
1	**Off task** Response is irrelevant or "I don't know." Student writes some text, but it does not answer the question being asked.		
2	**Irrelevant/Incorrect** Have relevant ideas but fail to recognize links between them. Make links between relevant and irrelevant ideas. Have incorrect/ irrelevant ideas.	There is no evidence for evolution. Disputed about evolution cannot be resolved.	"No, of course not, things change too much for anyone to know." (Student 1, pre, 5th)
3	**Partial** Have relevant ideas but do not fully elaborate links between them in a given context.	One of the above ideas (process, outcome, or impact) or a relevant example.	"Because fossils of dinosaurs and other animals are good evidence supporting evolution." (Student 2, post, 2nd)
4	**Basic** Elaborate a scientifically valid link between two ideas relevant to a given context.	A full link (see above): Between process, out-come, or impact.	"They can use the bones and fossils to compare them to animals that are still here." (Student 3, post, 2nd)

		OR Mention of process, outcome, or impact + relevant example. Note: Fossil reference must mention *comparison* between fossils or change over time.	
5	**Complex** Elaborate two or more scientifically valid links among ideas relevant to a given context.	Complex link (link between *three* of the above categories of ideas a, b, and c) + example. OR Full link (link between *two* of the above categories of ideas, a, b, and c) + that illustrated the ideas. Note: Fossil reference must mention *comparison* between fossils or change over time.	"Yes, they can show how dinosaurs evolved by fossils. The fossils can show changes in species. The scientists can decide on what they think and if their ideas are the same."

FIGURE 7.1.1 Rubric for "Can scientists use evidence to resolve disputes about evolution?"

Question	Pretest Response	Posttest Response
The science principles and facts will always be true.	Yes, because they were proven by scientists with wise ideas and they delivered [it] to students to teach them.	No.
Throughout history scientists have agreed on how to explain the process of evolution.	I think that they mostly explain [evolution] like each other.	I think no because Darwin and Lamarck have different ways of how to explain the process of evolution
Scientists analyzing the same data all reach the same conclusions.	Other scientific communities believe in something different, that's why people have agreements and different opinions. If two scientists do an experiment they don't always have to get the same conclusion. They could make a mistake.	No, because just like the two scientists we were learning about, they were sort of analyzing the same data but they had different theorems and thoughts about it. They can prove that some species have bones like the ones that we have today.

FIGURE 7.1.2 Pretest/posttest responses to selected questions

Embedded Assessment Responses

"When interpreting evidence to support evolution we think Darwin and Lamarck would not interpret it the same. Because they each have their own ideas and theories about evolution because Lamarck will think that the animals develop better arms etc. by using it more while Darwin thinks that the animals develop by adapting to the environment."

"Lamarck would explain the existence of the larger bird beaks by saying that the bird could have used the beak a lot so that the beak became stronger and larger. Darwin would explain the existence of the larger bird beaks by where the bird lived becau)se if you had a bigger beak it would help it get its food depending on its location or area."

"Darwin could use observations from the fossil record to support his theory by comparing the sketches and fossil findings to the species that live today, and can see a path of evolution."

"The evidence from the fossil record is more convincing now than during Darwin's time because back then, Christianity was widely accepted all throughout Europe, and building a theory against the church was treason and punishable by death. Also, back then, people didn't know about the DNA of living things."

Results

Students made significant gains on both evolution concepts and ideas about the nature of science (F = 15.9, p<.001). The dimensions were highly correlated (r = .75). This outcome occurred in a typical WISE unit (approximately 5 class periods). By adding emphasis on the nature of scientific advance into the unit, the study of evolution was strengthened as was understanding of the nature of science. By connecting evolution concepts with discussions of nature of scientific argumentation students were able to integrate their ideas about evolution and the nature of science. By encouraging discussion, asking probing questions, and inquiring how these topics connect, students gained robust understanding that linked evolution and the nature of science.

Source: Mazzei, P. (2008). *Using Evolution as a Context to Promote Student Understanding of Nature of Science.* Unpublished Master's Thesis, submitted in partial fulfillment of Master's of Arts degree in Education, University of California, Berkeley.

Use Varied Contexts for Investigation

An important goal for science instruction is to characterize the variation in scientific research across disciplines. Science courses often limit experimentation to applications of the controlling variables strategy and study of situations that involve primarily linear relationships. Yet, in many important scientific domains, it is not possible to directly manipulate the variables and the variables do not have linear impacts on outcomes.

Investigations of dinosaur extinction, global climate change, or plate tectonics require analysis of the geological/paleoclimate record, often followed by computer modeling. Students can explore these complex topics using virtual experimentation environments. Broadening the types of evidence used in science can help students appreciate that evidence for claims about events such as meteors or worldwide epidemics varies in reliability and validity. Using virtual experiments students can compare alternative claims and evaluate computer projections of their effects. For example, a unit on global climate change uses a NetLogo model to allow students to test the impact of decisions such as recycling, taking public transportation, and adopting a vegetarian diet on climate change (see Box 7.2).

BOX 7.2 CONCEPTS ILLUSTRATED IN THE NETLOGO GLOBAL CLIMATE SITUATION

The Global Climate Change unit uses NetLogo visualizations to illustrate factors impacting global climate change. Students made significant gains from pretest to posttest

The Global Climate Change unit engages students in exploring a complex system while exploring the role of energy in NetLogo visualizations. Students investigate factors impacting global climate change and connect their findings to personal decisions about driving versus walking and eating vegetables versus meat. The unit elicits ideas about factors contributing to greenhouse gas emissions. Surprisingly, students often report that littering is a major factor.

NetLogo climate experiments

To add ideas students conduct virtual experiments using a series of NetLogo visualizations (Tinker & Staudt, 2005). Students explore the role of solar energy, infrared energy, greenhouse gases, clouds, pollutants, and albedo (see screenshot). They investigate the impact of greenhouse gases on climate change. To distinguish ideas they assess the role of littering, eating meat, driving a car, and increasing the area of the oceans (reducing global levels of albedo) on climate.

NetLogo virtual experiment. The solid line represents the surface of the Earth. The red dots represent heat energy, the yellow triangles represent solar radiation, the purple triangles represent infrared radiation, and the black dots represent pollutants.

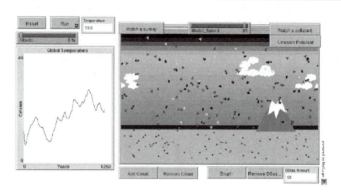

FIGURE 7.2.1 NetLogo simulation

Reflection and assessment

To reflect, students respond to embedded questions, write energy stories, and build MySystem diagrams (Svihla, Ryoo, Sato, Swanson, & Linn, 2010).

Assessment Questions and Sample Responses.

TABLE 7.2.1 Assessment Questions and Sample Responses

Pre and Post Question	Pretest Responses (KI score)	Posttest Responses (KI Score)
What is the role of albedo in the greenhouse effect?	I don't know what albedo is. (1)	Albedo bounces off sunlight. (1)
		Albedo is the ability of a surface to reflect light. (3)
		Open water absorbs heat while white ice and snow reflect it. (3)
What is the role of clouds in the greenhouse effect?	To cool off the solar energy. (2)	Clouds in the greenhouse effect make the earth's temperature cooler. (3)
	Clouds make rain. (2)	
	It makes a mist. (2)	Clouds help solar energy go away by a little. (3)
		They help cool down the Earth and reflect some of the solar energy. (4)

What is the role of greenhouse gases in global warming?	I think the greenhouse gases contaminate the air. (2)	Greenhouse gases reflect the heat causing a steady rise of temperature. (4)
	I think the greenhouse gases make the air polluted. (2)	
	The gasses make it humid and really wet and hot. (2)	

Energy story: Write a story to explain to Gwen how the Earth is warmed by the Sun.

Sample posttest response: UV radiation comes from the Sun. UV radiation goes through the atmosphere into the ozone layer and absorbs into the Earth. Once in the Earth, and becomes heat energy. Then when the energy comes out, it comes out as IR radiation. The IR radiation hits the greenhouse gases and goes back into the Earth and becomes heat energy. As a result this makes the Earth warmer. Some IR radiation doesn't hit greenhouse gases and goes back into space.

Results

The global climate unit leads to improved understanding of the role of energy in climate change as shown in pretest posttest studies involving knowledge integration items and energy stories (Svihla et al., 2010). Middle school students gain insight into energy transmission but have difficulty with energy transformation. Students report changes in their beliefs about the causes of green house gas emissions (fewer believe that littering is important, more believe that gasoline engines and meat eating contribute).

Assuming linearity may discourage students from developing robust experimentation strategies that include testing boundary conditions, honing in on thresholds, or disentangling collinear relationships as illustrated by Inhelder and Piaget (1958/1972) in studies of pendulums and curvilinear motion. For example, in a study of the factors that make airbags safe for drivers, McElhaney (2010) showed that students often assume that all variables are linearly related and neglect more complex relationships. Varying driver height results in understanding that there is a point where the driver is too close to the steering wheel and will be injured by the expanding airbag. Often students compare two heights, see that they are both safe, and move on without noticing there could be a threshold where short drivers are unsafe (see Box 7.3).

BOX 7.3 AIRBAGS

In Airbags, students conduct virtual experiments to explore airbag safety. They first observe a video of a crash dummy. Then they conduct experiments where they can vary the position of the driver, the velocity of the car, and the time required for the car to crumple. They indicate whether the driver was safe or not. The rubric shows how the virtual experimentation is coded for knowledge integration. Students get credit for their choice of experiments combined with the justifications they provide

To gain insight into complex experimentation contexts and apply physics ideas about kinematics, students conduct virtual experiments to explore airbag safety (McElhaney, 2010). Students observe a video of a crash using a dummy (see screenshot 1 below). They make predictions about the factors that contribute to a safe or unsafe experience in a car crash.

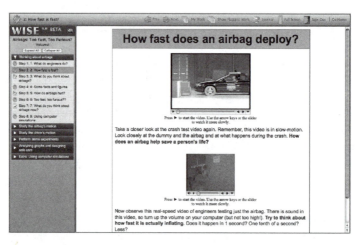

FIGURE 7.3.1 Screenshot from WISE4 Airbags unit

To add ideas, students conduct virtual experiments using the visualization shown in screenshot 2. Students can vary the position of the driver, the velocity of the car, and the time required for the car to crumple. They indicate the goal for the experiment, run the experiment, and indicate whether the driver was safe or not. Students respond to embedded assessments asking them to explain the conditions under which the driver will be safe.

Students often conduct experiments without really understanding the complex relationships among the variables. For example, a student might vary the distance of the driver from the steering wheel and discover that the driver is save for both trials. Some students then conclude that the distance from the steering wheel is not a safety concern. If they had tried a position closer to the steering wheel they would have discovered that there are conditions when position of the driver matters.

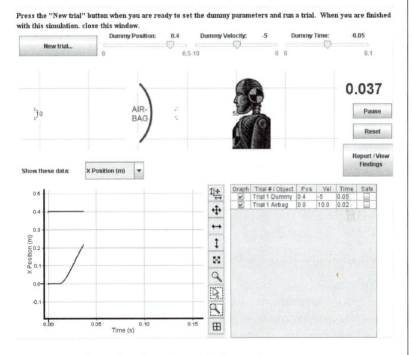

FIGURE 7.3.2   Screenshot from WISE4 Airbags unit

Students are prompted to review their experiments. They are asked to analyze their findings and distinguish the effect of the combinations of variables. In reflection questions they consider how the variables interact to impact tall drivers (who are usually far enough from the steering wheel to avoid danger) and short drivers (who need to consider their distance from the steering wheel, especially if they are pregnant).

Assessments and results

To assess student understanding we analyzed the log of experimentation activities for knowledge integration. The rubric (below) shows how the series of virtual experiments is coded for knowledge integration by combining an emphasis on controlling variables with an emphasis on conducting experiments that reveal the impact of the variables (McElhaney & Linn, in press). We created a separate score for each variable. The experimentation score was the average of the separate scores. Only students at the highest level were able to explain the role of the interactions among the variables and to appreciate that the experimental situation involved a threshold.

Rubric: Experimentation Score

KI level	Score	Description
blank	0	Conduct zero trials
none	1	Conduct exactly one trial
invalid/ isolated	2	Change all three variables between trials or hold the investigation variable constant
partial	3	Change exactly two variables between trials, including the investigation variable
basic	4	Change only the investigation variable between trials that produce the same outcome
complex	5	Change only the investigation variable between trials that produce opposite outcomes or conduct two separate sets of controlled trials

To examine ability to make sense of results of experiments we analyzed embedded assessment and posttest questions asking students to interpret results of an airbag experiment (see example below). Students who conducted meaningful experiments were also able to interpret a new experiment.

Assessment Question: Interpreting Results

[Refers to the graph.] Describe what happened between the driver and airbag in this crash. Was the driver injured by the airbag? Explain based on the graph.

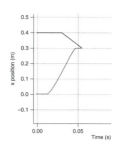

FIGURE 7.3.3 Interpreting results of the assessment question

Analysis of the results showed that students often followed a controlling variables procedure without interpreting the results. Students benefit from investigating complex settings where they need to combine the science principles and the experimentation procedures to reach insights. Furthermore, these results show that studying how students conduct virtual experiments can illustrate ways to improve instruction on experimentation.

Source: McElhaney, K. W. (2010). *Making Controlled Experimentation More Informative in Inquiry Investigations.* Unpublished doctoral dissertation, University of California, Berkeley.

Providing complex examples of experimentation is essential to ensure that learners appreciate the importance of understanding the variables. Even very young children know how to control variables (Case, Griffin, & Kelly, 1999). Children will not allow their peers to arrange unfair footraces or other contests. Of course it is possible to trick children into unfair decisions when they do not understand the variables. For example, children might evaluate the amount of juice in wide and narrow glasses based on the height of the juice. The child may select the juice that is higher in the glass even if it has less volume.

Even scientists fail to control variables when they are unaware of their importance or function. For example, researchers believed that heat had mass in the form of phlogiston and designed experiments based on this belief. Psychologists neglected the role of time of day in measuring intellectual performance until they realized that students' circadian rhythms contributed to performance on many indices. Learners need opportunities to investigate a wide range of situations so they can appreciate the varieties of evidence scientists use and the wide range of impacts variables can have.

Incorporate Contemporary Technologies

Technology advances can strengthen experimentation in science classes in several ways. First, students can use real-time data collection with probeware and conduct virtual experiments. Second, online learning environments like WISE can guide investigations. Third, new technologies can enable students to develop computation-based contemporary skills such as fluency with information technology (Snyder et al., 1999) and computational thinking (NRC, 2010). Business leaders call for 21st century skills to help students succeed in the workplace.

Both the National Academy of Sciences committee on Fluency with Information Technology (Snyder et al., 1999) and the American Association of University Women report entitled *Tech-Savvy* (2000) call for ensuring that all students gain fluency with information technology (see Box 7.4). In addition, the National Academy of Sciences committee on Computational Thinking (NRC, 2010) has identified new, emerging goals for experimentation (see Box 7.5).

BOX 7.4 FLUENCY WITH INFORMATION TECHNOLOGY

Capabilities, skills, and concepts associated with fluency with information technology

Snyder et al. (1999) characterized what everyone should know about technology to ensure that individuals could learn new technologies and work effectively with technologies.

Individuals need:

- **Capabilities** that include planning and innovation, diagnosing unintended consequences, refining an innovation, critiquing other innovations, collaborating with experts in varied disciplines, and debugging solutions.
- **Contemporary skills** that include electronic communication, word processing, spreadsheets, social networking sites, web 2.0 technologies such as wikis, various applications for collaborating when not co-located, computational tools, and other applications compatible with their everyday activities.
- **Concepts** that include intellectual property, privacy, multitasking, networking, computer security, modeling, and ecommerce.

The committee emphasized that fluency with information technology was not synonymous with computer programming. Many technological tools such as financial planning software, architectural design tools, design environments for theatrical productions, web-authoring tools, and social networking utilities require fluency with information technology.

Developing these capabilities, contemporary skills, and essential concepts calls for learners to engage in sustained, complex projects using relevant applications, to learn new applications—often from online resources—and to critique both the societal and personal impacts of the technologies. Individuals who are fluent with information technology have not only the capability of using the technology but an understanding and sensitivity to policies about technology.

Fluency with information technology applies across disciplines (e.g., designing new buildings; designing the blocking of a theatrical production; creating budgets for families, cities, daycare centers, and institutions; designing brochures for organizations; or modeling scientific processes). To develop this fluency, ideally, students would have the opportunity to carry out complex projects using various technological environments in and across different disciplines to learn about unintended consequences, debugging, testing, communication, anticipating changing technologies, and managing complexity in multiple contexts.

Source: Snyder, L., Aho, A. V., Linn, M. C., Packer, A., Tucker, A., Ullman, J., et al. (1999). *Be FIT! Being Fluent with Information Technology.* Washington, D.C.: The National Academies Press.

BOX 7.5 COMPUTATIONAL THINKING
Elements of computational thinking

Computational thinking

Virtually everyone sees substance in the notion of computational thinking, but there are more views of computational thinking than there are individuals.

Computational thinking is important in new specialties that integrate disciplinary knowledge and computational algorithms. Two examples are:

Human genome sequencing
Computational thinking:

- Algorithm is repeatedly applied precisely formulated unambiguous procedure
- Search, pattern matching, and iterative refinement
- Randomization as an asset in repeated fragmentation.

Disciplinary knowledge:

- DNA as a long string of base pairs.

Modeling of economic or sociological systems
Computational thinking:

- Aggregation of multiple independently specified rule-based agents
- Sensitivity to initial conditions.

Disciplinary knowledge:
- Knowledge of community as collection of independent decision-makers

Why is computational thinking important for everyone?

- Succeeding in a technological society
- Increasing interest in the information technology professions
- Maintaining and enhancing U.S. economic competitiveness
- Supporting inquiry in other disciplines
- Enabling personal empowerment.

Source: National Research Council (NRC). (2010). *Report of a Workshop on The Scope and Nature of Computational Thinking.* Washington, DC: The National Academies Press.

Individuals fluent with information technology have an edge when it comes to learning new technologies for personal or career goals and when called upon to evaluate the claims for technological innovations such as cloning or electronic commerce. Ensuring that all learners develop fluency with information technology advances the goal of ensuring equitable access to careers and to educational programs. Recent reports include these goals in definitions of 21st century skills (Hilton & NRC, 2010).

Recent advances in technology make these goals for both classroom and virtual experiments feasible. Technologies such as WISE can guide students in experimental procedures and activities. Students can use modeling environments such as Logo, NetLogo, Scratch, and Molecule Workbench to design experiments and test their ideas about phenomena such as global climate change, airbag safety, or energy efficiency.

Align Assessment with the Goals of Instruction

Assessing coherent understanding resulting from experimentation requires analysis of the methods students use and their justifications. Instruction emphasizing KI is best assessed with tests that also require KI (Clark & Linn, 2003; Linn et al., 2006; Ruiz-Primo, Li, Tsai, & Schneider, 2010). Multiple-choice items are often insensitive to the benefits of instruction that emphasizes writing explanations of experimental findings (e.g., Clark & Linn, 2003; Lee, Liu, & Linn, in press; Liu, Lee, Hofstetter, & Linn, 2008).

For experimentation tests that ask for explanations clarify outcomes. For example, in the Airbags unit (McElhaney, 2010), students conduct virtual experiments to explore the factors (height of the driver, speed of the vehicle, crumpling of the car) that make an airbag deployment safe (see Box 7.3). Students get higher scores based on the sophistication of the logistics of their experiment (are the variables controlled, is it possible to identify the threshold where a short driver is safe), and the conceptual interpretation of the variables (does the student appreciate the meaning of their experiments).

Many assessments of experimentation are inadequate or even invalid. Assessments may be limited to questions about linear relationships in straightforward experiments, to ability to use experimental apparatus, or to recall of details from the experiments. Students are often assessed on their laboratory reports and given points for procedural details such as the correct order for adding chemicals to test an outcome, correct findings, and clear descriptions. These outcomes are not sufficient to assess KI.

Skills such as identifying the variables, critiquing conclusions, and selecting evidence to form an argument need to be assessed to establish student understanding of experimentation. Furthermore, nonlinearly-related variables, nuanced interpretation of results, identification of threats to validity, and social context issues concerning how questions are framed, all key to sophisticated reasoning in science, are rarely included in assessments of experimentation.

Valid assessments of experiments help designers increase the impact of instruction. By requiring students to link and connect ideas, the KI rubric rewards this skill. For example, in a unit on global climate, students conduct virtual experiments to analyze the impact of accumulation of greenhouse gases in the atmosphere (Varma & Linn, in press). To assess student understanding, students are asked to compare the greenhouse effect to the mechanism governing a greenhouse (see Box 7.2). They explain similarities and use evidence from their virtual NetLogo experiments to support their claims. Researchers have used these assessments to redesign the activity with the result that the instruction has become more effective (Svihla, 2010).

KI assessments draw on the rich complex contexts that are also the goals of the curriculum such as global climate, airbag safety, recycling, home insulation, curing cancer, or preventing malaria. Including personally relevant contexts in assessments increases the validity of the assessment. These assessments can motivate curriculum designers to include personally-relevant topics in courses.

International assessments have begun to feature more complex contexts in science assessments. Analysis of TIMSS shows that very few items have the potential to tap KI (Linn et al., 2006). Furthermore, the TIMSS scoring rubrics often fail to reward using evidence to support outcomes and therefore do not measure KI. Comparing the TIMSS and KI scoring for the greenhouse item used for Global Climate (see Figure 10.7) shows that TIMSS scoring does not reward students who display coherent ideas warranted with evidence. Instead, students get full credit for recall of any detail about the situation.

TIMSS Rubric			Knowledge Integration Rubric		
Category	Description	Examples	Link(s)	Description	Examples
Correct	Protection against UV from the Sun or too strong rays from the Sun. Health concerns such as skin cancer/sunburn.	Because it keeps the Sun's rays from being too strong. Protects the UV radiation from the Sun. We do not get sunburned.	Complex	Elaborate two or more scientifically valid links among relevant ideas.	Blocks UV from the Sun and connects to legitimate health concerns.
			Full	Elaborate a scientifically valid link between two relevant ideas.	Blocks UV from the Sun (specific range is specified) from reaching earth's surface.
			Partial	Elicit relevant ideas but do not fully elaborate the link between relevant ideas.	Keeps us from radiation (does not specify specific range of radiation); Legitimate health related concerns (e.g. skin cancer)
Incorrect	Have non-normative ideas.		No	Have non-normative ideas or links.	Protects from meteorite strike. It helps us alive.
Off Task/Blank			Off Task/Blank		

FIGURE 7.1 Comparing TIMSS and KI scoring for a question on greenhouse gases

The Programme for International Student Assessment (PISA) is a recently developed test that emphasizes reasoning in many consequential contexts. It was administered in 41 to 65 countries in 2000, 2003, 2006, and 2009. Fensham (2009) reports that including the contextual items adds validity to the scores of the 2006 science test. In addition, these items alert instructors to the importance of linking science to realistic situations. To fully align experiments in the curriculum with assessments the outcome measures should feature KI items and tap a range of contexts that students find personally relevant and that professional scientists deem important for citizens.

Assessment of skills learned in laboratories including procedural and interpretive activities has been attempted in several international comparison studies but has substantial pitfalls (Ruiz-Primo & Shavelson, 1996). Implementation of a practical assessment in TIMSS was costly and did not add valid information to the overall score (Vos & Kuiper, 2005).

In summary, the goals for experimentation in *America's Lab Report* align with the goals for KI. Those that are particularly neglected in most classrooms include communicating the nature of experimentation, expanding the types of contexts included in experiments, and emphasizing the connection between experimental methods and the experimental question. Experimentation goals cannot be assessed unless the tests align with the goals of experimentation and include questions that require students to use evidence to support their arguments.

Experimentation Activities and KI

Research on experimentation underscores the need to guide and scaffold inquiry learning so that teachers are freed to mentor individuals and small groups on their specific questions. In addition, research demonstrates the importance of selecting personally relevant problems to ensure that students build on the cultural experiences and develop autonomous learning skills from science experiments. Research also offers support for the individual processes in the KI pattern. We review selected literature to illustrate the evidence for the KI approach.

Address Compelling Questions

The KI framework emphasizes selecting inquiry contexts that build on what students know and connect to problems they consider important and relevant to their lives. As described in Chapter 5, students draw on cultural, deliberate, and intentional processes to generate ideas about science.

WISE projects engage students in investigating topics such as frog deformities, animal extinctions, earthquakes, and recycling. These problems are likely to come up in the future and permit students to reuse and build on their ideas.

Similarly, Krajcik, Czerniak, and Berger (1999) stress the importance of designing good driving questions to organize inquiry. They spell out criteria to make these questions effective: feasibility (students should be able to design and perform the investigations in hands-on or simulated experiments), worth (they should deal with rich science content and match local curriculum standards), relevance (questions should be anchored in lives of learners and deal with important and real-world questions), meaning (projects should be interesting and exciting), and sustainability (projects should sustain student interest over time).

Scaffold Inquiry

Researchers debate the importance of autonomous versus guided experimentation. The constructivist perspective stresses the importance of independent inquiry, but teachers complain that even scaffolded inquiry can be chaotic and unproductive. Often teachers spend all their time answering procedural questions such as telling students the next step in a procedure. Scaffolding can also go too far, making an investigation like following a recipe (Hofstein & Lunetta, 2004).

Making experimentation efficient is a key goal, given restrictions on instructional time (see Box 7.6). Polman (2000) describes how a skilled teacher created a set of milestones and guidelines to enable students to conduct projects spanning six weeks. Students were able to refine their questions, develop feasible plans, gather data, and interpret their findings. While valuable, this lengthy process is not always feasible.

BOX 7.6 INSTRUCTIONAL TIME

Comparison of the time allocated to science topics in the United States and Japan

The science standards are packed. Current science standards require fleeting coverage of far too many topics. For example, in California the eighth grade standards include:

- *9* general topics such as motion, forces, reactions, solar system, and buoyancy;
- *46* specific topics such as velocity, gravity, electrons, molecules, galaxy, conservation of matter, role of carbon in living systems, inert gases, and density.

Consider this:

- California requires 180 days of instruction of which 15 or more are devoted to state testing and school-wide activities.
- That leaves about 165 days for the 55 topics or around 3 days per topic.

In contrast:

- Japanese students cover just eight topics in eighth grade.
- Japanese students continuously outperform American students on international tests.

The only area where we have been able to control this proliferation is in the weight of the textbooks.

Those concerned with stress injuries to children have succeeded in curtailing the weight of textbooks—for the moment.

For example, in California, the following maximum weight standards are in effect for each student textbook in elementary and secondary school:

Grades K–4	Grades 5–8	Grades 9–12
Three Pounds	Four Pounds	Five Pounds

Of course, as states replace textbooks with electronic materials even these minor constraints will disappear. Publishers are already putting textbooks on electronic page turning devices—neglecting all the potential of more powerful computers.

Source: http://www.cde.ca.gov/be/st/ss

Many researchers report that students cannot identify a researchable question or carry out a project without guidance (Edelson, Gordin, & Pea, 1999; Feldman, 2000; Linn, 1980b; Linn & Hsi, 2000). Scaffolding can increase the efficiency of experimentation activities, help students identify promising questions, and free teachers to work with individuals and small groups.

Even when the experiment is specified, students often face challenges in gathering valid evidence and benefit from guidance. Koslowski (1996) discusses the difficulties students face in designing effective experimental conditions. He argues that the interpretations students place on data depend on whether they can imagine an underlying mechanism that might account for the patterns observed. As shown in the Airbags example (see Box 7.3), students often miss the main point of an experiment. In Airbags, students needed to focus on the safety of the driver to make sense of their experiments. McElhaney (2010) achieved this focus for the unit by iterative refinement of the scaffolds for experimentation.

Many have argued that students should be given realistic data sets (such as data on bird migration, weather patterns, or disease vectors) to enhance experimentation opportunities (Feldman, 2000; Newman, Griffin, and Cole, 1989). Scientists spend years learning how to make sense of these datasets. They can overwhelm and confuse learners. For example, Feldman, Konold, and Coulter (2005) studied forty classes using networked science databases to support student investigations. Students found the data sets confusing and could not frame manageable questions independently. A few teachers discovered ways to model the process of using these resources. Most teachers struggled to help students in narrowing and refining their questions.

To guide learning, researchers have shown the benefit of scaffolds that sequence activities and provide social and logistic supports (Davis & Miyake, 2004; Linn & Hsi, 2000; Puntambekar & Kolodner, 1998; Quintana et al., 2004; Sherin, Reiser, & Edelson, 2004). Scaffolds can help learners use an apparatus they could not easily use on their own (Rogoff, 1990). For example, Geological Information Systems (GIS) have often required considerable simplification of the software to be effective (Kali & Orion, 1996; Liben, Kastens, & Stevenson, 2002).

Research describes scaffolds that support language learners, non-readers, or students lacking necessary mathematics skills (e.g. Clark & Jorde, 2004; Krajcik et al., 2000; Tabak, 2004). For example, Model-It is more successful when students are guided to use qualitative language when building relationships between variables in a model (Metcalf, Krajcik, & Soloway, 2000). Scaffolds can give students multiple paths to the same goal (e.g., Puntambekar & Kolodner, 1998) and support activities that allow investigation of complex questions (Tabak & Reiser, 1997).

Scaffolds have the added value of freeing the teacher to tutor individuals while the learning environment provides help and guidance (Linn & Hsi, 2000). As illustrated in the case studies (Chapters 3 and 4), instructional patterns can serve as a guide for design of scaffolds. Ideally, scaffolds help students appreciate the nature of investigation and guide them to take responsibility for performing the activities themselves. Several types of scaffolds show promise.

Inquiry Maps or Cycles

Many technology-enhanced learning environments and some worksheets scaffold the process of inquiry using a map or cycle. Environments such as WISE (Chapter 3; Linn & Slotta, 2000), WorldWatcher (Edelson et al., 1999), Thinker Tools (White & Frederiksen, 1995, 1998, 2000; White, Shimoda, & Frederiksen, 1999), the Cognitive Tutor (Koedinger, Anderson, Hadley, & Mark, 1997; Koedinger & Anderson, 1998), and BGuILE (Tabak & Reiser, 1997) have such maps.

The WISE authoring system enables designers to create personalized inquiry activities aligned with a combination of instructional patterns. WISE specifically characterized inquiry maps for the goals of promoting debate, critique, investigation, or design (Linn, Clark, & Slotta, 2003). These maps make the KI pattern visible to teachers and students.

Inquiry cycles are used in many projects to capture the iterative nature of scientific investigations. The Thinker Tools activities follow the cycle: question, hypothesize, investigate, analyze, model, and evaluate (White & Frederiksen, 1995). Legacy (Bransford et al., 1996) follows the cycle: generate ideas, multiple perspectives, research & revise, test your mettle, and go public. Barab and Hay (2001) describe inquiry as following the cycle: questioning, collecting fundamental facts, enacting facts into a model, addressing the question, presenting the results. The various maps and cycles offer similar sequences of activities that all translate into curriculum patterns that are more likely to promote KI than the lists of steps found in many textbooks. Some textbooks have recently replaced lists of the scientific method steps with cycles.

In summary, scaffolding the complex process of inquiry offers promise for implementing effective experiment activities in classrooms. By scaffolding experimentation the designer focuses student attention on the goals of the project. This means that scaffolds can guide students to conduct consequential tests (see Box 7.3), highlight issues regarding the nature of science (see Box 7.1), and ensure that key ideas are investigated (see Box 7.2).

Scaffolds can increase the emphasis on KI and encourage coherent understanding. Scaffolds increase the impact of teachers by freeing them to mentor students and monitor class progress. When teachers can access embedded assessments in technology-enhanced learning environments to review student work in real time, they can use this information to determine when to interrupt the class and discuss student difficulties as well as to orchestrate discussions of student work.

Guide KI Processes

Designers have created many effective ways to scaffold individual KI processes such as eliciting ideas, distinguishing ideas, adding ideas, and reflecting as well as combination of these processes. We highlight some promising practices.

Make Predictions

As described in the "Computer as Learning Partner" example in Chapter 3 and the "Give and Take" method in learning about materials in Chapter 4, making predictions elicits the repertoire of student ideas and permits students to consider all their views while engaging in inquiry. Many activities including prediction prompts, collaborative discussions, critiques, and brainstorm sessions support the process of eliciting ideas and show benefit for learning (e.g., Linn & Eylon, 2006; Linn & Hsi, 2000). Research shows that adding predictions as part of experimentation improves outcomes (Crouch, Fagen, Callan, & Mazur, 2004; Songer & Linn, 1991; White & Gunstone, 1992). When instructors publicly list all of the ideas held by students as in the Ikatura method (see Chapter 2) and Minstrell's benchmark lessons (diSessa & Minstrell, 1998; van Zee & Minstrell, 1997) they help students generate all of the relevant ideas they hold.

Organize and Represent Data

Several research programs show the importance of designing helpful ways to represent data so that students can distinguish among ideas. Representations can help students focus their attention and interpret the results of their experiments by narrowing the investigation and organizing evidence (Kali, 2006).

The BioKIDS project created representations that helped students organize their data while exploring an ecosystem. For example, the BioKIDS Cyber-Tracker incorporates taxonomic common sense to guide students to categorize animals with accurate but understandable intuitive classification schemes (Lee & Songer, 2003). Starting with expert tools, they refined the representation of data to make it manageable for students. They designed the tools to help students interpret distinct ecosystems to achieve understanding of habitat while also learning basic biological concepts (Lee & Songer, 2003). They found that students appreciated the opportunity to compare their observations of separate ecosystems around the school.

Many technologies support data collection and representation using real time data collection and graphs. The WISE Malaria unit enables interactions with hand-held devices and guides students to explore the spread of malaria (Slotta & Aleahmad, 2002). The WISE Graphing Stories unit incorporates real time data collection to help students understand position and motion graphs. The team found that the increased class sizes in many states (up to 40 students in middle school science in California) meant that students sometimes graphed data from another team by accident. Nevertheless, the activity helped students make sense of position and time graphs. Asking students to critique graphs from different teams helps students develop skill in interpreting graphs and improved ability to interpret graphs of novel situations (Wells, 2010).

Reiser (2004) describes problematizing and structuring experimentation to focus investigations. Problematizing involves the selection of a problem for investigation. For example, the BGuILE curriculum challenges students to explain the adaptation of finches in the Galapagos. Students begin by developing hypotheses, consistent with the eliciting ideas process. They add ideas by performing experiments using a database of Darwin's studies in the Galapagos (Reiser et al., 2001). The software structures experimentation by asking students to give a rationale for their question, interpret their results, and identify their criteria. Students use a table to record conjectures and results of analyses of variables such as beak shape and size. The structure constrains investigation by preventing learners from changing more than one variable at a time (Tabak, 2004). Structuring involves narrowing and focusing attention on salient aspects of the data (Tabak & Reiser, 1997). With this support, students still have difficulty determining effective ways to sort out the complex data set. Students gain experience in testing unpromising ideas and critiquing far-fetched arguments. To help students distinguish ideas, research shows that students are more successful when the teacher models the process of making sense of the information (Tabak & Reiser, 1997).

Masnick and Klahr (2003) also show that structuring experimentation results for young children can increase their ability to distinguish among alternatives and identify sources of experimental error. Using both easily manipulated materials and clear guidelines, they found that 16% of 2nd graders and 40% of 4th graders could conduct controlled experiments and identify possible sources of error. They show that young students have a rich but unsystematic and poorly integrated conception of experimental error and its possible sources.

In all of these examples software or classroom guidance that helps students organize and represent data improves the effectiveness and efficiency of experimentation. Students benefit from representations that reduce the complexity of the experimentation task. They are more successful when the data is structured to reveal relationships and make experimental errors salient. Ultimately, students need to become more autonomous in conducting experiments but first, they need experience interpreting data.

Identify Alternatives

Many research studies show the benefit of guidance that focuses students on identifying alternatives. This supports the KI process of distinguishing ideas. When students distinguish ideas, they develop criteria to select among the existing and new ideas.

Kanari and Millar (2004) argue that students need guidance to identify variables that covary and those that do not covary. They claim that interpreting experimental outcomes is particularly demanding in situations where the variables do not covary. To investigate the role of complexity in experiments, Kanari and Millar (2004) asked 10-, 12- and 14-year-olds to investigate the motion of a pendulum and the force required to move boxes that varied in surface area. Students had much greater difficulty interpreting the results of experiments where the variables did not co-vary (like the weight of the pendulum bob) than in interpreting experiments involving co-variation (like surface area). This finding is consistent with the airbags research where students had difficulty identifying thresholds (see Box 7.3). In these situations providing hints and guidance to help students identify alternatives was effective for improving outcomes.

Support Argumentation

Another way to encourage students to distinguish ideas is to support argument construction. Howe et al. (Howe & Tolmie, 2003; Howe; Tolmie, Duchak-Tanner, & Rattray, 2000) show how inquiry instruction can help students integrate disciplinary and methodological ideas by emphasizing argumentation. Howe (2002) studied the topics of shadow size and heat transfer with 9–12-year-old students. They found that argument construction played an important role in integrating disciplinary and methodological ideas. Howe and Tolmie (2003) show that argument construction varies depending on the discipline (shadows and heat transfer) and the repertoire of ideas students bring to the situation. They found that students' ideas about shadows were descriptive, based on observations and photographs rather than on the nature of light consistent with the work of Osborne (Osborne, Black, Smith, & Meadows, 1990). As a result, students were receptive to integrating results from investigations of how light travels.

When they extended this approach to heat transfer the situation was different (Howe, 1998). Students' inaccurate beliefs were adequate for the initial version of the curriculum so the accurate ideas were not integrated. The designers modified the forms of empirical evidence and anecdotal evidence in numerous design iterations to create instruction that led to arguments that distinguished ideas.

These results show the difficulty of designing experiments that connect to student ideas. Designers need to test the activities with users to ensure that student ideas about the discipline are engaged.

Encourage Critique

Although critique activities help learners interpret experiments, critique is often neglected (Linn, Chang, Chiu, Zhang, & McElhaney, 2010). One challenge with critique is ensuring that students use valid criteria. Many groups report that students use schoolish criteria to evaluate the work of their peers, focusing on formatting, spelling, or grammar (Chang & Quintana, 2006; Linn & Hsi, 2000; White, Shimoda, & Frederiksen, 1999) or implicit and idiosyncratic criteria (Izsak, 2004; diSessa, 2002, 2004). Peers generally offer less valid critiques than instructors (Falchikov & Goldfinch, 2000; Topping, 2003, 2005). Helping students make their criteria explicit as well as focusing critique on whether an experiment answers the research question, distinguishes between competing accounts of a situation, or uses valid measurement techniques could advance scientific understanding.

Scientists engage in critique when the review grants or papers, evaluate the results of competitors' experiments, and analyze the progress of their students. Intriguingly, students do not always understand how critique contributes to scientific advance (Mathison, 1996; Tabak & Reiser, 2008). Students often think that when scientists disagree it is because they prefer to be argumentative rather than because they have an alternative interpretation of the evidence (Linn & Hsi, 2000). Several research programs have explored how critique activities could advance the goal of helping students understand the nature of science or develop meta-strategic knowledge (Zohar, 2006; Zohar & Peled, 2008).

Several investigations show the benefit of instruction that scaffolds learners to engage in critique as part of the KI pattern. In these studies, students critique the experiments of fictitious students to ensure consistent experiences. Linn, Chang, Chiu, Zhang, and McElhaney (2010) show that critique of thermodynamics experiments using a simulation is as effective as interacting with the simulation and more effective than observing the simulation. Shen and Linn (in press) demonstrate that critique adds value to understanding of an electrostatics simulation. Zhang (2010), studying student interactions with a molecular workbench simulation of chemical reactions, found that asking students to critique was as effective as asking them to generate a drawing of bond breaking and bond formation (see Chapter 8).

When studies implemented critique as part of the KI pattern it improved outcomes. In every case, asking students to critique an experiment generated by a fictitious student using criteria supplied in the project resulted in deeper understanding of complex science than did interacting with the simulation. Peer critique, while less dependable for promoting KI because students do not necessarily use valid criteria, ultimately contributes to the ability to distinguish ideas and resonates with calls for promoting 21st century skills (Hilton, 2010).

Prompt for Explanations

Asking students to write explanations of their interpretation of experiments has proven beneficial for science learning (Davis & Linn, 2000; Linn & Hsi, 2000; Ruiz-Primo, Li, Tsai, & Schneider, 2010). Consistent with research on generation prompts (Richland et al., 2007) and on self-explanations (Chi, Bassok, Lewis, Reimann, & Glaser, 1989; Chi, de Leeuw, Chiu, & LaVancher, 1994; Slotta,

Chi, & Joram, 1995) students who explain their ideas either spontaneously or as the result of prompts reconsider their interpretation of experimental findings and may revisit an experiment to clarify their views (Davis & Linn, 2000). Writing explanations supports the reflection step of the KI framework. When students reflect they can check the logic of their reasoning, consider adding ideas to their arguments, and monitor their own progress.

Inquiry Island (White, Shimoda, & Frederiksen, 1999) combines hands-on investigations, Thinker Tools computer models, and simulations along with intelligent agents to help middle school students learn basic mechanics content (Newton's 1st and 2nd laws; White, Shimoda, & Frederiksen, 1999). In this program, avatars guide students to critique their peers and to reflect on their ideas using a process called *reflective assessment*. The instructional approach is inspired by the success of reciprocal teaching (Palincsar & Brown, 1984). Students are scaffolded by teachers, peers, or intelligent agents to learn about and reflect on the processes of scientific inquiry as they construct increasingly more complex models of force and motion phenomena.

In a comparative study investigating the impact of reflective assessment White and Frederiksen (2000) found that the curriculum succeeded in improving understanding of both content and inquiry. Students in the reflective assessment group had greater gains than those in the comparison group. Low achievers gained more than high achievers although both groups made significant progress. Nevertheless, White and Frederiksen (2000) report that some students struggled with the idea of a model. Many students persisted with their beliefs in impetus theory while also exploring normative ideas. Students were reluctant to criticize each other's work. Some students appeared to transfer their skills to other topics and to their science fair projects. Ten of the thirteen winners of a science fair carried out during the period of the study participated in the reflective assessment condition.

In summary, as these studies suggest, experiments benefit from carefully designed activities that emphasize the processes of KI (see Chapter 5). To increase the impact of inquiry on coherent understanding, instructional designers need to scaffold investigations of questions that connect to the lives of students and address all the inquiry goals including understanding of the nature of science (see Box 7.1). They need to ensure that experiments add new ideas and showcase the variations of inquiry processes associated with diverse contexts of investigation (see Box 7.3). Inquiry projects are most successful when they include activities that implement each of the KI processes. Combining these processes to create a successful unit involves incorporating all of the separate processes and ensuring that the scaffolds free teachers to mentor students.

KI Pattern

The KI pattern introduced in Chapter 5 emphasizes activities that enable students to develop coherent understanding while conducting experiments. Researchers

Table 7.1 KI Patterns in Experimentation Frameworks

Approach	Elicit Ideas	Add Ideas	Distinguish Ideas	Reflect And Sort Out Ideas	Commentary
National Standards	Engage in question (motivate)	Gather evidence	Formulate explanations using the evidence	Connect explanations to scientific knowledge & communicate	Neglects eliciting ideas; focuses distinguishing narrowly
5Es	Engage & assess prior knowledge	Learner exploration	Explanation	Elaboration, application + evaluation	Neglects distinguishing ideas
Learning Cycle	Explore	Teachers invent	Discover	Discover	Abstract, may limit inquiry
Predict, Observe, Explain	Predict	Learners observe	Explain	Explain	Neglects distinguishing ideas
Learning-for-use	Motivate, excite curiosity and elicit student ideas	Construct, gather data and get teacher input	Refine, reflect on ideas	Refine, apply ideas to new situations	Distinguishing ideas is implied but not articulated
Learning by Design	Hypothesize and mess about	Learn science ideas from teacher or text	Create design and get feedback from peers in pin-up or gallery walk	Reflect on feedback	Distinguishing ideas depends on feedback from peers & teacher

have identified and tested several alternative frameworks intended to guide the design of experimentation activities. These frameworks often resonate with the KI pattern and lend credibility to the call for inquiry instruction (Duschl et al., 2007; Singer et al., 2005). They range from goals articulated in standards documents to more specific efforts to identify processes consistent with the messy and complex interactions found in typical scientific laboratories. In this section we describe how the KI pattern works for experimentation and briefly compare it to several other approaches (see Table 7.1).

KI Experimentation Pattern

Inspired by constructivist theory (see Chapter 5), the KI pattern for experimentation takes advantage of students' classroom research (as illustrated in Box 7.2 and Box 7.3) and encourages students to become lifelong learners. It involves:

- *Eliciting ideas.* From the standpoint of KI, it is essential to elicit ideas so they can be explored and distinguished from the new ideas. Explicit activities such as making predictions or generating hypotheses are most successful. These activities also serve the role of assessing students' prior knowledge and can help teachers plan the pace and scope of the unit. When instruction elicits ideas about a compelling science topic, it can be motivating for learners.

- *Adding ideas.* The primary goal of experiments is to add new ideas about the science topic and the methods used to investigate the topic. Both hands-on and virtual experiments can add ideas. Technologies such as real-time data collection and logging of student activities can make experiments more informative. But, designers need to create experiments that make the idea compelling (serve as a pivotal case, for example) for the learner. In addition, adding ideas is not sufficient to ensure that the ideas are integrated.

- *Distinguishing ideas.* From the KI standpoint, the most important and neglected aspect of experimentation is distinguishing ideas. If students lack sufficient insight into the differences between their own ideas and those in the experiment they are likely to continue to hold their own ideas or to add the new ideas but use them sparingly. Designers have conjectured that adding new ideas will induce conflict and lead to distinguishing ideas (Caravita & Halldén, 1994; Strike & Posner, 1985). However, research refutes this view (Inhelder & Piaget, 1958/1972). Students often generate explanations that support both views by saying for example, that heating and cooling are just different (Linn & Hsi, 2000). Activities such as data representation, argumen-tation, critique, and debate help students distinguish ideas.

- *Sorting out ideas.* To complete the process of KI, students need to reflect on their whole repertoire of ideas as well as the connections of their repertoire to related topics. Many science courses place little to no emphasis on cumulative learning and therefore never require students to sort out their ideas, identify gaps in their understanding, and build a more coherent account of a science topic. Some refer to this process as self-monitoring, or metacognition (Chiu & Linn, in press). For experiments to achieve the goal of promoting lifelong learning, they need to instill in students the propensity to reflect on their own ideas and look for gaps or contradictions in the arguments they encounter.

A cohort comparison study of typical instruction and instruction designed using the pattern shows clear benefit for the pattern (Linn et al., 2006). Details on the study are reported in Chapter 10.

National Standards

The National Science Education standards (National Research Council, 2000) build on constructivist theory to describe inquiry as involving: (a) *Engage* in scientifically oriented questions, (b) gather *Evidence* to respond to questions,

(c) formulate *Explanations* from evidence, (d) connect explanations to scientific *Knowledge*, and (e) *Communicate and justify* explanations. This account of inquiry emphasizes warranting explanations with evidence and stresses the collaborative nature of science inquiry by emphasizing communication and justification of explanations. From the KI standpoint, eliciting ideas and distinguishing new and existing ideas could use more emphasis. Furthermore the steps in this description of inquiry could be interpreted as the typical scientific method. The engage step could be narrowly construed to refer to hypothesizing. The formulating explanations step could be captured in a laboratory report.

BSCS 5Es

The Biological Sciences Curriculum Study (BSCS) developed an instructional model to guide experimentation that informed the national standards (Bybee et al., 2006). This model informed the elements in the National Standards (NRC, 1996). It includes: engagement, exploration, explanation, elaboration, and evaluation. The model guides design of lessons, units, and whole curricula. Ideally teachers also use this model to make classroom decisions.

A cohort comparison study shows that instruction using the 5Es is more successful than typical instruction (Wilson, Taylor, Kowalski, & Carlson, 2010). In addition, Coulson (2002) explored the relationship between fidelity to BSCS 5Es and student learning. She found that students whose teachers taught with medium or high levels of fidelity to the BSCS 5E instructional model experienced learning gains that were nearly double that of student whose teachers did not use the model or used it with low levels of fidelity.

Predict, Observe, Explain

As discussed in Chapters 2 and 3, the *predict, observe, explain* (POE) approach to experimentation has roots in constructivism (White & Gunstone, 1992). The POE pattern involves asking students to make a prediction, observe a demonstration or experiment, and explain their thinking. The *prediction* part of POE serves the role of eliciting ideas and is also consistent with making hypotheses before conducting experiments. Considerable research supports the value of predictions (see above). The *observation* part of the pattern involves either doing an experiment or observing a demonstration as a way to add ideas. The *explanation* step in the pattern encourages learners to reflect on their observations and give an explanation of the situation. The explain step combines the distinguish ideas and reflection step of the instructional pattern introduced in Chapter 5. The process in the instructional pattern of distinguishing ideas is implied but not articulated in the POE pattern and may be neglected.

Many research groups have demonstrated the value of scaffolding the POE pattern. In the Model-It software, students build a model of how they believe the variables in a water quality situation will interact, gather data, run the model, and compare their prediction to the outcome (Krajcik, Blumenfeld, Marx, & Soloway, 1994). In a genetics modeling project, Gobert and Pallant (2004), ask students to make predictions about the genotypes of individuals with particular phenotypes and use virtual experiments with Biologica to test their predictions. Learners repeat the *predict, observe, explain* pattern until they have enough evidence to describe the genotype. Scaffolding the POE pattern is more successful that trial-and-error without guidance (Krajcik et al., 1999).

The Learning Cycle

Robert Karplus, a physicist, inspired by Piaget (Inhelder & Piaget, 1958/1972), described the learning cycle that includes three activities: *exploration, invention, and discovery* (see Karplus & Thier, 1971). The cycle guided design of the Science Curriculum Improvement Study (Karplus & Thier, 1971). Exploration refers to a process typically involving hands-on materials where students investigate a scientific situation. For example, students might test whether a wide range of objects float or sink. Often these activities involve a worksheet where students make predictions and then test their ideas. Invention refers to explaining the scientific phenomena to students. For example, teachers might "invent" the concept of density to help students interpret why objects sink or float. One author (Linn) was often discouraged when visiting SCIS classrooms to discover that the teacher was on the invention part of the cycle and giving a lecture. Overusing this step reduces the inquiry aspect of the learning cycle. Discovery refers to systematic experimentation sometimes combined with making a report. For example, students might compare objects of the same volume but with different density and record their observations.

Materials designed with the learning cycle proved more effective than typical instruction in numerous studies (Abraham, 1998). A longitudinal comparison study of SCIS versus typical instruction showed that students learned more about experimentation from materials designed using the learning cycle (Bowyer, 1975). Comparisons from a national sample of schools showed that lessons designed using the learning cycle were more successful than typical lessons for teaching students how to design experiments (Linn & Thier, 1975).

Learning for Use

Learning for use grew out of work on software design. Soloway adapted emerging practices in human-computer-interaction to advocate for incorporating more sophisticated understanding of the cultural and social aspects of the learner into the design of innovations (Soloway, Guzdial, & Hay, 1994). Many projects adapted and refined this approach. In a series of projects starting with CoVis (Pea, 1993) and culminating with WorldWatcher (Edelson, Gordin, & Pea, 1999) designers adapted atmospheric visualization tools for learners (see Box 7.7). Edelson (2001) articulated a framework called learning-for-use that emerged from this research. It has three steps:

Motivate

To motivate learners, designers create a demand for knowledge by posing a challenging problem and elicit curiosity by illustrating the problem with surprising findings. For example, in the create-a-world project students are motivated to design a fictitious world and articulate their ideas about landmasses and temperature.

Construct

To construct knowledge students directly interact with environments and receive communications from their teachers. For example, in the create-a-world project students use mapping tools to test conjectures about features of the planet, observe the impact of features such as proximity to the ocean or the equator, and receive explanations about the factors they identify from their teachers.

Refine

To refine their ideas students reflect during discussions with peers and apply their ideas to related problems. For example, in the create-a-world project students design new worlds and explain their temperature predictions.

Edelson (2001) compared learning-for-use with the learning cycle and found the two to have many similarities. They both allow students to explore and then fill in new ideas—often in teacher presentations. They both encourage students to refine their ideas. From a KI perspective, learning-for-use often elicits ideas during the motivation activity but may neglect distinguishing ideas in the construct activity. The impact of the refine activity depends on the supports learners receive from teachers and peers. The framework has resulted in gains in understanding (see Box 7.7).

Learning by Design

The Learning by Design project is inspired by case-based reasoning (Kolodner, 1993; Schank, 1982, 1999) and problem-based learning (Barrows, 1985; Koschmann, Myers, & Feltovich, 1994). It draws on the cognitive apprenticeship approach to constructivism (Collins, Brown, & Newman, 1989; Lave & Wenger, 1991). Kolodner and her colleagues have designed ways to guide students in conducting design projects. The designers assume that learners are goal directed and will engage in activities such as trying out alternatives to achieve their goals.

BOX 7.7 WORLDWATCHER
WorldWatcher curriculum materials

The WorldWatcher software supports experimentation about factors that contribute to the weather. The software draws on weather databases and simulations to support experimentation. The research on WorldWatcher resulted in the learning-for-use framework (Edelson, 2001).

The WorldWatcher software uses interactive maps that illustrate temperature gradients in color consistent with depictions in newspapers and on televised weather reports. The software allows users to customize by adjusting the color scheme, magnification, and spatial resolution (see http://www.geode. northwestern.edu/softwareWW.htm). Students can use energy balance diagrams to explore conjectures about weather impacts (Edelson, 2001).

Learning by Design engages learners in design challenges such as building a bridge or developing an erosion control system (Kolodner et al., 2003). Students follow a process of design and redesign based on feedback from peers. The authors define a series of skills and practices that students need and specific activities in the context of design to develop these skills and practices. The skills include making decisions, understanding and discussing devices, construction, collaborating, reflecting, keeping records, and designing and running experiments. It also introduces them to the repeated practices and activities they will engage in, e.g., messing about, poster sessions, pin-up sessions, and gallery walks. Students are introduced to the process of design by a launcher project and guided by worksheets as well as their teachers to complete their designs. Results show that students perform as well or better than students in typical courses on science knowledge and excel in use of design skills (Kolodner et al., 2003).

In summary, many groups have researched patterns to guide design of science experiments (see Table 7.1). The similarities in patterns show that the KI pattern resonates with research conducted by a wide range of research groups. As these examples show, instruction incorporating the elements of the KI pattern leads to better understanding of science.

Elicit Ideas

Patterns vary in their emphasis on eliciting ideas. Some use predictions (POE) or pretests (5Es). Some elicit ideas in explorations (learning cycle) or discussions of planning (learning by design) but others neglect this step. Some focus on motivation more than on eliciting ideas (the National Standards, 5Es, learning-for-use).

Add Ideas

All the patterns use experiments to add ideas, some in teacher demonstrations and others in hands-on or virtual student investigations. In the learning cycle teachers invent the concepts that students have explored. Similarly, the learning-for-use approach features many opportunities for teachers or worksheets to add scientific ideas. As expected, the learning by design approach emphasizes student inquiry for learning new ideas.

Distinguish Ideas

Patterns differ the most in their emphasis on distinguishing ideas. Some patterns imply this process while others address it with peer or teacher feedback and comparison activities. From the KI perspective when students distinguish ideas they use evidence from their experimental findings and have the chance to evaluate their methods. Distinguishing ideas with help from peers is consistent with cognitive apprenticeship and highlighted in learning-by-design and learning-for-use. The national standards and 5Es include formulating explanations from connecting explanations to scientific knowledge which could include distinguishing ideas.

Reflect and Sort Out Ideas

Patterns vary in their inclusion of opportunities to reflect by sorting out ideas. Many of the patterns combine distinguishing ideas and sorting out of ideas rather than keeping these activities distinct. Most of the patterns emphasize explaining results or new ideas, sometimes implying that it will be straightforward for students to explain. This disregards the need for students to distinguish new ideas from the well-established alternative ideas that many students have developed from their interactions with the natural world.

All the patterns are intended to help learners learn to carry out their own investigations. Practice of a consistent inquiry pattern in a supportive environment may enable learners to develop a manageable set of investigative practices and know when to consult experts or peers to become more successful. Making the pattern explicit, as is characteristic of learning-by-design and implemented in many learning environments including WISE can help learners appreciate how inquiry works in varied contexts. When designers structure activities using the KI pattern, students have the chance to test out their own ideas, go down wrong paths, recognize the weaknesses of their approach, and develop the skill of guiding their own inquiry.

Conclusions

This chapter shows that the KI pattern provides excellent guidance for creating effective virtual or hands-on experiments that lead to integrated understanding.

Research can help designers create activities that use experiments to help students integrate their ideas about a science topic as well as their ideas about scientific methods and scientific advance. Using the KI pattern in the design process can improve the image of experimentation that students acquire as well as the robustness of their understanding. This approach can extend understanding to include the economic, policy, and interpersonal dimensions of experimentation.

More research is needed to determine effective ways to help students develop a realistic image of the nature of scientific research. In addition, we need to explore ways to help students learn to guide their own investigations.

Reflection Activity

Identify a classroom or laboratory experiment that you either (a) performed or (b) assigned to students. Describe the experiment using the KI pattern. Identify how (or whether) the activity (a) elicited ideas, (b) added ideas, (c) enabled participants to distinguish ideas, and (d) encouraged reflection. Discuss how the experiment could be improved.

8

MAKING VISUALIZATIONS VALUABLE

Introduction

Visualizations that take advantage of advances in technology can enable learners to explore phenomena that are too small (molecules), fast (electrons), abstract (forces), or massive (the solar system) to observe directly. We explore the promise of this powerful technology for improving science learning. We contrast uses based on absorption with those informed by KI. We discuss the considerable challenge of designing effective visualizations and the added challenge of designing curriculum materials that take advantage of the visualizations.

We define visualizations as *interactive*, computer-based animations of scientific phenomena including models and simulations. We focus in this chapter on visualizations designed to add ideas that cannot be directly observed such as atomic interactions (chemical reactions, electrostatics), cellular processes (mitosis, meiosis), and astronomical phenomena (solar system, seasons). By interactive, we mean visualizations that allow users to change parameters, select views, contrast conditions, and analyze alternatives. Visualizations that implement virtual experiments such as Airbags and Global Climate Change were discussed in Chapter 7.

Controversy and Confusion

Research concerning the educational value of dynamic visualizations is contradictory and inconclusive. For example in 2002, Tversky (Tversky, Morrison, & Betrancourt, 2002) concluded, ". . . the research on the efficacy of animated over static graphics is not encouraging" (p. 251). Recent reviews of the literature report uneven results (e.g., Chang et al., 2008; Hoffler & Leutner, 2007). These results show that, as is the case for textbooks, lectures, and classroom experiments, designing instruction with visualizations is complicated. Like lectures, visualizations can transmit information that does not connect to the learner. Like experiments, visualizations can be interactive but not informative. This chapter clarifies the controversy about the potential benefit of visualizations.

New Technologies

Recently, powerful visualization environments have emerged to illustrate complex science phenomena. These include Molecular Workbench (Pallant & Tinker, 2004), Biologica (Buckley et al., 2004), WorldWatcher (Geographic Data in Education (GEODE) Initiative, 2003), NetLogo (Wilensky & Rand, in press), and Physics Education Technology (PhET 2010, Wieman, Adams & Perkins, 2008). By embedding visualizations in learning environments such as WISE, research can take advantage of rapid prototyping, iterative refinement, user customization, embedded assessment, and logging of student interactions. Part of the controversy about visualizations stems from the challenge of designing effective instruction that uses these technologies (Gilbert, 1991; Justi & Gilbert, 2002; Loh et al., 1997).

For example, these advances in technology recently enabled researchers to explore using a molecular kinetic model for middle school thermodynamics. In Chapter 3 we discussed the decision of the Computer as Learning Partner project to abandon the molecular kinetic model in favor of heat flow for explaining thermal events. This decision reflected the difficulty students had interpreting the textbook explanation and the lack of good alternatives (Linn & Hsi, 2000). With the availability of the molecular workbench software researchers tried introducing a molecular kinetic visualization for teaching thermal equilibrium (Clark & Jorde, 2004).

A refined version of the Clark and Jorde (2004) unit illustrates the opportunities new technologies afford and the many choices that face designers. Chang et al. (2008) revised the unit and compared three methods for using the visualization. All students started the unit with a hands-on thermal equilibrium activity where they predicted the temperature of objects in the room and then used a probe to measure the temperatures. To explore these experimental findings about thermal equilibrium students used the molecular visualization of a cup of liquid on a table (see Figure 3.4). All three conditions followed the KI pattern. To elicit ideas about the visualization, students identified a research question and made predictions about the temperature of a cup of hot liquid on a table. To distinguish ideas, students either observed, experimented, or critiqued an experiment. To reflect, students explained how the new ideas and investigations answered their research question about thermal equilibrium.

They explored three conditions:

- In the *observe condition*, students predicted, observed experiments that varied starting temperature for the table and the cup, and explained the visualization of how the molecular movement and temperature graph change when the hot cup is placed on the cold counter.
- In the *interactive condition* students predicted outcomes, conducted experiments by varying starting temperature for the table and the cup, and explained their observations. They then reviewed guidelines for effective experiments.
- In the *critique condition* students predicted outcomes, conducted experiments by varying starting temperature for the table and the cup, and explained their observations. They then critiqued responses of a fictitious student (see Box 8.1).

All three groups made significant gains on KI questions. Questions included an item that asked students to draw pictures to show how heat is transferred and explain their drawings. In addition, the critique group outperformed the other two groups, consistent with findings for critique reported in Chapter 7. These results suggest that critique is very effective for helping students distinguish ideas presented in visualizations. This example suggests that powerful visualizations could add ideas about molecular kinetic theory that were difficult to understand in textbook-based courses. It also suggests that well-designed KI activities can

---

BOX 8.1 THERMODYNAMICS CRITIQUE

Students in the Critique Treatment responded to this item asking them to determine whether a fictitious student named Mary conducted an informative experiment. Responses were scored using the knowledge integration rubric shown

In the Thermodynamics unit students investigate thermal equilibrium. They link experiments and visualizations showing heat propagation at the atomic level. Students investigate heat propagation in a visualization with a cup of hot liquid on a counter. In a comparison study (Chang & Linn, in press) students were assigned to the Critique, Interaction, or Observation condition. The Observation group watched experiments with the visualization while the Interaction group conducted their own virtual experiments. They varied the temperatures and studied the outcomes. The Critique group conducted fewer experiments than the Interaction group and also explained whether a fictitious student named Mary conducted an informative experiment (see Critique Activity). Responses were scored using the knowledge integration rubric.

Critique activity

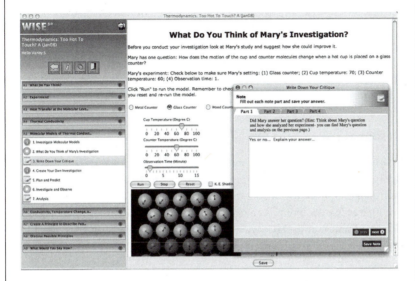

FIGURE 8.1.1 Critique activity

Student responses

Example responses to embedded assessment in the Interaction condition.

Prediction:

"After a REALLY long time, the molecules will start to slow down."

Explanation:

"The cup's molecule's motion in the beginning was faster than the counter's motion, then after a while, the cup's motion started to slow down while the counter's speeds up until they have the same speed."

TABLE 8.1.1 Coding Rubric

Coding rubric for the pre and posttests

KI Level	Score	Description
Complex link	5	Three or more normative and relevant ideas and elaborate two or more scientifically valid links among the ideas
Full link	4	Two normative and relevant ideas and elaborate one scientifically valid link between the two ideas

Partial link	3	Normative and relevant ideas but cannot fully elaborate the links among them
No link	2	Relevant ideas that are not non-normative but make non-normative links among them, or ideas that are relevant to the science context but are non-normative
Irrelevant	1	Ideas that are irrelevant to the science context
No information	0	Did not answer the item

Results

The Critique group outperformed the other groups (Critique Effect Size = 1.21; Interaction Effect Size .63; Observation Effect Size = .57). This result stems, in part, from the unsystematic approach typically used by students in the Interaction condition. As a result the Observation and Interaction conditions had similar impact. Critique seemed to be more successful because the students were guided to distinguish alternatives and develop criteria (Chang et al., 2008).

help students develop more coherent views when using visualizations. In this chapter we explore these suggestions by considering additional research.

Absorption and Deceptive Clarity

Recent research suggests that one reason students fail to benefit from visualizations is that, without guidance, they underestimate the demands of interpreting the instruction (Chiu, 2010; Linn, Chang, Chiu, Zhang, & McElhaney, 2010). Instruction aimed at transmitting information could overwhelm learners with visualizations that are too complicated to understand.

Research on *judgment of learning* helps clarify how students view their understanding of visualizations and monitor their progress. To assess students' perceptions of their ability to learn from scientific visualizations, Chiu studied judgment of learning from the chemical reactions visualization (see Box 8.2). Chiu (2010) asked students to rate their understanding at one of two points: right after they had experimented with the chemical reactions visualization (consistent with the absorption approach) or after they had written an explanation of what they thought the chemical reactions visualization illustrated (consistent with the reflection process of the KI pattern). Take a moment to predict what you think students will say. Will they rate their understanding right after the visualization higher or lower than their understanding after they write an explanation?

BOX 8.2 CHEMICAL REACTIONS UNIT AND ASSESSMENT

In Chemical Reactions students compare chemical reactions that contribute to greenhouse gases (hydrocarbon combustion), and chemical reactions that may be more environmentally friendly (hydrogen combustion). They use the evidence from their explorations to write a letter to their congressperson (Chiu, 2010).

Curriculum

The unit implements the KI pattern as follows.

Eliciting ideas in a brainstorm
The unit uses an online brainstorming step to elicit students' ideas about the greenhouse effect and global warming.

Adding ideas from a visualization

To add ideas, students experiment with a visualization of hydrogen combustion (see Figure 8.4). Students can observe intermediate states in a reaction, determine the effect of adding heat on molecular motion, or trace the path of a single atom.

Distinguishing ideas using peer critique

To distinguish ideas, pairs of students develop criteria by discussing the new ideas and compare them to their existing ideas. Teachers model the process of evaluating ideas and help students develop criteria to use in comparing ideas. Students create a rubric that makes explicit the criteria for a well-supported decision and use it to critique the responses of their peers.

Students draft a letter to their congressperson describing how chemistry relates to climate change. Students are encouraged to use notes from the entire project to construct their letter. The letter is posted in an online discussion for peer critique.

In a peer critique students use the rubric to critique each other's arguments. The peer feedback informs not only revisions to the justifications, but also the connections students make between new and existing ideas.

Sorting out ideas

To sort out ideas, students revise their letters based on the feedback from their peers. They are encouraged to use the class rubric to evaluate their revised response.

Assessment and scoring rubric

To assess outcomes students take pretests and posttests. One question asks students to draw their ideas about chemical reactions.

Question: If a grey circle represents hydrogen, a white circle represents oxygen, and a bond is represented with a line, draw a molecular picture of the following balanced equation: $2H_2 + O_2 \rightarrow 2H_2O$.

(Possible ideas to integrate: Conservation of mass, molecular understanding of subscripts and/or coefficients, dynamic nature of reaction)

Score	Description	Student Example
4	Complex link: Two or more scientifically valid links among ideas.	
3	Full link: Complete connection among ideas. Students understand how two scientific concepts interact.	
2	Partial link: Partial connections among ideas, students consider relevant ideas but not consistent throughout response (i.e. correct molecules but incorrect number).	
1	No link: Students have non-normative links or ideas in a given context.	
0	No answer/Irrelevant: Students do not engage in given science context.	I don't know

Results

FIGURE 8.2.1 Assessment and scoring rubric

Overall, students gain insight into chemical reactions. Many students received responses to the letters they wrote to Congress.

Under conditions consistent with the absorption approach, where the visualization transmitted information, students asked after viewing the visualization believed they had better understanding than those asked after writing the explanation (see Figure 8.1). Analysis of subsequent performance showed that students who rated their understanding of the process of chemical reactions after viewing the visualization overestimated their progress. This finding suggests that the visualization is deceptively clear.

Experience with watching the visualization is sufficient to convince students that they understand chemical reactions better than when they are asked to articulate

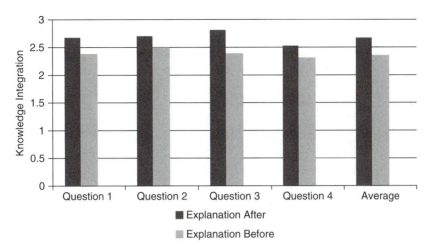

FIGURE 8.1 Deceptive clarity. Students rate their understanding of a chemical reactions visualization higher right after viewing than they do after generating an explanation of the visualization

Source: Chiu, J. L. (2010). Supporting students' knowledge integration with technology-enhanced inquiry curricula. Unpublished doctoral dissertation, University of California, Berkeley, CA.

their ideas. This finding is consistent with research asking people whether they learn best from text, visual materials, or auditory presentations has demonstrated that almost all learners report that they learn better from visual materials (Linn & Hsi, 2000).

Deceptive clarity may deter students from further review of the ideas in the visualization. These results add weight to the view that students' ideas about their own learning are not always consistent with evidence from their own experiences (Linn & Hsi, 2000). Learners also prefer active, hands-on learning to more passive activities, such as lectures (Light, 2001). In addition, students often select unproductive study habits and inaccurately monitor their own learning (Dweck, 2006; Dweck & Master, 2008). Rather than selecting the activities that lead to the most understanding, students seem to select activities they find pleasing (like visualizations and hands-on experiments) and that take minimal intellectual effort (like watching a visualization or underlining text in the book).

This finding helps explain study habits that involve rereading text or underlining in multiple colors (see Chapter 6). In research on memory, studies show that learners are prone to overestimate their ability to remember even relatively straightforward information like telephone numbers or names unless prompted to test their beliefs (Bjork, 1994). Similarly, learners suffer from an "illusion of explanatory depth" for complex processes, especially for phenomena that can be mentally visualized or animated (Rozenblit & Keil, 2002).

These findings help explain why transmission is appealing to learners as well as teachers. Consistent with Sinapuelas' (2010) investigation of test preparation, students may not test their understanding. The deceptive clarity of visualizations supports the importance of embedding visualizations in KI patterns.

The growing popularity of weather visualizations on websites and in news broadcasts illustrates both the apparent interest that visualizations generate and their deceptive clarity. Most people have difficulty explaining the role of pressure, temperature, and wind speed shown in weather visualizations (Edelson, 2001). Educational programs such as World Watcher (Edelson, 2001) and Kids as Global Scientists (Songer, 1996) found that weather visualizations required extensive refinement before they could be used as evidence in an argument. Studies that ask students to write explanations of their observations, show that this sort of prompt for reflection leads students to realize that they have gaps in their understanding (Chiu & Linn, in press). The recognition of those gaps leads to a decline in the estimate understanding but also motivates the learner to fill the gap. Without prompting, students seem satisfied with superficial exposure to a topic.

In summary, both designers and learners are tempted to assume that visualizations on their own can teach complex ideas. Like lectures and experiments, such materials could succeed if students autonomously applied KI strategies to make predictions, observe the outcomes, question their own ideas, use evidence to distinguish ideas, and reflect on the results. Since students rarely use these strategies spontaneously, designers seek instructional activities that take advantage of powerful visualizations and help students integrate the new ideas they encounter.

Static versus Dynamic Representations

The main issue in the controversy about visualizations concerns their dynamic nature. Psychologists and science educators have compared dynamic and static approaches to teaching the same topic. Research syntheses have found small overall effects for dynamic materials compared to static materials but large effects favoring each side in individual studies (Höffler & Leutner, 2007). The heterogeneous findings reflect the heterogeneity of the research agendas of those conducting the research. Most of the comparison studies are conducted by psychologists whose goals and methods differ from those in science education (see Richland et al., 2007).

Psychologists often compare static and dynamic instruction to clarify basic processes of communicating information, improving memory for events, and, sometimes, improving understanding of phenomena. Often the goal of the design is to make the treatments equal, not to exploit the strengths of one format or another. Visualizations may be formed by animating static diagrams (e.g., Hegarty, Kriz, & Cate, 2003; Mayer, Hegarty, Mayer, & Campbell, 2005; Tversky et al., 2002). These studies generally are conducted in laboratories with undergraduates and have a duration of one or two hours. The studies often use multiple indicators of progress including measures of spatial reasoning, recall of information, reasoning processes, and sometimes argument construction. This suite of tests often means that the actual instruction is quite short (often minutes or even seconds). Assessments aligned with the instruction often focus on recall of the information presented.

Most studies in science education focus on understanding complex topics. Visualizations are generally used to illustrate dynamic processes (chemical reactions, force and motion, mitosis). Students typically start with a repertoire of ideas about the phenomena. Designers often construct visualizations as pivotal cases that respond to the repertoire of ideas (Chapters 3 and 7). Designers of scientific visualizations study the characteristics of effective designs and seek to align the designs with learner knowledge (NRC, 2006; Tinker & Xie, 2008; Wieman et al., 2008). Science curriculum designers have studied activities such as critique of visualizations to help students integrate their ideas (Kozma, 2003; Linn et al., 2006; Schank & Kozma, 2002). Science education studies typically last a week or longer, involve precollege students in regular classes, and use outcome measures that assess ability to interpret or explain complex science concepts.

In science education, comparison studies are difficult to design because the dynamic versions may add information that is difficult or impossible to communicate with static materials. Research in science education has commonly sought to add value to typical instruction with visualizations. For example, the process of bond breaking and bond formation in chemical reactions requires appreciation of how molecules in an aggregate interact (see Box 8.1).

To illustrate the agendas of psychologists and science educators, we compare studies that used the same method for constructing the visualizations but report very different outcomes. Both studies started with static pictures and animated them to create the dynamic instruction. This approach ensures that the dynamic condition presents the identical images as found in the static condition. Neither study was designed to take advantage of the dynamic format. In the psychology study, college students studied observable phenomena such as lightning. They either viewed static pictures and read accompanying explanations or viewed the same pictures displayed quickly in a flipbook format and listened to a narration using the same explanations (Mayer et al., 2005). They could not interact with the materials or control the pacing. In the science education study, Kehoe, Stasko, and Taylor (2001) asked students to interact with a static diagram (of a computer algorithm for the binomial heap) or to view a flipbook animation of the same diagrams. Students could control the flipbook and were able to go forward as well as backward to explore the workings of the binomial heap.

Duration of instruction and outcome measures were very different. In the psychology study, instruction was between 50 seconds and seven minutes in duration. For the binomial heap, students had unlimited time to interact with the materials. For the binomial heap, the outcome measure required students to solve problems. Mayer et al. (2005) asked students to list all the information they could recall.

Results of the studies were completely opposite to each other. On average, Mayer et al. (2005) report an effect size of −0.59, students recalled more from the static condition than the dynamic condition. Kehoe et al. (2001) found that animations were very effective with an effect size of 1.47. Comparing these studies showcases the difficult decisions faced by designers and the importance of the outcome measure.

These studies differed in duration, opportunity to interact, and opportunity to control one's own learning. In addition, as Mayer et al. (2005) acknowledge, the psychology study increases demand on working memory since students could not review the materials.

One confound in the Mayer et al. (2005) study concerns the alignment of assessment and condition. The flipbook had narrated explanations presented at a predetermined rate while students were able to read the explanations for the static pictures at their own rate. Performance on the written assessment might have been easier for students who read the information rather than hearing it. When students read the information they had a chance to see the spelling and formatting of the words. Since the outcome measure required them to write down their recollections, they might have had an easier time producing what they saw. This may help to explain why the flipbook and narration was less successful than the static and written explanation approach, although the results were uneven across visualizations.

In a another study, Holyoak and his colleagues compared dynamic and static representations in a series of laboratory studies and report a similar benefit for dynamic visualizations using assessments that required students to integrate ideas from two contexts (Pedone et al., 2001). Their work illustrates the importance of the alignment of the outcome measure with the goals of instruction. They studied the role of analogies in helping students understand relatively complex phenomena such as radiation therapy. In this study the goal was to understand how to impact a target with strong radiation without damaging surrounding tissue. The analogy was to an army infiltrating an enemy camp by sending small groups of soldiers into the area from multiple locations around the perimeter. Holyoak and colleagues tried multiple ways to help students recognize the similarities between radiation therapy and infiltrating armies. Holyoak and colleagues compared narrative explanations, static arrows, and moving arrows to show the direction of the radiation and the paths of the small groups of soldiers. Only the dynamic arrows succeeded (Pedone, Hummel, & Holyoak, 2001). The animations were more successful than static diagrams in helping students make an analogy between the two situations and explain the similarities. The Holyoak studies show the value added by animation over a static diagram when the goal is KI. The animations illustrate the mechanism in each situations even though the phenomena are different. In this study the goal of instruction is fundamentally a dynamic process.

These studies clarify when and how visualizations could have value in science. They show that visualizations are especially effective for science topics that are fundamentally dynamic (such as chemical reactions or mitosis). These studies suggest that visualizations can help students sort out ideas about complex situations. They illustrate the importance of focusing the visualization on information that is difficult to infer from static materials. They show the importance of aligning outcome measures with the demands of the task.

Assessment of Visualizations

Visualizations are well suited to adding ideas about complex, dynamic processes. As illustrated, when embedded in appropriate instruction visualizations can help students link symbolic equations and molecular representations, everyday situations and kinetic theory, or radiation therapy and armies infiltrating an enemy camp. To measure the impact of this instruction, assessments need to require similar forms of reasoning.

For example, assessments may require students to distinguish the ideas in the visualization from their own, integrate disparate views, or critique a conjecture using evidence from the visualization. For a unit where students use a visualization of the role of energy in photosynthesis, students were asked to explain the role of the Sun in feeding a rabbit (see Box 8.3). When students studied chemical reactions, items asked students to use one explanation to connect such diverse events as explosions, the rusting of metal, or blood sugar metabolism. Assessments that ask students to relate ideas about these dynamic processes can also serve as a mini lesson, requiring students to integrate ideas.

BOX 8.3 PHOTOSYNTHESIS ASSESSMENT

New assessment items for energy concepts use MySystem and Energy Stories. Responses are scored using the knowledge integration rubric

To improve our ability to understand how students make sense of the role of energy in complex systems such as global climate and photosynthesis the Cumulative Learning using Embedded Assessment Results (CLEAR) project developed two new forms of assessment (see also Box 7.3, Global Climate, for an example of an energy story). The new assessments were designed to capture a narrative account of energy transfer and transformation (Energy Stories) and to offer students a graphical representation tool to capture their ideas (MySystem). These item types also enable students to learn while they are performing assessments. Responses are all scored using the knowledge integration rubric as shown.

Example Assessments Using Energy Stories and MySystem

Energy Stories	MySystem
Write a story using scientific evidence to explain to Mary how plants use sunlight to grow.	Create a MySystem diagram that tells Mary how plants use sunlight to grow.
Make sure your story explains:	Make sure your diagram shows:
• where plants get energy to grow • how the energy is transformed • what happens to the energy in the plants • where the energy ends up.	• where plants get energy to grow • how the energy is transformed • what happens to the energy in the plants • where the energy ends up.

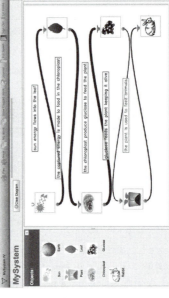

FIGURE 8.3.2 MySystem

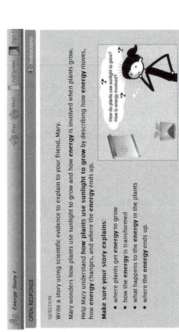

FIGURE 8.3.1 Energy Story

Knowledge Integration Rubric for Energy Stories and MySystem

Score	KI Level	Description	Sample Student Responses: Energy Stories	Sample Student Responses: MySystem
1	**Off-task**	Invalid ideas or I don't know.	— I don't know.	Icons for the system are not linked to each other.
2	**No Link**	One valid idea plus non-normative or scientifically invalid links and ideas.	— The sun energy travels through the air which goes into the oxygen which helps the rabbit get energy. The energy is produced into different minerals which helps the plant grow. It ends up helping the plant grow and produce food for animals.	At least two icons are linked and the links are not valid. For example, the rabbit is linked to glucose and the link has the label "flow."
3	**Partial Link**	Normative ideas but no valid link.	— The chloroplast produces glucose which the glucose is food for the plant and the food helps the bunny produce energy to move around. The sun then uses its sunlight for the chloroplast that is needed to grow the plant then the bunny or any animal eats the plant to help it survive.	Icons are linked but the links are not accurately labels. For example, all the labels say "flow."
4	**Full Link**	One scientifically valid and elaborated link between.	— Well Mary, energy is very important because it is basically the main ingredient to photosynthesis, or the growth of plants. The energy from the Sun goes to the Earth then it gets into plants and the	Icons are linked and the links have one label. See Figure MySystem Scored 4.

Continued

		normative and relevant energy ideas.	photosynthesis begins. The energy is then transformed into chemical energy which makes the food. The energy stays in the plant and keeps going through the photosynthesis cycle until the plant dies and the energy stops the cycle.	Icons are linked and there are several accurate labels.
5	Complex Link	Two scientifically valid and elaborated links between normative and relevant energy ideas.	— The sunlight energy is beamed down to Earth, and hits the plants. When the energy reaches them, the chloroplast in them absorbs the energy. The energy is then converted into glucose during photosynthesis, which uses CO_2, H_2O, and the energy to form glucose, and release oxygen. The plant then uses the glucose to survive and grow, repeating the same process over and over again.	
6	Advanced Complex Link	Three or more scientifically valid and elaborated links between normative and relevant energy ideas.	— Plants use the process called photosynthesis to grow. It is started by leaves absorbing the sunlight and CO_2. The CO_2 comes from the humans. Plants also needs water. When sunlight, CO_2, and water enters the chloroplast, it brakes apart then recombined to make glucose and oxygen. The glucose helps plant grow and the oxygen helps human live. The energy ends up in the animals stomach when they eat the leaves.	Icons are accurately linked and the labels are normative and relevant. See Figure MySystem scored 6.

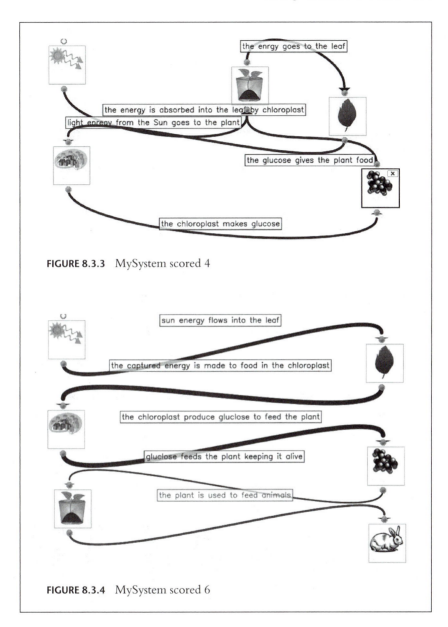

FIGURE 8.3.3 MySystem scored 4

FIGURE 8.3.4 MySystem scored 6

Typical versus Visualization-Rich Instruction

The Technology-Enhanced Learning in Science (TELS) National Science Foundation funded center conducted a cohort comparison study to test the impact of visualizations embedded in inquiry projects designed using the KI pattern. Participants in the center used a partnership design process to create 12 units.

The units were designed for middle school earth science, life science, and physical science and for high school biology, chemistry, and physics. For a discussion of the partnership design process and the professional development program see Chapter 10.

In this study, 25 teachers were recruited in the spring and agreed to test their current students. The following year they taught TELS 5-day units and tested their new cohort of students (Linn et al., 2006). The students using the visualization-enhanced curriculum ($N = 4520$) performed almost one-third of a standard deviation better (effect size of .32 (p <.001)) than the typical cohort ($N = 3712$). These effects were found across middle school and high school science courses (see Figure 8.2).

The features of the TELS curriculum include: implementation of the KI pattern; guided inquiry using interactive visualizations, models, and probeware; relevant contexts that interest students; ample time for reflection; a focus on integrating prior experiences with new observations; student collaboration (see discussion in Chapter 9); and easy implementation (Lee, Linn, Varma, & Liu, 2009).

The cumulative impact of the TELS curriculum is reinforced by studies that track the trajectory of student learning during the year (see Figure 8.3). Students took pretest, posttest, and annual assessments. High school students learned about unseen processes involving molecules (chemical reactions), electrons (electrostatics), population-based genetics (evolution), and chromosomes (meiosis).

TELS followed these students ($N = 764$) taught by 11 teachers from 6 schools in 3 states as they completed pretests and posttests immediately before and after the unit

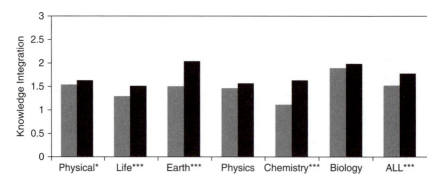

FIGURE 8.2   Cohort comparison study. This study compared students studying the typical curriculum [grey bars] and students studying the visualization-enhanced inquiry curriculum [black bars] taught by the same teachers. Overall, the inquiry cohort significantly outperformed the typical cohort

Source: Linn, M. C., Lee, H.-S., Tinker, R., Husic, F., & Chiu, J. L. (2006). Teaching and Assessing Knowledge Integration in Science. *Science, 313*(5790), 1049–1050.

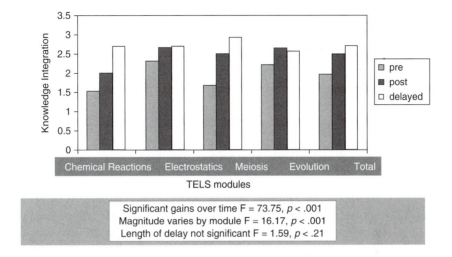

FIGURE 8.3   TELS longitudinal results. Performance on pretest, posttest, and delayed
posttest for students studying Chemical Reactions, Electrostatics, Meiosis, and Evolution as well as overall performance

Source: Chiu, J. L. (2010). *Supporting Students' Knowledge Integration with Technology-Enhanced
Inquiry Curricula.* Unpublished doctoral dissertation, University of California, Berkeley, CA.

enactment, and delayed posttests at the end of the school year. Where delayed posttests were administered, analysis shows that mean KI values significantly increased
from pretest to posttest and delayed posttest. Scores either remained the same or
increased from posttest to delayed posttest across four different TELS curriculum
units, $F(2, 1867) = 73.75$, $p < .001$ (Lee et al., in press). For example, for Chemical
Reactions the delayed posttest was significantly higher than the immediate posttest
(Chiu, 2010). In addition, for electrostatics, the delayed posttest is slightly higher
than the immediate posttest (Shen & Linn, in press). Considering that typical studies
show forgetting by the delayed posttests, these results indicate that instruction with
TELS units can nurture and sustain student understanding.

In summary, controversy surrounds the potential of visualizations for teaching
science. When used to transmit information they often result in deceptive clarity. If students expect that learning from visualizations is straightforward due to
their deceptive clarity, then they may not monitor their understanding as well as
if they expect that visualizations will be confusing. Students might add ideas to
their repertoire but not distinguish new ideas from existing ideas. Often students
adopt a minimalist or cognitive economist perspective when learning complex
science and fail to explore all the implications of new ideas (Linn & Hsi, 2000).
This propensity helps explain the many studies showing that static and dynamic
materials have similar impacts (Hoffler & Leutner, 2007).

Visualizations can contribute to KI as shown by the cohort comparison study. Both the design of the visualization and the design of the curriculum that includes the visualization contributed to the impact. To detect the impact, assessments were aligned with instruction and measured the ability of students to use evidence from the visualization to explain complex science. To clarify the findings, we explore the design of visualizations and the design of curriculum materials featuring visualizations.

Designing Visualizations

Overcoming deceptive clarity and taking advantage of the dynamic nature of science are both important in design of visualizations. In addition, designers need to tailor instruction with visualizations to the prior knowledge of students and design instruction to promote KI. The value of iterative refinement is apparent in all aspects of this work. Design studies have resulted in powerful materials (Chang & Quintana, 2006; Chang et al., 2008; Clark & Jorde, 2004; Edelson et al., 1999; Linn, Davis, & Bell, 2004).

In some cases, researchers refined powerful visualizations designed for experts to make them accessible for students (e.g., Edelson et al., 1999). The CoVis project (see Chapter 7) made numerous refinements to atmospheric data to create the World Watcher software to help students interpret weather patterns.

Tinker and collaborators at the Concord Consortium tried many designs of visualizations of molecular interactions before creating Molecular Workbench (Pallant & Tinker, 2004; Xie & Tinker, 2006). Their software is compelling because random processes such as the paths of atoms are represented. In addition, Molecular Workbench accurately captures the vibrations of atoms and molecules. Many complicated decisions were necessary to create Molecular Workbench. For example, the representation is basically two-and-a-half dimensional (allowing objects to collide and interact). Decisions concerning whether the molecules in the visualization should bounce off the walls or disappear, as well as decisions about whether molecules should pass in front or behind each other, were important in the overall design process.

The Physics Education Technology (PhET) project has created over 50 physics visualizations especially for students. These materials are downloadable from a website (http://phet.colorado.edu). Developed under the leadership of Carl Weiman, at the University of Colorado and University of British Columbia, the website encourages users to design the curriculum to go with them (see Box 8.4). PhET materials are intended to enhance student understanding of physics through exploration, often of everyday experiences (e.g., learning about buoyancy with hot air and helium balloons in the *ideal gas* simulation).

The authors report that the PhET materials add value to classroom instruction featuring hands-on experiments (Finkelstein et al., 2005). They report several studies of the materials. One study carried out with two groups of students

BOX 8.4 IDEAL FUELS UNIT

A study comparing Molecular Workbench and PhET visualizations found they were equally effective and both units led to increased student understanding of activation energy as a feature of an energy efficient fuel

To explore the value of visualizations, we designed a unit on the chemical properties of fuels and implemented it using both PhET and Molecular Workbench (Chiu, Zhang, Miller, & Linn, 2010). The visualizations illustrated the same underlying chemical principles.

The molecular workbench visualization appeared less complicated than the PhET visualization. Students interacted similarly with the two visualizations during this two-day unit.

Molecular Workbench visualization

Exothermic | <u>Endothermic</u> | <u>Explosion can do work.</u>

What is the difference between exothermic and endothermic reactions?

This simulation represents an exothermic reaction, with its accompanying energy diagram. The red bar graph on the right represents the kinetic energy of the system. You can start, stop, reset, and replay the simulation using the contols on the model below.

Instructions:

Push the play button. Using the simulation, answer the following questions:

1. What happens to the molecules in this reaction?

2. What happens to the kinetic energy of the system?

3. How does what is happening to the molecules relate relate to the energy graph?

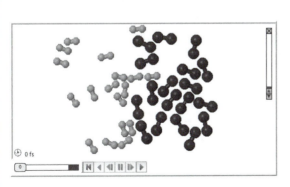

FIGURE 8.4.1 Screenshot of Molecular Workbench visualization

PhET visualization

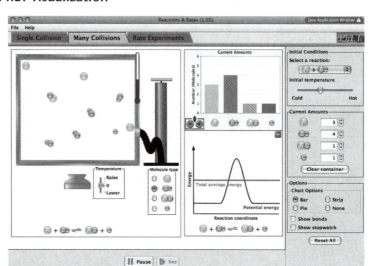

FIGURE 8.4.2 Screenshot of PhET visualization

Results

Comparing the unit with Molecular Workbench and PhET visualizations, we found they were equally effective and both units led to increased student understanding of activation energy as a feature of an energy efficient fuel.

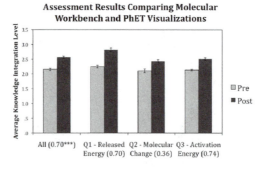

FIGURE 8.4.3 Assessment results comparing Molecular Workbench and PhET visualizations

All pretest to posttest differences were significant at $p < 001$. Error bars represent standard error of the mean.

These results illustrate that the important contribution of the visualization, that it illustrates unobservable processes, is equally achieved by both approaches.

(N = 363) in introductory physics compared *the circuit construction kit* that explicitly models electron flow to an equivalent hands-on laboratory experiment. PhET electricity visualizations capture unseen interactions caused by the fields created by electric charges. Students can explore cause-and-effect relationships, quantitative relationships, and qualitative connections. The students who used the PhET experiment outperformed the hands-on group on a conceptual survey of the domain as well as on the task of assembling a real circuit and describing how it works.

Researchers have studied how students represent chemical reactions using visualization environments either during instruction or for assessment. Chang and Quintana (2006) showed advantages for using Chemation software to make flipbooks illustrating their ideas about chemical reactions. They also identified areas for refinement of the software. They report that some students ignore conservation of mass and simply erase atoms that are unbonded in the reaction. The ChemSense software (Schank & Kozma, 2002) allows students to edit animations of chemistry concepts. Students can discuss their artifacts with their peers. When students design their own reactions they reveal their ideas about forming and breaking bonds.

As these studies suggest, creating effective visualizations for complex science topics has great promise. So far, these studies have focused on a small number of complex topics. Visualizations are needed for other difficult topics such as convection, the seasons, and evolution.

Aligning Visualizations with Learner Knowledge

Matching visualizations to the knowledge levels of students is essential for the visualizations to succeed. For example, one study reported that novice students with low prior knowledge learned better with static graphics, while experienced students with high prior knowledge learned equally well with dynamic visualization or static graphics (ChanLin, 2001). Another study reports that when students are able to construct a dynamic mental model from a series of static images, viewing an external dynamic visualization is not essential (Hegarty et al., 2003). The study of the Scanning Tunneling Microscope (STM) reported in Chapter 4 (Margel, Eylon, & Scherz 2004) showed that students' initial ideas about the particulate nature of matter influenced the degree to which they could benefit from the microscopic structure using the STM. Students who started with microscopic views had more significant benefits.

Matching instruction to the knowledge of learners holds for expertise in spatial reasoning as well. A study by Yang and others (2003) found that college students with expertise in visual processing learned more from an animation of the electrochemical phenomena than their peers who had limited expertise in visual processing. This suggests that some visualizations could overload students with limited skill in processing spatially presented information. However, Hays (1996) found that among middle school students with limited skill in visual processing, those who used computer animations demonstrated greater learning gains than those using static pictures or text only. Moreover, low expertise students using computer animations made learning gains as great as high expertise students. In the Yang, Andre, and Greenbowe (2003) study the visualization was projected in a lecture session for a college class, inhibiting individual efforts to interpret the visualization. In the Hays (1996) study, the middle school students used self-guided exploration. These interactions with the visualization may have been sufficient for all students to become experts in interpreting the spatially-presented information. These studies suggest that designers need to pay attention to the spatial strategies necessary for learning from their materials as they refine instruction.

Research suggests that students learn ways to interpret spatially presented information relatively quickly (Linn & Petersen, 1985; Sorby, 2009). For example, when students learn one video game or one programming language, they develop strategies that will enable them to learn new video games or programming languages more rapidly and more effectively (Clancy & Linn, 1996). This expertise development also applies to programming VCRs, watches, and phones.

Several research groups report on instruction that promotes development of generalizable visualization strategies (e.g., The Agam Program, Razel & Eylon, 1986). For example, students learn to restart the visualization or return the visualization to the initial state when it becomes confusing. They develop ways to represent visually presented information in drawings and to articulate their observations. As a result, exposure to instruction featuring visualizations can make it easier to interpret the next visualization.

In summary, overcoming deceptive clarity and designing effective visualizations for science requires refining the visualization to reduce complexity and to build on what students know. Effective visualizations target crucial scientific ideas that are fundamentally dynamic and supports learners to interact with the visualization to resolve their own questions. With experience, students develop ways to interpret new visualizations.

Visualizations in Curricular Units

To support learners in using evidence from visualizations and to promote distinguishing ideas with this evidence has been the focus of numerous studies of curriculum refinement. Curricular refinements are essential to take full advantage of visualizations.

Guidance for Exploring the Visualization

Many studies show that both experts and novices benefit from guidance to interpret visualizations designed by others. Users of Molecular Workbench visualizations often see balls bouncing around rather than observing molecules or explosions (see Figure 8.4). Students may initially see a pong game instead of realizing that they are observing the interaction of atoms and molecules. Refining

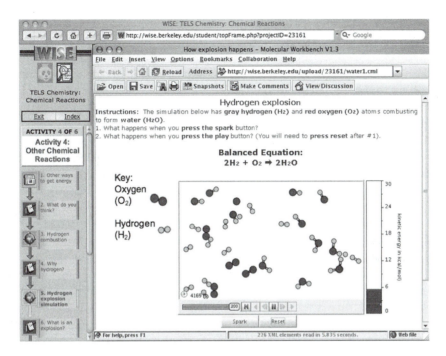

FIGURE 8.4 Screenshot from the WISE Chemical Reactions unit showing the Molecular Workbench visualization

instruction to elicit predictions, guide interpretation of the dynamic visualizations, and reflect on alternatives has motivated the design of many scaffolding frameworks such as those discussed in Chapter 7 (e.g., Edelson, 2001; Quintana et al., 2004) and the KI pattern (Linn & Eylon, 2006).

Refining Molecular Workbench Units

Using evidence from student learning, the TELS researchers refined use of Molecular Workbench instruction so that students with low and high prior knowledge were equally advantaged by visualizations (Chang et al., 2008; Chiu & Linn, 2008; Shen & Linn, in press). For example the TELS design partnership initially implemented the dynamic visualizations in chemical reactions pretty much as the software engineers designed them. However, after tryouts with students, they eliminated distracting details to focus students' attention on the key information and added the KI pattern.

The designers used the KI pattern to design the curriculum around the visualization. They elicited ideas, asking students to predict what happens when molecules interact.

They engaged students in linking the molecular interactions to the symbolic equation and to observable events. In the case of hydrogen combustion they showed a video of a hydrogen balloon explosion, for example, and guided students to link the explosion in the video to the explosion in the molecular workbench visualization. They also came up with ways to help students interpret complex chemical reactions, such as asking students to follow a single atom or stop the visualization when the first bond breaking occurred.

These refinement studies also revealed gaps in knowledge that needed attention. Students failed to understand the role of energy in a chemical reaction (Shen & Linn, in press). Students often interpreted the arrow in a chemical equation as an equal sign. Students did not realize that energy was necessary to start the reaction between hydrogen and oxygen.

Chiu refined chemical reactions by adding a pivotal case (see Chapter 3; Linn, 2005). The pivotal case compared the visualization with no spark to the visualization with a spark that added energy (see Figure 8.4). Without the spark, students saw molecules moving but no change in the bonds represented in the visualization. Bonds did not break and did not get reformed. In the comparison condition, with a spark shaped sort of like a lightning bolt, bond-breaking and bond-formation occurred. As students observed the visualization, they started to notice that after they added the spark, the reaction sped up, and the level of kinetic energy also increased. Students clearly appreciate that this is a controlled experiment: The only difference between the two conditions is the addition of the spark. Furthermore, they can create a narrative—or tell a story—about what happens if there is no spark, and what happens when a spark is added. In addition, comparing the situation with-and-without the spark provokes dialogue between students and spurs them to connect the visualization to the video of the balloon explosion. Students conjecture a variety of different explanations concerning the role of the spark. For example, some students think that the spark directly leads to the increase in kinetic energy, and others argue that it takes some time for the spark to start the reaction and for the reaction to produce increases in kinetic energy. By adding this pivotal case that focuses on the role of energy in the chemical reaction, Chiu was able to refine the instruction and help students understand both the symbolic equation and the visualization.

In summary, consistent with results in the chapter on Experimentation, instruction benefits from implementing the KI pattern as well as reducing complexity of the visualizations and adjusting for learners' initial ideas (Casperson & Linn, 2006; Chiu & Linn, 2008; Zhang & Linn, 2008). Chiu (2010) eliminated most of the complexity of the Molecular Workbench visualization. She added eliciting ideas, distinguishing ideas, and reflecting to ensure that precollege students could interpret how oxygen and hydrogen interact to form water.

Distinguishing Ideas

A series of experiments conducted by Helen Zhang (Zhang, 2010; Zhang & Linn, 2008) illustrate several ways to help students distinguish ideas. Zhang studied molecular workbench visualizations of chemical reactions in the context of a project where students explore the benefits of hydrogen fuel cells over gasoline to power cars.

Zhang developed a KI assessment that asked students to draw the state of the chemical reaction before it started, when it has just started, after it had been going for some time, and when it was completed. For many students the chemical formula tells the whole story. They neglect bond breaking and formation and believe that relationships represented on one side of the equation instantaneously change into the configuration represented on the other side of the equation. These students left the middle two drawings blank and only represented the beginning and end condition. Some students show that the reaction starts with all the atoms separated from each other. Other students drew intermediate states and final states that were not accurate. Some showed all the molecules breaking into atoms and then forming one gigantic molecule. Others showed all molecules following a common path, rather than some bonds breaking and some being formed.

To help students distinguish these ideas from the normative ideas represented in the visualization, Zhang asked them to draw their ideas during instruction. In her first study, Zhang compared a drawing condition with the exploration condition where students had the opportunity to perform more experiments with the visualization. It was difficult to get students to spend as much time experimenting with the visualization as they spent drawing. Zhang found that the drawing condition was significantly more successful than the exploration condition (Zhang & Linn, 2008).

Zhang wondered why the drawing condition was successful. Was generation necessary or was the main issue distinguishing among ideas? To test this question she compared drawing to selection. In selection, students were given possible drawings, created by identifying the most common incorrect drawings that students create. Students were asked to select among drawings to show the sequence that would occur during the chemical reaction.

In her first selection study, Zhang gave students a small set of drawings. She found that students were quite good at recognizing the order in which drawings should occur. They could do many more selection tasks than drawing tasks in the allotted time. However, the selection activity was not as successful as drawing. The outcome measure required students to draw chemical reactions and to explain chemical reactions. Students were more successful when they were assigned to the drawing condition.

The drawing task helps students to distinguish accurate from inaccurate ideas. When students are asked to link the symbolic equation to their drawings, they revisit their ideas about the symbolic equation. They can determine that the intermediate states are not represented in the symbolic equation.

Analyzing performance on drawing led Zhang to realize that the selection task in the first study was very easy. She extended the research program by increasing the difficulty of the selection task. In the hard selection condition, she offered 16 choices, forcing students to carefully discriminate among the possibilities. The time required for hard selection and drawing turned out to be quite similar. The performance of students in these two conditions was quite similar. These results suggest that the importance of the drawing task is that it guides students to discriminate among ideas. When students have to select from many drawings they analyze nuances. Students have to analyze intermediate states where bonds have been broken, but new bonds have not yet been formed and decide which representations are most accurate.

Zhang also found that for students who started with few ideas about intermediate states in chemical reactions, drawing remained more successful than selection. For these students selecting among the drawings is somewhat random because they lack criteria for deciding among them. Going back to the visualization could help them develop criteria but they might not do this when confronted with choices for selection. This finding is clarified by examining specific student responses. Often students who benefit from drawing but not selection have no ideas about the intermediate states. For students who leave the intermediate boxes blank, the drawing condition is more helpful than the selection condition.

These studies show that drawing or selecting from a large number of alternatives that represent intermediate conditions helps most students distinguish their ideas about bond breaking and bond formation. These tasks motivate students to distinguish among intermediate conditions and revisit the visualization. Consistent with findings for deceptive clarity, studies where researchers log how students interact with the visualizations show that when students are asked to represent intermediate states, they frequently go back to the visualization and run it again to figure out what is happening.

In many research studies, generation is more successful in promoting distinguishing ideas than selection. Thus this series of studies about chemical reactions is particularly important. The studies show that when students have the choice of selecting among a large set of alternatives, the selection task and the drawing task are similar for students who have some preliminary ideas. In both generation and selection, the goal for students is to discriminate among a large space of alternatives. In contrast, when students were given a smaller set of alternatives, selection was less effective than generation. The selection tasks do not tap as broad a range of understandings as are tapped in generation tasks, thereby making generation tasks more effective for the full range of learners.

Understanding of the Validity of Visualizations

Successful interpretation of visualizations requires understanding of the validity of the evidence presented in the visualization (Hofer & Pintrich, 2002). Sophisticated users need to consider the compromises that the designers made in order to create the visualization. To help students interpret the validity of visualizations, many instructors discuss the nature of simulations, modeling, and visualizations. Mazzei (2008; see Box 7.1) modified a unit on evolution to strengthen student understanding of the limitations and strengths of models. Students gained understanding of evolution as well as of the nature of science.

Visualizations and the KI Pattern

These studies of curriculum refinement show the value of implementing the KI pattern. Embedding visualizations in instruction designed using the KI pattern not only strengthens the impact of the visualization, but also enhances the overall goal of KI, as illustrated for experiments in Chapter 7.

Adding Ideas

The studies reported above show how visualizations can add ideas to make complex scientific thinking visible. As discussed above, visualizations are most likely to succeed with these features:

- Illustrate fundamental, dynamic information that students need
- Provide pivotal cases or comparisons to reduce confusions
- Be comprehensible to the audience
- Support interactions about central dimensions of the topic
- Allow learners to test personal conjectures
- Provide evidence that learners can use for constructing arguments.

Adding new ideas using visualization is not sufficient to ensure that students can understand the ideas or that they will distinguish them from their other ideas. For example, deceptive clarity can deter students from integrating the new ideas.

Eliciting Ideas

As reported for lectures and experiments, eliciting ideas in the form of predictions or brainstorms leads to improved outcomes (Crouch & Mazur, 2001; Linn & Hsi, 2000). For visualizations, predictions are especially useful in focusing students on the salient information.

Often ideas elicited prior to using a visualization need to be augmented by ideas that arise when observing the visualization. In chemical reactions, when students have the opportunity to view the visualization and generate ideas, they are spurred to generate their ideas about what happens between the initial and final state.

Eliciting ideas also helps teachers gain insight into the ideas that students bring to the situation and the challenges that they face in trying to understand the visualization. By using predictions teachers discovered that textbooks reinforce the instantaneous view of chemical reactions by emphasizing chemical formulas (Zhang, 2010). Teachers were surprised by these student interpretations of visualizations as well as by students who regularly anthropomorphized the reactions, talking about molecules wanting to separate their atoms and atoms wanting to find other elements in order to form reactions (Ben-Zvi et al., 1987).

Distinguishing Among Ideas

Helping students distinguish among their ideas contributes to the success of visualizations as it does for experiments (e.g., McElhaney, 2010). To distinguish among ideas, students need to generate criteria and to recognize the value of scientific evidence in determining which ideas are most productive. Many comparison studies show that students do not spontaneously distinguish among ideas. They need guidance to recognize that one idea is not the same as another. As discussed above, several practices including generating explanations, critiquing ideas of peers, and drawing ideas have promise.

Explanations

Chiu (2010) showed, in her study of deceptive clarity, described above, that explanation led students to identify gaps in their knowledge while just observing the visualization convinced them they already understood. Subsequent analysis of logs of student activities revealed that when answering explanation questions, students often returned to the visualization to study it in greater depth. When asked to explain, students detected gaps in their knowledge and sought additional information to distinguish among ideas. Generating an explanation also led students to monitor their own learning more effectively.

Critique

When students critique views of others, they are motivated to think about why one idea might take precedence over another. The value of critique was illustrated in the Chang et al. (2008) study described above and in the Zhang & Linn (2010) study. Asking students to analyze the reasoning of a hypothetical student in their class motivated them to examine their own reasoning.

Chang found that students made considerable progress in understanding thermodynamics in both the experimentation and critique conditions. Looking more closely, she found that on experiment questions, the two groups performed equally, but on critique questions, the critique group was more successful than the experiment group. Students developed better criteria for evaluating experiments by doing both experiments and critiques than when only experimenting. She concluded that combining experimenting and critiquing was more effective for helping students distinguish among their ideas than using either one alone.

Zhang (2010) also found that critique helps students distinguish among ideas, Zhang found that critique was as successful as drawing and selection for improving performance on the hydrogen fuel cell car project. Critique has some of the same characteristics as selection in that the respondent needs criteria to distinguish between their own response and the ideas presented in the response to be critiqued.

In summary, studies of explanation, drawing, selection, and critique illustrate ways to help students use evidence from visualizations to distinguish among ideas. They motivate students to consider the ideas in the visualization carefully, often returning to the visualization to clarify how interactions occur.

Sorting Out Ideas

Ultimately, the KI pattern has the goal of helping students sort out their ideas and develop a more coherent understanding of the topic that they are investigating. When sorting out ideas, students have an opportunity to grapple with various types of evidence, including evidence from visualizations and evidence from empirical studies. They have the opportunity to review the visualization to prepare their argument, making it easier to include nuanced information from the visualization. They can extend the visualization to naturally-occurring, personally-relevant problems that are not necessarily obvious when just working with the visualization.

For example, to help students sort out their ideas about the connections between chemical reactions and global climate, Chiu included an activity in chemical reactions where students wrote letters to policymakers. In these letters, students combined the scientific information they gathered with their understanding of global climate change to create a coherent argument. Chiu found that these letters were coherent and informative. Students benefitted from the opportunity to organize their ideas into a compelling narrative. And many members of Congress responded.

In summary, combining all of the processes in the KI pattern—eliciting ideas, adding ideas, distinguishing ideas, and sorting out ideas—has the potential to make visualizations effective. Visualizations add ideas and help students to elicit all of their ideas by prompting students to consider more alternatives. The other KI processes are also necessary to promote coherent understanding.

Conclusions

In conclusion, although there is controversy about the value of visualizations for science learning, the real question concerns how to take advantage of visualizations to add value to instruction. Research shows that visualizations have the potential to improve outcomes from science instruction when they are well-designed, align with student knowledge, and illustrate dynamic aspects of science. Curriculum materials that take advantage of the KI pattern enhance their value.

Effective designs require trial and refinement to achieve their full potential. Part of the refinement process involves matching the visualization to the audience. Students with high prior knowledge of the discipline learn from dynamic visualizations that extend their insights while those with low prior knowledge need to start with visualizations matched to their level of understanding. In addition, students with high spatial reasoning skills benefit from dynamic visualizations and students low in spatial reasoning need visualizations matched to their skills. This pattern of findings demonstrates the complexity of creating effective materials. All students benefit from instruction that develops their ability to monitor their own progress.

The research on visualizations provides insight into patterns and principles to guide future designers. A major benefit of scientific visualizations is to add new ideas to the mix held by students. As we have seen in extensive research (Chapter 2), adding new ideas, whether it is in a visualization, lecture, text, or other source of information, is not sufficient to impart integrated understanding. These and related studies show that visualizations embedded in inquiry activities have a broad and general impact on student understanding (Linn et al., 2006).

Visualization and Desirable Difficulties

To improve coherent understanding researchers have identified ways to guide students to attempt more detailed and systematic analysis of their ideas. A number of activities (explaining, drawing interactions, and critiquing) showed promise for helping students to distinguish among ideas and develop coherent understanding. For example, in eliciting explanations, students are asked to distinguish between alternative ideas and to provide evidence to support their assertions (Chiu, 2006; McElhaney, 2010).

To interpret results for activities that help students distinguish their ideas (Linn, Chang, Chiu, Zhang, & McElhaney, 2010) explored the role of desirable difficulties. Research on desirable difficulties (Bjork 1994, 1999) addresses the gaps in understanding revealed by the findings for deceptive clarity. Bjork (1994) argued that students benefit from certain difficult activities that generally slow down or prolong learning by increasing errors. Ultimately resolving these errors by self-initiated study leads to better understanding.

Bjork studied desirable difficulties in the context of memory. For memory research involving recall of paired items or lists of items, desirable difficulties involve things like interspersing irrelevant tasks or asking students to generate responses on practice trials rather than study presented items. These activities result in more errors during learning and lead to improved recall of the items. Richland, Linn, and Bjork (2007) showed that desirable difficulties could be effective for complex tasks such as learning science concepts.

For science learning, the tasks are more complicated and the outcome measures are more difficult to achieve. For these tasks, generating explanations or drawings, selecting from numerous alternatives, and critiquing experiments are potential desirable difficulties. They increase errors compared to activities such as conducting experiments. Rather than refining connections, these activities seem to focus students on distinguishing among ideas.

These studies support the value of distinguishing ideas as a method for promoting coherent understanding. Students more precisely distinguish ideas when they experiment, draw, select, or critique. When students engage in a series of activities designed to help them distinguish ideas about a complex topic, they are more successful than when they experiment with or observe visualizations.

In summary, research findings offer guidance to designers incorporating visualizations. Visualizations may offer a deceptively clear account of a scientific phenomenon or confuse learners who interpret them in unintended ways. Using the KI pattern overcomes these obstacles and can also help students develop strategies for taking advantage of future visualizations.

Reflection Activity

Identify an interactive visualization (model, simulation) that helped you or your students understand a science topic. Identify how the activity that included the visualization implemented the KI pattern. Discuss how it (a) elicited ideas, (b) added ideas, (c) enabled participants to distinguish ideas, and (d) encouraged reflection. Discuss whether or not users of the visualization experienced deceptive clarity.

9

COLLABORATION FOR KNOWLEDGE INTEGRATION

Introduction

Collaborative skills such as communication, respect for others, and ability to appreciate the roles of one's collaborators are central to the 21st-century workplace (Hilton & NRC, 2010; NRC, 2010; Nuffield Foundation & University of York, 2006; Snyder et al., 1999). These skills can be developed when students collaborate on complex science topics in classrooms. Many describe advantages for collaborative learning (e.g., Brown & Campione, 1994; Burbules & Linn, 1988; Cohen, 1994; Johnson & Johnson, 1999; Linn & Hsi, 2000; Scardamalia & Bereiter, 2006; Slavin, 1990). These include learning from others, achieving integrated understanding, learning to jointly solve problems, developing ability to monitor progress, and autonomous learning. Collaborative activities help students appreciate the ideas of others, learn how to negotiate meaning, take advantage of distributed expertise, become effective teachers, evaluate arguments, and develop community-wide criteria. Collaborative activities make the diverse ideas of students visible. They can give participants insight into culturally distinct views and encourage them to integrate these ideas.

This chapter provides examples of effective collaborative activities such as debates, design of innovations, and construction of arguments that both develop collaborative skills and increase understanding of science. We illustrate how the KI patterns can make collaboration among diverse students effective and discuss issues that need resolution for these activities to succeed.

Foundations of Collaborative Learning

Historically, theorists including Dewey (1901), Vygotsky (1978), Piaget (1970a), and Bruner (1962) have argued for the importance of learning from others.

Dewey argued that all learning is social, pointing out that even when individuals appear to be solitary learners, they often have inner dialogues and benefit from considering the perceived views of others. Vygotsky described the zone of proximal development, explaining that a more able collaborator could spur a student to achieve beyond their capability when working alone. Vygotsky pointed out that the social supports and hints provided by collaborators could provide a learning environment that might be internalized to foster future and increased understanding.

Ideas about the zone of proximal development contributed to the emergence of constructivism as a framework for design of instruction. Papert (1968) stressed that individuals jointly construct meaning with guidance such as critique and suggestions from other participants. Papert and his collaborators (diSessa, 2000; Kafai et al., 2009; Wilensky & Rand, in press) argued for using environments such as Logo to promote design of artifacts that implemented the ideas of the group (see also Chapter 8).

Collaborative activities where individuals have diverse forms of expertise provide multiple zones of proximal development. Each participant can simultaneously provide supports in their area of expertise and benefit from the supports provided by others with complementary expertise. KI is a form of constructivism that has been refined based on longitudinal study of students learning complex science concepts (Linn & Hsi, 2000). The emphasis on the repertoire of ideas in KI takes advantage of the varied cultural ideas of the participants in a collaborative group. Incorporating the diverse, often culturally embedded, ideas of participants in a collaborative group requires sensitivity and respect for others, skills that have substantial value in an increasingly multicultural society.

Features of Collaborative Learning

Collaboration is particularly effective for complex, controversial topics, such at topics in science, where weighing evidence from multiple sources is essential and culturally motivated ideas are useful. For example, when students study global climate change, genetically modified foods, or alternative sources of energy they need to weigh evidence, evaluate sources, recognize conflicts of interest, and resolve disagreements. Successful collaboration involves ability to appreciate the views of others, monitor ones' own progress, communicate successfully, learn from others, and evaluate the emerging views of the group. To succeed groups need to take advantage of multiple forms of expertise. They have the opportunity to agree on the criteria they apply to potential sources of evidence.

We define collaboration as occurring when two or more individuals are engaged in a learning activity. Of more importance, we argue that in order for collaboration to succeed, participants must communicate with each other, seek feedback from each other, and jointly approach a problem, situation, challenge, or dilemma. Successful collaborations require respect for all the participants, appreciation of the roles played by each participant including oneself, and ability to help others contribute and succeed.

The role of guiding or supporting other participants is unique to the collaborative situation. Developing the ability to help others learn (and as a result to test one's own understanding) is typically neglected in school. In addition, as we have shown, much of science education involves knowledge transmission so it is at least likely that participants in collaborative groups might emulate knowledge-telling practices and simply assume their peers will absorb their ideas without communicating the process of KI.

In this chapter, we focus on the collaborative activities that inevitably arise when students are using computers in typical school settings where the number of computers is usually fewer than the number of participants. We identify promising ways to guide students to work with peers to negotiate solutions to complex problems. We discuss how collaboration can improve understanding of science topics. This chapter explores ways to make opportunities for collaboration successful and productive.

Absorption and Collaborative Learning

Collaborative activities are not guaranteed to promote integrated understanding. Often, students inform their peers rather than negotiating meaning. Many times collaboration stops at the point of brainstorming rather than implementing the whole KI pattern. Brainstorming elicits ideas but does not ensure that the most effective ideas are selected. Participants may express their ideas but ignore the ideas of others and neglect the process of distinguishing ideas. Unguided collaboration where students express ideas but do not learn how to select among them may lead students to endorse non-normative ideas. If students were to vote on many science principles without instruction they would get them wrong. Students need criteria to select the most promising ideas.

Some collaborative activities are included in instructional situations primarily to motivate participation. These activities take advantage of students' interest in interacting with peers and expressing their ideas. The popularity of social networking opportunities including customer ratings of products or books, Facebook groups, photo sharing sites, blogging, and online repositories of recipes all attest to the interest people have in sharing their ideas and keeping up with the views of others. In these cases collaborative activities implement a pattern that could be called *motivate, assess*.

KI and Collaborative Learning

Collaboration is a central part of KI. One of the principles associated with KI is to encourage students to learn from each other (see Chapter 5). When students learn from each other, they gain insights from their efforts to teach others as well as from the insights that they acquire from their peers. Students benefit from the feedback and questions they receive while teaching others. When peers indicate what they do, and do not, understand, the student who is communicating gets valuable feedback. Another principle, making thinking visible, stresses the advantages when diverse learners make their ideas visible so others can build on them. The KI patterns have helped designers create effective collaborative activities (Bell, 2004a; Hoadley, 2004; Seethaler & Linn, 2004; Shear, Bell, & Linn, 2004; Svihla, 2010). Each of the KI processes contributes to effective collaborative learning. Most collaborative activities involve eliciting ideas or brainstorming (e.g., Hoadley, Hsi, & Berman, 1995). Many studies emphasize adding ideas in collaborative activities by using seeded discussions (e.g., Hoadley, 2004), jigsaws (Aronson, 2002), or distributed expertise (Brown et al., 1993; Hutchins, 2001). Distinguishing ideas in collaborative groups is supported by debate activities (Bell, 2004a), argument construction (Clark, D'Angelo, & Menekse, 2009; Erduran, Simon, & Osborne, 2004; Sampson & Clark, 2009; Zohar & Nemet, 2002), and collaboration software such as Knowledge Forum (Scardamalia & Bereiter, 2006), CaMILE (Guzdial, Turns, Rappin, & Carlson, 1995), or WISE (Hoadley, 2004). Reflection on the insights gained from collaborative learning is often best accomplished when students write individual notes, reports, or journals to integrate the insights from their collaborative experiences (Bell, 2004a; Clark, Varma, McElhaney, & Chiu, 2008).

In this chapter we highlight ways that the KI patterns can guide and shape collaborative activities. We distinguish productive and ineffective collaborative experiences. We illustrate how online learning environments can support effective uses of collaboration.

Assessing Collaborative Outcomes

Assessments of collaborative activities reveal the goals of instructional designers. Many studies assess how students learn from each other and how they interact in the group. Studies generally evaluate progress in understanding the science being studied and the quality of final products. Products of collaboration that require contributions of all participants include plans to reduce suffering from asthma, design of an environment-friendly fuel, a computer model of planetary motion, or a poster communicating the fate of an endangered species. These outcomes could be assessed using the KI rubric or another set of criteria that reward activities reflecting productive collaboration (see Box 9.1).

When researchers investigate interactions in collaborative groups they find that the dynamics of each group differ. Some groups succeed and others fail (Barron, 2003). Chi and her colleagues (Jeong & Chi, 2007) found that few groups created new ideas that built on the ideas of others in relatively short collaborative activities. But, most groups benefitted from the need to explain their thinking to their peers. Sampson and Clark (2011), studied how students select, access, and use ideas to collaboratively formulate an explanation for discrepant events. For example, they code: (1) the number of unique ideas introduced into the conversation, (2) how individuals responded to these ideas, (3) how often individuals challenged ideas when discussing them, (4) the criteria individuals used to distinguish between ideas, and (5) how group members used the available corpus of data. This and other studies looking at the interactions in small groups report that progress is uneven across groups (e.g., Hoadley, 2004).

BOX 9.1 KI ASSESSMENT ASTHMA
Design and assessment of the TELS Asthma unit

Questions

- **Oxygen Inhalation**—*Kris is breathing normally. Explain how oxygen (O_2) gets to cells in her body.* This item assesses how students make connections between the structures, functions, and behaviors of the respiratory and circulatory systems as they describe the trajectory of O_2 in the body.
- **Carbon Dioxide Exhalation**—*Explain how her body gets rid of carbon dioxide (CO_2).* This item assesses how students make connections between the structures, functions, and behaviors of the respiratory and circulatory systems as they describe the trajectory of CO_2 as it is removed from the body.
- **Asthma Attack**—*Joe is having an asthma attack. It is hard for him to breathe. What is happening in Joe's body that makes it hard to breathe?* This item assesses students' ability to identify the physiological asthma symptoms (e.g., inflammation of the airways) and causally link them to the narrowing of airways or the restriction of airflow.
- **Allergic Immune Response**—*Juan is allergic to pollen. It causes him to have asthma attacks. Explain how pollen causes Juan's asthma attack.* This item assesses how students understand the allergic immune response (allergic reaction) as the causal physiological mechanism for asthma attacks caused by allergens, particles that people are allergic to.
- **Allergen/Irritant Difference**—*Do allergens and irritants cause an asthma attack in the same way? Explain your answer.* This item assesses whether students distinguished how irritants and allergen affect the body on a physiological level.

See accompanying Knowledge Integration Scoring Rubric.

Score	Oxygen (O_2) Inhalation Item	Carbon Dioxide (CO_2) Exhalation Item	Asthma Attack Item	Allergic Immune Response Item	Allergen/Irritant Difference Item
0 No Answer **1 Irrelevant** **2 No KI**	She breathes oxygen in.	The body gets rid of carbon dioxide by breathing out through the mouth and nose.	There could be many factors such as his asthma is strong and he didn't have his inhaler. The air is very polluted and he just completed a vigorous workout.	The pollen clogs the nose so Juan doesn't get enough air.	Allergens clog your airways and irritants just irritate them.
3 Partial KI incomplete connections	Oxygen enters through the mouth and nose, which travels down the windpipe and fills the lungs	The body exhales the air where it comes out from the lungs up the trachea and out the mouth.	What's causing Joe to not get enough air is his bronchial tube are swelling up and get tighter.	When pollen is breathed in by Juan, it goes down the trachea and into the airways of his lungs, which would trigger an allergic reaction and irritate the passageway.	No. An irritant irritates the airways. An allergen causes an allergic reaction.
4 Full KI 1 complete connection	Air goes in through your mouth then down the windpipe and finally gets in branches in your lungs	Blood cells bring CO_2 back and it is exhaled.	His airpipes are involuntarily contracting, hence not letting air pass through... Joes bronchial tubes are going into what's called "bronchioconstriction," where the tubes become inflamed and mucusy, and the muscles in the tubes tighten. This results in a smaller space in which air can pass.	Histamines are released and that causes his airways to constrict and cause an asthma attack. When pollen comes into Juan's body, Juan's antibodies attack & produce histamines as a product. Histamines cause the reaction that lead to asthma attacks.	Irritants – initiate when they reach the lungs. allergens – make histamines that initiate the symptoms of asthma. Allergens activate antibodies which trigger the asthma attacks. Irritants directly cause the attacks by attaching to the wall of the bronchi.
5 Complex KI 2 or more complete connections	Oxygen enters through the mouth/nose travels into the lungs, goes through the air passageways and comes to the little sacs at the end of each passageway, alveoli. Inside the sacs, oxygen is transferred to red blood cells in the capillaries to be transported to the rest of your body.	Carbon dioxide leaves the body by going through the capillaries into alveoli into air passage ways and out the lungs.			

FIGURE 9.1.1 Assessment rubric

Many research projects assess the development of collaborative and workplace skills such as listening to others, communicating effectively, and making useful contributions. One approach is to have participants rate each other and themselves on their collaborative practices (Hackbert, 2004). This exercise can be used to assess self-monitoring by comparing the ratings of peers to self-ratings.

Assessing the respect participants have for others often requires subtle methods. Respondents generally self-report that they are respectful. Observations of collaborative interactions may not reveal stereotypes. And, impacts on respect for diversity may be gradual. One useful approach is to measure implicit stereotyping (Banaji, Hardin, & Rothman, 1993).

Assigning valid grades for collaborative productions is difficult because teachers cannot monitor all the activities that contribute to a final product. Usually classes have both individual and group outcome measures. Students worry that their contributions are underappreciated. Parents often complain that their students have been unfairly graded in collaborative projects. Some parents question the value of collaboration, arguing that teachers (not students) should instruct other students. Although there is considerable evidence that those who teach others also learn, parents do not always see teaching peers as beneficial. Instructors often respond by grading collaborative activities but keeping the points for the activity low. By reducing the total amount of points for collaborative activities instructors reduce the impact of unequal participation but miss the chance to emphasize the quality of the collaborative activity.

Managing Collaborative Learning

Managing collaborative investigations to achieve KI requires establishing norms, designing or selecting effective activities, modeling promising ways to work with others, grouping students so they can help each other learn, and implementing valid means for assessing individual as well as group products (Cohen, 1994; Saxe, 1999). Teachers often complain that establishing effective norms for collaboration is difficult because students have extensive experience with less productive collaborative activities. In addition, stereotypes about who can succeed in science may influence how students respond to peers (Burbules & Linn, 1988; Linn & Hsi, 2000).

Instructors need to find ways to encourage individuals in the classroom to display respect for each other, deal with stereotyped expectations about participants, remain on task, and communicate effectively to the other participants. Helping students not only monitor their own learning but also appreciate the roles of others in the group is important and difficult. Instructors need to ensure that participation is reasonably even and that projects have challenging goals and scope.

Grouping students who have the potential to work together is part of managing collaboration. Considerable research on grouping strategies suggests that, under most circumstances, heterogeneous groups are more successful than homogeneous groups, consistent with research on the zone of proximal development. For example, Dunbar (1999) worked with industry groups and found that better results were achieved when the members of the group came from different backgrounds, or different laboratories, than when they shared the same history. Chiu (2010) carried out a study involving grouping students who have similar and dissimilar pretest scores. She found that students with dissimilar pretest scores were more successful with collaboration in a WISE project. She documented that the collaboration among heterogeneous pairs was helpful for both parties, but especially for the underachieving individual. Grouping students who both have low scores appeared to be less successful that heterogeneous pairs, in part, because both students struggled to make sense of the material in the unit.

The responsibilities for implementing collaborative activities increase the complexity of teaching inquiry science. When using computer inquiry environments teachers typically have students working in groups of two or three. Designers have added features to environments such as WISE that guide students to respect each other and help students provide hints rather than engaging in knowledge transmission. For example, WISE discussions include prompts that guide students to explain how they reach conclusions so that they can model their use of evidence for others. They also allow students to make anonymous comments, to encourage participation. Creating prompts to support self-monitoring has also been a feature of several environments (Davis & Linn, 2000; Scardamalia & Bereiter, 1999). Implementing the KI pattern in environments such as WISE has the potential of improving collaborative activities.

Establishing Classroom Norms

Managing a classroom when students are working in pairs or small groups is ultimately rewarding, but can be difficult before students have developed effective norms for interaction and teachers have implemented successful activity structures associated with collaborative learning. When teachers implement collaborative activities for the first time, they frequently find that students have not developed a culture of respect for the contributions of their peers. Students may be unaccustomed to engaging in science talk. In addition, students frequently engage in what teachers regard as off-task behavior but what students undoubtedly believe is important social talk. In addition, when implementing classroom interactions and collaborative learning for the first time, teachers frequently report uneven participation in groups, with certain students telling others the answers, doing the work, or dominating others. All of these issues contribute to the uneven results across groups reported in many studies (Barron, 2003; Sampson & Clark, 2011). Teachers need to establish classroom norms that reward respect for others, illustrate the nature of science talk, encourage guiding rather than transmitting knowledge, and increase the likelihood that students will voice their opinions and concerns. Teachers need to translate these norms into criteria for assessment.

For instance, when projects are carried out by teams, teachers can specify which aspects of the assessment will be based on collaborative artifacts and which on individual ones.

Student beliefs about learning can thwart participation in collaborative groups. For example, students may not respect individuals who are different from them, or students may look on collaborative activities as opportunities to take a minimalist approach to learning. In addition, students may have difficulty determining when a collaborative activity will benefit from planning and review by the group and when it is good to divide the task into pieces and assign a part to each member. These aspects of collaboration need, at least initially, guidance from the teacher. To make collaboration successful, teacher activities, student activities, assessment, and curriculum need to be aligned and supportive of the participants.

Educational systems such as the Japanese system that emphasizes collaboration starting in preschool (Lewis, 1995; Linn, Lewis, Tsuchida, & Songer, 2000) establish procedures for collaborative learning that make it easy for teachers to implement this approach. From the earliest grades, students work in groups of four called hans, often break into pairs and then report back to their groups of four, and typically report back to the class. In Japan, classes are of size 40, and as soon as the class size of 40 is exceeded, a new class is formed.

In the Japanese system, students develop respect for the ideas of their peers early on and learn ways to negotiate meaning that help others understand complex topics. Students articulate their ideas and disagree with each other. Groups are rewarded for the accomplishments of their group *as well as for individual accomplishments*. Group success becomes an important expectation for all students starting in the early grades.

Implementing a collaborative culture in US classrooms is difficult because only some classes or topics emphasize it. When collaboration is not a common practice, teachers who desire to establish the skills or expectations for collaborative learning have to overcome alternative expectations. Several programs have studied the value of implementing a collaborative approach across grade levels and found considerable value for consistent practices and expectations from year to year in precollege settings (Lewis, 1995; Schaps, 2003; Schaps, Battistich, & Solomon, 2004). As discussed below, researchers have also worked with teachers to set up classrooms that succeed (Brown & Campione, 1994; Scardamalia & Bereiter, 1999; Watson & Ecken, 2003).

Many programs have investigated methods for developing norms and classroom practices to deal with groups of varying sizes. Linn and Hsi (2000) compared two-person groups to larger groups and reported that two person groups reduce the likelihood of uneven participation, take advantage of small computer screens by allowing both participants to be able to see the screen, and mean that there is no audience for putdowns or insults. For larger groups, research on scripting discussed below shows that implementing roles for participants is a common practice but can fail (Fischer & Mandl, 2005).

One important issue in establishing classroom norms concerns the propensity of students to hold stereotypes, expecting individuals different from themselves to make smaller contributions or have other weaknesses in a collaborative setting. In addition, students may believe that certain cultural groups are more likely to succeed in science and accord special status to, for example, white males. Teachers and students need to monitor for stereotyped behavior and clearly indicate that such behavior is unacceptable.

For example, Agogino and Linn (1992), report on an engineering capstone design course, where students worked in groups of four. Agogino asked groups to record their collaborative experiences after each group meeting to monitor progress. Agogino, in reviewing the comments, discovered a group where the individuals had very different perceptions of the contributions of their peers. The three men reported that the woman was not contributing while the woman reported that the men were not listening to her ideas. Documentation of group progress supported the viewpoint of the lone female. Fortunately, the instructor was able to intervene and get the group back on track, but not before relatively strong negative opinions had been expressed by the male members of the group concerning the female participant.

Another factor that has caused teachers to worry about collaborative learning concerns the possibility that the group will embrace a non-normative or suboptimal solution. One form of this phenomenon has been labeled groupthink (Janis, 1971). Groupthink involves a whole group endorsing non-normative ideas based on partial evidence for their value or lack of serious consideration of alternatives. Often a strong member of a group can reinforce an idea, such as the notion that heat and temperature are the same, and inhibit the ability of the group to reason about the question. Groupthink has arisen historically when experts inhibit their concerns about alternatives to reach consensus. This phenomenon led to the failure to anticipate Pearl Harbor and the failure to assess the risks in the Bay of Pigs according to Janis (1971). The KI principle of eliciting all ideas reduces the likelihood of groupthink as does the requirement that groups distinguish among alternatives rather than only finding support for their preferred view.

To overcome tendencies towards groupthink, teachers need to monitor group progress, encourage peer review, and establish evidentiary norms. In classrooms it helps for instructors to be aware of common beliefs students might have based on, for example, colloquial evidence or everyday observations and make sure these are compared to alternative ideas. As noted in Chapter 3, students might reasonably assume that heat and temperature is the same thing because the terms are used interchangeably in some utterances such as "turn up the heat" or "turn up the temperature." When students study, for example, insulation and conduction, it is essential to distinguish between heat and temperature in order to understand the rate of heat flow. Thus, activities exploring insulation can help learners appreciate the difference between the terms. As this example illustrates, instructors need to be diligent about identifying the different kinds of ideas that students might have and monitoring group interactions to be sure that groups are not falling into a groupthink approach and supporting non-normative ideas.

In summary, collaborative learning is almost inevitable in technology-enhanced learning. It has the potential to contribute to KI while also developing valuable workplace skills. Making collaborative opportunities succeed requires establishing supportive classroom norms, developing assessments aligned with the learning goals, and careful design of the collaborative activities. Collaborative activities can be inefficient, difficult to evaluate, and more useful for some learners than others. This chapter focuses on the potential of KI patterns to guide design of successful instruction featuring collaboration. Collaborative groups can augment and strengthen the effectiveness of classroom learning and instruction. To succeed, collaborative groups need supports from teachers and curriculum.

In this chapter we argue that collaboration is an important aspect of lifelong learning. We seek ways to ensure that students develop the capability of contributing to a group and of monitoring their own progress while participating in a group.

Impact of Collaborative Learning

Researchers have developed more and more precise understanding of the impact of collaborative learning. Studies that contrasted collaboration with similar instruction, which did not include collaboration, have shown that collaboration led to greater understanding but did not isolate the factors contributing to the success (e.g., Cohen, 1994; Cooper, Cox, Nammouz, Case, & Stevens, 2008; Johnson & Johnson, 1999; Slavin, 1990). Studies that included collaboration as part of science inquiry show advantages for inquiry in combination with other activities (Blumenfeld, Fishman, Krajcik, Marx, & Soloway, 2000; Tabak & Reiser, 1997). Studies of the KI framework show that collaborative learning contributes to the success of instruction (Davis & Linn, 2000; Gerard, Tate, Chiu, Corliss, & Linn, 2009; Linn, Davis, & Bell, 2004; Linn, Lee, Tinker, Husic, & Chiu, 2006). Several research directions help clarify the outcomes of collaboration and some of the elements that contribute to success.

Scripting Collaboration

To isolate the successful aspects of collaborating researchers have used scripting where participants are directly guided to assume specific roles and make comments in an online environment. Scripted interactions include supposed features of collaboration. Scripting, however, may inhibit generation of culturally motivated ideas and constrain interactions.

For example, Kollar, Fischer, and Slotta (2007) created explicit scripts for participants in a collaborative activity, including roles for each participant. Scripted groups had greater respect for each other than unscripted groups but had equal learning outcomes. Weinberger et al. (2007a, 2007b) compared macro-scripting that orchestrated classroom activities with micro-scripting that orchestrated individual contributions. They found that micro-scripting in the form of roles, turn-taking, and prompts for critique was not particularly effective. Students had difficulty complying with the scripting recommendations. They found that macro-scripting to orchestrate classroom activities and organize phases of lessons into sequences improved throughput of lessons but did not change student learning outcomes (Kollar, Fischer, & Slotta, 2005). Scripting roles can fail if students are assigned roles they cannot perform. Assignment of roles that do not take advantage of the expertise of the individuals obviates the advantages of having more expert students mentor others. Determining roles for participants that allow students to help each other such as coordinating the group, recording data, or monitoring equipment requires that students have the skills to perform the roles as well as the credibility of their peers. Scripting studies show that efforts to make conditions equivalent inhibit spontaneous efforts of students to develop or take advantage of their own expertise. Scripting may also reduce generation of culturally unique contributions, another potential advantage of collaboration.

Refinement of Classroom Culture

Several research groups have developed classroom cultures and supportive uses of technology to help students identify their own roles and to take advantage of culturally unique ideas. The Fostering Communities of Learners (FCL) project established classrooms where students collaboratively investigated complex topics and supported each other (Brown & Campione, 1990, 1994). One promising student practice designed to create distributed expertise was to assign subgroups responsibility for portions of a book, or concept and then to teach peers that aspect of the domain. To elicit culturally valuable ideas, teachers used practices such as cross-talk where responsibility for selecting the next participant in a discussion was held by the students. Teachers also modeled the collaborative process and guided students to monitor their own progress. The FCL program demonstrated impact by describing the products students create when they collaborate, as well as individual understandings of the domain under investigation (Brown & Campione, 1990, 1994).

Knowledge building classrooms take advantage of software such as Knowledge Forum to create community repositories of knowledge (Scardamalia & Bereiter, 2006). Scardamalia and Bereiter describe the sophisticated discourse that successful groups use to build the community knowledge base. For example, students might contribute an idea and recognize that they need to find evidence to support their view so the audience can use it. They are guided by prompts in the Knowledge Forum software that ask them to elaborate on their contributions.

Encouraging students to analyze and build on ideas from peers can motivate students to develop criteria for the information they encounter and to recognize gaps in their understanding (Scardamalia & Bereiter, 1994).

Research to create collaborative classroom cultures has identified promising practices. Classes using the practices have produced sophisticated classroom artifacts including reports, repositories of knowledge, and designs. Demonstrating the long-term benefits of these activities remains an important research topic.

Analyzing Collaborative Interactions

Analyses of collaborative interactions clarify when and how these activities help students learn. Several research groups have identified the conditions under which students co-construct new ideas (Fischer & Mandl, 2005; Jeong & Chi, 2007; Teasley, 1997). These studies show that starting with divergent knowledge is advantageous but that the benefits of collaboration are uneven. They illustrate the benefit of scripts that scaffold students to contrast their ideas.

Clark (Clark & Jorde, 2004) and his colleagues analyzed interactions in collaborative groups charged with explaining why an ice cube on a metal block melts faster than one on a plastic block. All groups had lists of alternative ideas to consider as well as opportunities to learn the normative ideas. Clark found that the groups who came up with stronger arguments also considered more ideas, discussed new ideas when they were proposed, challenged ideas more often, and engaged in critique more regularly. Thus, the successful groups compared to the unsuccessful groups both generated more ideas on their own and considered more of the ideas in the list of alternative explanations that they could use as part of instruction. Considering more ideas to start with means that the successful groups engaged in more comprehensive efforts to integrate ideas. All the groups gained insights from the same instructional materials. The successful groups discussed new ideas as they came up while the unproductive groups often ignored ideas. In addition, to distinguish ideas the successful groups used challenges and critiques. The use of challenges and critiques can be seen as guiding students who might prefer these ideas to look at them with a more critical eye. The guidance can be seen as moving students through their zone of proximal development to achieve more sophisticated understanding.

Thus, careful analysis of student interactions in collaborative groups shows that successful groups, compared to unsuccessful groups, generated and considered more alternatives. They also show that successful groups benefit from guidance that engages them in considering each others' ideas. Furthermore, the analysis clarifies how students might learn from others by responding to challenges or critiques. It also shows how students might become more able to monitor their own learning by developing the ability to recognize reasons to challenge or critique ideas. These findings help focus the analysis of other studies where the specific interactions are not analyzed.

Collaboration for Inquiry

Several research programs study how students learn from each other when doing inquiry projects (Bell & Linn, 2000; Clark & Sampson, 2007, 2008; deVries, Lund, & Baker, 2002; Hoadley, 2004; Osborne, Erduran, & Simon, 2004; Sandoval & Reiser, 2004; Songer, 1996). Consistent with the Clark analysis of collaborative interactions, inquiry projects endeavor to engage students in generating many ideas, including ideas that reflect their cultural experiences. They also pose questions that require critique and analysis to distinguish ideas. To take advantage of the varied ideas that students have including unique ideas based on their cultural experiences many collaborative activities feature debate, creating a group artifact, and constructing an argument (Linn, Clark, & Slotta, 2003; Slotta & Linn, 2009). Debates can highlight ideas and connect them to an argument in ways that might otherwise be missed. When students jointly create an artifact like a design they advocate for their own perspective and develop joint standards (Bransford et al., 1999). Encouraging students to generate all of their diverse ideas and respond to the ideas of others can elicit stereotyped comments and even marginalize comments from some students. Classroom norms that encourage students to listen and learn from others and take advantage of the collective knowledge in the classroom community can ameliorate stereotyped comments.

To facilitate collaborative inquiry learning, technology-enhanced environments use scaffolding as discussed in the experimentation chapter. Software like WISE can add elements from the KI pattern. Technologies include clickers, where students can vote on a particular idea in a classroom, tools to automatically group students based on their responses, group discussion tools, and peer review tools. These tools are often embedded in learning environments such as WISE. Researchers have designed and refined a variety of software for collaboration (e.g., Dori, Barak, & Adir, 2003; Hoadley, Hsi, & Berman, 1995; Linn & Hsi, 2000; Sadler, Barab, & Scott, 2007; Suthers & Hundhausen, 2001).

Debate

Many approaches have been studied to help students compare alternatives and develop criteria for their viewpoints. For example, Bell (2004a) studied debate practices in classrooms. These debates concerned the question: "How far does light go?" Students debated the normative view that light goes forever until it is absorbed and a visual acuity view, that light dies out. The visual acuity view is supported by the observation that a light source becomes dimmer as you move further from the source. Bell explored what he called partial scope and full scope debate activities. In partial scope, students were allowed to support their own viewpoint or were assigned a viewpoint to support. In a full scope debate students prepare for a discussion on either side of the question and are assigned one as the debate starts. Bell found that students were better able to articulate criteria for distinguishing among viewpoints in the full scope condition than they were when they prepared to support a single point of view, independent of whether that view was their own or was assigned. Thus, Bell showed that it is important for students to distinguish among alternative views in order to develop criteria and advance their understanding (Bell, 2004a).

Collaborative Construction of Principles

Clark and colleagues (Clark & Sampson, 2008; Sampson & Clark, 2007) have devised an explanation-oriented argumentation tool that takes advantage of collaborative contributions and they have tested it in the context of thermodynamics. Argumentation involves constructing a scientific explanation by gathering and interpreting data, using the evidence to justify an explanation, and critiquing alternative views. Argumentation gives students both understanding of the science topic, and appreciation of the nature of scientific discourse. In this approach students create and refine principles to explain their understanding of phenomena, such as thermal equilibrium. Students use drop-down menus to construct these principles so they are also interpretable by WISE. The software can create collaborative groups with different viewpoints, based on these principles. Once groups have been formed, then the participants comment on each other's viewpoints and jointly negotiate a common principle to explain the situation.

In research studies, Clark contrasted ways to compose the groups and tasks that the groups might perform, testing the best ways to stimulate productive argumentation. Like Chiu (2010) and Bell (2004a), he found that heterogeneous groups learned more than homogeneous groups. He contrasted groups that critiqued ideas from peers in the group with groups that critiqued a comprehensive set of viewpoints generated by the experimenters from the work of prior students (Clark & Sampson, 2008; Sampson & Clark, 2007). Clark found that it was more valuable for students to resolve a dispute among the comprehensive explanations than to negotiate about their own explanations. Students learned more and solved the problem more efficiently when they negotiated among views that spanned the full range of perspectives. Students reached effective conclusions and were able to maintain that understanding for subsequent problems. This finding demonstrates the importance of helping students integrate all the ideas they hold. In most groups, comprehensive comments were more effective in spurring students to construct a robust principle than were the set of ideas from the diverse participants assigned to the group.

This work supports the KI principle to design instruction where students can learn from each other since participants use evidence to support the diverse explanations (see Chapter 5). It also demonstrates that the instructional pattern of first generating ideas (in the principles), then adding ideas (in the comprehensive comments or peer comments), then distinguishing ideas (by comparing and contrasting the ideas), and then sorting out the ideas (in constructing a new principle) is effective. This example clearly differentiates distinguishing ideas where students use evidence to contrast their ideas and sorting out ideas where students construct a principle that reflects all of their contributions.

Seeded Discussions

To improve the KI potential of a discussion, designers have experimented with seeding discussions with ideas to ensure that students consider the full range of views. This is consistent with the value of experimenter-selected ideas over peer ideas in the Clark argumentation study (Sampson & Clark, 2007). Sources of ideas include ideas that other students have generated, ideas selected by the instructor, or ideas from experts. The design of the seeded comments is important. If seeded comments are attributed to a cognitive guide or another student they may be ignored by other participants. When ideas are attributed to an expert, students might simply accept the expert views without any real understanding of those views.

Hoadley (2004) studied ways to strengthen student learning by seeding an online argumentation activity. Using WISE, Hoadley overcame the limitations of attributing ideas to an expert by featuring two scientists who held differing views. He seeded a discussion with ideas about light attributed to Newton and Kepler. He motivated respect for the scientists by placing their views in historical context and providing accessible evidence for each perspective. Hoadley contrasted the expert-attributed ideas with guide-attributed ideas where all comments were attributed to a fictional character. The expert-attributed comments were more compelling to students and by seeding the discussion with conflicting ideas, Hoadley was able to advance KI. The opportunity for students to observe how experts might use evidence to respond to each other served as a model of effective argumentation strategies. Since all the ideas on both sides of the argument were attributed to the guide, it was difficult to appreciate the argumentation in the guide condition.

The discussion entries attributed to Newton and Kepler illustrate how discussion participants can support their viewpoint, provide evidence for their views, and respond to the evidence provided by others. In this research, the scientists do not change their views. They do encourage participants in the discussion to revise their ideas by using the information added. Modeling the process of changing ideas due to new evidence could also be accomplished, for example, by seeding a discussion with a character whose ideas change. This research shows the range of ways that designers can use seed comments. These comments do not have a very strong impact on learners by themselves, just as we found for other efforts to add ideas.

Bell also found that debate was not sufficient to motivate KI. Students often added ideas from debate but did not reconcile alternatives. Adding a reflection activity after the debate increased the impact of the debate, consistent with the KI framework (Bell, 2004a).

Peer Evaluation and Feedbacks

When students explain their thoughts to other students, they can clarify their own thinking as well as serve as a tutor (Sandoval & Reiser, 2004). Students can help their peers understand an idea by articulating concepts using familiar vocabulary and relevant examples (e.g., Songer, 1996). Researchers have studied the process of automating peer evaluation. CeLS (Collaborative, e-Learning Structure, http://www.mycels.net) enables instructors to construct online structured collaborative activities, including peer-evaluation. CeLS automatically gathers and analyzes information submitted by students and displays it in various customizable forms. A peer evaluation activity designed in CeLS can include statistical analysis, a histogram, and a collection of student justifications for their decisions (presented anonymously). Kali and Ronen (2005) used a peer-evaluation activity designed with CELS in a philosophy of education course. Undergraduate students constructed a conceptual model of their "ideal school" and developed more sophisticated epistemologies, as a result of using the peer evaluation process. In this example, students got new ideas from their peers and integrated them in the next version of their project.

Another example of technology support that encourages learners to learn from others is the eStep system (Derry, Seymour, Steinkuehler, Lee, & Siegel, 2004; Hmelo-Silver, Derry, Woods, DelMarcelle, & Chernobilsky, 2005). In eStep learners read and view a case study that presents a classroom dilemma. They individually reflect on the dilemma and propose an initial solution. Then they collaborate with other learners to collectively arrive at a revised solution. The lesson ends with individual critiques of the group solution, and reflection on the learning, collaboration, lesson design, and usefulness of the solution to their own professional practice. Derry et al. (2004) report that eStep produced significant increases in teachers' abilities to think deeply about student understanding. The course was more effective at producing transfer than a traditional lecture-based approach covering the same material.

As reported in the chapter on lectures, researchers investigating collaboration in classes, using student response systems such as clickers, can assign students to heterogeneous groups. These studies were not able to show an advantage for collaboration compared to making predictions without collaboration but instructors and students thought the collaboration was valuable (Crouch & Mazur, 2001).

These studies illustrate ways to support inquiry that includes collaboration. Collaboration can strengthen the process of eliciting ideas and increase the mix of ideas considered in KI. Collaborative inquiry activities can take advantage of the ideas students develop in unique cultural experiences or deliberate undertakings. Eliciting these ideas in a group activity increases the repertoire of ideas that a group considers.

Well-designed curricula can help learners guide their peers to interpret these ideas, appreciate their origins, and develop criteria for distinguishing among possible explanations. When students critique ideas they model the process of distinguishing ideas for others and may allow students who are collaborating with them to advance their own understanding.

Collaboration and Patterns

Incorporating collaboration into science cases can succeed when the instructional pattern is followed. To illustrate how collaboration can contribute to each of the processes within the instructional pattern, we discuss these processes and provide examples of projects or activities to illustrate each process (see Box 9.2, Box 9.3, Box 8.2, and Box 9.4).

BOX 9.2 FORMULA IN PHYSICS
Collaborative learning for linking mathematics and physics understanding

A partnership of physics teachers and science educators sought to strengthen links between the interpretation of symbols, units, conditions of applicability, and special cases using collaborative learning about formulas in physics. They designed an activity following the knowledge integration instructional pattern that involves individual and group activities (Bagno, Berger, & Eylon, 2008).

1. Individual work: *Elicit ideas*

Consider the formula: $x = x_0 + v_0 t + \frac{1}{2}at^2$

Using physics terms, write the meaning of each component of the formula (including units):

Component	Meaning in Physics	Units
v_0	Initial velocity (at time 0)	m/sec

  a) Show that the units on the right side of the formula are identical to the units on its left side.
  b) Describe the conditions under which the formula can be applied.
  c) Describe the relationship between the components of the formula either by a graph or by a drawing.
  d) Using the following table, analyze special/boundary cases for the formula (for example, one of the components is zero).

The special case	The form of the formula in this case	The meaning of the formula in this case
$a = 0$	$x = x_0 + v_0 t$	Formula for position of object at any time moving with constant velocity v_0

Write down, using your own words, the meaning of the formula.
Sample response: The formula expresses the position of an object at any time, starting with a specific initial velocity and moving at constant acceleration.

2. Group collaboration: *Add ideas and distinguish ideas*
Discuss with your group mates each of the questions in the individual work. Negotiate a common answer.

3. Class discussion and refinement of ideas. *Reflect on ideas*
Compare the approaches of each group. Develop a class-wide solution.

4. Individual reflection on homework assignment. *Reflect on ideas*
Reflection on physics:
   a) Does this formula make sense to you? Why (or why not)?
   b) Describe an everyday scenario or a physics problem in which the formula applies.
   c) Describe a special case of the above scenario or the everyday physics problem
   d) What change do you have to make in the everyday scenario or problem so that the formula no longer applies?

Reflection on learning:
   a) What did you learn from the activity?
   b) What did the group discussion add to your understanding?
   c) What did the class discussion add to your understanding?
   d) What is still unclear to you?

Results

The unit was implemented as designed by 9 teachers and 260 students. The group collaboration and guided discussion increased normative connections between mathematics and physics (see Figure 9.2.1). Teacher comments:

Eliciting ideas: *"There are always students who prefer to be passive and wait till their peers would answer the question. The individual worksheets forced each of them to answer the questions by him/her and not hide behind somebody else."*

Collaboration: According to the teachers, the **group phase** had an enormous contribution to the improvement of their students' learning. *"In the group work the students exchanged knowledge; each learned and contributed something new to his or her peers."* *"When a student works by himself he has only his own point of view, but when he listens to others, he becomes aware to other points of view."*

Reflection: *"While reflecting on their work, the students became more aware of their understanding; they had to go over all what they had learned and to decide what they realize what they really understood and what still required review."*

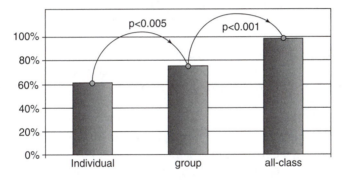

FIGURE 9.2.1 Learning outcomes

Elicit Ideas

Collaborating to elicit ideas means that groups typically come up with a larger repertoire of ideas than when they work alone. Culturally motivated ideas are more likely to arise in large diverse groups. Individuals often spur others to generate ideas by mentioning their own insights. Students might recall or find words to express ideas they had not considered. To ensure that students feel free to contribute all of their ideas, participants should not criticize ideas during the eliciting ideas activity.

Nevertheless, a danger when groups generate ideas together is that some students might be inhibited by the ideas or reactions of others. An effective procedure is to balance group and individual generation of ideas by first having individuals note their own ideas. Students can add more ideas after they hear the views of

BOX 9.3 ASTHMA TEACHERS' GUIDE
Design of the Asthma teachers' guide

To support teachers' enactment of the Asthma unit, the design team, comprised of education, science, and community partners, developed the online Teacher's Guide (Gerard, Tate, Chiu, Corliss, & Linn, 2009). Teachers collaborated to create resources for their peers.

Teaching resources

A repository for teachers' print materials such as evidence organizer worksheets, lab instructions, and scoring rubrics.

Pedagogical resources

Teachers' descriptions of normative explanations for the topic and common alternative ideas students' hold. For example, teachers contributed these comments:

"The unit teaches three physiological symptoms of an asthma attack—airway inflammation, mucus production, and bronchial muscle constriction. Students often focus on the ideas that oxygen is restricted from entering the body. The unit also points out that carbon dioxide is restricted from exiting the body." (Teacher 1)

"Making the Best Decision: The Supporting Your Decision step is a good point to stop the class and have a discussion. Often students are at different points in the unit, so it may be best to review this page at the beginning of a class session." (Teacher 2)

Customization suggestions

To help their peers customize instruction effectively, teachers came up with several versions of the debate activity and the critique activity and recorded their discussions.

Debate activity

First version. The first Teacher's Guide offered worksheets students could use to plan for the debate and options to help teachers facilitate the activity. Teachers struggled to appropriately scaffold students to participate in the highly interactive debate and were frustrated when unsubstantiated arguments went unquestioned.

Revisions. In year two, three teachers revised the Guide to include tips based on successful implementation of the debate. One teacher's revisions included adding more structure, clarifying presentation types (e.g., opening statement, rebuttal, response, and closing statement), setting time limits, and adding work periods where students come together to plan for their next presentation. The new debate format was added to the online Teacher's Guide and three new teachers implemented it.

Critique activity

The Teacher's Guide presented a basic set of instructions to guide teachers' implementation of this peer critique activity. Teachers added alternatives and distinguished their ideas.

Knowledge integration alternative: One teacher designed an introductory activity where she elicited students' ideas about what "critique" meant to them and helped students develop class criteria for critique. To scaffold the critique process, she asked the class to apply the criteria to a composite response she constructed from past student work.

Absorption alternative: Another teacher created a PowerPoint presentation to explain rubrics and introduce a rating system.

Teachers had evidence from their courses that the absorption option would not succeed but also worried that the knowledge integration option would lead to many critiques of spelling and grammar. One teacher suggested modifying the project to add a critique activity where students first criticized spelling and grammar and then criticized the scientific argument. The teachers also reflected on their own grading criteria and noted that they often gave rather general feedback rather than specific guidance for improving the outcomes. Several teachers decided to use the same distinction between spelling and science ideas in their own feedback.

Spontaneous student cross talk was limited so that students thoughtfully used their evidence to support their arguments and counter arguments. In addition, this teacher created planning worksheets and scoring rubrics for students and for teacher grading of student contributions following the knowledge integration framework.

their peers. This has been used successfully in the Multimedia Forum Kiosk (Linn & Hsi, 2000) and in gated discussions.

Gated discussion has proven effective in computer science (Clancy et al., 2003). Titterton et al. (2010) used this approach for generating ideas to solve computer programming problems such as *Tower of Hanoi*. In a gated discussion, individuals first enter their own ideas about a complex problem. Once they contribute, they

BOX 9.4 COLLABORATIVE DIAGNOSIS OF CONCEPTIONS
Collaborative diagnosis of conceptions for geometrical optics

Collaborative Diagnosis of Conceptions (CDC) implements the KI pattern. It has been studied in the context of geometric optics (Eldar, Eylon, & Ronen, in press).

1) **To elicit ideas,** learners are asked to generate their ideas about a task.

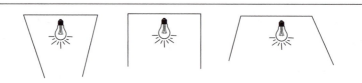

Three light bulbs are surrounded by different lampshades. Describe the light propagation for each case (draw and explain your drawing).

FIGURE 9.4.1 Eliciting ideas

Sample responses:

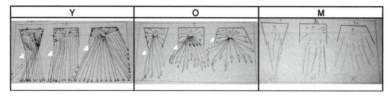

FIGURE 9.4.2 Sample student responses

2) **To add and distinguish ideas** collaborators:

(a) Discuss differences in solutions and develop criteria to characterize the features of the responses. Often students expected the three lampshades to have the same effect. Teacher guidance was needed to distinguish alternatives. Teachers asked questions such as: *Does the direction of the light rays change when the rays encounter an obstacle?*

(b) Negotiate a common solution by discussing the evidence for their own ideas and considering the evidence of their peers. Students often carry out experiments, run simulations, and ask for teacher help. The teacher asked students guiding questions such as: *what is similar and different between your answers?*

3) **To sort out ideas** collaborators:

   (a) Reflect on the activity and reorganize their thoughts about the content. They clarify what they have learned.
   (b) Share their reflections with the class and comment on reflections of others using the CeLS (Collaborative, e-Learning Structure) (http://www.mycels.net) environment.

Sample Responses:
I learned something new: that light is scattered to a large area and that it is not only near the barrier.

   How light is scattered and how to convince other learners to choose the right answer.

   I liked the group work because we gathered different views and we helped each other.

Comparison study

A study compared using the CDC approach alone in a course on geometrical optics for elementary science teachers to augmenting the learning with KI professional development activities. In the KI version, teachers wrote a blog about their ideas about the discipline and their pedagogy (*Eliciting ideas about pedagogy*). They read the blog entries of the other teachers (*Adding new ideas*). They compared pedagogical alternatives and developed criteria in a facilitated discussion (*Distinguishing ideas*). They participated in small-group discussions of student work to understand how the pedagogy could contribute to student learning. They examined specific examples of student work and developed ways to customize the instruction for students (*Reflect and sort out ideas*).

   The posttest included qualitative tasks (eliciting ideas) diagnostic tasks (see geometric optics example in Figure 9.4.1), and application tasks:

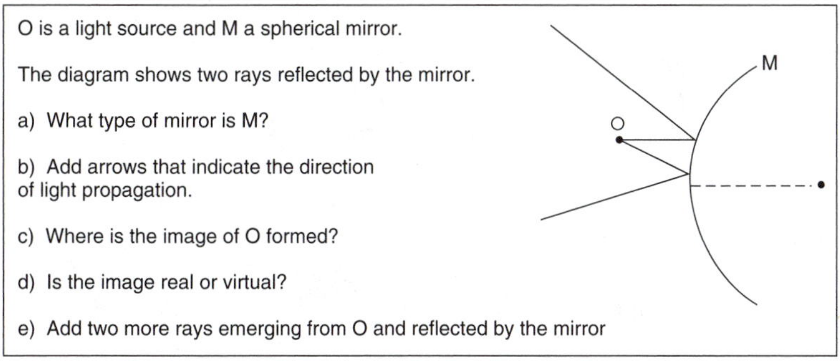

O is a light source and M a spherical mirror.

The diagram shows two rays reflected by the mirror.

a) What type of mirror is M?

b) Add arrows that indicate the direction of light propagation.

c) Where is the image of O formed?

d) Is the image real or virtual?

e) Add two more rays emerging from O and reflected by the mirror

FIGURE 9.4.3 Application task

All teachers achieved acceptable levels of understanding of the science:

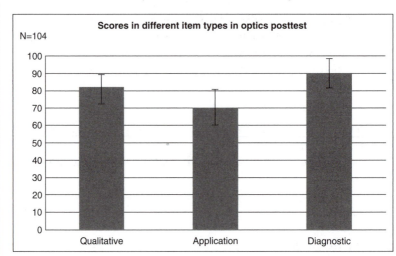

FIGURE 9.4.4 Scoring

The results indicated significant advantages of the KI professional development activities for teachers' pedagogical knowledge (see Table Teacher Learning). Both groups of teachers learned the geometric optics content from the course but only those who specifically participated in activities intended to integrate their ideas were able to develop sophisticated ideas about pedagogy.

TABLE 9.4.1 Teacher Learning: teacher performance on content and pedagogy

Version	Achievement mean (standard deviation)	
	Content	Pedagogy
CDC Alone	89.0 (7.2)	32 (15)
CDC + KI Professional Development	81.9 (13.7)	75 (20)
Kruskal–Wallis	$\chi^2{}_1 = 1.45$ (NS)	$\chi^2{}_1 = 7$ p < 0.005

Source: Eldar, O., Eylon, B.-S., & Ronen, M. (in press). A Metacognitive Teaching Strategy for Pre-service Teachers: Collaborative Diagnosis of Conceptual Understanding in Science. In A. Zohar & Y. J. Dori (Eds.), *Metacognition and Science Education: Trends in Current Research*. London, UK: Springer-Verlag.

As Bell (2004a) reported, students need the opportunity to reflect to fully benefit from debate activities and can achieve this by writing a report. Tate (2009) shows that when students debate and then create a poster advocating for their position, they benefit more than when they do not construct a poster.

Reflection activities can develop students' ability to communicate to new audiences. When individuals are motivated to explain their ideas to others in a coherent and cohesive way, they have the chance to think about their varied ideas and consolidate them. In several WISE activities, including chemical reactions and the asthma project (see Box 9.3), individuals communicate to policy makers, such as Congress or city councils or health professionals, advocating for their point of view. Reflection activities are advantageous because they reinforce the communication skills that are valuable for 21st-century tasks and will serve students well in future collaborative activities.

In summary, collaborative opportunities can strengthen all four of the processes in the KI pattern. Collaborative activities motivate students to explain their ideas to others and add culturally unique ideas to the mix. They provide an opportunity for students to guide each other and therefore move students along in their zone of proximal development. The heterogeneity of student ideas in a collaborative setting can help students make sense of their own ideas and even enable students to articulate ideas that might otherwise go unnoticed and unexamined. Collaborative opportunities can support the process of negotiating meaning, although this is not a straightforward or guaranteed outcome of collaborative work. Rather, effort is needed to ensure that groups generate all the relevant ideas, negotiate meaning, use valid evidence, develop criteria for distinguishing ideas, and reconcile diverse views.

Conclusions

Collaboration occurs in most technology-enhanced learning programs. It can benefit both teachers and students. Implementing collaborative activities in classrooms, however, is neither straightforward nor guaranteed to succeed.

New technologies offer advantages. They can document the process of collaboration for multiple groups in a classroom. Collaborative discussion tools can scaffold interactions, keep track of contributions in a repository, and encourage students to use evidence to support their views.

Collaboration is beneficial for eliciting ideas. Students generate a larger repertoire of ideas when they collaborate than when they work alone. New technologies such as instant messaging, chat, and Twitter increase opportunities to elicit ideas from friends.

Collaborative activities can be implemented in a well-designed learning environment. By implementing the KI pattern, a learning environment can guide students to take advantage of the ideas of their peers and to also focus on integrating and coordinating their views.

can view the ideas of other students and add more ideas. After eliciting ideas, participants might critique ideas, respond to comments on their ideas, and add new ideas that combine their own solutions with the ideas they gained from observing the work of others.

In classroom implementations of gated discussions, a somewhat unanticipated finding was that students were genuinely surprised about the multitude of different possible approaches taken by their peers (Linn, Bell, & Davis, 2004). This finding supports the value of eliciting ideas and comparing alternative views.

Clickers are also used to elicit ideas. To take advantage of eliciting ideas, instructors could start with a brainstorm and then ask students to vote on the generated list. When instructors use lists of ideas supplied by textbook publishers they may neglect some of the ideas held by class members.

In summary, collaborative groups can help each other elicit ideas. Technology can support effective practices such as allowing students to make their own contributions before permitting them to see the ideas of their peers.

Add Ideas

Collaborative groups can develop a large set of ideas. They still may need new ideas to achieve KI. They may need normative ideas such as insights into molecular kinetic theory. The may also need pivotal cases to help them distinguish among alternatives. The seeded discussions outlined above are one way to add ideas. Peers can add ideas in the group work and share ideas in class discussion to integrate scientific and mathematical ideas (see Box 9.2).

Individuals can add new ideas that extend the zone of proximal development of their peers. This could occur when a student suggests a structure a peer could use to clarify some ideas. For example, to contrast the metal and plastic in the ice melting experiment, a student might suggest using insulation and conduction to explain the result. Peers can help make scientifically normative ideas accessible by explaining how they have used the ideas or translating the ideas into more accessible vocabulary. For example, to explain why ice melts faster on a metal block, a student remarked that insulators block heat, like a cooler (Clark & Sampson, 2008). This example makes the concept of insulation more accessible by connecting to a typical experience.

Another way that collaboration can add new ideas is when participants ask questions. Research suggests that those who ask questions and those who answer questions both benefit from collaboration (Webb & Palincsar, 1996). Unanswered questions are frustrating for participants and could be answered by someone monitoring the collaboration. In addition, if students just tell students the correct answer the situation devolves to a lecture. To help students become effective tutors teachers can encourage individuals to specialize in a topic and to develop pivotal cases to explain their area of expertise to others.

Technologies to support adding ideas include repositories and discussion tools. Repositories store ideas in a database. Organizing the database for easy access and revision is valuable.

Thus, collaborative discussions can add ideas when individuals describe their ideas to others. Participants help their peers clarify their ideas. Seeded discussions and teacher-monitored discussions using a repository can ensure that normative ideas are available to groups. Preparing students to tutor others by developing expertise and generating effective examples could enhance outcomes. Scaffolding and guidance can help, but the most important issue is ensuring that participants consider multiple alternative viewpoints and are required to reconcile these viewpoints into a well-supported common argument.

Distinguish Alternatives

Activities that require students to distinguish alternative views take advantage of the variety of views that students generate. When students advocate for their own ideas they get feedback from their peers on the adequacy of their argument. When students point out weaknesses in the ideas of others they can extend the zone of proximal development for their peers. Thus, distinguishing alternatives can give students insight into monitoring their own understanding.

To synthesize and coalesce the many alternatives they generate, students need to negotiate meaning and construct a common understanding (Fischer & Mandl, 2005; Jeong & Chi, 2007). Guiding social interactions promotes knowledge construction as does teacher mentored online discussion (Scardamalia, Bereiter, Hewitt, & Webb, 1996; Weinberger, Stegmann, & Fischer, 2007; see also Box 9.3). Creating groups with differing views often leads to productive discussions, consistent with findings contrasting heterogeneous groups with homogeneous groups (Chiu, 2010; Clark & Sampson, 2008). The CDC strategy (see Box 9.4) is designed to promote such interactions but enabling students to negotiate qualitative understanding.

To achieve synthesis, students need to negotiate a single set of criteria for distinguishing among ideas. When student have distinct criteria they can support conflicting views. For example, if some students base their decisions about heat flow on the way objects feel and others base their decisions on the reading of a thermometer, they may reach distinct conclusions. Furthermore, if consensus is not reached, students may believe that intuitive but wrong ideas are accurate because they were not refuted. Thus part of supporting collaboration is supporting the negotiation of criteria for distinguishing among ideas.

Critique activities help students develop criteria for distinguishing ideas. To establish class norms, an expert teacher, Mr. K., created a class activity that involved critiquing a fictitious report created to illustrate the arguments made by small groups. The students critiqued the report and developed criteria for using scientific evidence to warrant assertions (Linn & Hsi, 2000). They posted the class

activities for all to use. Similarly, studies have shown that critique questions help students develop criteria for distinguishing among ideas in discussions and enable them to be more active critics in the future (Chang et al., 2008; Chiu & Linn, 2008).

Efforts to scaffold argumentation have mixed impact. Effective software can provide guidance for argumentation by structuring ideas, similar to the benefits of structuring discussed for experimentation. For example Sensemaker (Bell, 1997), the Multimedia Forum Kiosk and SpeakEasy (Hoadley, Hsi, & Berman, 1995), as well as charts and graphs (Baker & Lund, 1997) support structuring.

Fischer and his collaborators have found benefits for scripting social interactions versus no scripting (Fischer & Mandl, 2005). Systems like Belvedere that guide individuals to provide warrants for their assertions and evaluate their arguments reveal the difficulty students have linking and connecting ideas with evidence (Lesgold, 1984). Often more generic guidance to use evidence or identify gaps in reasoning aligns better with students' comprehension of construction of an argument (Davis, 2004a). The findings of Tate concerning the asthma debate (see Box 9.3) and of Chiu concerning chemical reactions (see Box 8.2) illustrate the progress students make when encouraged to use evidence in arguments. In both cases, students needed opportunities to develop criteria, and support for the process of distinguishing ideas.

In summary, distinguishing among ideas and identifying those that are most promising is important for cumulative, integrated understanding of science. Students need guidance but can learn to monitor their own understanding when distinguishing and integrating ideas. Scaffolding the process of distinguishing ideas needs to align with the capabilities of the students. Students often seek confirmatory evidence rather than negotiating meaning. Although negotiating meaning has been a central tenet of constructivism from the beginning, evidence for programs that have large-scale benefits for developing the ability to negotiate meaning is scarce.

Reflection

Reflecting on personal understanding after collaborating to construct meaning consolidates ideas and engages students in explaining their own viewpoint. It guides students to monitor their progress and identify gaps as found for spontaneous explanations during learning (Chi, de Leeuw, Chiu, & LaVancher, 199; Linn & Hsi, 2000). Reflection requires students not only to pay attention to t evidence that they reviewed, but also to organize that evidence into a coher argument. Ultimately this is an autonomous process that can instill a feelin agency.

Reflection encourages students to incorporate the perspectives of their into their own framework. Many different techniques can be used to mo reflection.

Learning environments can prompt students to use evidence to support their claims. When students are required to back their assertions with evidence they often recognize the weakness of their arguments, gaps in their understanding, or their inability to distinguish their own views from those articulated by others.

Learning environments have the opportunity of extending collaboration beyond the classroom. They can support home users and connect students who are geographically diverse. A broad community can contribute a rich range of ideas to the learning setting. This was particularly evident in the asthma case study, where teachers implementing the project in diverse contexts developed patterns for instruction relative to their geographical area.

The KI framework can support successful collaborations in the classroom and in the design of curriculum. The chemical reaction unit illustrates how the collaborative opportunities can help students develop integrated understanding of complex science. The collaboration around the online teacher's guide for the Asthma unit illustrates how teachers can build on their past practices, incorporate customizations made by their peers, and reuse effective materials. The support for evidence-based customization and professional development illustrates how communities of teachers can create curricular revisions that result in improved student understanding.

These collaborative experiences succeed in part because of the alignment of the curriculum, assessment, and professional development with the KI framework. Using a common framework for all of these activities makes sure that every aspect of the instructional setting contributes to KI, and that teachers and students implement effective practices that support each other. For example, when students respond to embedded assessment activities or contribute to discussions, they provide teachers with evidence for how KI is progressing and enable teachers to modify instruction to benefit student learning.

Evidence from a broad range of research suggests that the instructional patterns add value to collaborative experiences. Combining the patterns and new technologies amplifies the impact of collaboration on teacher and student learning.

Reflection Activity

Describe either (a) a time when you collaborated to design science instruction or (b) a collaboration among students that you observed. Analyze the pattern of interaction that arose. Discuss how the KI pattern could have improved the outcome.

10

PROFESSIONAL DEVELOPMENT FOR KNOWLEDGE INTEGRATION

Introduction

The chapters on experimentation, lecturing, collaboration, and visualization suggest that teaching inquiry according to KI patterns can improve learning outcomes. In this chapter we discuss ways to align instruction and professional development to enhance learning outcomes. We contrast typical professional development informed by the absorption approach with professional development that is informed by a KI perspective.

Professional development for inquiry teaching is especially important in the U.S. because of the deep entrenchment of the absorption approach in our current educational system (from curriculum design to every level of instruction). Strauss (2005) argues that most people have intuitive views of teaching as transmitting knowledge and of learners as absorbing information. This can lead teachers to be skeptical of inquiry teaching, particularly as they have most likely engaged primarily in absorption-based models of learning and instruction themselves.

This chapter discusses professional development that takes advantage of technology-enhanced inquiry environments such as WISE. It addresses the challenges of teaching with technology such as managing small groups and taking advantage of embedded assessments. Previous chapters show the value of technology-enhanced units that guide learners to use hands-on materials, virtual experiments, visualizations, and collaboration.

Technology-enhanced materials such as WISE provide evidence for teachers in the form of embedded assessments of student work. This evidence supports more nuanced exchanges between teachers and students. Evidence from student work allows teachers to adapt their instructional strategies and customize curriculum materials to improve their practice (Davis & Varma, 2008; Eylon, Berger, &

Bagno, 2008; Slotta, 2004; Slotta & Linn, 2009). When teachers customize technology-enhanced units, they create a curriculum tailored to their students (Gerard, Spitulnik, & Linn, 2010). Teachers can use evidence to customize instruction in three time frames: during class, from day-to-day, and between enactments. Such technology environments also provide evidence for professional development, in the form of teacher's online comments to students. These comments inform our understanding of how teachers use such environments.

We describe the results from recent research on professional development, contrasting two projects that align instruction, assessment, and professional development using the KI approach. The Technology-Enhanced Learning in Science (TELS) center and the Mentored and Online Development of Educational Leaders in Science (MODELS) project differ in the depth of interactions with teachers. These programs engaged teachers for three or more years in the process of customizing their instruction to include elements of inquiry and technology. The projects linked professional development to student learning outcomes by using embedded assessments, end of unit tests, and annual assessments.

Absorption and Professional Development

A common approach to professional development in science follows the *motivate, inform, assess* pattern of instruction. In this approach a motivational presentation is combined with lectures on a science topic, often delivered by a well-known scientist.

Motivation can indeed reinvigorate teachers. One of the authors (Linn) had the honor of introducing Nobel Laureate Glenn Seaborg at a professional development event held at the Lawrence Hall of Science. Teachers came from great distances to attend. After the lecture they clamored to have their photograph taken with Dr. Seaborg and assured him that they would discuss the lecture with their students next day in class. While exciting, these experiences are not sufficient to change teaching and learning (Borko, 2004; Gerard et al., 2010; Little, 2003).

A second popular approach to professional development engages teachers in enacting the activities that they will then use subsequently with their own students (Borko, 2004; Ford & Wargo, 2007; Rogers et al., 2007; Supovitz & Turner, 2000). This approach implements the *motivate, interact, assess* pattern (Chapter 2) and aligns with instruction that follows the same pattern.

Starting in the 1960s, NSF sponsored summer institutes that engaged teachers in this practice of participating as students. These institutes, developed with government funding, served as dissemination opportunities. They alerted teachers to the materials, often supplemented disciplinary knowledge, and, most importantly, developed a community of teachers who led local workshops and continued to support each other for years to come. One of our collaborators (Mr. K., see Chapter 3) participated in such workshops during the 1960s, and continued to work with teachers he met at those workshops throughout his career. These teachers, with support from the curriculum publishers, spread the word about the new materials and supported each other to develop skills for teaching programs such as the Science Curriculum Improvement Study. NSF institutes show the value of intensive, long-term programs for building community.

Many programs continue the tradition of dissemination through workshops. Some provide summer laboratory research experiences for teachers (i.e., where teachers work alongside bench scientists in research laboratories). Others provide workshops that involve using new curriculum materials and learning new disciplinary knowledge. These programs augment teacher salaries, build communities, and build morale. They most certainly motivate teachers to remain in the field.

Assessment of the impact of such professional development often consists of surveys about satisfaction or self-report of impacts. However, these results—even when favorable—do not necessarily translate into improved teaching and learning (Borko, 2004; Supovitz & Turner, 2000). We still need to find solutions that change teacher practice and have impact on student learning.

Studies showing the impact of professional development on student learning are extremely rare (Davis, Petish & Smithey, 2006; Gerard et al., 2010). Even teachers who explicitly report on the importance of introducing changes into their practice (e.g., taking into account the repertoire of students' ideas, or teaching by inquiry) often do not align their teaching with these claims. Hence, it is not surprising that most successful professional development programs fail to impact students' learning.

Assessing Impacts of Professional Development

Aligning assessments of professional development with the instruction including goals for student outcomes is important but rare (Pellegrino, Chudowsky, & Glaser, 2001). It is essential to measure changes in teacher practice and student learning using observations of classrooms and assessments that tap the instructional goals. To evaluate KI professional development researchers need to examine classroom practices to see if students engage in inquiry and to measure student learning using KI items and rubrics (see examples of materials and assessments in Chapters 5, 6, 7, and 8).

Even large and impressive studies rarely assess impacts on students. For example, in one comprehensive study of professional development, teachers were followed as they participated in a systemic reform effort over three years (Supovitz, Mayer, & Kahle, 2000). To enhance their interest and use of inquiry methods, teachers engaged in inquiry units just like the ones they would implement with their students. They also received inquiry teaching materials. Based on self-report of teaching practices, the study showed that increased experience in learning about inquiry science resulted in increases in reported use of inquiry teaching.

During the first year, teachers indicated increased interest in inquiry but the level of interest remained flat between the second and third year. Over the three years of the project, teachers reported using more and more inquiry teaching strategies but only after extensive professional development. Changes in reported teaching practices (such as use of hands-on materials) only emerged after 80 hours of instruction and changes in reported classroom culture (such as use of evidence to support claims or use of collaborative groups) emerged after 160 hours of instruction (as well as after implementation of the new inquiry materials). The study demonstrates that interest precedes implementation of new practices. It did not measure impact of these self-reported changes on student learning (Supovitz & Turner, 2000).

Professional Development for Inquiry

Reviews of the literature on professional development for inquiry teaching emphasize the multiple skills teachers need (Davis, Petish, & Smithey, 2006; Higgins & Spitulnik, 2008; Kali & Linn, 2008; Lawless, & Pellegrino, 2007; Linn & Hsi, 2000; Sisk-Hilton, 2009; Williams, Linn, Ammon, & Gearhart, 2004). These include:

- Ways to monitor inquiry teaching to ensure that it helps students learn science.
- Strategies for guiding students, setting up small groups, asking inquiry questions, and encouraging KI.
- Ability to assess student inquiry units.
- Skill in teaching with technology-enhanced materials (if used), including how to troubleshoot the system and how to use the tools designed for teachers.
- Ability to articulate the goals of inquiry teaching to parents, administrators, and their students.

Research on science inquiry and professional development is sparse. Only a few studies explore linkages between inquiry strategies, instructional materials, and learning outcomes (Borko, 2004; Davis et al., 2006; Fishman, Marx, Blumenfeld, Krajcik, & Soloway, 2004; Lawless & Pellegrino, 2007; Little, 2003). Few studies have followed teachers for multiple years (Supovitz & Turner, 2000) and fewer still have linked teaching with student learning (Gerard et al., 2010).

Detailed reviews of preservice programs show that even well-designed and intensive programs rarely set teachers on a path towards lifelong inquiry teaching (Davis et al., 2006). Beginning science teachers face multiple challenges to facilitate inquiry. Davis et al. (2006) report that most programs provide limited insight into issues specifically associated with technology or inquiry science. The review reported that most science teachers abandoned inquiry instruction for a more didactic approach by the 3rd year of teaching.

Only a few preservice programs provide opportunities for teachers to test new technology-enhanced teaching strategies. Two studies used questionnaires, interviews, and observations of classroom teaching practices to assess impacts of these opportunities (Justi & van Driel, 2005; Niess, 2005). At the end of the preservice courses in these studies, a majority of teachers could implement a technology-enhanced inquiry lesson in a secondary school classroom. These teachers could communicate the meaning of modeling in chemistry, elicit student ideas during the inquiry process, and support students to analyze the limitations of scientific models. Even the teachers who attempted to enact modeling-based inquiry but eventually substituted a didactic approach reported a value for the inquiry approach.

Professional development in the area of technology integration often focuses on helping teachers develop skill in using word-processing or presentation software rather than on inquiry teaching. Studies published between 1997 and 2005 on integrating technology across disciplines show that professional development was primarily aimed at developing teachers' technology skill (Lawless & Pellegrino, 2007). The studies, as expected, showed that teachers gained skill in using productivity software but did not typically track changes in teacher practice.

Research on in-service teaching using technology primarily involves short-term (one year or less) interventions (Gerard et al., 2010). These studies suggest that short term programs can help add new technology-enhanced tools to practice when the tool extends, rather than changes, the teacher's existing approach. These programs are generally not successful in promoting inquiry teaching unless teachers are already using inquiry (Yarnall et al., 2006). In one study, teachers resisted using a technology-enhanced data collection tool because they did not think it supported their instructional goals (Penuel, Fishman, Gallagher, Korbak, & Lopez-Prado, 2008).

Studies show that during the first year of using technology-enhanced inquiry, teachers generally focus on dealing with the technology rather than teaching inquiry (e.g., Songer, Lee, & Kam, 2002; Songer et al., 2003; Varma, Husic, & Linn, 2008). A few programs report that having a mentor available to guide reflection on practice benefits teachers (e.g., Songer, Lee, & McDonald, 2003). Overall, these studies suggest that short-term professional development did not result in increases in inquiry teaching because teachers often substituted a more direct style even when the materials called for inquiry (e.g., Henze, van Driel, & Verloop, 2007; Schneider, Krajcik, & Blumenfeld, 2005; van Driel & Verloop, 2002).

Research focusing on interventions of two or more years has demonstrated some impacts on inquiry teaching. Geir et al. (2008), Fishman, Marx, Best, and Tal (2003), Rivet and Krajcik (2004), and Slotta (2004) all found that students made significant learning gains over two or three years when teachers participate in professional development. All these groups guided teachers to use evidence from student assessments to customize, test, and refine their instruction. Much of the research on long-term professional development has been conducted by two

NSF funded centers for teaching and learning: TELS and the Center for Learning Technologies in Urban Schools (LeTUS).

Long-term interventions generally include opportunities for teachers to adapt or customize their curriculum materials as well as their teaching strategies. Teachers constantly adapt instruction to available resources, instructional time, and student interests. When guided to make adaptations based on evidence from student learning teachers can impact outcomes (Gerard, Spitulnik, & Linn, 2010). Davis created a program called Curriculum Access System for Elementary Science (CASES), a technologically-mediated environment that features educative materials for teachers including resources, diagnoses of student difficulties, and adaptable unit plans (see http://cases.soe.umich.edu/; Davis, 2004b; Davis & Varma, 2008).

Professional Development for KI

Research on inquiry-oriented professional development shows that programs aligned with the KI approach have promise for changing teaching strategies and improving learning outcomes. Many research groups have found the KI framework useful for guiding design of professional development (Davis, 2004a; Eldar, Eylon & Ronen, 2010, Eylon, Berger & Bagno, 2008; Gerard, Spitulnik, & Linn, in press; Sisk-Hilton, 2009; Williams, Linn, Ammon & Gearhart, 2004).

A review of the literature on professional development for technology-enhanced learning shows that KI patterns are associated with improved classroom practices and, in a few cases, improved performance on KI assessments (Gerard, Varma, Corliss, & Linn, in press). We report on two projects that align professional development, curriculum materials, and assessments using KI (see examples of materials and assessments in Chapters 5, 6, 7, and 8). Each project implements professional development using KI processes by eliciting ideas, adding ideas, distinguishing ideas, and reflecting on ideas.

Eliciting Ideas

Eliciting ideas from teachers as they design, customize, or review technology-enhanced inquiry units reveals important beliefs that deserve attention in professional development (Varma, Husic, & Linn, 2008). Teachers have many reservations about inquiry learning. They frequently wonder whether they can implement inquiry activities in their classrooms. They worry about classroom management. They have doubts about the value of inquiry learning for helping students on typical state tests. They worry that they lack sufficient disciplinary knowledge and sufficient technological skills. They would prefer to teach the basic ideas of each topic before starting on inquiry.

The eliciting ideas activity gave the teachers a chance to hear the views of their peers and also allowed the professional developers to gain insight into the concerns of the teachers (Higgins, 2008). Eliciting ideas is important to ensure that professional development addresses the ideas held by the teachers.

Adding Ideas

Teachers unfamiliar with technology-enhanced inquiry science face many new ideas. They usually encounter new ideas about curriculum, assessment, and teaching. They may be unfamiliar with rubrics for scoring inquiry tasks. They may lack pedagogical content knowledge including strategies for guiding students, setting up small groups, respecting the diverse ideas of students, and encouraging KI that helps with inquiry.

Effective inquiry materials add ideas about inquiry and can be educative in the sense that they help teachers learn about the science discipline and about teaching strategies (Davis & Krajcik, 2005). WISE materials illustrate how inquiry works and show the possibilities of technology-enhanced instruction. For example, they guide students to engage in inquiry using the inquiry map (see Chapter 3). Teachers can observe students doing inquiry with online guidance. Using WISE enables teachers to observe the impact of inquiry lessons in their classrooms even when they are skeptical.

Several research projects have designed videos of classroom practice to introduce ideas about inquiry teaching. The development of video cases is rooted in apprenticeship learning and social networking theory (e.g., Lave & Wenger, 1991; Vygotsky, 1978). Effects of video cases have been uneven as designers find ways to use this technology (Barab et al., 2004; Derry et al., 2004; Falk & Drayton, 2009; Renninger & Shumar, 2002a). Interpretation of a video, because of its complexity, can be contentious unless viewers have agreed-upon criteria. Often audiences do not agree on interpretations of video cases and the ideas added by the video may not be the ones that the designers hoped to emphasize.

Video cases have special appeal for online communities of teachers (Falk & Drayton, 2009). In many cases, programs have succeeded in creating a repository of materials (e.g., the Math Forum, Renninger & Shumar, 2002b) or supporting discussion of an aspect of instruction such as using representations in science (Rubin & Doubler, 2009). Often evaluation involves demonstrating widespread use of the site. Impacts on teaching and learning are more illusive.

Demonstration lessons have been used to add new ideas about inquiry teaching in Japan (e.g., see Lewis & Tsuchida, 1998; Linn, Lewis, Tsuchida, & Songer, 2000). In lesson study, a group of teachers plan a demonstration lesson. They explain their goals and then teach the lesson while visitors observe in the classroom. It is often possible to interact with the students. After the lesson the teacher comments on the strengths and weaknesses of the lesson and responds to questions. Observers often suggest alternatives and discuss criteria for effective instruction. For example, they might discuss how well students reconciled alternative ideas.

Another approach for adding ideas is to pair teachers with a mentor. The mentor might model effective teaching, observe and critique the mentee, or discuss alternatives with the mentee.

In summary, designers have explored many ways to add ideas about inquiry. Curriculum materials can illustrate student inquiry activities. To communicate teaching strategies, video cases and lesson study have been used. To communicate, these cases need to engage teachers in distinguishing ideas.

Distinguishing Ideas

Helping teachers to add new ideas (e.g., about student learning) is not sufficient in itself for them to adopt inquiry practices. Changing teaching practices, like changing other interpersonal practices takes time, especially because most teachers primarily learned from courses that implemented the absorption approach. Teachers need to distinguish new ideas from their established ones.

Professional development activities for distinguishing ideas are similar to the ones introduced in other chapters such as debate, critique, interpreting pivotal cases, and developing arguments. Teachers are accustomed to critiquing new curriculum materials so this is often a good place to start. Enticing teachers to evaluate instruction materials for emphasis on inquiry can reveal some important issues. For example, teachers might look for examples of the *inform and assess* or *motivate and assess* patterns (see Chapter 2). Asking teachers to use KI criteria to evaluate instructional or customize the materials has shown promise (Higgins, 2008).

Reflecting and Sorting Out Ideas

The final aspect of the KI pattern concerns reflection. During the reflection process, individuals sort out their ideas, refine their criteria for evaluating new materials, and identify questions. Reflection is an important part of many successful professional development programs (e.g., Schon, 1983).

Encouraging reflection on practice and ensuring that the reflective process contributes to improved teaching takes time and energy. Many schools and school districts change curriculum materials, standards, teaching assignments, and class schedules with little consultation of teachers. This diminishes professional confidence and can thwart reflection on professional practice. Strengthening opportunities for reflection and encouraging teachers to act on their reflections and test their ideas in their classrooms strengthens classroom teaching and can contribute to lifelong learning.

Ultimately teachers need to develop the skills to independently and autonomously teach for inquiry. This can happen when communities of teachers at a school meet together to support each other's development of more coherent understanding and more effective teaching (see Box 9.4). This is the goal of the lesson study approach to professional development (Lewis, 2002; Lewis & Tsuchida, 1998; Sisk-Hilton, 2009).

In earlier chapters, we argued that the KI pattern is important for student learning. In this chapter we illustrate its value for designing teacher inquiry supporting professional development. Using the pattern to inform design of professional development is likely to promote effective teaching and ultimately enable teachers to engage in lifelong learning.

Two Professional Development Programs

To highlight the features of KI professional development, we discuss two research projects that support teachers as they adopt and customize technology-enhanced science lessons (using WISE) for their courses. Both projects provided sustained, in-depth professional development, running for at least 2 years, and included summer workshops and mentoring components.

First, the Technology-Enhanced Learning in Science (TELS) center explored ways to encourage over 100 teachers in participating schools in seven states to make effective use of technology-enhanced materials (Varma, Husic, & Linn, 2008). TELS was a large NSF center that included researchers from several different institutions. TELS was focused on understanding the role of scientific visualizations within WISE inquiry units. TELS recruited schools with many teachers who had never enacted any WISE unit before.

TELS professional development consisted of:

- A short (1 to 2 hour) workshop that introduced the WISE units, helped teachers select a unit for their class, and guided teachers to schedule the classroom run,
- An on-site guide (either a staff member or an experienced teacher at the school) to help the teacher get started including registering students and accessing WISE teacher tools,
- On-demand half-day workshops on relevant topics,
- On-demand email and phone mentoring.

In addition, the TELS project recruited a total of twelve teachers to join the TELS instructional *design partnerships*. TELS selected 2 teachers from each of six courses (middle school earth science, life science, and physical science, and high school biology, chemistry, and physics). Teachers needed to be available to participate in the summer design retreat.

Second, the Mentored and Online Development of Educational Leaders for Science (MODELS) program that worked with teachers from just two middle schools. Compared to TELS, MODELS collaborated more intensively with teachers. MODELS offered an intensive weeklong summer workshop, as well as a school-based mentor who was released for one period each day to help with implementation of technology-enhanced learning at the school. In the week-long workshop, the MODELS teachers established goals, identified WISE units aligned with their curriculum, and planned how they would incorporate this new material into their instructional program. The MODELS teachers agreed upon a school-wide goal for their implementation of the units each year. For example, in the first year MODELS teachers selected the goal of helping students read to learn (as opposed to helping students learn to read).

In the next two sections, we analyze the trajectories of teacher learning for three groups: (1) TELS teachers who *implemented* units, (2) TELS teachers who participated in the *design* of units, and (3) MODELS teachers, who generally customized WISE units and enacted them. Both the TELS and MODELS professional development programs tested comprehensive approaches for improving the implementation of inquiry science.

TELS Design Activities and Teacher Participants

The teachers who participated in the design of TELS units contributed to two summer workshops. TELS inquiry science units were designed at the first summer retreat and refined at the second retreat. Design partnerships included the classroom teachers, researchers, evaluators, technologists, discipline specialists, and TELS graduate students or postdoctoral scholars with expertise in the topic. At the retreat the participants took advantage of the inquiry unit topic selection process, benchmark assessments, and resources for units including visualizations, curriculum reviews, and research findings:

Inquiry Unit Topic Selection

To identify topics for the units, TELS asked more than 50 teachers from participating schools to identify topics for potential curriculum units that met three criteria:

- Aligned with the state standards
- Traditionally difficult to teach or poorly articulated in the textbook
- Amenable to visualization and technology enhancement.

The teachers generated a long list of topics. At the TELS inaugural meeting, participating teachers narrowed the list to 12 topics (see Table 10.1).

Benchmark Assessments

Once the topics were identified, TELS reviewed standardized tests and research papers to identify assessments that aligned with the topics. TELS sought KI items that asked students to link and connect ideas. Tests for each grade level included some multiple choice items from published tests such as NAEP and several KI

Table 10.1 TELS Units. Units Designed for the Cohort Comparison Study

GRADE LEVEL	SCIENCE BRANCH	PROJECT
Middle School	Earth Science	Solid Earth—Rock Cycle Global Climate Change
	Physical Science	Heat and Temperature Kinematics
	Life Science	Mitosis Cell Processes Genetics and Inheritance
High School	Chemistry	Phase Change Chemical Reactions (Stoichiometry & Global Warming)
	Physics	Position, Time, and Velocity Electricity
	Biology	Genetics and Evolution Genetics, Mitosis and Meiosis

items that required generation of explanations. TELS designed the benchmark assessments to take about one class period. TELS administered benchmark assessments in all participating teachers' classrooms not long after they were recruited in late May. The results of these assessments were available for the design partnerships at the design retreat.

Resources: Visualizations, Curriculum, and Research

To inform the design of the new curriculum units, TELS graduate students, postdoctoral scholars, and technology experts began by identifying driving questions that would make the science accessible. They then sought visualizations and existing curriculum materials as starting points for each of the 12 topics. In addition, for each topic, TELS graduate students reviewed textbook depictions and research studies of learning about the topic to identify promising activities and commonly used assessments.

In some cases, researchers were able to identify an existing WISE unit or an existing Concord Consortium model that could be used to stimulate the design process. At the summer retreat, these materials were introduced as new ideas to be considered in the design process.

Design Activities

At the curriculum design retreat, TELS formed six partnerships—one for each grade from 6 through 12—to plan two WISE curriculum units each. These partnerships followed an established design process to prototype and review the curriculum units (see Figure 10.1).

Each partnership started by reviewing the overall performance of students on the Benchmark tests and diagnosing the ideas that students had when they took the assessment. Consistent with research reported earlier (e.g., Hake, 1998; Halloun & Hestenes, 1985b), teachers expected that their students performed better than the average. When teachers had an opportunity to look at the responses from their students, they were generally disappointed in student performance and motivated to design better instruction.

The TELS group hoped that this evidence would motivate teachers to be receptive to inquiry instruction. Reactions were mixed, consistent with other research (Blumenfeld et al., 2000; Strauss, 2005). Some teachers felt that more rigorous text and lecture instruction, consistent with the absorption approach, would be the ideal solution. An often-heated debate occurred between teachers who advocated for adding more text and details, and researchers who advocated for focusing more on students' interactions with informative materials such as the visualizations. The discussions were difficult to resolve because both groups had evidence for their point of view. Most teachers had been using lectures and text-

A central design goal for TELS is to explore the role of new technologies within an inquiry framework as in this example where a charged particle model is integrated into the Electricity project.

FIGURE 10.1   The TELS design review process

books for some time, and felt that such an approach was successful. The researchers felt that the evidence from the benchmark assessments suggested that the textbook approach had limitations.

TELS encouraged the partnerships to identify visualizations and create an inquiry activity that implemented the KI approach. The teachers liked the visualizations and thought they might help students. Thus the two groups differed with regard to their criteria for effective instruction but everyone thought the visualizations might be helpful. The researchers and teachers negotiated activities to address the gaps and intuitive ideas revealed in the benchmark assessments.

The teams created prototypes and engaged in a process of collaborative design involving a series of design reviews. All the participants reviewed other units and each group of experts reviewed all the units using criteria based on KI (see Table 10.2). This process resulted in units that had consistent inquiry activities.

TABLE 10.2 TELS Design Review Activities

Design Review for TELS

Community review

To enable all participants to appreciate the challenges of their peers and find connections across units, TELS started with a community review. Each design team created a poster highlighting their current plan, pedagogical features, challenges, and opportunities. The other design team for their grade or course reviewed the poster for overlap and connections on content. After revisions, groups that included representatives from at least 4 other units reviewed the poster for overall coherence of the design, implementation of inquiry, and integration of visualizations. This review pushed the community to grapple with the nature of inquiry and the advantages of technology.

Assessment Review

To spur co-design of assessments and instruction and to ensure that embedded assessments called for knowledge integration the TELS assessment leaders reviewed every unit. They examined how the team incorporated available published items, evaluated the knowledge integration potential of embedded assessments and pretests/posttests, and reviewed alignment of the unit with the assessments. The assessment review stimulated discussion about the nature of knowledge integration items.

Design Principles Review

To take advantage of prior research, design teams identified instructional challenges and used the proven features in the Design Principles Database (Kali, 2007) and design patterns (Linn & Eylon, 2006) to craft a solution. For example, one group found that the debate pattern documented by Bell (his dissertation) strengthened the knowledge integration potential of evolution. This review stimulated discussion of research on knowledge integration.

Technology Review

Retreat participants included technologists who were familiar with technologies used in schools as well as individuals able to evaluate requests for new technologies. Teams met with the technologists and explained their ideas for adding visualizations. The experts considered what was possible given the time frame and current resources. This review helped the project identify visualizations that could work for multiple units.

Discipline Review

Each design team had one or more discipline specialists. For this review, specialists in life, physical, and earth science reviewed all the units in their subject area for disciplinary connections and sequencing. The discipline specialists found it challenging to identify how topics such as energy were represented across units, in part due to the neglect of cross cutting themes in most standards for science.

Grade Level and Equity Review

Each unit had one or more expert in classroom teaching. As in the discipline review, the classroom teachers reviewed the reading level of the materials, the pacing of the unit, the opportunities for connections to other aspects of the curriculum, and the overall emphasis on science literacy, technology literacy and language literacy for all units at their grade level. They looked for inadvertent stereotyping of science and suggested ways to ameliorate the situation. They also compared units across grades to ensure there was an appropriate progression of sophistication.

Inquiry Review

Prior research on inquiry instruction has identified a set of criteria for successful units such as making science personally relevant, making thinking visible, helping students learn from others, and encouraging students to monitor their own progress (e.g., Bransford, Brown, & Cocking, 1999). TELS created an inquiry feedback form and each design team used the form to evaluate another unit.

External Advisory Board Review

The TELS advisory board had members with expertise in policy, science disciplines, curriculum, classroom teaching, learning, and technology. The design teams prepared posters integrating the recommendations from all the reviews and presented their plans to the advisory board at the end of the retreat. The advisory board commended TELS on progress, gave specific feedback, and warned that iterative refinement studies would reveal more challenges.

Immediately following the retreat the TELS advisory board joined the group and reviewed the designs.

This TELS iterative design process followed the KI approach. Topics for the units emerged from a survey of ideas held by teachers. The partnerships generated a wealth of ideas before they settled on a plan. The benchmark assessments, existing curriculum materials, research findings, and visualizations all added ideas. The partnerships debated alternatives and used evidence to distinguish among their ideas in the design reviews. The design partnerships generated embedded assessments that included prompts for explanations, drawings, and selections among alternatives. They also designed pretests and posttests for each unit. Throughout the retreat, participants regularly reflected on their progress.

In summary, the partnership design process benefitted from the assessments, existing curriculum materials, research findings, and visualizations but would not have succeeded without the continued discussion, debate, and negotiation among the members of the design partnership. The formation of teams with a broad range of expertise was essential as were the eight design reviews. Participants remained energized for the 8 days of the retreat, but reported exhaustion at the end. Following the retreat the teams completed the units, continued to review the plans of other teams, and prepared to deploy the units in classrooms. The participating teachers were eager to gather evidence from students using the new units.

TELS Professional Development: A Targeted Approach

TELS professional development followed the KI pattern. Activities were targeted to the requests of teachers. Some of the highlights are described here.

Eliciting and Adding Ideas Before Enactment

To introduce inquiry teaching, TELS held a short workshop at the school. At the workshop the teachers shared their ideas about using visualizations for inquiry learning. The leaders introduced the units. The teachers selected units for their classes and scheduled enactments. Teachers were encouraged to review the unit prior to enactment but often had little time. Many teachers enacted the units with limited prior knowledge of the content.

Eliciting and Adding New Ideas During Enactment

A TELS guide (either a staff member or an experienced teacher at the school) scaffolded enactment of the units so that all teachers could succeed. TELS staff visited the school before the run to test the technology and answer questions. On the first day of instruction, the guide helped the new teacher register students and get started. Typically, the guide illustrated ways to manage the class, establish ground rules for students working in pairs, use the teacher portal, and manage inquiry.

In some cases the guide taught the class for the first few class periods and then turned the instruction over to the teacher (teachers had up to seven classes using the WISE units). Guides offered solutions to technology glitches and encouraged teachers to contact the project by phone or email if problems arose.

Students could follow the online steps in the WISE inquiry map to complete the activities within the curriculum unit (see Figure 10.2). Students differed substantially in the quality of responses they wrote to embedded notes and in the attention that they gave to the evidence pages and the visualizations.

The guide illustrated inquiry support strategies, solicited ideas from teachers concerning how they might solve problems, and negotiated effective approaches to monitoring and supporting inquiry learning (Higgins & Spitulnik, 2008). The guide encouraged the teacher to monitor progress by interacting with each group of students to find out what they were thinking. The guide illustrated ways to encourage students to attend to the details of the curriculum, interact with the visualizations in depth, and write responses to prompts that used evidence from the unit. One teacher remarked that a guide, Mr. K., convinced her to talk to students so she could identify when many of the students had similar problems and interrupt the class to discuss the issues (see also Linn, 2005).

The guide showed the teacher how to access student work in the teacher portal and encouraged teachers to use the portal to review student notes and ask students to add details if responses were superficial. The guide also helped teachers identify enrichment activities (such as using the visualization to answer a question related to the unit) for groups who completed the unit early. Students who were progressing rapidly could also assist groups who were having difficulty but ensur-

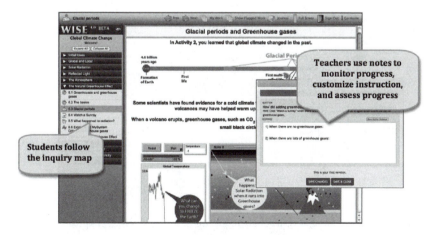

FIGURE 10.2   Classroom supports for WISE. Features of the Web-based Inquiry Science Environment (WISE) that help teachers plan instruction and assess progress

ing that students encourage inquiry is challenging. Rather than tutoring, students often use the *inform, assess* pattern (Webb & Farivar, 1994).

The TELS guide helped teachers use the portal to read comments, send feedback, assign grades, compose reusable comments, and monitor progress of the class. A few teachers found they could look at student work during class. Most teachers found looking at student work from one day to the next was a good way to improve their teaching (Slotta, 2004).

Typically, teachers asked the guide to stay for all their classes on the first day. Often, teachers asked the guide to return on subsequent days. As shown in Figure 10.3, during the first year teachers often required extensive support, having a guide there for almost every day of the enactment (Varma, Husic, & Linn, 2008). Although TELS technology experts tested the school computers and network prior to enactment, teachers requested help mostly for dealing with the

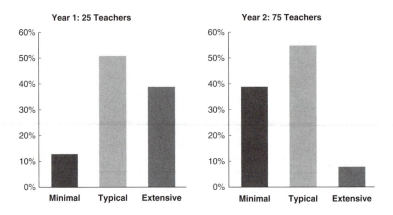

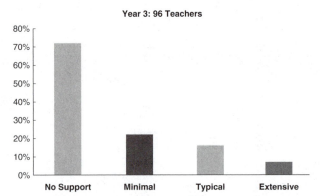

FIGURE 10.3 Percentages of teachers requiring different levels of support during the first 3 years of TELS

Source: Varma, K., Husic, F., & Linn, M. (2008). Targeted support for using technology–enhanced science inquiry modules. *Journal of Science Education and Technology, 17*(4), 341–356.

technology (see Figure 10.4). Guides helped teachers diagnose network connection problems, deal with slow download times for the visualizations, and identify when firewalls were interfering with the implementation of the units.

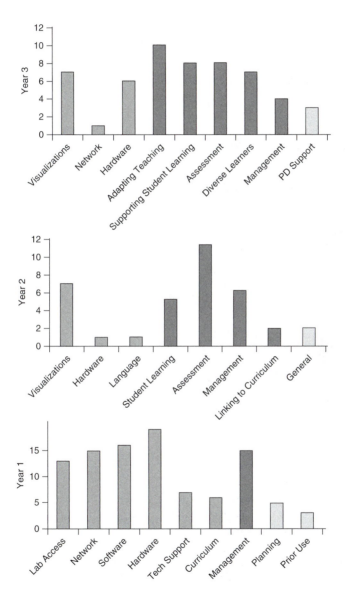

FIGURE 10.4   Teacher obstacles in first year of using TELS—Logistics, Instruction, and General

Source: Varma, K., Husic, F., & Linn, M. C. (2008). Targeted support for using technology–enhanced science inquiry modules. *Journal of Science Education and Technology, 17*(4), 341–356.

Sorting Out Ideas in Interviews

Teachers reflected on their experiences implementing WISE units, identified obstacles, and requested professional development in annual reflection interviews (Varma, Husic, & Linn, 2008). As can be seen in Figure 10.4, in the first year almost all the obstacles had to do with the logistics of implementing the project but these were largely solved in subsequent years. Teachers at participating schools helped each other resolve problems.

The degree of support teachers requested and the number of obstacles that teachers reported declined dramatically from year one to year three, while at the same time the number of teachers participating increased from about 25 to close to 100. Each year, some teachers were unable to continue teaching in the program so the total number of teachers served was over 100.

Distinguishing Ideas in Workshops

In targeted professional development teachers could request workshops. During the first year, teachers often wrote down the questions the guide asked the class and were eager for help in asking inquiry questions. In subsequent years teachers also asked for help in using visualizations and encouraging collaborative learning.

At the half-day workshops, TELS focused on helping teachers distinguish among their ideas about the selected topic. Teachers refined their inquiry teaching strategies and suggested ways to customize the units. A subset of teachers attended the TELS retreat to help improve the units. The TELS targeted approach had the advantage of quickly enabling teachers to enact inquiry instruction and supporting them with a guide as they identified immediate professional development needs. Nevertheless, TELS teachers found many challenges in teaching for inquiry.

Impact of TELS: A Cohort Comparison

To assess the impact of the TELS units combined with the professional development, TELS conducted a cohort comparison study. Teachers administered the original benchmarks, enacted the units with a new cohort of students, and administered the benchmarks to these students. As discussed in Chapter 9, 24 teachers from four states completed all the activities: first year benchmarks, unit implementations, second year benchmarks. During the first year 10 of the 12 units were enacted. TELS also analyzed embedded assessments and pretests and posttests. Results showed that students who used the WISE activities for the topic under consideration were in general more successful on the benchmark tests (see Figure 8.2) than the cohort of students taught by the same teacher who took the benchmark tests the year before (Linn et al., 2006).

Furthermore, the researchers found that students with high and low pretest scores made similar gains, a concern of many teachers (Chiu & Linn, 2008; Shen and Linn, in press; Tate, 2009). Students who start the unit with very little information as well as those who start the unit with an extensive repertoire of ideas all make gains.

Student, Class, and Teacher Impacts in TELS

To clarify the role of professional development in student learning, TELS analyzed the typical versus TELS cohort using data from interviews and teacher surveys. Liu, Lee, and Linn (2010b) conducted a hierarchical linear model (HLM) analysis with student, class, and teacher levels. At the student level there was no effect for gender, confirming observations in classrooms that boys and girls were equally engaged with the visualizations. This finding is important because some believe that spatial reasoning may be more developed in boys than girls. The finding is consistent with recent findings that spatial skills are responsive to instruction (Sorby, 2009). At the class level there was a main effect for cohort consistent with the cohort comparison study findings (Linn et al., 2006). There was also an effect for high school compared to middle school (see Figure 10.5).

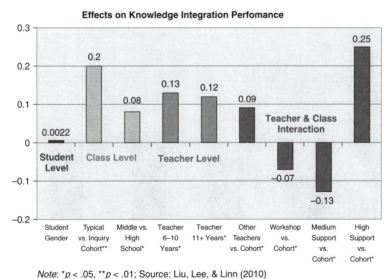

Note: *p < .05, **p < .01; Source: Liu, Lee, & Linn (2010)

FIGURE 10.5   Analysis of the impact of TELS using a Hierarchical Linear Model

Source: Liu, O. L., Lee, H.-S., & Linn, M. C. (2010, March 23). *Investigating Teacher Impact on Student Inquiry Science Learning Using a Hierarchical Linear Model.* Paper presented at the annual meeting of the National Association of Research in Science Teaching (NARST), Philadelphia, PA.

At the teacher level, there was a main effect for experience with more experienced teachers having more successful students on all the benchmarks. This is consistent with higher performing schools having more experienced teachers. Interactions between class and cohort showed that having a partner teacher at the school resulted in greater student gains from cohort 1 to cohort 2 than not having a partner teacher. In addition, teachers who were members of the partnership design team had more substantial student outcomes than the other teachers. This finding suggests that teachers benefitted from familiarity with the unit. In addition, when teachers required medium or extensive support during enactment their students were less successful that those for teachers who required minimal support, suggesting that difficulties with the technology may have interrupted the flow of the units.

Longitudinal Impact of WISE Units

Instructional programs generally have their highest impact on tests administered at the end of the program. Typically students forget some of what they learned and are less successful on delayed posttests. As discussed in Chapter 9, Chiu found that between the posttest and the delayed posttest, rather than forgetting information students either remained at the same level of understanding or actually improved in their understanding (see Figure 10.6). This surprising finding that students gained understanding for some topics and remained at the same level for others between the posttests in the delayed posttest can be attributed to a number of factors.

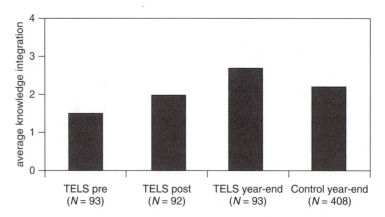

FIGURE 10.6   Comparison Study of TELS Chemical Reactions. The average knowledge integration scores for TELS Chemistry increased over the pre, post, delayed tests. A control group was less successful on the end of year test

Source: Chiu, J. L. (2010). *Supporting Students' Knowledge Integration with Technology-Enhanced Inquiry Curricula*. Unpublished doctoral dissertation, University of California, Berkeley, CA.

First, many teachers reported revisiting the visualizations or ideas from the WISE activities after they had completed the WISE curriculum. This suggests that the visualizations and other aspects of the units were sufficiently powerful that they merited integration with other parts of the curriculum. As a result, students may have had additional opportunities to revisit the ideas and integrate them.

Ozone Layer:
Comparing open-ended scoring schemes

TIMSS Rubric			Knowledge Integration Rubric		
Category	Description	Examples	Link(s)	Description	Examples
Correct	Protection against UV from the Sun or too strong rays from the Sun. Health concerns such as skin cancer/sunburn.	Because it keeps the Sun's rays from being too strong. Protects the UV radiation from the Sun. We do not get sunburned.	Complex	Elaborate two or more scientifically valid links among relevant ideas.	Blocks UV from the Sun and connects to legitimate health concerns.
			Full	Elaborate a scientifically valid link between two relevant ideas.	Blocks UV from the Sun (specific range is specified) from reaching earth's surface.
			Partial	Elicit relevant ideas but do not fully elaborate the link between relevant ideas.	Keeps us from radiation (does not specify specific range of radiation) Legitimate health related concerns, e.g. skin cancer.
Incorrect	Have non-normative ideas.		No	Have non-normative ideas or linked.	Protects from meteorite strike. It helps us alive.
Off Task/Blank			Off Task/Blank		

- Picture "A" shows a real greenhouse where light from the Sun passes through the glass panels and heats the inside. The glass panels of the greenhouse keep the heat energy from escaping.

  Multiple Choice Claim

- Picture "B" shows the greenhouse effect that happens on Earth.

- Which part of the picture is like the glass of the greenhouse?

- (Choose one) __ Sun __ Space __ Atmosphere __ Earth

  Explanation
  Open-ended

- Explain your answer.

Picture A   Picture B

FIGURE 10.7   Comparing rubrics for TELS and TIMSS. Using the KI Rubric converted this TIMSS item to a KI item

Second, the personally-relevant examples such as airbags, global climate change, and cancer remedies in the units may have reinforced the ideas. Students could have encountered these questions outside of science class and used their science knowledge.

Third, inquiry learning may be more effective than traditional instruction and enhance the chance for students to maintain their ideas. Students may continue to reflect on the inquiry activities. This possibility is consistent with the finding that students used evidence from the WISE inquiry experiments when they responded to the benchmark assessments.

In addition, students may have developed a propensity to explain their ideas using evidence as a result of the WISE unit. The assessments used to assess the units (see Figure 10.7), required students to write several sentences using evidence to support their point of view. The propensity to explain science may have helped them maintain their ideas from posttest to delayed posttest.

In summary, students gained integrated understanding from the TELS units. This success stems from both the units and the professional development. Teachers who participated in the curriculum design partnerships, and were therefore more familiar with the units, were more successful than those in the targeted group. Students benefitted when their teachers had collaborators at the school. These findings show that the KI patterns can align curriculum and professional development to improve learning outcomes.

MODELS Professional Development

The MODELS project used the KI patterns to create professional development. Since they all came from two schools, the teachers were eager to help each other learn. MODELS, compared to TELS, provided more extensive mentoring for teachers and supported teachers to customize instruction.

MODELS teachers worked with experienced designers to select units from the WISE library and to commission units that would enhance their practice. The MODELS teachers enacted two to four inquiry units each year. TELS teachers enacted one to two units (Higgins, 2008). As in TELS, initially the MODELS teachers were inclined to increase the non-inquiry aspects of the units. The researchers encouraged them to instead focus on customizations that would make the units more relevant to their students. Thus, in the first year, one MODELS teacher customized the water quality unit to a local creek. Most teachers customized the text based on the language capabilities of their students. This involved simplifying language in cases where students had difficulties with English, and putting language alternatives into the text, for example, creating Spanish-language versions of units (Spitulnik & Linn, 2007). They also improved alignment of units with curricular standards.

The teachers critiqued each other's customizations and planned their implementation of the units during the summer workshop. During the school year, the school-based mentor observed enactments. The mentor helped teachers focus on inquiry and initiated activities that involved distinguishing among alternative approaches to instruction. Teachers had regular opportunities for reflection on their teaching and for review of the progress of their students.

MODELS Customization Workshops

During the second and third years, unlike TELS, the MODELS teachers attended workshops where they used students' work to guide customization and refinement. They met in grade-level groups, examined their students' embedded notes as well as pretest and posttest scores, identified areas where improvement was needed, and made customizations based on these observations to improve the unit. Typically all the teachers agreed to use the customized versions.

Gerard et al. (2010) reported on the activities of a participating teacher referred to as Ted who customized the Plate Tectonics unit. Ted concluded that several of the embedded questions could be refined to elicit more informative responses. In addition, he noted that the Plate Tectonics unit needed to be customized to the local area to increase relevance to students. Therefore, he added an activity about the plate movement in the local region. Finally, Ted was concerned about the alignment of the unit with the standards, and he added some elaborations to pages of the activity to ensure full coverage of the standards. These customizations resulted in improved student learning (see Figure 10.8).

MODELS teachers refined text, sometimes added activities, and often streamlined activities to increase alignment with their instructional goals and the state standards. When teachers wanted to add text to elaborate on topics, the researchers reminded teachers of the difficulties students have reading online material and suggested giving an assignment from the textbook instead.

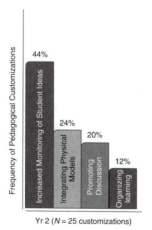
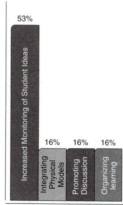

FIGURE 10.8 Impact of teacher customization of instruction on student learning
Source: Gerard et al., 2010.

In the third year, MODELS teachers made fewer changes to the curriculum, and identified more ways that they themselves could teach effectively to improve learning outcomes. For example, they identified questions that they could ask, ways that they could improve understanding of the visualizations, and ways to use student work during science class to orchestrate effective discussions (see Gerard et al., 2010). This focus reflected their deepening understanding of inquiry learning and led to improvements in student learning (Gerard et al., 2010).

MODELS Dilemmas

The MODELS teachers, like the TELS teachers, identified areas for professional development, including questioning strategies and teaching with visualizations. The MODELS researchers and mentors created what they called dilemmas to respond to the teachers.

Dilemmas are inquiry activities for teachers that elicit ideas about an aspect of practice such as asking inquiry questions. To add ideas, the designers gathered video segments showing alternative ways that members of the teacher community have implemented the practice. Teachers then distinguish among the alternative approaches, seeking criteria and evidence to select the most promising approach. At the end, teachers reflect on the connections between the dilemma and their own practice. MODELS followed up on the dilemmas by observing in classrooms to see if teaching practices changed. TELS also used these dilemmas for targeted professional development.

Questioning Dilemma

Research shows that initially teachers have great difficulty asking questions in inquiry situations, especially when the science topic is unfamiliar. Over time teachers develop this capability (Williams et al., 2004; Williams, 2008). The researchers created the questioning dilemma to address the issue.

They began by asking teachers how they were using questioning strategies and eliciting a large number of ideas. Many teachers indicated that they were not sure they were asking appropriate questions and that they wanted to know about the experiences of other teachers. The MODELS team then introduced evidence for the dilemmas from videos they had made in classrooms, showing the actual questions that teachers in the MODELS program were asking. The MODELS team had gathered video segments over the year, identified segments where teachers asked questions, and coded the questions from those segments (see Table 10.3). They found that teachers asked many types of questions. Some were recall questions. Some were similar to the KI assessments, asking for evidence to resolve a conundrum. The dilemma illustrated different types of questions and engaged teachers in the process of distinguishing among them. The participants developed

TABLE 10.3 Teacher Generated Guiding Questions for Teaching with Models and Visualizations

Important Considerations for Teaching Models			
Purpose of Models	*Models as Teaching Science Content*	*Mechanics/ Management*	*Models as Experiment*
• What are models? • What do models represent? • How does the model map onto nature or natural processes? • What are limitations of the model? • What do the colors and symbols represent? • What do students "see" in the model?	• What is the science content? • What part of the science is the model representing? • Is the model connecting representations (pictures, equations)? • Relating to enrichment • How does the model connect elements of the phenomena? • How does the process in the model relate to real world phenomena?	• What is the meaning of the model? • Why use the model instead of another approach? • What is the value of the model? • When should the model be used? Why is it there? • How do you assess understanding of the model? • What do you want to emphasize?	• How do you run or use the model? • How do you introduce the model? • What are the goals of using the model? • Make observations • Gather data —many trials • Ask questions • Make sense of phenomena

criteria for identifying questions that encouraged KI. Then the teachers reflected on their practice.

Many teachers, responding to the dilemma, noted that their knowledge of the science topic impeded their ability to ask complex questions. They sought examples from other teachers and from the researchers to help them identify more sophisticated discipline-specific KI questions.

In their reflections, some teachers argued that a mix of questions is important for promoting inquiry. Asking questions that clarify basic understanding is often helpful for diagnosing why students are neglecting evidence that seems relevant but can interfere with inquiry.

Visualization Dilemma

The MODELS teachers also noted that students often rush through visualizations and do not fully appreciate them. The researchers concurred in this observation, based on their classroom visits. The researchers identified video footage illustrating this difficulty as well as some of the strategies that MODELS teachers had used to overcome it.

FIGURE 10.9 MODELS visualization dilemma. Suggestions for improving benefits of visualizations generated by teachers during the dilemma activity

This dilemma, like the questioning one, engaged teachers in distinguishing ideas. The teachers wanted ways for students to explore the visualizations in more detail (see Figure 10.9). Many of the teachers concurred with the findings of Chiu (Chiu & Linn, in press) that reported on the deceptive clarity of the visualizations (see Chapter 8). The teachers pooled their ideas about teaching with visualizations and reflected on their own practice. They made plans to implement their insights during the next school year.

Impact of Dilemmas

After the workshop, classroom observations showed the impact of the MODELS professional development activities. First, teachers asked far more questions during WISE enactments and used questions that were more KI oriented that those used the previous year, consistent with the taxonomy that emerged (Figure 10.10; Corliss & Spitulnik, 2008; Gerard et al., 2009). In research studies, Corliss and Spitulnik (2008) found that teachers asked more questions during lessons that involved the visualizations than during other parts of instruction (Figure 10.10).

The MODELS dilemmas informed the design of short workshops offered to the TELS teachers on questioning strategies and visualization strategies. Some of the MODELS professional developers assisted in the implementation of these workshops, ensuring that the expertise from MODELS was extended to the participants in TELS. Participants found the workshops helpful and often communicated their experience to other teachers at their school.

% of total questions	Purpose	Examples
58%	Monitor comprehension	Can you explain what albedo is? What do clouds do to global warming?
46%	Prompt connection	If sunlight goes into a greenhouse, why are the plants inside instead of outside in the Sun? What happens to the ocean if the Earth gets too warm?
13%	Activate prior knowledge	What is the connection between the experiment we did last week and global warming? What do molecules and atoms have to do with what we are studying today?
6%	Planning/check progress	What are you going to do today? Who is on activity 7?
3%	Clear up misconception	What happened to sunlight when you added CO2 to the model? Can sunlight actually slow down?

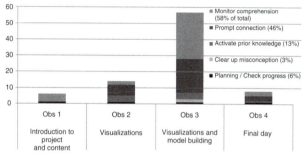

Purpose of Teacher Questions

FIGURE 10.10   Teacher customization of questions for specific activities. Teachers asked questions to monitor comprehension and prompt connections on days that students worked with visualizations

Source: Corliss, S., & Spitulnik, M. (2008). Student and teacher regulation of learning in technology-enhanced science instruction. In *International Perspectives in the Learning Sciences: Cre8ting a Learning World. Proceedings of the 8th International Conference of the Learning Sciences* (Vol. 1, pp. 167–174). Utrecht, The Netherlands: International Society of the Learning Sciences, Inc.

In summary, both TELS and MODELS created professional development based on KI. The projects have very different levels of support for teachers so the intensity differs considerably. Only in MODELS was it possible to link professional development to student learning outcomes.

Both projects found that teachers initially tended to eliminate inquiry and add elements of the *inform, assess* pattern. The MODELS professional development mitigated this effect. When teachers reviewed evidence from student work and customized instruction the units became more aligned with the goals of inquiry rather than the goals of absorption. TELS teachers did not customize instruction.

Both projects impacted student learning. As the TELS cohort comparison study shows, adding new inquiry units and professional development results in student gains over typical instruction (Linn et al., 2006). As the MODELS customization studies show, review of student work motivates teachers to align the curriculum and their teaching strategies with KI and leads to enhanced student learning (Gerard, Spitulnik, & Linn, 2010).

The WISE curriculum units, facilitated by teachers' beliefs that visualizations are valuable, add important ideas about inquiry. The materials are educative in that teachers learn about the discipline and about student progress while using them. All the teachers were motivated to make the visualizations succeed to help students learn.

Using the units helped teachers appreciate inquiry learning but also raised concerns. The teachers felt inquiry took longer than using the *inform, assess* pattern. In addition, problems with technology and difficulties managing inquiry (especially dealing with students who worked at different paces) posed challenges. Although the cohort comparison studies show that *inform, assess* is not as effective as KI, this finding seems abstract to teachers. Furthermore, since the effects of inquiry are more pronounced for KI questions than for multiple choice questions teachers need to rely on the embedded assessments for evidence of this impact (Linn et al., 2006).

The major difference between MODELS and TELS is the intensity of professional development. In a comparison study of student progress MODELS has a greater impact than TELS on student outcomes (Varma, Gerard, Liu, Corliss, & Linn, submitted). This appears to stem primarily from the customization opportunities in MODELS, consistent with other work on adapting curriculum materials (Davis & Varma, 2008).

Discussion

The pedagogical content knowledge necessary to teach inquiry science is substantial. Most professional development programs are too short and too narrow to impact teacher beliefs. Longer programs have an impact on beliefs and some also impact student learning.

Most programs rely on a knowledge transmission approach to professional development, consistent with the curriculum materials available for students. To encourage inquiry teaching successful programs align professional development, assessment, and curriculum design.

The professional development programs created by TELS and MODELS help teachers develop pedagogical content knowledge. They take advantage of the embedded assessments to provide evidence for customization of teaching strategies. They augment the information available in the curriculum materials and respond to teacher requests for guidance (specifically with regard to asking inquiry questions and supporting student use of visualizations). An outcome of these efforts to improve pedagogical content knowledge is that student learning is improved.

Refining and Customizing

The professional development programs in both TELS and MODELS featured iterative refinement of curriculum materials. These refinements were strengthened by comparison studies where researchers identified successful inquiry practices (see Chapters 7 and 8).

In summary, these findings combined with results from other studies suggest that evidence-based customization of instruction is a successful way to improve inquiry teaching and impact student learning (Corliss & Spitulnik, 2008; Davis & Varma, 2008; Gerard, Spitulnik, & Linn, 2010; Fishman, Marx, Best, & Tal, 2003; Slotta, 2004; Tal, Krajcik, & Blumenfeld, 2006; Williams et al., 2004). Customizing motivates teachers to distinguish among instructional approaches. In multiyear professional development programs, teachers can see the benefit of their customizations on student learning.

Video and Professional Development

Unlike many studies using video cases (e.g., Barab et al., 2004; Falk & Drayton, 2009; Renninger & Shumar, 2002a) the use of video for the questioning and visualization dilemmas in MODELS led to improved practice, although it was difficult to link to improved student outcomes. Several factors probably contributed to improved practice. Since the videos were from the classrooms of participating teachers, they had extensive contextual information that might be missing in some online courses where videos are prepared for a large audience. In addition, the topics of the videos, questioning and visualization, were identified by the teachers as important. Furthermore, following the KI pattern, the teachers developed criteria for inquiry that they could use to distinguish their practice from the video examples. The success of the MODELS videos parallels the success of the video club approach where teachers bring their own videos and develop criteria in collaboration (Frederiksen & White, 1992).

Recruiting and Sustaining Teacher Participants

Ensuring that the technology infrastructure remains viable is essential to sustain these projects beyond the initial funding. None of the schools in either TELS or MODELS had ideal ways to do this. Maintaining the technology infrastructure is the biggest drawback to scalability and sustainability of technology-enhanced materials. Until schools can solve this in a dependable way, there will always be ups and downs in implementation of technology-enhanced materials.

Both TELS and MODELS sustained and increased participation over four years. Both projects recruited new teachers and TELS also added new schools in participating districts. Teachers often joined the projects to take advantage of mentoring and social networking. The MODELS use of a school-based mentor requires an economic model that districts can no longer sustain. In the economic climate in 2010, this became impossible.

Mentoring can be an effective approach to professional development as shown in several studies (Songer et al., 2002; Yarnall et al., 2006) but is not always successful (Penuel et al., 2008). The MODELS project engaged almost every science teacher in the participating schools in using the curriculum and all teachers reported benefits from the school-based mentor. TELS showed the value of having a partner teacher using the same unit at the school. In both cases the collaborating teachers developed criteria for critiquing inquiry-oriented materials over time. Teachers often reported on insights that they gained from discussing inquiry teaching with their peers. This is consistent with results reported from lesson study (e.g., Lewis, Perry, & Murata, 2006; Linn, Lewis, Tsuchida, & Songer, 2000).

Gerard et al. (2009) found that a strong, supportive principal was a factor in recruiting new teachers. In all cases, principals were contacted, agreed to the use of WISE materials in their schools, and were supportive of teachers using the materials. Schools where the principals participated in a principal community had more teacher participation than schools where the principals were not members of the principal community (Gerard, Bowyer, & Linn, 2008).

For TELS, having a partner teacher and a supportive principal at the school was important for expansion. The various incentives offered by TELS, such as a small stipend for enacting units to cover the costs of administering pretests and posttests and other inconveniences also helped. In addition, the opportunity to participate in professional development was viewed favorably by most teachers. In addition, several unanticipated factors contributed to teachers embracing the project. Upon visiting schools where some teachers were using WISE materials, we learned that teachers who had not yet used the materials were frequently encouraged to do so by students who asked, "When are we going to do WISE?" This student enthusiasm for the curriculum materials was a factor in teachers' decisions to use WISE curriculum materials. In addition, teachers reported that other teachers motivated them to use WISE materials.

All the evidence from both TELS and MODELS points to the value of the school community in supporting sustainability and scalability of inquiry-oriented, technology-enhanced instruction. Many suggest using online teacher communities to strengthen professional development but others report obstacles. Research suggests that successful communities require face-to-face opportunities as well as online support, they benefit from strong leadership, and they are more successful when implementing a consistent and articulated philosophy (Falk & Drayton, 2009). For WISE, many teachers take advantage of the publically available curriculum materials but few participate in online discussions, consistent with other work on repositories (e.g., Borgman et al., 2008).

In summary, sustaining participation in innovative, inquiry-oriented science requires resources, supportive administrators, effective communities, and ongoing professional development. The technology needs to be maintained, mentors need time to mentor, and teachers need time to meet with their peers. All of these supports are expensive and rarely available in the United States. In contrast, in many countries such as Japan and the Netherlands, these supports are available. Teachers have time to meet with peers and observe each other teaching. They distinguish alternatives and reflect on their practice. These differences in professional supports probably contribute to the differential findings reported in the TIMSS classroom study discussed in Chapter 2 (Roth et al., 2006).

Conclusions

The trajectory that teachers follow in building understanding of inquiry teaching and using inquiry instruction in the classroom is complex. As teachers participate in TELS or MODELS, their confidence in the value of inquiry teaching increases. Initially, many teachers resisted inquiry and wished to customize inquiry units to make them less inquiry-oriented. Teachers began to see the value of inquiry by the second year. This change in belief was typically not immediately accompanied by changes in teaching strategy. Consistent with research on behavior change in many areas, teachers embraced the practice by recognizing its advantages, but took a longer time to change behavior to align with their beliefs.

The growing understanding of how the curriculum helps students learn was a factor in increasing confidence in the inquiry approach to instruction. As teachers gained a deeper understanding of the kind of instructional goals represented in inquiry units, they were more able to distinguish between their typical practices and the valuable inquiry strategies like asking complex questions and encouraging students to use evidence to support their responses to embedded questions. Thus, belief in inquiry teaching led to efforts to develop strategies for questioning and use of visualizations.

Given the difficulty of understanding how inquiry works and the need for evidence that inquiry can be successful, the pace of reform is often slow and uneven. Coordinated programs that include community-building, customization based on evidence from student work, and support for the process of KI seem to be the most promising.

Reflection Activity

Identify a professional development program you have designed, attended, or led. Describe one instructional pattern used in the program. Discuss how the KI pattern could improve the program.

11

THE CASE FOR KNOWLEDGE INTEGRATION

Introduction

This book makes the case for the KI approach to learning and instruction. We contrast KI with the absorption approach that characterizes much of science instruction in the United States and many other countries. We show that KI instruction compared to typical instruction results in more coherent and generative understanding of science. Students remember difficult science concepts longer and build on them during subsequent instruction when they learn from KI curriculum materials. Moreover, students who use materials designed to promote KI become skilled in monitoring their own learning. Ultimately all learners rely on KI processes. Everyone can make sense of materials intended to transmit information or to persuade if they use KI processes to interpret the information.

Building on Ideas of Designers

The goal of the KI approach to instruction is to encourage students to learn science by building on their natural inquisitiveness and ability to link and connect their observations. Directing children's interest in making sense of the world by building on their existing ideas enables them to gain insights and take advantage of scientific resources. We illustrated how this worked for 4-year-old Ben when he tried to explain dinosaur extinction (see Chapter 1).

KI emerges from the goal of helping learners make sense of the repertoire of ideas that they develop about the same scientific topic. People develop ideas by intentionally observing the natural world, deliberately interrogating their surroundings, and drawing on their cultural experiences (Chapter 1). The repertoire of ideas that people develop provides a rich resource for making sense of science.

Take a moment to jot down your ideas about instructional design. Check the ideas you generated when reading Chapter 1 if they are available. What beliefs do you have about how students learn?

On the surface, KI is inconsistent with several important intuitions many people have about learning. We examine these intuitions and show how KI can build on them.

See if these arguments build on your intuitions.

First, promoting KI runs counter to the intuitive belief that transmitting *information is key to learning.* Many textbook designers, lecturers, and even some classroom experiments follow the intuitive belief that if they just find the ideal explanation, students will learn the material. Lectures get more packed, books get longer and longer, but students only get more and more confused. Transmission without attention to the ideas held by the learner leads to adding but not integrating ideas. Students often remember the new ideas only long enough to repeat them on the next classroom test. The KI approach emphasizes *adding ideas* to the mix of ideas held by students but argues that effective ideas need to serve as pivotal cases that help students develop more coherent understanding. This means that new ideas may require careful design and extensive classroom testing.

Second, rather than designing new ideas to promote KI, when transmission fails, designers and lecturers often believe in the value of *adding motivating features* such as attractive photographs or humorous anecdotes to capture the attention of students. Motivating features may attract attention and please students but they may also distract students. Comparisons between instruction in the United States (where students scored in the middle, 18th of 38 countries) and instruction is some of the highest scoring countries on TIMSS (Roth et al., 2006) shows that successful countries pay far more attention to making science coherent (Chapter 2). To build on the belief in the value of motivating students, the KI approach emphasizes making science accessible. This is accomplished by adding ideas that connect to the interests of students and are relevant to their lives.

Third, building on the ideas of students conflicts with the intuitive belief that students *have misconceptions that need to be eradicated or at least replaced by accurate ideas.* Many lecturers and designers distrust students' ability to distinguish new ideas from their misconceptions—and this is indeed difficult. Many hundreds of physics instructors have been shocked when they administer the Force Concept Inventory and discover that their well-designed instruction has failed (Hake, 1998). The KI approach emphasizes that successful instruction engages students in distinguishing existing and new ideas rather than substituting one set of ideas for another.

The KI approach emphasizes finding ways to help students use evidence to distinguish new ideas from the ones they have developed already. Rather than viewing the ideas held by students as unworthy of consideration, the KI approach seeks to engage students in analyzing all of their ideas. Many promising ways to encourage distinguishing ideas such as engaging students in critiques have been identified (see Chapters 7 and 8).

Fourth, many instructors and designers believe that *students learn more when they are actively involved than when they are passive.* The belief in active learning is consistent with the KI process of distinguishing ideas. But some examples of active learning do not result in KI. It is common for students to actively conduct experiments but not appreciate the goals or outcomes of the experience (see Chapter 7).

The goal for KI is to make sure that active learning is geared towards coherent understanding. This means not only distinguishing ideas but reflecting on the outcome. Students can engage in a debate where they distinguish ideas and even make an excellent case for a specific viewpoint. Often, however, they do not consolidate the arguments from the debate and end up with fragmented understanding. To help students benefit from efforts to distinguish ideas, KI emphasizes reflecting on the results of experiments, debates, critiques, or other efforts to make sense of their repertoire. The goal of reflecting is to help students learn to identify gaps in understanding, monitor their own progress, weigh alternatives, and form a coherent argument. The process of reflection may include promoting new, normative ideas that have broad application and reconceptualizing ideas that seemed valuable but proved to have limitations. Reflection emphasizes the ultimate goal of science instruction—to become a lifelong science learner.

Did any of these four beliefs about instructional design resonate with your ideas? Look back over the arguments above and identify the ones you find compelling and the ones you find questionable.

Often designers are skeptical about elements of KI. In this book, we have provided evidence for each of the processes of KI but primarily for the advantages of the processes in combination. Evidence supports the value of eliciting student ideas. Studies suggest that helping students build on their ideas by supporting the process of distinguishing ideas can succeed (see Chapters 6, 7, and 8). Studies show that designing new ideas to add to the mix is challenging but pivotal cases can help (see Chapters 3 and 7, especially). Adding reflection to an activity strengthens student learning and increases the chance that students will use the ideas they learn in new contexts (see Chapters 6, 7, 8, and 9).

Use evidence from the book and from your own experience to construct an argument for one of your intuitive beliefs about instructional design. Did your argument support or question KI? What sort of evidence would help you decide?

Developing a coherent view of instructional design means building on useful intuitions about students and considering evidence about how students learn. The intuitions that govern the absorption approach also play a role in the KI approach. Evidence that adding accurate ideas is not in itself sufficient for long-term retention has cast doubt on the absorption approach. We illustrate how the negotiation of these alternatives occurs in a hypothetical example that merges experiences leading professional development workshops from both of the authors.

Professional Development Example

This example stems from our many experiences with design partnerships. In this example we illustrate the challenge of designing a new activity to develop coherent understanding of chemistry. We use interchanges that have occurred in typical workshops where teachers, technology experts, researchers, and curriculum designers brainstorm about how best to teach chemistry concepts. This example focuses on concepts of electronegativity, bond polarity, molecular polarity, and intermolecular forces in high school. Our partner chemistry teachers said that they first taught the rules and then assigned problems, which was not overly successful. The design team came up with the idea of connecting these concepts to the clean up of the recent oil spill. They suggested that these ideas would come to life if students explored why oil and water do not mix (because water molecules are more attracted to each other than to oil particles) and investigated why detergents were successful in dispersing the oil spill (detergents have both polar and non-polar ends, allowing oil and water to mix). The partnership identified a classroom experiment using detergents, a molecular visualization, and some assessment items building on observations of oil and vinegar. A tentative plan was developed and everyone went to the workshop banquet.

The next day, the partnership revisited the discussion and several teachers wanted to ask a question. They asked why the unit needed the detergent example. They said it might take extra time, it had some weaknesses, and it might be better to start with the rules. We asked them whether their students even asked why they had to learn about these concepts. They said, "all the time." We asked whether this example might help students understand the usefulness of chemistry. They said that their students enjoyed active learning, so the experiments sounded promising. But the teachers were still unsure about adding the investigation of detergents.

The next agenda item for the workshop, by chance, was a discussion with Mr. K., an experienced KI teacher, who started the session by reporting that, although he was now retired, he often received email from former students reporting on their activities. These students frequently wrote about news articles connected to the topics they had studied, such as designing energy efficient houses. One thing Mr. K. noticed was that students almost universally told him that the best part of his eighth grade class was that they understood why they were learning science. The teachers then asked Mr. K. about the detergent example, wondering if the example was necessary. Mr. K. asked the teachers what they wanted. They wanted an active approach but thought it should focus on the rules. They were not sure about the potential benefits of the detergent example. In response, Mr. K. built on the teachers' idea that active learning is good while clarifying that a personally relevant example might make science relevant.

The teachers agreed to include the notion of dispersing oil through the use of detergents as a personally relevant problem. They decided it would be helpful to compare the new instruction to their past practice. They worked with the other partners to create assessments that captured their goals for learners. By the time the partnership had finished developing the unit, all the teachers decided to use it with all of their students because it did seem more powerful than their past practices.

Reflect on your own intuitions about instruction and the views of the participants in this hypothetical example.

Evidence for KI

The chapters in this book provide evidence for the advantages of designing instruction that is consistent with KI. This is true for:

- Lectures (Chapter 2: Box 2.1; Chapter 6: Clancy & Linn, 1999; Crouch & Mazur, 2001);
- Experiments (Chapter 7: McElhaney & Linn, 2008; Lee & Songer, 2003; Wilson, Taylor, Kowalski, & Carlson, in press);
- Visualizations (Chapter 8: Linn et al., 2006; Shen & Linn, 2010);
- Collaboration (Chapter 9: Sampson & Clark, 2009; Fischer & Mandl, 2005);
- Professional development (Chapter 10: Fishman et al., 2003; Gerard et al., 2010; Williams et al., 2004).

To show the impact of KI, the studies generally use assessments that asked students to link and connect ideas and to support their arguments with evidence. The studies reveal that students learn more, and often in less time than was devoted to typical instruction, when they participate in courses designed following the KI pattern.

Specifically, successful materials include four KI processes:

- *Elicit student ideas* using brainstorms, predictions, and pretests to build on the cultural and intellectual diversity of learners.
- *Add new ideas* designed to meet criteria of pivotal cases, often in the form of classroom experiments, virtual experiments, or visualizations that illustrate unseen processes or large-scale phenomena.
- Engage students in *distinguishing ideas* by generating explanations, drawing their ideas, critiquing experiments of others, or using evidence to negotiate with peers who hold different ideas.
- Guide students to *reflect and sort out* their ideas in summative reports, persuasive letters to policy makers, journal entries, or poster presentations.

The four processes work together to enable students to integrate ideas. The contribution of each of the processes is important as we discuss in the next sections. Together the processes contribute to the ability of everyone to become a lifelong science learner. Below, we summarize the processes along with supporting evidence from studies comparing absorption to KI instruction.

Elicit Ideas

KI generally starts with eliciting ideas but these activities are much less common in absorption-oriented instruction. As a result, adding predictions or opportunities to generate ideas has been a big advantage in numerous studies. Studies of experiments (Linn & Songer, 1993), visualizations (Linn & Hsi, 2000), collaborations (Clancy et al., 1999; Fischer & Mandl, 2005), and lectures (Crouch & Mazur, 2001) all show the value of predictions.

The main purpose of eliciting ideas is to focus the learner on identifying and testing out their views. When students make predictions they become committed to investigating them. Stating a point of view can focus the learner on comparing their own ideas to those they might encounter. Research on self-explanations can be seen as supporting the idea of eliciting ideas. When students are prompted to explain an observation or when they spontaneously generate an explanation they are clarifying their own ideas and predicting how the scientific situation works (Chi et al., 1989).

Another essential reason for eliciting ideas is to promote equity. By asking students for their ideas, instruction validates culturally-relevant ideas that might not be found in typical curriculum materials but make sense to students (Bell et al., 2009). For example, in Israel where many immigrants have diverse experiences, some programs build on ideas about navigation, measurement, and food preparation that illustrate complex scientific concepts. Honoring culturally relevant ideas provides students with respect for their views and for themselves. As a result, students gain a sense of agency—they are empowered to explore their ideas and develop more coherent ideas—where otherwise they might develop a sense of isolation or helplessness.

A third important reason to elicit ideas is to help students to integrate all of their ideas. Neglected ideas may later be embraced because they have not been compared to or distinguished from new ideas (Linn & Hsi, 2000).

A fourth important reason to elicit ideas is that some of these views serve as stepping stones for students to achieve more coherent understanding. Thus, in thermodynamics, students build on their idea that metals are naturally cold to distinguish the difference between the temperature of their hand and the temperature of objects they touch (see pivotal case, Chapter 3).

To elicit ideas, the designer needs to ask the right question. Asking a reasonably narrow question is a good idea for getting a manageable set of responses but might constrain respondents unnecessarily. In addition, since students have a repertoire of ideas, not just one, instruction is more successful when students consider all their views. Having students first generate ideas with a peer and then contribute to the class can increase the number of ideas generated. Often seeing a visualization motivates students to generate more ideas than they generated initially.

Many activities and technologies can be used to elicit ideas. Students can make predictions individually or in a brainstorm (or gated collaboration). The use of embedded assessments in online learning environments can both elicit ideas and promote reflection. In lectures, students can contribute predictions using systems such as networked tablet PCs and can communicate their ideas in one-minute summaries. Personal response systems such as clickers often ask students to select from predetermined alternatives. If students are required to select among alternatives, they may not find their personal view represented. Nuanced use of these systems could include ways to elicit additional possibilities.

Eliciting ideas helps teachers appreciate the views that students hold. To increase equity, instructors need ways to ensure that all the ideas held by students including culturally relevant ideas are captured.

Add Ideas

Both KI and absorption embrace the idea of adding ideas. Everyone thinks it is a good idea to add ideas to the mix held by the student. Extensive evidence shows that adding ideas in lectures and textbooks is often either confusing, unsuccessful, or associated with short-term gains (Clancy et al., 1999; Kulik & Kulik, 1979; Kulik, Kulik, & Cohen, 1980; Mazur, 1997; Odubunmi & Balogun, 1991; Roseman et al., 1999; Roseman et al., 2008).

Research on KI stresses the importance of designing the ideas that are added to the mix held by the student with care. Most successful ideas fit the definition of a pivotal case in that they build on the ideas held by learners, compare scientifically transparent conditions, offer valid arguments, encourage students to incorporate the ideas into a narrative, and illustrate new ideas in personally-relevant contexts (Chapters 3 and 7; Linn, 2003). The value of pivotal cases rather than whole lectures has led many instructors to shorten or even eliminate lectures (Crouch & Mazur, 2001; Titterton et al., 2010). Careful design of visualizations so that they do add information has demonstrated their value (Lee, Linn, Varma, & Liu, 2009; Linn et al., 2006; Liu, Lee, & Linn, 2010a). When teachers use curriculum materials that have been refined their students learn more.

Ideally new ideas resonate with student ideas and supply evidence for distinguishing new and existing ideas. Several instructional approaches can increase the likelihood that new ideas are considered. Collaborators or peers can provide hints and guidance to enable students to make sense of new ideas based on Vygotsky's (1978) notion of the Zone of Proximal Development. Vygotsky argued that social supports and hints provided by collaborators could spur students to appreciate ideas that at first seemed confusing.

Adding ideas is especially important as new technologies provide insight into unobservable processes and allow for virtual experimentation (Chapters 6 and 7).

Designing effective ideas to add is only part of the KI process. If these ideas are deceptively clear they could inhibit KI. If new ideas get isolated rather than integrated or misconstrued they may actually interfere with lifelong science learning by convincing students that they cannot understand science.

Distinguish Ideas

Distinguishing ideas is essential for KI. Those who view the learner as absorbing information do not emphasize distinguishing ideas. As a result, this process is often neglected in instruction. It is common for students to encounter critique for the first time when doing a KI unit. Debates in science class are rare and often viewed by teachers as inappropriate given that science is established by empirical studies (Shear et al., 2004).

When students distinguish ideas they need to develop criteria for selecting among alternative views. Developing these criteria can become a goal of instruction by itself. Students need to decide about the validity of evidence available to them. For complex topics such as global climate change, they have to find criteria that allow them to sort out persuasive messages and biased opinions. This activity also provides insight into the nature of scientific advance, a topic that is often neglected in science courses.

Finding effective ways to support the process of distinguishing ideas is key to the research on lectures (Chapter 6), experiments (Chapter 7), visualizations (Chapter 8), and collaboration (Chapter 9). Distinguishing ideas requires that students have generated ideas and added new ideas—so they have something to distinguish.

Research has revealed some promising practices to support distinguishing ideas:

- Generation questions or explanations as used in most KI units (Chiu & Linn, in press).
- Drawing activities such as used for chemical reactions (Chiu & Linn, 2008; Zhang & Linn, 2008).
- Selecting among alternatives as used for chemical reactions (Zhang & Linn, 2008).
- Critique activities as used in chemical reactions as well as thermodynamics (Chang et al., 2008) and electrostatics (Shen & Linn, in press).
- Collaborative negotiation of views as used in collaborative learning (Eldar, Eylon, & Ronen, in press; Sampson & Clark, 2009) and customization of instruction (Gerard et al., 2010). When students with distinct views negotiate understanding they distinguish ideas. Often this process involves critique and requires students teach and learn from peers (Clark & Sampson, 2009). Several studies suggest that collaborative negotiation can succeed even when the viewpoints that students integrate are supplied by the curriculum (Fischer & Mandl, 2005; Sampson & Clark, 2011). When teachers

customize instruction they also negotiate viewpoints supported by evidence from student work.

Desirable difficulties, identified by Bjork (1994), may help elaborate the nature of distinguishing ideas. Bjork found that some conditions of learning that appear optimal during instruction (because students are successful in completing tasks) can fail to support long-term retention and transfer of knowledge. He described desirable difficulties as activities that appear suboptimal because they increase errors and prolong learning but, remarkably, enhance long-term retention and transfer. Desirable difficulties include some of the same activities that help students distinguish ideas such as generating explanations (which could be in the form of drawings) and using tests such as critiques as learning events (see Chapter 8). Other possible desirable difficulties such as spacing rather than massing study sessions, interleaving practice on distinct topics, varying presentation of material, and reducing feedback deserve further study as potential methods for helping students to distinguish ideas.

Distinguishing ideas can be supported by technology that guides students to structure their ideas (Reiser, 2004) or represent experimental findings in a table (McElhaney & Linn, 2008). Learning environment such as WISE scaffold students to write explanations, draw their ideas, select among alternatives, critique, and collaborate.

Reflect on Ideas

An essential aspect of lifelong learning is to reflect on ideas about new information or perplexing questions. The KI approach emphasizes reflection as a way to consolidate and organize the many ideas students develop. In contrast the absorption approach is more likely to emphasize recall of accurate information, consistent with the items on most state and national tests.

To take advantage of predictions, new ideas, and efforts to distinguish ideas students benefit from opportunities to reflect. Distinguishing ideas is not always sufficient for KI. Bell (2004a) found that students accurately distinguished ideas but needed to reflect and consolidate their ideas in order to benefit from activities such as debates.

To develop coherent ideas about science, students need to reflect on their views. When students reflect on ideas about a topic they have the opportunity to reexamine the links and connections among their ideas and to build a more coherent account of the topic. Reflection involves considering all the ideas developed in instruction, the ideas developed before instruction, and the evidence gained from distinguishing ideas. Reflection is an essential aspect of self-monitoring. Ideally, students would continue to approach scientific dilemmas by reflecting on what they know, identifying gaps in their knowledge, and seeking information to resolve uncertainties all during their lives.

Often assessments of KI instruction call for reflection, providing additional opportunities to practice integrating ideas. The KI rubric rewards students who have made progress in integrating their ideas and does not penalize students for making inaccurate conjectures.

Reflection is typically implemented in learning environments as a prompt for reflection. Learning environments can encourage self-monitoring by helping students keep track of their ideas, compare predictions to outcomes, and identify gaps in their knowledge. Students are also regularly asked to reflect in collaborative online environments such as Knowledge Forum (Scardamalia & Bereiter, 1998). Reflection also occurs when students write persuasive arguments to support scientific issues such as protecting endangered species or consolidate their ideas in reports and posters.

In summary, the four processes of KI work in synergy. They are all needed to enable students to develop coherent understanding of science. Fortunately they also engage students in the specific activities they will need to become lifelong science learners.

KI and Lifelong Learning

The KI approach to instruction has the potential of both promoting coherent understanding and developing lifelong learning processes. Curriculum materials can improve coherent understanding of science by emphasizing the four processes of KI along with the principles of *making science accessible, making thinking visible, learning from each other,* and *promoting autonomy* (see Chapter 5). KI instruction can help everyone become an autonomous integrator of ideas by giving students practice using KI processes in many different units and contexts.

Becoming an autonomous learner is facilitated by making science accessible. This means ensuring that KI units feature personally-relevant problems such as airbag safety (Chapter 7) or asthma (Chapter 9). As illustrated for experiments, when students study problems such as global climate that arise in their lives, they can build on their ideas when they encounter the problem again.

KI instruction can also help students and teachers alike learn to monitor their understanding so that they know when to use autonomous learning processes. As discussed for lectures (Chapter 6), students who develop the autonomous ability to engage in KI can benefit from instruction featuring transmission of information, even when instruction does not make it easy. People will also be prepared to question persuasive messages if they learn processes for distinguishing ideas such as critique (see Chapter 7).

Successful autonomous learners:

- Elicit their own ideas about new science topics and compare them to the instructed ideas.
- Distinguish among their own and the new ideas.

- Reflect on their progress.
- Apply their ideas to new, relevant problems they encounter.

Thus, teaching for KI has the potential of creating lifelong science learners. The same KI processes implemented in curriculum materials succeed when individual learners follow them to guide their own learning. To become autonomous learners, everyone needs to spontaneously monitor their progress and identify gaps in their knowledge.

Assessment of Science Learning

Achieving coherent understanding of science is a lifelong process. To document the value of KI designers, instructors, and learners need appropriate outcome measures. KI has the goal of developing coherent understanding of science. This means that learners can link and connect ideas using evidence. As understanding becomes more coherent, individuals connect more of the ideas in their repertoire. This generally means that learners promote promising ideas that are supported by evidence and pay less attention to views that have limited support. Items that measure this process usually require reflection on what has been learned. KI instruction, when aligned with KI assessment allows teachers to diagnose student strengths and limitations, make decisions about customizing materials, and measure progress in developing coherent ideas (see KI assessment items and rubrics in Chapters 2–10).

Design of KI Assessments

KI assessments require careful design (Liu, Lee, Hofstetter, & Linn, 2008). The KI rubric rewards answers that have normative ideas and connections among those ideas. It does not penalize learners who also include inaccurate, intuitive ideas and non-normative links among their ideas. Students get credit for the most sophisticated idea and link that they include in their response.

At the same time, the KI rubric encourages students to seek links among their ideas. Knowing that they can make conjectures without penalty encourages students to practice linking and connecting their ideas Items that encourage students to generate links and attempt to support them with evidence serve as learning opportunities. Thus, KI assessments can serve as learning events as well as outcome measures.

When students generate inaccurate links they reveal their inclination to make links and provide teachers with valuable information about their thinking. Teachers can use the information to customize instruction.

Instruction-Sensitive Assessment

Ensuring that assessments are aligned with instruction is especially important for KI. Assessments that primarily measure recall are quite insensitive to KI instruction—and probably to other forms of instruction as well (Clark & Linn, 2003; Linn et al., 2006). This makes sense because recall tests measure only a small part of the goal of KI—acquiring isolated ideas. They do not measure the coherence of ideas.

Even when state tests are aligned with the standards it has been difficult to show benefits from changes in instructional practice. Specifically, many dramatic improvements on state tests have been attributed to familiarity with the item types, elimination of students who should not be taking the test (such as those who do not speak English), and demographic changes in the school population—not changes in understanding of the topic (Koretz, 2008). Even when schools make quite substantial changes in instructional practice they often find minimal gains in student performance due to the nature of the test used to assess gains.

Measuring Coherent Understanding

To capture progress in KI, we need tests than measure coherent understanding. Comparing KI items to typical state and national science items, shows that typical multiple choice items fail to measure the sophisticated ideas captured in KI items (see Box 7.2). In one study, available items measured performance at level 2 of the KI rubric: one valid idea (Lee, Liu, & Linn, in press). It is possible to create multiple-choice items for level three and sometimes for level four but these are rare. A study comparing constructed response items to multiple choice items found that the constructed response items always added valid information about KI (Liu, Lee, & Linn, 2010a).

Unfortunately most of the state and national assessments fail to measure KI. For example, in an analysis of 246 studies of mathematics performance conducted between 1990 and 2007, Lindberg, Hyde, Petersen, and Linn (2010) coded all available items using a depth of knowledge framework (Webb, 1999). The framework has four levels: Level 1 (Recall) includes the recall of information such as facts or definitions and using simple algorithms such as addition. Level 2 (Skill/Concept) includes items that require students to make decisions about a concept. These items typically ask students to classify, organize, estimate, or compare information. Level 3 (Strategic Thinking) includes complex and abstract items that require students to reason, plan, and use evidence. Level 4 (Extended Thinking) requires complex reasoning, planning, developing, and thinking over an extended period of time. Level 4 requires students to connect ideas within the content area or among content areas. Level 3 and 4 items can reasonably be assumed to require some KI. Of the 120 studies where it was possible to code the depth of knowledge used in the assessment, only 9 studies (7.5%) had tests that measured performance at levels 3 or 4.

The dearth of measures of KI among high stakes tests sends a clear message to teachers that quick regurgitation of facts is of paramount importance, especially compared to a deep, coherent understanding of science principles. With the increased emphasis on testing associated with No Child Left Behind, increasing numbers of teachers teach to the test (Au, 2007). If the tests only measure recall or straightforward understanding of concepts, then teaching for KI appears to be unnecessary. Most American textbooks already neglect KI and fail to support coherent understanding (Roseman, Linn, & Koppal, 2008). Reliance on recall-oriented tests is likely to further disadvantage American students relative to their counterparts in countries that emphasize more coherent understanding (Chapter 2; Roth et al., 2006).

This situation is exacerbated by classroom testing practices that focus on short-term recall rather than cumulative understanding. Research on KI instruction typically includes tests of cumulative understanding at the end of the semester or end of the year. These tests alert teachers and students to the importance of maintaining their understanding at least for the remainder of the course. Many teachers, frustrated by the number of weeks they need to devote to state tests, have reduced their use of cumulative tests. When they only need to prepare for a single end of unit test, students rightfully argue that memorizing is successful (Linn & Hsi, 2000).

In summary, the studies reported in this book provide evidence that teaching for KI can improve performance on tests that measure coherent understanding. This means that KI instruction leads to greater gains on the instructed topics than does typical instruction (Lee, Linn, Varma, & Liu, 2009; Linn et al., 2006; Liu, Lee, & Linn, 2010a). KI instruction also has long-term benefits. Several studies show that rather than forgetting what they learned, students perform better on delayed tests, than they did on unit tests (Chapter 8; Chiu, 2010). We attribute these gains to the coherent understanding that is the goal of KI instruction.

Furthermore, the studies show that aligning instruction with assessment is crucial to effective implementation of KI practices. Tests that measure KI typically require generation of explanations although several new item types such as creating a MySystem diagram (see Box 8.3) offer alternatives. High-stakes assessments have become more prevalent and consequential for science. If these tests primarily measure recall of isolated ideas then students and teachers get the feeling that coherent understanding is not valued.

Technology and KI

Technologies for education have benefitted from decades of trial and refinement. As the research in this book shows, technologies such as online, interactive visualizations, virtual experiments, and guidance for inquiry learning can be important contributors to effective instruction. Early efforts to use technology for teaching often followed the absorption approach and used electronic books or videos of experiments to transmit information. These early efforts to take advantage of technology failed but promising alternatives emerged (Collins & Halverson, 2009; Linn, 1998).

Recently the National Science Foundation convened a task force to make recommendations about cyberlearning. One author of this book (Linn) served on the task force. Cyberlearning refers to instruction that is supported by networked computing and communications technologies including laptop computers, handhelds, location sensing devices, immersive worlds, games, and cloud computing. The task force identified opportunities for education at the intersection of cyberinfrastructure and the learning sciences. The task force concluded that cyberlearning has the potential to take advantage of computer programming, social networking, maps, art, and other cultural artifacts to improve learning outcomes (Borgman et al., 2008). Today, cyberlearning is a major research initiative at the National Science Foundation and the question is not so much whether to use technology but how to use it effectively.

While technology cannot solve all the educational problems, the cyberlearning report identifies places where networked computing and communications technology, if properly leveraged, can enhance educational opportunities and strengthen proven methods of learning (Borgman et al., 2008). Examples of the promise of technology are delineated in this book (see Chapters 6, 7, 8, 9, and 10). For example, environments like WISE have many promising features that can support teaching and learning such as,

- Incorporating interactive scientific visualizations to help students understand unobservable processes.
- Scaffolding students in inquiry practices.
- Supporting teachers to efficiently comment on student work.
- Providing authoring tools that simplify use of the KI pattern for new materials.
- Enabling co-design of assessments delivered using the same technologies.
- Incorporating open source innovations like PhET, and Molecular Workbench.
- Supporting interoperability with other effective student design environments.
- Gathering continuous indicators of student progress using embedded assessments.

Teachers report that guidance from WISE allows them to focus on helping their students learn. They can respond to substantive questions from individuals. They can identify issues that apply to most students and interrupt the class to discuss the topic.

The cyberlearning report recommends that the community adopt policies to promote open educational resources so developers can work together to create useful innovations. By building an open source community it will be possible for educators to create more powerful and effective materials than they could by working alone. We hope that readers of this book will join the effort.

New Goals for Science Instruction

As discussed in Chapter 1, technology both enables and demands that citizens develop new skills. To prepare the next generation of scientists and ensure that all citizens lead fruitful lives, policy leaders have called for instruction that promotes 21st century reasoning skills and computational thinking. These new goals for science courses align well with the KI approach.

- *21st century reasoning skills.* Recent reports in the United States (Hilton, 2010), England (Nuffield, 2006), Israel (Tomorrow 98, 1992) and other countries, often funded by industry leaders, call for preparing students to develop new skills that are needed in today's workplace (see Table 11.1). These skills are consistent with a KI approach to curriculum, which requires *adaptability* in dealing with new evidence, *communication* skills when students work in teams, and *non-routine problem solving* to deal with everyday problems such as airbag safety or asthma prevention (Chapters 7 and 9). As discussed above, KI processes can help students become *autonomous* learners, and can engage students in systems thinking around problems such as global climate change.
- *Computational thinking.* A new form of reasoning, called computational thinking, is emerging at the intersection of computer science and other disciplines. For example, to appreciate the mapping of the human genome, people need to combine understanding of the nature of DNA with understanding of a variety of computational approaches including the famous "shotgun algorithm." Many in the computer science community argue that students will not be prepared to reason about problems at the intersection of computer science and other disciplines without educational experiences that emphasize integrating ideas from multiple disciplines. Defining this form of thinking was the goal of the first workshop (NRC, 2010). Evidence that teenagers can do email, use VoIP to talk to a friend in Italy, watch a fantasy video, and finish homework simultaneously suggests that computational thinking may be achievable. Making sense of analyses of contemporary problems such as global climate change requires people to combine understanding of powerful computational tools with advances in the discipline. Creating computational thinkers could be the focus of KI units.

In summary, the KI approach to learning and instruction capitalizes on new technologies and has the potential of helping students develop new technology-relevant skills and capabilities. The cyberlearning initiative highlights important directions for technology-enhanced learning. Recent reports that call for preparing students to thrive in a rapidly changing technology environment resonate with the goals of KI instruction.

TABLE 11.1 21st Century Skills

21st CENTURY SKILLS
Adaptability
The ability and willingness to cope with uncertain, new, and rapidly-changing conditions, tasks, technologies, and cultures.
Complex communications/social skills
The ability to interpret both verbal and non-verbal information, including persuasive messages and respond effectively. This might mean decomposing complex tasks, asking questions to clarify messages, or arguing a point using scientific evidence.
Non-routine problem solving
The ability to deal with imprecise information, recognize patterns, conduct investigations, diagnose a dilemma, synthesize information, and create solutions.
Self-management/self-development
The ability to work remotely, to autonomously attack problems, to identify needed skills and acquire them, and to monitor progress.
Systems thinking
The ability to comprehend and interrogate an entire system. This includes investigating how a system works, documenting how an action, change, or malfunction in one part of the system affects the rest of the system, and using judgment and decision making to evaluate alternative impacts on the system.

Next Steps, Open Questions and New Directions

The findings reported here raise new questions and suggest new research programs. We identify some prominent directions and encourage partnerships to explore these and related questions.

Refining Patterns

The research reported in this book builds on the specific patterns we reported earlier (Linn & Eylon, 2006) and synthesizes the research to support a general KI pattern. We illustrate this pattern for specific activities such as lectures, experiments, and professional development. We also show that this general pattern can help improve instruction in many diverse science disciplines.

While we synthesized findings into a general pattern it is the specific examples that best illustrate the value of the KI approach. The pattern offers a starting point for design of instruction aimed at coherent understanding of science. For each curriculum unit we describe, substantial user testing and refinement was needed to make it successful for a wide range of learners. This book identifies some of the specific features of instruction that emerged from this process of trial and refinement. Examples include encouraging students to make drawings of their interpretations of visualizations to distinguish ideas, using gated discussions to elicit ideas, and designing pivotal cases to introduce new ideas.

For each disciplinary topic, analysis of the science concepts, repertoire of ideas held by students, and relevant visualizations were essential. Most units we have studied are quite short—lasting from one to several weeks. In some cases, we have studied effective sequences of activities that build on each other. It is also important to determine best practices for each discipline. Research using the patterns reveals unique challenges for each discipline (e.g., electrostatics, Casperson & Linn, 2006; Shen & Linn, in press; photosynthesis and plate tectonics, Svihla et al., 2010; electricity and magnetism, Bagno & Eylon, 1997). These studies reveal that we need more research to create pivotal cases for perplexing science topics.

The next steps for our own refinement of KI patterns include study of longer sequences of instruction, study of features of KI in each discipline, and study of techniques for promoting cumulative learning across science courses. We argued that students benefit from integrating their ideas using visualizations, experiments, collaboration, and other activities. We suspect that when instruction includes varied activities, everyone benefits. Students can refine the processes of KI when they have the chance to practice with varied activities. They benefit from using a wide range of specific patterns for experiments, collaborative investigations, visualizations, and debates, for example (Linn & Eylon, 2006).

Thus, to elaborate the implications of the KI pattern it is important to study sustained use of the pattern across whole courses. It is also important to study the features that are important for specific topics and disciplines.

Developing Research Methods

Research on instructional patterns has benefitted from advances in methods for studying iterative refinement of instruction and classroom learning. Methods for developing assessments to measure coherent understanding across topics and disciplines allow for comparison of progress across courses (Linn et al., 2006; Liu, Lee, Hofstetter, & Linn, 2008; Liu, Lee, & Linn, 2010a). These methods have improved but need further refinement. We need better techniques for analyzing the interactions of small groups responding to KI instruction. We have made progress, but we need more ways to capture the impact of professional development on student learning (Gerard et al., 2010). We can now log student interactions with visualizations and virtual experiments. We need better methods for analyzing these findings.

Promoting Equity

We have made progress in ensuring that science instruction is equitable. KI patterns respect the ideas of all learners and incorporate culturally relevant views by eliciting ideas and building on student experiences. All of the studies of KI have a common finding of no differences between boys and girls. This is true even for units that require extensive use of spatial reasoning skills (Liu, Lee, & Linn, 2010a).

Collaborative activities have the potential of reinforcing stereotypes, but we find little evidence of this when students work in two person groups. Furthermore, we find that both students benefit when groups are formed based on diverse performance on the pretest (Chiu, 2010).

By drawing on personally-relevant examples, we can connect to varied student experiences. Selecting examples that reflect the interests and experiences of individuals can help students identify with the role of a scientist (Tate, 2009). Students who participate in KI activities often develop a sense of agency. They feel empowered to make sense of new information.

We need to investigate these aspects of KI and student learning in broader cultural contexts and for more extended periods of time. Researchers in Taiwan, China, Israel, Singapore, and Germany are beginning to illustrate the role of diverse school systems on efforts to promote KI. Ensuring that diverse individuals all develop a sense of agency and identify themselves as lifelong science learners is essential to the success of science education.

Improving Professional Development

Professional development to enable teachers to prepare the next generation of scientists, citizens, and lifelong science learning is challenging (see Chapter 10). Teachers are starting to see the benefit of this approach. At a recent workshop, one teacher reacted to the emphasis on eliciting student ideas by remarking:

> I love that idea. Eliciting ideas. It is like martial arts instead of attacking blindly. I never thought of that. Starting with the ideas instead of a blank slate.

Another teacher, after participating in KI professional development where eliciting ideas, critiquing units, and customizing with student work, was central to the activities, commented:

> I have been attending professional development workshops for over 20 years. This is the first time that the leaders were interested in my opinion and ideas.

These comments reveal the need for more widespread and effective professional development to promote KI and encourage inquiry teaching. There are currently many obstacles to inquiry teaching. Many teachers argue that students are not able to reason about science and choose to postpone implementing activities that depend on student reasoning (Sisk-Hilton, 2009). Others complain that they lack the time, are constrained by the standards, or need smaller classes before they can teach for coherent understanding. Research including investigation of educational policies is needed to find effective solutions to these dilemmas.

Supporting Autonomy and Self-Monitoring

We have made some progress in helping students become autonomous learners. We need better insights into this process and more detailed understanding of ways to develop learners who integrate their ideas even when patterns are not apparent in the materials. Much of science instruction remains designed based on the absorption approach. To prepare successful learners we need to ensure that they can integrate ideas even when the instructional materials offer no help or guidance.

Conclusions

We have made the case for the KI approach to science teaching and learning. We argue that everyone can learn science when courses implement activities that feature the KI instructional pattern. Evidence in every chapter supports this claim. Teachers and schools can start now with KI by using WISE units that are free and available (wise.berkeley.edu) and by customizing instruction to add the KI pattern.

We have distinguished the KI and absorption approach to instruction and shown the limitations of absorption. Both approaches agree on the need to add ideas to those held by the learner—but KI emphasizes the importance of careful design of the ideas and shows that new ideas need to be interspersed with opportunities to distinguish among ideas and reflect. Both seek to motivate the learner, but KI takes advantage of student interest in personally-relevant problems while absorption often uses distracting photographs or anecdotes. Both see advantages of active learning but KI engages students in distinguishing ideas while absorption activities can even engage the learner in developing incoherent ideas.

KI emphasizes the need to build on student ideas using brainstorms or predictions while absorption focuses on transmitting the information that students lack.

For KI, when instructors are aware of student ideas they are much more likely to succeed because they can build on the views of their students. When instructors have an absorption view of student ideas they often seek—unsuccessfully—to eradicate the ideas.

In addition, KI stresses the importance of reflecting on understanding, monitoring progress, and directing ones' own learning. Absorption privileges transmission rather than encouraging monitoring and therefore is less likely to promote lifelong learning.

If instructors could only make one change in their teaching, every chapter shows that eliciting ideas or asking for predictions and encouraging students to reconcile predictions with new evidence is a quick and effective way to improve learning outcomes.

The most valuable outcome of KI instruction is the ability to engage in lifelong science learning. When students learn KI processes they can use them for all their learning. This means they are prepared to learn even from materials that are designed to transmit information. As a result, learners can continuously improve the coherence of their ideas.

This book underscores the importance of promoting autonomous, lifelong learning, improving state and national assessments, ensuring equitable access to instruction, and using technology effectively. Supporting cumulative under-standing of science remains challenging. We encourage readers to explore these and other open questions to refine our understanding of science learning and teaching.

Reflection Activity

Explore the availability of open source software for a science topic of your choice. Identify a favorite online activity for the topic. Find out if the software is open source or proprietary. Discuss the advantages and drawbacks of open source software.

REFERENCES

Abell, S. K., Martini, M., & George, M. D. (2001). "That's what scientists have to do": Preservice elementary teachers' conceptions of the nature of science during a moon investigation. *International Journal of Science Education, 23*(11), 1095–1109.

Abelson, H., & Sussman, G. (1985). *Structure and interpretation of computer programs.* Cambridge: MIT Press.

Abraham, M. R. (1998). The learning cycle approach as a strategy for instruction in science. In B. J. Fraser & K. G. Tobin (Eds.), *International handbook of science education* (pp. 513–524). Dordrecht, The Netherlands: Kluwers.

Agogino, A. M., & Linn, M. C. (1992). Retaining female engineering students: Will early design experiences help? [Viewpoint Editorial]. M. Wilson (Ed.). *National Science Foundation Directions, 5*(2), 8–9.

Alexander, C., Ishikawa, S., & Silverstein, M. (1977). *A pattern language: Towns, buildings, construction.* New York: Oxford University Press.

Allen, S. (2002). Looking for learning in visitor talk: A methodological exploration. In G. Leinhardt, K. Crowley & K. Knutson (Eds.), *Learning conversations in museums* (pp. 259–303). Mahwah, NJ: Lawrence Erlbaum Associates.

American Association for the Advancement of Science. (2002). Middle grades science textbooks: A benchmarks-based evaluation. Retrieved May 24, 2007, from http://www.project2061.org/publications/textbook/mgsci/report/index.htm

American Association for the Advancement of Science, A. (1994). *Benchmarks for science literacy: Project 2061.* New York: Oxford University Press.

American Association of University Women (AAUW) Educational Foundation. (2000). *Tech-savvy: Educating girls in the new computer age.* Washington, DC: AAUW.

Anderson, J. R. (1983). *The architecture of cognition.* Cambridge, MA: Harvard University Press.

Anderson, J. R., Corbett, A. T., Koedinger, K. R., & Pelletier, R. (1995). Cognitive tutors: Lessons learned. *The Journal of the Learning Sciences, 4*(2), 167–207.

Anderson, R., Anderson, R., Simon, B., Wolfman, S. A., VanDeGrift, T., & Yasuhara,

K. (2004). Experiences with a tablet PC based lecture presentation system in computer science courses. In *Proceedings of the 35th SIGCSE technical symposium on computer science education*. Norfolk, VA: Association for Computing Machinery (ACM).

Andersson, B. (1990). Pupils' conceptions of matter and its transformations (age 12–16). *Studies in Science Education 18*(1), 53–85.

Ardac, D., & Akaygun, S. (2005). Using static and dynamic visuals to represent chemical change at molecular level. *International Journal of Science Education, 27*(11), 1269–1298.

Aronson, J. (Ed.). (2002). *Improving academic achievement: Impact of psychological factors on education*. San Diego, CA: Academic Press.

Ashburn, E. A., & Floden, R. E. (Eds.). (2006). *Meaningful learning using technology: What educators need to know and do*. New York: Teachers College Press.

Au, W. (2007). High-stakes testing and curricular control: A qualitative metasynthesis. *Educational Researcher, 36*(5), 258–267.

Bagno, E., & Eylon, B.-S. (1997). From problem-solving to a knowledge structure: An example from the domain of electromagnetism. *The American Journal of Physics, 65*(8), 726–736.

Bagno, E., Berger, H., & Eylon, B.-S. (2008). Meeting the challenge of students' understanding of formulas in high-school physics: A learning tool. *Physics Education, 43*, 75–82. Available also at: http://stacks.iop.org/0031-9120/43/75

Baker, M., & Lund, K. (1997). Promoting reflective interactions in a CSCL environment. *Journal of Computer Assisted Learning, 13*(3), 175–193.

Ball, D. L., & Feiman-Nemser, S. (1988). Using textbooks and teachers' guides: A dilemma for beginning teachers and teacher educators. *Curriculum Inquiry, 18*(4), 401–423.

Banaji, M. R., Hardin, C., & Rothman, A. J. (1993). Implicit stereotyping in person judgement. *Journal of Personality and Social Psychology, 65*(2), 272–281.

Barab, S., Kling, R., & Gray, J. H. (Eds.). (2004). *Designing For virtual communities in the service of learning*. Cambridge, MA: Cambridge University Press.

Barab, S. A., & Hay, K. E. (2001). Doing science at the elbows of experts: Issues related to the science apprenticeship camp. *Journal of Research in Science Teaching, 38*(1), 70–102.

Barak, M., & Dori, Y. J. (2005). Enhancing undergraduate students' chemistry understanding through project-based learning in an IT environment. *Science Education, 89*(1), 117–139.

Baram-Tsabari, A., & Yarden, A. (2009). Identifying meta–clusters of students' interest in science and their change with age. *Journal of Research in Science Teaching, 46*(9), 999–1022.

Barron, B. (2000). Achieving coordination in collaborative problem solving groups. *Journal of the Learning Sciences, 9*(4), 403–436.

Barron, B. (2003). When smart groups fail. *The Journal of the Learning Sciences, 12*(3), 307–359.

Barrows, H. S. (1985). *How to design a problem-based curriculum for the predinical years*. New York: Springer.

Beck, S., Bertholle, L., & Child, J. (1961). *Mastering the art of French cooking*. New York: Knopf.

Becker, H. J. (1999). *Internet use by teachers: Conditions of professional use and teacher-directed student use* (Report No. 1). Irvine, CA: Center for Research on Information Technology and Organizations, University of California, Irvine, and the University of Minnesota.

Beichner, R. (2000). Student-centered activities for large enrollment university physics

(SCALE-UP). In *Proceedings of the Sigma Xi forum "reshaping undergraduate science and engineering education: Tools for better learning"* (pp. 43–52). Minneapolis, MN.

Beichner, R. J. (2008). The SCALE-UP project: A student–centered active learning environment for undergraduate programs. Invited white paper for the National Academy of Sciences: The National Academies Press, Washington, DC.

Bell, P. (1997). Using argument representations to make thinking visible for individuals and groups. In R. Hall, N. Miyake & N. Enyedy (Eds.), *Proceedings of CSCL '97: The Second International Conference on Computer Support for Collaborative Learning* (pp. 10–19). Toronto, Canada: University of Toronto Press.

Bell, P. (2004a). Promoting students' argument construction and collaborative debate in the science classroom. In M. C. Linn, E. A. Davis & P. Bell (Eds.), *Internet environments for science education* (pp. 115–144). Mahwah, NJ: Lawrence Erlbaum Associates.

Bell, P. (2004b). The educational opportunities of contemporary controversies in science. In M. C. Linn, E. A. Davis, & P. Bell (Eds.), *Internet environments for science education* (pp. 233–260). Mahwah, NJ: Lawrence Erlbaum Associates.

Bell, P., Davis, E. A., & Linn, M. C. (1995). The knowledge integration environment: Theory and design. In J. L. Schnase & E. L. Cunnius (Eds.), *Proceedings of the Computer Supported Collaborative Learning Conference, CSCL '95* (pp. 14–21). Mahwah, NJ: Lawrence Erlbaum Associates.

Bell, P., Hoadley, C., & Linn, M. C. (2004). Design-based research in education. In M. C. Linn, E. A. Davis & P. Bell (Eds.), *Internet environments for science education* (pp. 73–88). Mahwah, NJ: Lawrence Erlbaum Associates.

Bell, P., Lewenstein, B., Shouse, A. W., Feder, M. A., & National Research Council (NRC) (Eds.). (2009). *Learning science in informal environments: People, places, and pursuits.* Washington, DC: The National Academies Press.

Bell, P., & Linn, M. C. (2000). Scientific arguments as learning artifacts: Designing for learning from the web with KIE. *International Journal of Science Education, 22*(8), 797–817.

Bell, P., & Linn, M. C. (2002). Beliefs about science: How does science instruction contribute? In B. K. Hofer & P. R. Pintrich (Eds.), *Personal epistemology: The psychology of beliefs about knowledge and knowing* (pp. 321–346). Mahwah, NJ: Lawrence Erlbaum Associates.

Ben–Zvi, R., Eylon, B.-S., & Silberstein, J. (1986a). Is an atom of copper malleable? *Journal of Chemical Education, 63*(1), 64–66.

Ben–Zvi, R., Eylon, B.-S., & Silberstein, J. (1986b). Revision of course materials on the basis of research on conceptual difficulties. *Studies in Educational Evaluation, 12*(2), 213–223.

Ben-Zvi, R., Eylon, B.-S., & Silberstein, J. (1987). Students' visualization of a chemical reaction. *Education in Chemistry, 24*(4), 117–120.

Ben–Zvi, R., Eylon, B.-S., & Silberstein, J. (1988). Theories, principles and laws. *Education in Chemistry, 25*(3), 89–92.

Ben-Zvi, R., & Hofstein, A. (1996). Strategies for remediating learning difficulties in chemistry. In D. F. Treagust, R. Duit & B. J. Fraser (Eds.), *Improving teaching and learning in science and mathematics* (pp. 109–119). New York: Teachers College Press.

Ben-Zvi, R., & Silberstein, Y. (1986). *Chemistry a challenge.* Rehovot, Israel: The Weizmann Institute of Science.

Bereiter, C., & Scardamalia, M. (1989). Intentional learning as a goal of instruction. In L. B. Resnick (Ed.), *Knowing, learning, and instruction: Essays in honor of Robert Glaser* (pp. 361–392). Hillsdale, NJ: Lawrence Erlbaum Associates.

Billings-Gagliardi, S., & Mazor, K. M. (2007). Student Decisions about Lecture Attendance: Do Electronic Course Materials Matter? *Academic Medicine: Journal of the Association of American Medical Colleges, 82*(10), S73–S76.

Bjork, E. L., & Bjork, R. A. (2011). Making things hard on yourself, but in a good way: Creating desirable difficulties to enhance learning. In M. A. Gernsbacher, R. W. Pew, L. M. Hough & J. R. Pomerantz (Eds.), *Psychology and the real world: Essays illustrating fundamental contributions to society* (pp. 235–258). New York: Worth Publishers.

Bjork, R. A. (1994). Memory and metamemory considerations in the training of human beings. In J. Metcalfe & A. Shimamura (Eds.), *Metacognition: Knowing about knowing* (pp. 185–205). Cambridge, MA: MIT Press.

Bjork, R. A. (1999). Assessing our own competence: Heuristics and illusions. In D. Gopher & A. Koriat (Eds.), *Attention and performance XVII. Cognitive regulation of performance: Interaction of theory and application* (pp. 435–459). Cambridge, MA: MIT Press.

Blumenfeld, P., Fishman, B., Krajcik, J., Marx, R. W., & Soloway, E. (2000). Creating usable innovations in systemic reform: Scaling up technology-embedded project-based science in urban schools. *Educational Psychologist, 35*(3), 149–164.

Borgman, C. L., Abelson, H., Dirks, L., Johnson, R., Koedinger, K. R., Linn, M. C., et al. (2008, June 24). *Fostering learning in the networked world: The cyberlearning opportunity and challenge.* Washington, DC: National Science Foundation.

Borko, H. (2004). Professional development and teacher learning: Mapping the terrain. *Educational Researcher, 33*(8), 3–15.

Bowyer, J. (1975). *Science curriculum improvement study and scientific literacy.* Unpublished doctoral dissertation, University of California at Berkeley, Berkeley, CA.

Bransford, J. D., Brown, A. L., & Cocking, R. R. (Eds.). (1999). *How people learn: Brain, mind, experience, and school.* Washington, DC: The National Academies Press.

Bransford, J. D., Zech, L., Schwartz, D., Barron, B., Vye, N., & The Cognition and Technology Group at Vanderbilt. (1996). Fostering mathematical thinking in middle school students: Lessons from research. In R. J. Sternberg & T. Ben-Zeev (Eds.), *The nature of mathematical thinking* (pp. 203–250). Mahwah, NJ: Lawrence Erlbaum Associates.

Braun, H., Coley, R., Jia, Y., & Trapani, C. (2009, May). *Exploring what works in science instruction: A look at the eight-grade science classroom* (Policy Information Report). Princeton, NJ: Educational Testing Services (ETS).

Bricker, L. A., & Bell, P. (2008). Conceptualizations of argumentation from science studies and the learning sciences and their implications for the practices of science education. *Science Education, 92*(3), 473–498.

Briggs, D., Alonzo, A., Schwab, C., & Wilson, M. (2006). Diagnostic assessment with ordered multiple-choice items. *Educational Assessment, 11*(1), 33–63.

Brook, A., Briggs, H., Bell, B., & Driver, R. (1984). *Aspects of secondary students' understanding of heat: Full report.* Leeds: CLIS Project.

Brown, A. (1987). Metacognition, executive control, self-regulation, and other more mysterious mechanisms. In F. E. Weinert and R. H. Kluwe (Eds.), *Metacognition, motivation, and understanding* (pp. 65–116). Hillsdale, NJ: Lawrence Erlbaum Associates.

Brown, A. (1992). Design experiments: Theoretical and methodological challenges in creating complex interventions in classroom settings. *The Journal of Learning Sciences,* *2*(2), 141–178.

Brown, A. L., Ash, D., Rutherford, M., Nakagawa, K., Gordon, A., & Campione, J. C. (1993). Distributed expertise in the classroom. In G. Salomon (Ed.), *Distributed cognitions: Psychological and educational considerations* (pp. 188–228). Cambridge, England: Cambridge University Press.

Brown, A. L., & Campione, J. C. (1990). Communities of learning and thinking, or a context by any other name. In D. Kuhn (Ed.), *Developmental Perspectives on teaching and learning thinking skills* (pp. 108–126). Basel, Switzerland: Karger.

Brown, A. L., & Campione, J. C. (1994). Guided discovery in a community of learners. In K. McGilly (Ed.), *Classroom lessons: Integrating cognitive theory and classroom practice* (pp. 229–270). Cambridge, MA: MIT Press/Bradford Books.

Brown, A. L., & Campione, J. C. (1996). Psychological learning theory and the design of innovative environments: On procedures, principles and systems. In L. Shauble & R. Glaser (Eds.), *Contributions of instructional innovation to understanding learning* (pp. 289–325). Hillsdale, NJ: Lawrence Erlbaum Associates.

Bruer, J. T. (1993). *Schools for thought: A science of learning in the classroom.* Cambridge, MA: MIT Press.

Bruner, J. S. (1962). *On knowing: Essays for the left hand.* Cambridge, MA: Harvard University Press.

Buckley, B., Gobert, J. D., Kindfield, A. C. H., Horwitz, P., Tinker, R., Gerlits, B., et al. (2004). Model-based teaching and learning with BioLogica: What do they learn? how do they learn? how do we know? *Journal of Science Education and Technology, 13*(1), 23–41.

Bumiller, E. (2010, April 26). We have met the enemy and he is PowerPoint [Electronic Version]. *The New York Times.* Retrieved August 12, 2010 from http://www.nytimes.com/2010/04/27/world/27powerpoint.html.

Burbules, N. C., & Linn, M. C. (1988). Response to contradiction: Scientific reasoning during adolescence. *Journal of Educational Psychology, 80*(1), 67–75.

Bybee, R. W., Taylor, J. A., Gardner, A., Scotter, P. V., Powell, J. C., Westbrook, A., et al. (2006). *The BSCS 5E instructional model: Origins and effectiveness.* Colorado Springs, CO: BSCS.

Caravita, S., & Halldén, O. (1994). Re-framing the problem of conceptual change. *Learning and Instruction, 4*(1), 89–111.

Cardall, S., Krupat, E., & Ulrich, M. (2008). Live lecture versus video-recorded lecture: are students voting with their feet? *Academic Medicine: Journal of the Association of American Medical Colleges, 83*(12), 1174–1178.

Carey, S. (1985). *Conceptual change in childhood.* Cambridge, MA, MIT Press.

Carey, S., & Smith, C. (1993). On understanding the nature of scientific knowledge. *Educational Psychologist, 28*(3), 235–251.

Case, R. (Ed.). (1978). *Implications of developmental psychology for the design of effective instruction.* New York: Plenum.

Case, R. (1980). Intellectual development from birth to adulthood: A neo–Piagetian interpretation. In R. Siegler (Ed.), *Children's thinking: What develops?* (pp. 37–72), Hillsdale, NJ, Lawrence Erlbaum Associates.

Case, R. (1985). *Intellectual development: Birth to adulthood.* Orlando, FL: Academic Press.

Case, R. S., Griffin, S., & Kelly, W. (1999). Socioeconomic gradients in mathematical ability and their responsiveness to intervention during early childhood. In D. P. Keating & C. Hertzman (Eds.), *Developmental health and the wealth of nations: Social, biological, and educational dynamics* (pp. 125–152). New York: Guilford Press.

Casperson, J. M., & Linn, M. C. (2006). Using visualizations to teach electrostatics. *American Journal of Physics, 74*(4), 316–323.

Chall, J. S., & Squire, J. R. (1991). The publishing industry and textbooks. In R. Barr, M. L. Kamil, P. Mosenthal & P. D. Pearson (Eds.), *Handbook of reading research* (Vol. 2, pp. 120–146). White Plains, NY: Longman.

Champagne, A. (1988). Kill all the mosquitoes or cure malaria, *Symposium conducted at the annual meeting of the American Association for the Advancement of Science (AAAS).* Philadelphia, PA.

Chang, H.-Y., & Quintana, C. (2006). Student-generated animations: supporting middle school students' visualization, interpretation and reasoning of chemical phenomena. In *Proceedings of the 7th International Conference of the Learning Sciences* (pp. 71–77). Bloomington, Indiana: International Society of the Learning Sciences, Inc.

Chang, H.-Y., Shen, J., Chiu, J., Clark, D., Menekse, M., D'Angelo, C., et al. (2008). Improving the design and impact of interactive, dynamic visualizations for science learning. In *International Perspectives in the Learning Sciences: Cre8ting a Learning World. Proceedings of the 8th International Conference of the Learning Sciences* (Vol. 3, pp. 221–228). Utrecht, The Netherlands: International Society of the Learning Sciences, Inc.

ChanLin, L.-J. (2001). Formats and prior knowledge on learning in a computer-based lesson. *Journal of Computer Assisted Learning, 17*(4), 409–419.

Chen, X. (1998). *What kinds of teaching practices do faculty use in their undergraduate classes?* Washington, DC: Institute of Education Sciences; Retrieved online from http://nces.ed.gov/das/epubs/2002209/what.asp.

Chi, M. T. H. (1992). Conceptual change within and across ontological categories: Examples from learning and discovery in science. In R. N. Giere (Ed.), *Minnesota studies in the philosophy of science* (pp. 129–186). Minneapolis: University of Minnesota Press.

Chi, M. T. H., Bassok, M., Lewis, M. W., Reimann, P., & Glaser, R. (1989). Self-explanations: How students study and use examples in learning to solve problems. *Cognitive Science, 13*(2), 145–182.

Chi, M. T. H., de Leeuw, N., Chiu, M., & LaVancher, C. (1994). Eliciting self-explanations improves understanding. *Cognitive Science, 18*(3), 439–477.

Chi, M. T. H., & Koeske, R. D. (1983). Network representation of child's dinosaur knowledge. *Developmental Psychology, 19*(1), 29–39.

Chi, M. T. H., & Slotta, J. D. (1993). The ontological coherence of intuitive physics. Commentary on A. diSessa's "Toward an epistemology of physics". *Cognition and Instruction, 10*(2/3), 249–260.

Chiu, J. L. (2006, April 9). *Using powerful computer models to promote integrated understandings of chemical reactions.* Paper presented at the annual meeting of the American Educational Research Association, San Francisco, CA.

Chiu, J. L. (2010). *Supporting students' knowledge integration with technology-enhanced inquiry curricula.* Unpublished doctoral dissertation, University of California, Berkeley, CA.

Chiu, J., & Linn, M. C. (2008). Self-assessment and self-explanation for learning chemistry using dynamic molecular visualizations. In *International Perspectives in the Learning Sciences: Cre8ting a Learning World: Proceedings of the 8th International Conference of the Learning Sciences* (Vol. 3, pp. 16–17). Utrecht, The Netherlands: International Society of the Learning Sciences, Inc.

Chiu, J., & Linn, M. C. (in press). The role of self-monitoring in learning chemistry with dynamic visualization. In A. Zohar & Y. J. Dori (Eds.), *Metacognition and science education: Trends in current research.* London, UK: Springer-Verlag.

Chiu, J. L., Zhang, H., Miller, D., & Linn, M. C. (2010). *Comparing PhET and Molecular Workbench as visualizations to illustrate the features of fuels. VISUAL Annual report.* Berkeley, CA: University of California, Berkeley.

Clancy, M., Titterton, N., Ryan, C., Slotta, J., & Linn, M. C. (2003). New roles for students, instructors, and computers in a lab-based introductory programming course. *ACM SIGCSE Bulletin, 35*(1), 132–136.

Clancy, M. J., & Linn, M. C. (1996). *Designing Pascal solutions: Case studies with data structures* (1st ed.). New York, NY: W.H. Freeman and Company.

Clancy, M. J., & Linn, M. C. (1999). Patterns and pedagogy. *Special Interest Group on Computer Science Education Bulletin, 31*(1), 37–42.

Clark, D. B. (2006). Longitudinal conceptual change in students' understanding of thermal equilibrium: An examination of the process of conceptual restructuring. *Cognition and Instruction, 24*(4), 467–563.

Clark, D. B., D'Angelo, C. M., & Menekse, M. (2009). Initial structuring of online discussions to improve learning and argumentation: Incorporating students' own explanations as seed comments versus an augmented-preset approach to seeding discussions. *Journal of Science Education and Technology, 18*(4), 321–333.

Clark, D. B., & Jorde, D. (2004). Helping students revise disruptive experientially supported ideas about thermodynamics: Computer visualizations and tactile models. *Journal of Research in Science Teaching, 41*(1), 1–23.

Clark, D. B., & Linn, M. C. (2003). Scaffolding knowledge integration through curricular depth. *Journal of Learning Sciences, 12*(4), 451–494.

Clark, D. B., & Sampson, V. (2007). Personally-seeded discussions to scaffold online argumentation. *International Journal of Science Education, 29*(3), 253–277.

Clark, D. B., & Sampson, V. (2008). Assessing dialogic argumentation in online environments to relate structure, grounds, and conceptual quality. *Journal of Research in Science Teaching, 45*(3), 293–321.

Clark, D. B., Sampson, V. D., Stegmann, K., Marttunen, M., Kollar, I., Janssen, J., et al. (2010). Online learning environments, scientific argumentation, and 21st century skills. In B. Ertl (Ed.), *E-collaborative knowledge construction: Learning from computer-supported and virtual environments* (pp. 1–39). New York: IGI Global.

Clark, D. B., Varma, K., McElhaney, K., & Chiu, J. (2008). Design rationale within TELS projects to support knowledge integration. In D. Robinson & G. Schraw (Eds.), *Recent innovations in educational technology that facilitate student learning* (pp. 157–193). Charlotte, NC: Information Age Publishing.

Clement, J. (1993). Using bridging analogies and anchoring intuitions to deal with students' preconceptions in physics. *Journal of Research in Science Teaching, 30*(10), 1241–1257.

Cohen, E. G. (1994). Restructuring the classroom: Conditions for productive small groups. *Review of Educational Research, 64*(1), 1–35.

Collaborative e-Learning Structures (CeLS). http://www.mycels.net. Retrieved March 25, 2010, from http://www.mycels.net

Collins, A., Brown, J. S., & Newman, S. E. (1989). Cognitive apprenticeship: Teaching the crafts of reading, writing, and mathematics. In L. B. Resnick (Ed.), *Knowing, learning and instruction: Essays in honor of Robert Glaser* (pp. 453–494). Hillsdale, NJ: Lawrence Erlbaum Associates.

Collins, A., & Halverson, R. (2009). *Rethinking education in the age of technology: The digital revolution and schooling in America.* New York, NY: Teachers College Press.

Committee on Science and Technology Education. (1992). *Tomorrow 98.* Israel: Ministry of Education.

Cooke, N. J., & Breedin, S. D. (1994). Constructing naive theories of motion on the fly. *Memory and Cognition, 22*(4), 474–493.

Cooper, M. M., Cox, C. T., Jr., Nammouz, M., Case, E., & Stevens, R. (2008). An assessment of the effect of collaborative groups on students' problem-solving strategies and abilities. *Journal of Chemical Education, 85*(6), 866–872.

Corliss, S., & Spitulnik, M. (2008). Student and teacher regulation of learning in technology-enhanced science instruction. In *International Perspectives in the Learning Sciences: Cre8ting a Learning World. Proceedings of the 8th International Conference of the Learning Sciences* (Vol. 1, pp. 167–174). Utrecht, The Netherlands: International Society of the Learning Sciences, Inc.

Coulson, D. (2002). *BSCS Science: An inquiry approach—2002 evaluation findings.* Annapolis, MD: PS International.

Crouch, C. H., Fagen, A. P., Callan, J. P., & Mazur, E. (2004). Classroom demonstrations: Learning tools or entertainment? *American Journal of Physics, 72*(6), 835–838.

Crouch, C. H., & Mazur, E. (2001). Peer Instruction: Ten years of experience and results. *American Journal of Physics, 69*(9), 970–977.

Crouse, L., Schneps, M. H., Sadler, P. M., Private Universe Project, & Annenberg/CPB Math and Science Project. (1989). *A private universe [teacher guide and video series].* Cambridge, MA: Private Universe Project, Harvard-Smithsonian Center for Astrophysics.

Davis, E. A. (2004a). Creating critique projects. In M. Linn, E. Davis & P. Bell (Eds.), *Internet environments for science education* (pp. 89–114). Mahwah, NJ: Lawrence Erlbaum Associates.

Davis, E. A. (2004b). Knowledge integration in science teaching: Analysing teachers' knowledge development. *Research in Science Education, 34*(1), 21–53.

Davis, E. A., & Krajcik, J. (2005). Designing educative curriculum materials to promote teacher learning. *Educational Researcher, 34*(3), 3–14.

Davis, E. A., & Linn, M. C. (2000). Scaffolding students' knowledge integration: Prompts for reflection in KIE. *International Journal of Science Education, 22*(8), 819–837.

Davis, E. A., & Miyake, M., (Eds.). (2004). Guest editors' introduction: Explorations of scaffolding in complex classroom systems (Special Issue on Scaffolding). *Journal of the Learning Sciences, 13*(3), 265–272.

Davis, E. A., Petish, D., & Smithey, J. (2006). Challenges new science teachers face. *Review of Educational Research, 76*(4), 607–651.

Davis, E. A., & Varma, K. (2008). Supporting teachers in productive adaptation. In Y. Kali, J. E. Roseman & M. C. Linn (Eds.), *Designing coherent science education* (pp. 94–122). New York: Teachers College Press.

Davis, K. S. (2003). "Change is hard": What science teachers are telling us about reform and teacher learning of innovative practices. *Science Education, 87*(1), 3–30.

del Pozo, R. M. (2001). Prospective teachers' ideas about the relationships between concepts describing the composition of matter. *International Journal of Science Education, 23*(4), 353–371.

Department for Education and Employment. (2000). *Science: The National Curriculum for England—Key Stages 1–4.* London: The Stationery Office.

Derry, S. J., Seymour, J., Steinkuehler, C., Lee, J., & Siegel, M. A. (2004). From ambitious vision to partially satisfying reality: An evolving socio-technical design supporting community and collaborative learning in teacher education. In S. A. Barab, R. Kling & J. H. Gray (Eds.), *Designing for virtual communities in the service of learning* (pp. 256–295). Cambridge, MA: Cambridge University Press.

deVries, E., Lund, K., & Baker, M. (2002). Computer-mediated epistemic dialogue: Explanation and argumentation as vehicles for understanding scientific notions. *Journal of the Learning Sciences, 11*(1), 63–103.

Dewey, J. (1901). *Psychology and social practice* (Vol. 11). Chicago: University of Chicago Press.

diSessa, A. (1983). Phenomenology and the evolution of intuition. In D. Gentner & A. L. Stevens (Eds.), *Mental models.* Hillsdale, NJ: Lawrence Erlbaum Associates.

diSessa, A. A. (1988). Knowledge in pieces. In G. Forman & P. Pufall (Eds.), *Constructivism in the computer age* (pp. 49–70). Hillsdale, NJ: Lawrence Erlbaum Associates.

diSessa, A. A. (2000). *Changing minds: Computers, learning and literacy.* Cambridge, MA: MIT Press.

diSessa, A. A. (2002). Why "conceptual ecology" is a good idea. In M. Limón & L. Mason (Eds.), *Reconsidering conceptual change: Issues in theory and practice* (pp. 29–60). Dordrecht: Kluwer.

diSessa, A. A. (2004). Metarepresentation: Native competence and targets for instruction. *Cognition and Instruction, 22*(3), 293–331.

diSessa, A. A., & Minstrell, J. (1998). Cultivating conceptual change with benchmark lessons. In J. G. Greeno & S. Goldman (Eds.), *Thinking practices* (pp. 155–187). Mahwah, NJ: Lawrence Erlbaum Associates.

Dolan, K. (2008). Comparing modes of instruction: The relative efficacy of on-line and in-person teaching for student learning. *PS: Political Science and Politics, 41*(2), 387–391.

Dori, Y. J., Barak, M., & Adir, N. (2003). A Web-based chemistry course as a means to foster freshmen learning. *Journal of Chemical Education, 80*(9), 1084–1092.

Dory, E., Orad, Y., Orpaz, N., Angelmann, Y., Dayan, S., Harel, R., et al. (1989). *Into the matter (In Hebrew).* Maalot, Israel.

Driver, R. (1985). Changing perspectives on science lessons. In N. Bennett & C. Desforges (Eds.), *Recent advances in classroom research, British Journal of Educational Psychology Monograph Series, No. 2* (pp. 58–74). Edinburgh: Scottish Academy Press.

Driver, R., Asoko, H., Leach, J., Mortimer, E., & Scott, P. (1994). Constructing scientific knowledge in the classroom. *Educational Researcher, 23*(7), 5–12.

Driver, R., Leach, J., Millar, R., & Scott, P. (1996). *Young people's images of science.* Buckingham, UK: Open University Press.

Dunbar, K. (1995). How scientists really reason: Scientific reasoning in real-world laboratories. In R. J. Sternberg & J. Davidson (Eds.), *Mechanisms of insight* (pp. 365–395). Cambridge, MA: MIT Press.

Dunbar, K. (1999). How scientists build models invivo science as a window on the scientific mind. In L. Magnani, N. J. Nersessian & P. Thagard (Eds.), *Model-based reasoning in scientific discovery* (pp. 85–99). New York: Kluwer Academic/Plenum Publishers.

Duschl, R. A., Schweingruber, H. A., & Shouse, A. W. (Eds.). (2007). *Taking science to school: Learning and teaching science in grades K-8.* Washington, DC: National Academies Press.

Dussault, M., Sadler, P., Coyle, H., Gould, R., Reinfeld, E., Steel, S., et al. (2005). What do students (and teachers) understand about the universe? Using qualitative and quantitative assessments to inform and improve astronomy education efforts. *Bulletin of the American Astronomical Society, 37,* 1210.

Dweck, C. S. (2006). *Mindset.* New York: Random House.

Dweck, C. S., & Master, A. (2008). Self-theories motivate self-regulated learning. In D. Schunk & B. Zimmerman (Eds.), *Motivation and self-regulated learning: Theory, research, and applications* (pp. 31–52). Mahwah, NJ: Erlbaum.

Eccles, J. (2009). Who am I and what am I going to do with my life? Personal and collective identities as motivators of action. *Educational Psychologist, 44*(2), 78–89.

Eccles, J., Wigfield, A., & Schiefele, U. (1998). Motivation to succeed. In W. Damon (Series Ed.) & N. Eisenberg (Vol. Ed.) (Eds.), *Handbook of child psychology: Vol. 3. Social, emotional, and personality development* (5th ed., pp. 1017–1095). New York: Wiley.

Eccles, J. S. (1994). Understanding women's educational and occupational choices: Applying the Eccles et al. model of achievement-related choices. *Psychology of Women Quarterly, 18*(4), 585–609.

Edelson, D. C. (2001). Learning-for-use: A framework for the design of technology-supported inquiry activities. *Journal of Research in Science Teaching, 38*(3), 355–385.

Edelson, D. C., Gordin, D. N., & Pea, R. D. (1999). Addressing the challenges of inquiry-based learning through technology and curriculum design. *Journal of the Learning Sciences, 8*(3/4), 391–450.

EduTube. (2008). What causes the different seasons (animation). Retrieved January 31, 2010, from http://www.edutube.org/en/video/what-causes-different-seasons-animation

Eldar, O., Eylon, B.-S., & Ronen, M. (in press). A metacognitive teaching strategy for pre-service teachers: Collaborative diagnosis of conceptual understanding in science. In A. Zohar & Y. J. Dori (Eds.), *Metacognition and science education: Trends in current research.* London, UK: Springer-Verlag.

Else-Quest, N. M., Hyde, J. S., & Linn, M. C. (2010). Cross-national patterns of gender differences in mathematics: A meta-analysis. *Psychological Bulletin, 136*(1), 103–127.

Erduran, S., Simon, S., & Osborne, J. (2004). TAPping into argumentation: Developments in the application of Toulmin's Argument Pattern for studying science discourse. *Science Education, 88*(6), 915–933.

Estes, W. K. (1960). Learning theory and the new "mental chemistry." *Psychological Review, 67*(4), 207–223.

Eylon, B., Berger, H., & Bagno, E. (2008). An evidence based continuous professional development program on knowledge integration in physics: A study of teachers' collective discourse. *International Journal of Science Education, 30*(5), 619–641.

Eylon, B.-S., & Linn, M. C. (1988). Learning and instruction: An examination of four research perspectives in science education. *Review of Educational Research, 58*(3), 251–301.

Eylon, B.-S., Ronen, M., & Ganiel, U. (1996). Computer simulations as tools for teaching and learning: Using a simulation environment in optics. *Journal of Science Education and Technology, 5*(2), 93–110.

Falchikov, N., & Goldfinch, J. (2000). Student peer assessment in higher education: A meta-analysis comparing peer and teacher marks. *Review of Educational Research, 70*(3), 287–322.

Falk, J., & Drayton, B. (Eds.). (2009). *Creating and sustaining online professional learning communities.* New York, NY: Teachers College Press.

Felder, R. M., & Brent, R. (2003). Learning by doing. *Chemical Engineering Education, 37*(4), 282–283.

Feldman, A. (2000). Decision making in the practical domain: A model of practical conceptual change. *Science Education, 84*(5), 606–623.

Feldman, A., Konold, C., & Coulter, B. (2000). *Network science, a decade later: The internet and classroom learning.* Mahwah, NJ: Lawrence Erlbaum Associates.

Feldon, D. F., Timmerman, B. C., Stowe, K. A., & Showman, R. (2010). Translating expertise into effective instruction: The impacts of cognitive task analysis (CTA) on lab report quality and student retention in the biological sciences. *Journal of Research in Science Teaching, 47*(10), 1165–1185.

Fensham, P. (1994). Beginning to teach chemistry. In P. Fensham, R. Gunstone & R. White (Eds.), *The content of science: A constructivist approach to its teaching and learning* (pp. 14–28). London: Falmer.

Fensham, P. J. (2009). Real world contexts in PISA science: Implications for context-based science education. *Journal of Research in Science Teaching, 46*(8), 884–896.

Feynman, R. P., Leighton, R. B., & Sands, M. L. (1963). *The Feynman lectures on physics.* Reading, MA: Addison-Wesley Pub. Co.

Figlio, D. N., Rush, M., & Yin, L. (2010). *Is it live or is it internet? Experimental estimates of the effects of online instruction on student learning (NBER Working Paper No. 16089).* Cambridge, MA: National Bureau of Economic Research.

Finkelstein, N. D., Adams, W. K., Keller, C. J., Kohl, P. B., Perkins, K. K., Podolefsky, N. S., et al. (2005). When learning about the real world is better done virtually: A study of substituting computer simulations for laboratory equipment. *Physical Review Special Topics—Physics Education Research, 1*(1), 010103.

Fischer, F., & Mandl, H. (2005). Knowledge convergence in computer-supported collaborative learning: The role of external representation tools. *The Journal of the Learning Sciences, 14*(3), 405–441.

Fishman, B., Marx, R., Best, S., & Tal, R. (2003). Linking teacher and student learning to improve professional development in systemic reform. *Teaching and Teacher Education, 19*(6), 643–658.

Fishman, B., Marx, R., Blumenfeld, P., Krajcik, J. S., & Soloway, E. (2004). Creating a framework for research on systemic technology innovations. *Journal of the Learning Sciences, 13*(1), 43–76.

Ford, M. J., & Wargo, B. M. (2007). Routines, roles, and responsibilities for aligning scientific and classroom practices. *Science Education, 91*(1), 133–157.

Frailich, M., Kesner, M., & Hofstein, A. (2009). Enhancing students' understanding of the concept of "chemical bonding" by using activities provided on an interactive website. *Journal of Research in Science Teaching, 46*(3), 289–310.

Frederiksen, J., & White, B. (1992). Mental models and understanding: A problem for science education. In E. Scanlon & T. O'Shea (Eds.), *New directions in educational technology* (pp. 211–226). New York: Springer Verlag.

Gabel, D. L. (1999). Improving teaching and learning through chemistry education research: A look to the future. *Journal of Chemical Education, 76*(4), 548–554.

Geir, R., Blumenfeld, P., Marx, R. W., Krajcik, J. S., Fishman, B., Soloway, E., et al. (2008). Standardized test outcomes for students engaged in inquiry-based science curricula in the context of urban reform. *Journal of Research in Science Teaching, 45*(8), 922–939.

Geographic Data in Education (GEODE) Initiative. (2003). WorldWatcher: Overview. Retrieved June 24, 2004, from http://www.worldwatcher.northwestern.edu/softwareWW.htm

Gerard, L. F., Bowyer, J. B., & Linn, M. C. (2008). Principal leadership for technology-enhanced science. *Journal of Science Education and Technology, 17*(1), 1–18.

Gerard, L. F., Spitulnik, M., & Linn, M. C. (2010). Teacher use of evidence to customize inquiry science instruction. *Journal of Research in Science Teaching, 47*(9): 1037–1063.

Gerard, L. F., Tate, E., Chiu, J., Corliss, S. B., & Linn, M. C. (2009). Computer support for collaborative learning. In C. O'Malley, D. Suthers, P. Reimann & A. Dimitracopoulou (Eds.), *Proceedings of the 8th International Conference on Computer Supported Collaborative Learning* (Vol. 1, pp. 188–193). Rhodes, Greece: International Society of the Learning Sciences, Inc.

Gerard, L. F., Varma, K., Corliss, S. C., & Linn, M. C. (in press). A review of the literature on professional development in technology-enhanced inquiry science. *Review of Educational Research.*

Gilbert, J. (1991). Model building and a definition of science. *Journal of Research in Science Teaching, 28*(1), 73–79.

Gildea, P. M., Miller, G. A., & Wurtenberg, C. L. (1990). Contextual enrichment by videodisc. In D. Nix & R. Spiro (Eds.), *Cognition, education, & multimedia* (pp. 1–30). Hillsdale, NJ: Lawrence Erlbaum Associates.

Gobert, J. D., & Pallant, A. (2004). Fostering students' epistemologies of models via authentic model-based tasks. *Journal of Science Education and Technology, 13*(1), 7–22.

Graesser, A. G., McNamara, D. S., & VanLehn, K. (2005). Scaffolding deep comprehension strategies through Point&Query, AutoTutor, and iSTART. *Educational Psychologist, 40*(4), 225–234.

Greene, J. (2007, June 7). Northgate High School anatomy students observe surgery at AGH [Electronic Version]. *Pittsburgh Tribune-Review.* Retrieved August 12, 2010 from http://www.pittsburghlive.com/x/pittsburghtrib/news/pittsburgh/s_511146.html.

Grigg, W., Lauko, M., & Brockway, D. (2006). *The nation's report card: Science 2005 (NCES 2006–466).* Washington, DC: U.S. Government Printing Office.

Gunstone, R. F., & Champagne, A. B. (1990). Promoting conceptual change in the laboratory. In E. Hegarty-Hazel (Ed.), *The Student laboratory and the science curriculum.* New York: Routledge.

Guzdial, M., Turns, J., Rappin, N., & Carlson, D. (1995). Collaborative support for learning in complex domains. In J. L. Schnase & E. L. Cunnius (Eds.), *Computer support for collaborative learning '95* (pp. 157–160). Hillsdale NJ: Erlbaum.

Hackbert, P. H. (2004). Building entrepreneurial teamwork competencies in collaborative learning via peer assessments. *Journal of College Teaching & Learning, 1*(12), 39–52.

Hake, R. R. (1998). Interactive-engagement vs. traditional methods: A six-thousand-student survey of mechanics test data for introductory physics courses. *American Journal of Physics, 66*(1), 64–74.

Halloun, I. A., & Hestenes, D. (1985a). The initial knowledge state of college physics students. *American Journal of Physics, 53*(11), 1043–1055.

Halloun, I. A., & Hestenes, D. (1985b). Common sense concepts about motion. *American Journal of Physics, 53*(11), 1056–1065.

Halloun, I. A., & Hestenes, D. (1998). Interpreting VASS dimensions and profiles for physics students. *Science and Education, 7*(6), 553–577.

Halsall, P. (1998). http://www.fordham.edu/halsall/mod/1859Faraday-forces.html. Retrieved January 28, 2010

Hartley, J., & Davies, I. K. (1978). Note-taking: A critical review. *Programmed Learning and Educational Technology, 15*(3), 207–224.

Hatano, G., & Inagaki, K. (Eds.). (1991). *Sharing cognition through collective comprehension activity.* Washington, DC: American Psychological Association.

Hatano, G., & Inagaki, K. (2003). When is conceptual change intended?: A cognitive-sociocultural view. In G. M. Sinatra & P. R. Pintrich (Eds.), *Intentional conceptual change* (pp. 407–427). Mahwah, NJ: Lawrence Erlbaum Associates.

Hays, T. (1996). Spatial abilities and the effects of computer animation on short-term and long-term comprehension. *Journal of Educational Computing Research, 14*(2), 139–155.

Hegarty, M., Kriz, S., & Cate, C. (2003). The roles of mental animations and external animations in understanding mechanical systems. *Cognition and Instruction, 21*(4), 325–360.

Heller, P., Keith, R., & Anderson, S. (1992). Teaching problem solving through cooperative grouping. Part 1: Group versus individual problem solving. *American Journal of Physics, 60*(7), 627–636.

Henze, I., van Driel, J. H., & Verloop, N. (2007). The change of science teachers personal knowledge about teaching models and modeling in the context of science education reform. *International Journal of Science Education, 29*(15), 1819–1846.

Hestenes, D., & Halloun, I. (1995). Interpreting the Force Concept Inventory: A response to March 1995 critique by Huffman and Heller. *The Physics Teacher, 33*(8), 502, 504–506.

Hestenes, D., Wells, M., & Swackhamer, G. (1992). Force Concept Inventory. *The Physics Teacher, 30*(3), 141–158.

Heubert, J. P., & Hauser, R. M. (Eds.). (1999). *High stakes: Testing for tracking, promotion, and graduation.* Washington, DC: The National Academies Press.

Hiebert, J. (1986). *Conceptual and procedural knowledge: The case of mathematics.* Hillsdale, NJ: Erlbaum.

Hiebert, J., Gallimore, R., Garnier, H., Givvin, K. B., Hollingsworth, H., Jacobs, J., et al. (2003). *Teaching mathematics in seven countries: Results from the TIMSS 1999 video study.* Washington, DC: National Center for Education Statistics.

Higgins, T. E. (2008). *Through the eyes of professional developers: Understanding the design of learning experiences for science teachers.* Unpublished doctoral dissertation, University of California, Berkeley.

Higgins, T. E., & Spitulnik, M. (2008). Supporting teachers' use of technology in science instruction through professional development: A literature review. *Journal of Science Education and Technology, 17*(5), 511–521.

Hilgard, E. R., & Bower, G. H. (1966). *Theories of learning* (3rd ed.). New York: Appleton-Century-Crofts.

Hilton, M., & National Research Council (NRC). (2010). *Exploring the intersection of science education and 21st Century Skills: A workshop summary.* Washington, DC: The National Academies Press.

Hmelo-Silver, C. E., Derry, S. J., Woods, D., DelMarcelle, M., & Chernobilsky, E. (2005). From parallel play to meshed interaction: The evolution of the eSTEP system. In T. Koschmann, D. D. Suthers & T.-W. Chan (Eds.), *Proceedings of CSCL 2005: Computer support for collaborative learning: The next 10 years!* (pp. 195–204). Mahwah, NJ: Lawrence Erlbaum Associates.

Hoadley, C. (2004). Fostering collaboration offline and online: Learning from each other. In M. C. Linn, E. A. Davis & P. L. Bell (Eds.), *Internet environments for science education* (pp. 145–174). Mahwah, NJ: Lawrence Erlbaum Associates.

Hoadley, C. M., Hsi, S., & Berman, B. P. (1995). The multimedia forum kiosk and SpeakEasy. In *Proceedings of the Third ACM International Conference on Multimedia* (pp. 363–364). San Francisco, CA: ACM Press.

Hoadley, C. M., & Linn, M. C. (2000). Teaching science through on-line, peer discussions: SpeakEasy in the knowledge integration environment. *International Journal of Science Education, 22*(8), 839–857.

Hofer, B. K., & Pintrich, P. R. (Eds.). (2002). *Personal epistemology: The psychology of beliefs about knowledge and knowing.* Mahwah, NJ: Lawrence Erlbaum Associates.

Hoffler, T. N., & Leutner, D. (2007). Instructional animation versus static pictures: A meta-analysis. *Learning and Instruction, 17*(6), 722–738.

Hofstein, A., & Lunetta, V. N. (1982). The role of the laboratory in science teaching: Neglected aspects of research. *Review of Educational Research, 52*(2), 201–217.

Hofstein, A., & Lunetta, V. N. (2004). The laboratory in science education: Foundations for the twenty-first century. *Science Education, 88*(1), 28–54.

Holton, G. (2003). What historians of science and science educators can do for one another. *Science & Education, 12*(7), 603–616.

Holyoak, K. J., & Thagard, P. (1995). *Mental leaps: Analogy in creative thought.* Cambridge, MA, MIT Press.

Horwitz, P., & Christie, M. (1999). Hypermodels: Embedding curriculum and assessment in computer-based manipulatives. *Journal of Education, 181*(2), 1–23.

Horwitz, P., & Tinker, R. (2001). Pedagogica to the rescue: A short history of hypermodels. *@CONCORD, 5*(1), 12–13.

Howe, A. (2002). *Engaging children in science.* Upper Saddle River, NJ: Merrill Prentice-Hall.

Howe, C., & Tolmie, A. (2003). Group work in primary school science: Discussion, consensus and guidance from experts. *International Journal of Educational Research, 39*(1–2), 51–72.

Howe, C., Tolmie, A., Duchak-Tanner, V., & Rattray, C. (2000). Hypothesis testing in science: Group consensus and the acquisition of conceptual and procedural knowledge. *Learning and Instruction, 10*(4), 361–391.

Howe, K. (1998). The interpretive turn and the new debate in education. *Educational Researcher, 27*(8), 13–21.

Hsi, S. (1997). *Facilitating knowledge integration in science through electronic discussion: The multimedia forum kiosk.* Unpublished doctoral dissertation, University of California, Berkeley, CA.

Hunt, E., & Minstrell, J. (1994). A cognitive approach to the teaching of physics. In K. McGilly (Ed.), *Classroom lessons: Integrating cognitive theory and classroom practice* (pp. 51–74). Cambridge, MA: MIT Press.

Hutchins, E. (2001). Distributed cognition. In N. J. Smelser & P. B. Baltes (Eds.), *International encyclopedia of the social & behavioral sciences* (4th ed., pp. 2068–2072). Amsterdam: Elsevier.

Hyde, J. S., Lindberg, S. M., Linn, M. C., Ellis, A. B., & Williams, C. C. (2008). Gender similarities characterize math performance. *Science, 321*(5888), 494–495.

Iles, A., Glaser, D., Kam, M., & Canny, J. (2002). Learning via distributed dialogue: Livenotes and handheld wireless technology [Electronic Version]. Retrieved March 25, 2010 from www.cs.berkeley.edu/~jfc/papers/02/IGKCcscl02.pdf.

Inhelder, B., & Piaget, J. (1958/1972). *The growth of logical thinking from childhood to adolescence: An essay on the construction of formal operational structures.* New York: Basic Books.

Inhelder, B., & Piaget, J. (1969). *The early growth of logic in the child.* New York: Norton.

Israeli Ministry of Education. (1996). *The Israeli national syllabus for junior high school (In Hebrew).* Jerusalem, Israel: Ministry of Education.

Israeli Ministry of Education. (1996). *Science and technology curriculum for junior high schools (In Hebrew).* Jerusalem, Israel: Ministry of Education.

Izsak, A. (2004). Students' coordination of knowledge when learning to model physical situations. *Cognition and Instruction, 22*(1), 81–128.

Janis, I. L. (1971). Groupthink. *Psychology Today, 5,* 43–46, 74–76.

Jeong, H., & Chi, M. T. H. (2007). Knowledge convergence and collaborative learning. *Instructional Science, 35*(4), 287–315.

Johnson, D. W., & Johnson, R. T. (1999). Making cooperative learning work. *Theory into Practice, 38*(2), 67–73.

Johnson, P. (1998). Progression in children's understanding of a 'basic' particle theory: A longitudinal study. *International Journal of Science Education, 20*(4), 393–412.

Johnstone, A. H. (1991). Why is science difficult to learn? Things are seldom what they seem. *Journal of Computer Assisted Learning, 7*(2), 75–83.

Johnstone, A. H., & Percival, F. (1976). Attention breaks in lectures. *Education in Chemistry, 13*(2), 49–50.

Joseph, D. (2004). The practice of design-based research: Uncovering the interplay between design, research, and the real-world context. *Educational Psychologist, 39*(4), 235–242.

Justi, R., & Gilbert, J. (2002). Models and modeling in chemical education. In J. K. Gilbert, O. D. Jong, R. Justi, D. F. Treagust & J. H. van Driel (Eds.), *Chemical education: Towards research-based practice* (pp. 47–68). Dordrecht: Kluwer.

Justi, R., & van Driel, J. (2005). The development of science teachers' knowledge on models and modeling: Promoting, characterizing, and understanding the process. *International Journal of Science Education, 27*(5), 549–573.

Kafai, Y. B., Peppler, K. A., & Chapman, R. N. (Eds.). (2009). *The computer clubhouse: Constructionism and creativity in youth communities*. New York: Teachers College Press.

Kali, Y. (2002). Design Principles Database. Retrieved January 28, from http://www. edu-design-principles.org

Kali, Y. (2006). Collaborative knowledge-building using the Design Principles Database. *International Journal of Computer Support for Collaborative Learning, 1*(2), 187–201.

Kali, Y., Bos, N., Linn, M. C., Underwood, J., & Hewitt, J. (2002). Design principles for educational software. In G. Stahl (Ed.), *Computer support for collaborative learning: Foundations for a CSCL community, proceedings of CSCL*. Hillsdale, NJ: Lawrence Erlbaum Associates.

Kali, Y., Levin-Peled, R., Ronen-Fuhrmann, T., & Hans, M. (2009). The Design Principles Database: A multipurpose tool for the educational technology community. *Design Principles & Practices: An International Journal, 3*(1): 55–65.

Kali, Y., & Linn, M. C. (2008). Technology-enhanced support strategies for inquiry learning. In J. M. Spector, M. D. Merrill, J. J. G. V. Merriënboer & M. P. Driscoll (Eds.), *Handbook of research on educational communications and technology* (3rd ed., pp. 145–161). New York: Lawrence Erlbaum Associates.

Kali, Y. & Linn, M. C. (2009). Designing effective visualizations for elementary school science. *Elementary School Journal, 109*(5): 181–198.

Kali, Y., Linn, M. C., & Roseman, J. E. (Eds.). (2008). *Designing coherent science education*. New York: Teachers College Press.

Kali, Y., & Orion, N. (1996). Spatial abilities of high-school students in the perception of geologic structures. *Journal of Research in Science Teaching, 33*(4), 369–391.

Kali, Y., Orion, N., & Mazor, E. (1997). Software for assisting high school students in the spatial perception of geological structures. *Journal of Geoscience Education, 45*(1), 10–21.

Kali, Y., & Ronen, M. (2005). Design principles for online peer-evaluation: Fostering objectivity. In T. Koschmann, D. Suthers & T. W. Chan (Eds.), *Proceedings of CSCL 2005: Computer support for collaborative learning: The next 10 years!* (pp. 247–251). Mahwah, NJ: Lawrence Erlbaum Associates.

Kali, Y., & Ronen-Fuhrmann, T. (2007). How can the design of educational technologies affect graduate students' epistemologies about learning? In C. A. Chinn, G. Erkens & S. Puntambekar (Eds.), *Proceedings of the Computer Supported Collaborative Learning (CSCL) 2007: Mice, minds and society* (pp. 320–322). Mahwah, NJ: Lawrence Erlbaum Associates.

Kam, M., Wang, J., Iles, A., Tse, E., Chiu, J., Glaser, D., et al. (2005). Livenotes: A system for cooperative and augmented note-taking in lectures. In *Proceedings of ACM conference on human factors in computing systems* (pp. 531–540). Portland, OR: ACM.

Kanari, Z., & Millar, R. (2004). Reasoning from data: How students collect and interpret data in scientific investigations. *Journal of Research in Science Teaching, 41*(7), 748–769.

Karplus, R., & Thier, H. D. (1971). *SCIS: The science curriculum improvement study*. New York: Macmillan.

Kehoe, C., Stasko, J., & Taylor, A. (2001). Rethinking the evaluation of algorithm animations as learning aids: An observational study. *International Journal of Human-Computer Studies, 54*(2), 265–284

Keller, E. F. (1985). *Reflections on gender and science*. New Haven, CT: Yale University Press.

Kesidou, S., & Roseman, J. E. (2002). How well do middle school science program measure up? Findings from Project 2061's Curriculum Review. *Journal of Research in Science Teaching, 39*(6), 522–549.

King, A. (1992). Comparison of self-questioning, summarizing, and notetaking-review as strategies for learning from lectures. *American Educational Research Journal, 29*(2), 303–323.

Klahr, D. (2000). *Exploring science: The cognition and development of discovery processes.* Cambridge, MA: MIT Press.

Klahr, D., & Dunbar, K. (1989). Developmental differences in scientific discovery processes. In D. Klahr & K. Kotovsky (Eds.), *Complex information processing: The impact of Herbert A. Simon* (pp. 109–143). Hillsdale, NJ: Lawrence Erlbaum Associates.

Klahr, D., & Nigam, M. (2004). The equivalence of learning paths in early science instruction. *Psychological Science, 15*(10), 661–667.

Koedinger, K. R., & Anderson, J. R. (1998). Illustrating principled design: The early evolution of a cognitive tutor for algebra symbolization. *Interactive Learning Environments, 5*, 161–180.

Koedinger, K. R., Anderson, J. R., Hadley, W. H., & Mark, M. A. (1997). Intelligent tutoring goes to school in the big city. In J. Greer (Ed.), *Proceedings of AI-ED 95: World Conference on Artificial Intelligence in Education* (pp. 421–428). Washington, DC: AACE.

Kokkotas, P., Vlachos, I., & Koulaidis, V. (1998). Teaching the topic of the particulate nature of matter inprospective teachers' training courses. *International Journal of Science Education, 20*(3), 291–303.

Kollar, I., Fischer, F., & Slotta, J. D. (2005). Internal and external collaboration scripts in web-based science learning at schools. In T. Koschmann, D. D. Suthers & T.-W. Chan (Eds.), *Proceedings of the 2005 Conference on Computer Support for Collaborative Learning: The next 10 years!* (pp. 331–340). Mahwah, NJ: Lawrence Erlbaum Associates.

Kollar, I., Fischer, F., & Slotta, J. D. (2007). Internal and external scripts in computer-supported collaborative inquiry learning. *Learning & Instruction, 17*(6), 708–721.

Kolodner, J. (1993). *Case-based reasoning.* San Mateo, CA: Morgan Kaufmann Publishers, Inc.

Kolodner, J. L., Crismond, D., Fasse, B., Gray, J., Holbrook, J., & Puntembakar, S. (2003). Putting a student-centered learning by Design™ Curriculum into Practice: Lessons learned. *Journal of the Learning Sciences, 12*(4), 495–548.

Kolodner, J. L., Gray, J. T., & Fasse, B. B. (2003). Promoting transfer through case-based reasoning: Rituals and practices in Learning by Design™ classrooms. *Cognitive Science Quarterly, 3*(2), 119–170.

Koretz, D. (2008). *Measuring up: What educational testing really tells us.* Cambridge, MA: Harvard University Press.

Koschmann, T., Myers, A. C., & Feltovich, P. J. (1994). Using technology to assist in realizing effective learning and instruction: A principled approach to the use of computers in collaborative learning. *The Journal of the Learning Sciences, 3*(3), 227–264.

Koslowski, B. (1996). *Theory and eficence: The development of scientific reasoning.* Cambridge, MA: MIT Press.

Kozma, R., Chin, E., Russell, J., & Marx, N. (2000). The roles of representations and tools in the chemistry laboratory and their implications for chemistry learning. *Journal of the Learning Sciences, 9*(2), 105–143.

Kozma, R., & Russell, J. (2005). Modelling students becoming chemists: Developing representational competence. In J. K. Gilbert (Ed.), *Visualization in science education* (pp. 121–145). Dordrecht: Springer.

Kozma, R. B. (2003). The material features of multiple representations and their cognitive and social affordances for science understanding. *Learning and Instruction, 13*(2), 205–226.

Krajcik, J., Blumenfeld, P. C., Marx, R., & Soloway, E. (2000). Instructional, curricular, and technological supports for inquiry in science classrooms. In J. Minstrell & E. H. van Zee (Eds.), *Inquiring into inquiry learning and teaching in science* (pp. 283–315). Washington, DC: American Association for the Advancement of Science.

Krajcik, J., Blumenfeld, P. C., Marx, R. W., Bass, K. M., Fredricks, J., & Soloway, E. (1998). Inquiry in project-based science classrooms: Initial attempts by middle school students. *The Journal of the Learning Sciences, 7*(3/4), 313–350.

Krajcik, J., Czerniak, C., & Berger, C. (1999). *Teaching children science: A project-based approach*. Boston, MA: McGraw-Hill.

Krajcik, J. S. (1991). Developing students' understanding of chemical concepts. In Y. S. M. Glynn, R. H. Yanny & B. K. Britton (Eds.), *The psychology of learning science: International perspective on the psychological foundations of technology-based learning environments* (pp. 117–145). Hillsdale, NJ: Lawrence Erlbaum Associates.

Krajcik, J. S., Blumenfeld, P. C., Marx, R. W., & Soloway, E. (1994). A collaborative model for helping middle grade science teachers learn project-based instruction. *The Elementary School Journal, 94*(5), 483–497.

Kraus, P. A. (1997). *Promoting active learning in lecture-based courses: Demonstrations, tutorials, and interactive tutorial lectures*. Unpublished Doctoral Dissertation with Lillian C. McDermott, Available from ProQuest Dissertations and Theses database. (UMI No. 9736313), University of Washington, Seattle, WA.

Kuhn, D., Amsel, E., O'Loughlin, M., & Schauble, L. (1988). *The development of scientific thinking skills*. Orlando, FL: Academic Press.

Kuhn, T. S. (1970). *The structure of scientific revolutions* (2nd ed.). Chicago: University of Chicago Press.

Kulik, J., & Kulik, C. L. (1979). College teaching. In P. L. Peterson & H. J. Walberg (Eds.), *Research on teaching: Concepts, findings and implications* (pp. 70–93). Berkeley, CA: McCutchan Pub. Corp.

Kulik, J. A., Kulik, C. L., & Cohen, P. A. (1980). Effectiveness of computer-based college teaching: A meta-analysis of findings. *Review of Educational Research, 50*(4), 525–544.

Larkin, J. H., & Simon, H. A. (1987). Why a diagram is (sometimes) worth ten thousand words. *Cognitive Science 11*, 65–99.

Larson, E. (2006). *Thunderstruck*. New York: Random House.

Latour, B. (1987). *Science in action: How to follow scientists and engineers through society*. Cambridge, MA: Harvard University Press.

Latour, B., & Woolgar, S. (1986). *Laboratory life: The construction of scientific facts*. Princeton, NJ: Princeton University Press.

Lave, J., & Wenger, E. (1991). Situated learning: Legitimate peripheral participation. In R. Pea & J. S. Brown (Eds.), *Learning in doing: Social, cognitive, and computational perspectives* (pp. 29–129). Cambridge, MA: Cambridge University Press.

Laverty, D. T., & McGarvey, J. E. B. (1991). A constructivist approach to learning. *Education in Chemistry, 28*(4), 99–102.

Lawless, K. A., & Pellegrino, J. W. (2007). Professional development in integrating technology into teaching and learning: Knowns, unknowns, and ways to pursue better questions and answers. *Review of Educational Research, 77*(4), 575–614.

Leach, J., Hind, A., & Ryder, J. (2003). Designing and evaluating short teaching interventions about the epistemology of science in high school classrooms. *Science Education, 87*(3), 831–848.

Lee, C. D. (1997). Bridging home and school literacies: Models for culturally responsive teaching, a case for African American English. In J. Flood, S. B. Heath & D. Lapp (Eds.), *A handbook for literacy educators: Research on teaching the communicative and visual arts* (pp. 334–345). New York: Macmillan Publishing Co.

Lee, C. D. (2009). Cultural influences on learning. In J. A. Banks (Ed.), *The Routledge international companion to multicultural education* (pp. 239–251). New York: Routledge.

Lee, H.-S., Linn, M. C., Varma, K., & Liu, O. L. (2009). How does technology-enhanced inquiry instruction with visualizations impact classroom learning? *Journal of Research in Science Teaching, 47*(1), 71–90.

Lee, H.-S., Liu, O. L., & Linn, M. C. (in press). Validating measurement of knowledge integration in science using multiple-choice and explanation items. *Applied Measurement in Education.*

Lee, H. S., & Songer, N. (2003). Making authentic science accessible to students. *International Journal of Science Education, 25*(8), 923–948.

Lee, V. R. (2010a). Adaptations and continuities in the use and design of visual representations in US middle school science textbooks. *International Journal of Science Education, 32*(8), 1099–1126.

Lee, V. R. (2010b). How different variants of orbit diagrams influence students' explanations of the seasons. *Science Education, 94*(6), 985–1007.

Leighton, H. B. (1984). The lantern slide and art history. *History of Photography, 8*(2), 107–119.

Leinhardt, G., Crowley, K., & Knutson, K. (2002). *Learning conversations in museums.* New Jersey: Lawrence Erlbaum Associates, Inc.

Leithwood, K., & Steinbach, R. (1991). Indicators of transformational leadership in the everyday problem solving of school administrators. *Journal of Personnel Evaluation in Education, 4*(3), 221–244.

Lepper, M. R. (1985). Microcomputers in education: Motivational and social issues. *American Psychologist, 40*(1), 1–18.

Lesgold, A. M. (1984). Acquiring expertise. In J. R. Anderson, & Kosslyn, S. M. (Ed.), *Tutorials in learning and memory: Essays in honor of Gordon Bower* (pp. 31–60). San Francisco: W. H. Freeman.

Lewis, C. (1995). *Educating hearts and minds: Reflections on Japanese preschool and elementary education.* New York: Cambridge University Press.

Lewis, C., Perry, R., & Murata, A. (2006). How Should Research Contribute to Instructional Improvement? The Case of Lesson Study. *Educational Researcher, 35*(3), 3–14.

Lewis, C., & Tsuchida, I. (1997). Planned educational change in Japan: The case of elementary science instruction. *Journal of Educational Policy, 12*(5), 313–331.

Lewis, C., & Tsuchida, I. (1998). A lesson is like a swiftly flowing river: How research lessons improve Japanese education. *American Educator, 22*(4), 12–17, 50–52.

Lewis, C. C. (2002). *Lesson study: A handbook of teacher-led instructional change.* Philadelphia, PA: RBS, Inc.

Lewis, E. L. (1996). Conceptual change among middle school students studying elementary thermodynamics. *Journal of Science Education and Technology, 5*(1), 3–31.

Lewis, S. E., & Lewis, J. E. (2008). Seeking effectiveness and equity in a large college chemistry course: An HLM investigation of Peer-Led Guided Inquiry. *Journal of Research in Science Teaching, 45*(7), 794–811.

Lewis, E. L., & Linn, M. C. (1994). Heat energy and temperature concepts of adolescents, adults, and experts: Implications for curricular improvements. *Journal of Research in Science Teaching, 31*(6), 657–677.

Lewis, E. L., Stern, J., & Linn, M. C. (1993). The effect of computer simulations on introductory thermodynamics understanding. *Educational Technology, 33*(1), 45–58.

Liben, L. S., Kastens, K. A., & Stevenson, L. M. (2002). Real-world knowledge through real-world maps: A developmental guide for navigating the educational terrain. *Developmental Review, 22*(2), 267–322.

Light, R. J. (1990). *Explorations with students and faculty about teaching, learning, and student life.* Cambridge, MA: Harvard University.

Light, R. J. (2001). *Making the most of college: Students speak their minds.* Cambridge, MA: Harvard University Press.

Lindberg, S. M., Hyde, J. S., Petersen, J. L., & Linn, M. C. (2010). New trends in gender and mathematics performance: A meta-analysis. *Psychological Bulletin, 136*(6), 1123–1135.

Linn, M. C. (1980a). Free-choice experiences: How do they help children learn? *Science Education, 64*(2), 237–248.

Linn, M. C. (1980b). Teaching children to control variables: Some investigations using free choice experiences. In S. Modgil & C. Modgil (Eds.), *Toward a theory of psychological development within the Piagetian framework* (pp. 673–697). Windsor, Berkshire, England: National Foundation for Educational Research Publishing Company.

Linn, M. C. (1995). Designing computer learning environments for engineering and computer science: The Scaffolded Knowledge Integration framework. *Journal of Science Education and Technology, 4*(2), 103–126.

Linn, M. C. (1998). The impact of technology on science instruction: Historical trends and current opportunities. In K. G. Tobin & B. J. Fraser (Eds.), *International handbook of science education* (Vol. 1, pp. 265–294). The Netherlands: Kluwer.

Linn, M. C. (2003). Technology and science education: Starting points, research programs, and trends. *International Journal of Science Education, 25*(6), 727–758.

Linn, M. C. (2005). WISE design for lifelong learning-Pivotal Cases. In P. Gärdenfors & P. Johansson (Eds.), *Cognition, education and communication technology* (pp. 223–256). Mahwah, NJ: Lawrence Erlbaum Associates.

Linn, M. C., Bell, P., & Davis, E. A., (2004). Specific design principles: Elaborating the scaffolded knowledge integration framework. In M. C. Linn, E. A. Davis & P. Bell (Eds.), *Internet environments for science education* (pp. 315–340). Mahwah, NJ: Lawrence Erlbaum Associates.

Linn, M. C., Chang, H.-Y., Chiu, J., Zhang, H., & McElhaney, K. (2010). Can desirable difficulties overcome deceptive clarity in scientific visualizations? In A. Benjamin (Ed.), *Successful remembering and successful forgetting: A Festschrift in honor of Robert A. Bjork* (pp. 239–262). New York: Routledge.

Linn, M. C., Chang, H.-Y., Chiu, J., Zhang, H., & McElhaney, K. (2010). Can desirable difficulties overcome deceptive clarity in scientific visualizations? In A. Benjamin

(Ed.), *Successful remembering and successful forgetting: A Festschrift in honor of Robert A. Bjork* (pp. 239–262). New York: Routledge.

Linn, M. C., & Clancy, M. J. (1992a). Can experts' explanations help students develop program design skills? *International Journal of Man-Machine Studies, 36*(4), 511–551.

Linn, M. C., & Clancy, M. J. (1992b). The case for case studies of programming problems. *Communications of the ACM, 35*(3), 121–132.

Linn, M. C., Clark, D., & Slotta, J. D. (2003). WISE design for knowledge integration. *Science Education, 87*(4), 517–538.

Linn, M. C., Clement, C., Pulos, S., & Sullivan, T. (1989). Scientific reasoning during adolescence: The influence of instruction in science knowledge and reasoning strategies. *Journal of Research in Science Teaching, 26*(2): 171–187.

Linn, M. C., Davis, E. A., & Bell, P. (Eds.). (2004). *Internet environments for science education.* Mahwah, NJ: Lawrence Erlbaum Associates.

Linn, M. C., Davis, E. A. & Eylon, B.-S. (2004). The knowledge integration perspective on learning. In M. C. Linn, E. A. Davis & P. Bell (Eds.), *Internet environments for science education* (pp. 29–46). Mahwah, NJ: Lawrence Erlbaum Associates.

Linn, M. C., & Eylon, B.-S. (1996). Lifelong science learning: A longitudinal case study. In *Proceedings of Cognitive Science Society, 1996* (pp. 597–602). Mahwah, NJ: Lawrence Erlbaum Associates.

Linn, M. C., & Eylon, B.-S. (2000). Knowledge integration and displaced volume. *Journal of Science Education and Technology, 9*(4), 287–310.

Linn, M. C., & Eylon, B.-S. (2006). Science education: Integrating views of learning and instruction. In P. A. Alexander & P. H. Winne (Eds.), *Handbook of educational psychology* (2nd ed., pp. 511–544). Mahwah, NJ: Lawrence Erlbaum Associates.

Linn, M. C., & Hsi, S. (2000). *Computers, teachers, peers: Science learning partners.* Mahwah, NJ: Lawrence Erlbaum Associates.

Linn, M. C., Husic, F., Slotta, J., & Tinker, R. (2006). Technology enhanced learning in science (TELS): Research Programs. *Educational Technology, 46*(3), 54–68.

Linn, M. C., & Kessel, C. (1996). Success in mathematics: Increasing talent and gender diversity among college majors. In J. Kaput, A. Schoenfeld & E. Dubinsky (Eds.), *Research in collegiate mathematics education* (Vol. 2, pp. 101–144). Providence, RI: American Mathematical Society.

Linn, M. C., Lee, H.-S., Tinker, R., Husic, F., & Chiu, J. L. (2006). Teaching and assessing knowledge integration in science. *Science, 313*(5790), 1049–1050.

Linn, M. C., Lewis, C., Tsuchida, I., & Songer, N. B. (2000). Beyond fourth-grade science: Why Do U.S. and Japanese students diverge? *Educational Researcher, 29*(3), 4–14.

Linn, M. C., & Muilenburg, L. (1996). Creating lifelong science learners: What models form a firm foundation? *Educational Researcher, 25*(5), 18–24.

Linn, M. C., & Petersen, A. C. (1985). Emergence and characterization of sex differences in spatial ability: A meta-analysis. *Child Development, 56*(6), 1479–1498.

Linn, M. C., & Slotta, J. D. (2000). WISE science. *Educational Leadership, 58*(2), 29–32.

Linn, M. C., & Songer, N. B. (1993). How do students make sense of science? *Merrill-Palmer Quarterly, 39*(1), 47–73.

Linn, M. C., Songer, N. B., & Eylon, B. S. (1996). Shifts and convergences in science learning and instruction. In R. Calfee & D. Berliner (Eds.), *Handbook of educational psychology* (pp. 438–490). Riverside, NJ: Macmillan.

Linn, M. C., & Thier, H. D. (1975). The effect of experiential science on the development of logical thinking in children. *Journal of Research in Science Teaching, 12*(1), 49–62.

Little, J. W. (2003). Inside teacher community: Representations of classroom practice. *Teachers College Record, 105*(6), 913–945.

Liu, O. L., Lee, H.-S., & Linn, M. C. (2010a). Multifaceted assessment of inquiry-based science learning. *Educational Assessment, 15*(2), 69–86.

Liu, O. L., Lee, H.-S., & Linn, M. C. (2010b). An investigation of teacher impact on student inquiry science performance using a hierarchical linear model. *Journal of Research in Science Teaching, 47*(7), 807–819.

Liu, O. L., Lee, H. S., Hofstetter, C., & Linn, M. C. (2008). Assessing knowledge integration in science: Construct, measures and evidence. *Educational Assessment, 13*(1), 33–55.

Loh, B., Radinsky, J., Reiser, B. J., Gomez, L. M., Edelson, D. C., & Russell, E. (1997). The progress portfolio: Promoting reflective inquiry in complex investigation environments. In R. Hall, N. Miyake & N. Enyedy (Eds.), *Proceedings of the 2nd International Conference on Computer Support for Collaborative Learning* (pp. 176–185). Toronto, Ontario: International Society of the Learning Sciences.

Longino, H. E. (1990). *Science as social knowledge: Values and objectivity in scientific inquiry.* Princeton, NJ: Princeton University Press.

Lorenzo, M., Crouch, C. H., & Mazur, E. (2006). Reducing the gender gap in the physics classroom. *American Journal of Physics, 74*(2), 118–122.

Lundberg, M., Levin, B., & Harrington, H. (Eds.). (1999). *Who learns what from cases and how? The research base for teaching and learning with cases.* Mahwah, NJ: Lawrence Earlbaum Associates.

Madhok, J. J. (2006). *The longitudinal impact of an eighth grade inquiry curriculum on students' beliefs and achievement in science.* Unpublished doctoral dissertation with J. Slotta & M. C. Linn—Advisors, University of California, Berkeley, CA. Available from ProQuest Dissertations and Theses database. (UMI No. 3228414).

Margel, H. (1999). *About fibers (In Hebrew).* Rehovot, Israel: Weizmann Institute of Science.

Margel, H., Eylon, B., & Scherz, Z. (2004). "We actually saw atoms with our own eyes": Conceptions and convictions in using the Scanning Tunneling Microscope in junior high school. *Journal of Chemical education, 81*(4), 558–566.

Margel, H., Eylon, B.-S., & Scherz, Z. (2006). From textiles to molecules—teaching about fibers to integrate students' macro- and microscale knowledge of materials. *Journal of Chemical Education, 83*(10), 1552.

Margel, H., Eylon, B., & Scherz, Z. (2008). A longitudinal study of junior high school students' conceptions of the structure of materials. *Journal of Research in Science Teaching, 45*(1), 132–152.

Masnick, A. M., & Klahr, D. (2003). Error matters: An initial exploration of elementary school children's understanding of experimental error. *Journal of Cognition and Development, 4*(1), 67–98.

Mathison, M. A. (1996). Writing the critique, a text about a text. *Written Communication, 13*(3), 314–354.

Mayer, R. E., Hegarty, M., Mayer, S., & Campbell, J. (2005). When static media promote active learning: Annotated illustrations versus narrated animations in multimedia instruction. *Journal of Educational Psychology, 11*(4), 256–265.

Mazur, E. (1997). *Peer instruction: A user's manual.* Upper Saddle River, NJ: Prentice-Hall.

Mazzei, P. (2008). *Using evolution as a context to promote student understanding of nature of science.* Unpublished Master's Thesis, submitted in partial fulfillment of Master's of Arts degree in Education, University of California, Berkeley.

McDermott, L. C. (1991). Millikan Lecture 1990: What we teach and what is learned — Closing the gap. *American Journal of Physics, 59*(4), 301–315.

McDermott, L. C. (2001). Oersted Medal Lecture 2001: Physics education research—The key to student learning. *American Journal of Physics, 69*(11), 1127–1137.

McDermott, L. C. (2006). Preparing K-12 teachers in physics: Insights from history, experience, and research. *American Journal of Physics, 74*(9), 758–762.

McElhaney, K., & Linn, M. C. (2010, May 4). *What can students learn by comparing rather than isolating variables?* Paper presented at the annual meeting of the American Educational Research Association (AERA), Denver, CO.

McElhaney, K. W. (2010). *Making controlled experimentation more informative in inquiry investigations.* Unpublished doctoral dissertation, University of California, Berkeley.

McElhaney, K. W., & Linn, M. C. (2008). Impacts of students' experimentation using a dynamic visualization on their understanding of motion. In *International Perspectives in the Learning Sciences: Cre8ting a learning world. Proceedings of the 8th International Conference of the Learning Sciences* (Vol. 2, pp. 51–58). Utrecht, The Netherlands: International Society of the Learning Sciences, Inc.

McLelland, C. V. (2006). *The nature of science and the scientific method.* Boulder, CO: Geological Society of America.

Mehan, H. (1979). *Learning lessons: Social organization in the classroom.* Cambridge, MA: Harvard University Press.

Metcalf, S. J., Krajcik, J., & Soloway, E. (2000). Model-It: A design retrospective. In J. M. Jacobson & R. B. Kozma (Eds.), *Innovations in science and mathematics education: Advanced design for technologies of learning* (pp. 77–115). Mahwah, NJ: Lawrence Erlbaum Associates.

Metz, K. E. (2000). Young children's inquiry in biology. Building the knowledge bases to empower independent inquiry. In J. Minstrell & E. H. van Zee (Eds.), *Inquiring into inquiry learning and teaching in science* (pp. 3–13). Washington, DC: American Association for the Advancement of Science.

Metz, K. E. (2004). Children's understanding of scientific inquiry: Their conceptualization of uncertainty in investigations of their own design. *Cognition and Instruction, 22*(2), 219–290.

Millar, R. (1990). Making sense: What use are particles to children? In P. Lijnse, P. Licht, W. d. Vos & A. J. Waarlo (Eds.), *Relating macroscopic phenomena to microscopic particles* (pp. 283–293). Utrecht: CD-ß Press.

Miyahara, K. (2007). The impact of the lantern slide on art-history lecturing in Britain. *British Art Journal*, Autumn.

Mokros, J. R., & Tinker, R. F. (1987). The impact of microcomputer-based labs on children's ability to interpret graphs. *Journal of Research in Science Teaching, 24*(4), 369–383.

Muller, R. A. (2010). *Physics and technology for future presidents: An introduction to the essential physics every world leader needs to know.* Princeton, NJ: Princeton University Press.

Mullis, I. V. S., Martin, M. O., Gonzalez, E. J., Gregory, K. D., Garden, R. A., O'Connor,

K. M., et al. (1999). *Trends in mathematics and science study: International mathematics report.* Boston, MA: International Study Center, Lynch School of Education, Boston College.

Nakhleh, M. B., Samarapungavan, A., & Saglam, Y. (2005). Middle school students' beliefs about matter. *Journal of Research in Science Teaching, 42*(5), 581–612.

National Center for Education Statistics. (2002). http://nces.ed.gov/. Retrieved March 23, 2010

National Educational Goals Panel. (1998). *Ready schools: A report of the goal 1 ready schools resource group.* Washington, DC: U.S. Government Printing Office.

National Geographic Society (U.S.). Berwald, J., Guazzotti, S. A., & Fisher, D. (2007). *Focus on earth science California, Grade 6.* Princeton, NJ: Glencoe/McGraw-Hill School Pub Co.

National Research Council (NRC). (1999). *Transforming undergraduate education in science, mathematics, engineering, and technology.* Washington, DC: The National Academies Press.

National Research Council (NRC). (1996). *National science education standards.* Washington, DC: The National Academies Press.

National Research Council (NRC). (2000). *National science education standards.* Washington, DC: The National Academies Press.

National Research Council (NRC). (2006). *Learning to think spatially.* Washington, DC: The National Academies Press.

National Research Council (NRC). (2010). *Report of a workshop on the scope and nature of computational thinking.* Washington, DC: The National Academies Press.

Newman, D., Griffin, P., & Cole, M. (1989). *The construction zone: Working for cognitive change in school.* London: Cambridge University Press.

Nicole, D. J., & Boyle, J. T. (2003). Peer instruction versus class-wide discussion in large classes: a comparison of two interaction methods in the wired classroom. *Studies in Higher Education, 28*(4), 457–473.

Niess, M. L. (2005). Preparing teachers to teach science and mathematics with technology: Developing a technology pedagogical content knowledge. *Teaching and Teacher Education, 21*(5), 509–523.

Novick, S., & Nussbaum, J. (1978). Junior high school pupils' understanding of the particulate nature of matter: An interview study. *Science Education, 62*, 273–281.

Nuffield Curriculum Centre/Foundation, & The University of York. (2006). *Twenty-first century science (curriculum suite).* London: Oxford University Press.

Nussbaum, J. (1985). The Earth as a cosmic body. In R. Driver, E. Guesne, & A. Tiberghien (Eds.), *Children's ideas in science* (pp. 170–192). Milton Keynes, UK: Open University Press.

Nussbaum, J. (1998). History and philosophy, philosophy of science and the preparation for constructivitist teaching: The case of particle theory. In J. J. Mintzes, J. H. Wandersee, & J. D. Novak (Eds.), *Teaching science for understanding: A human constructivist view* (pp. 165–192). San Diego, CA: Academic Press.

Nussbaum, J. (2000). *The structure of matter: Vacuum and particles.* Rehovot, Israel: Weizmann Institute of Science.

Nussbaum, J., & Novick, S. (1982). Alternative frameworks, conceptual conflict and accomodation: toward a principled teaching strategy. *Instructional Science, 11*, 183–200.

O'Sullivan, C. Y., Lauko, M. A., Grigg, W. S., Qian, J., & Zhang, J. (2003). *The nation's report card: Science 2000*. National Assessment of Educational Progress (NAEP).

Ochs, E., & Capps, L. (2000). *Living narrative*. Cambridge: Harvard University Press.

Odom, A. L., & Barrow, L. H. (1995). Development and application of a two-tier diagnostic test measuring college biology students' understanding of diffusion and osmosis after a course of instruction. *Journal of Research in Science Teaching, 32*(1), 45–61.

Odubunmi, O., & Balogun, T. A. (1991). The effect of laboratory and lecture teaching methods on cognitive achievement in integrated science. *Journal of Research in Science Teaching, 28*(3), 213–224.

Old Computers Online Database. (2009). http://oldcomputers.net/macportable.html. Retrieved June 2, 2010, from http://oldcomputers.net/macportable.html

Osborne, J., Black, P., Smith, M., & Meadows, J. (1990). *Space project research report: Light*. Liverpool: Liverpool University Press.

Osborne, J., Erduran, S., & Simon, S. (2004). Enhancing the quality of argumentation in school science. *Journal of Research in Science Teaching, 41*(10), 994–1020.

Palincsar, A. S., & Brown, A. L. (1984). Reciprocal teaching of comprehension-fostering and comprehension-monitoring activities. *Cognition and Instruction, 1*, 117–175.

Pallant, A., & Tinker, R. (2004). Reasoning with atomic-scale molecular dynamic models. *Journal of Science Education and Technology, 13*(1), 51–66.

Palmer, D. H. (2009). Student interest generated during an inquiry skills lesson. *Journal of Research in Science Teaching, 46*(2), 147–165.

Papert, S. (1968). *Mindstorms*. New York: Basic Books.

Pea, R., Wulf, W. A., Elliott, S. W., & Darling, M. A. (Eds.). (2003). *Planning for two transformations in education and learning technology: Report of a workshop*. Washington, DC: The National Academies Press.

Pedone, R., Hummel, J. E., & Holyoak, K. J. (2001). The use of diagrams in analogical problem solving. *Memory and Cognition, 29*(2), 214–221.

Pellegrino, J. W., Chudowsky, N., & Glaser, R. (Eds.). (2001). *Knowing what students know: The science and design of educational assessment*. Washington, DC: The National Academies Press.

Penuel, W. R., Fishman, B., Gallagher, L., Korbak, C., & Lopez-Prado, B. (2008). Is alignment enough? Investigating the effects of state policies and professional development on science curriculum implementation. *Science Education, 93*(4), 656–677.

Petrosino, A. J., Martin, T., & Svihla, V. (Eds.). (2007). *Developing student expertise and community: Lessons from how people learn: New directions for teaching and learning* (Vol. 108). San Francisco, CA: Jossey-Bass.

Pfundt, H., & Duit, R. (1991). *Students' alternative frameworks* (3rd ed.). Federal Republic of Germany: Institute for Science Education at the University of Kiel/Institut für die Pädagogik der Naturwissenschaften.

Pfundt, H., & Duit, R. (1994). *Bibliography: Students' alternative frameworks and science education* (4th ed.). Kiel, Germany: Institute for Science Education.

PhET. (2010). http://phet.colorado.edu/. Retrieved July 10, 2010

Piaget, J. (1964). *The psychology of intelligence*. London: Routledge & Kegan Paul.

Piaget, J. (1970a). *Science of education and the psychology of the child*. New York: Orion Press.

Piaget, J. (1970b). *Structuralism*. New York: Basic Books.

Pinker, S. (2010, June 10). Mind over mass media [Electronic version]. *The New York*

Times. Retrieved August 12, 2010 from http://www.nytimes.com/2010/06/11/opinion/11Pinker.html?_r=1&ref=intelligence.

Pintrich, P. R. (2003). A motivational science perspective on the role of student motivation in learning and teaching contexts. *Journal of Educational Psychology, 95*(4), 667–686.

Polman, J. L. (2000). *Designing project-based science: Connecting learners through guided inquiry.* New York: Teachers College Press.

Puntambekar, S., & Kolodner, J. L. (1998). The design diary: A tool to support students in learning science by design. In *Proceedings of the International Conference of the Learning Sciences (ICLS 98)* (pp. 35–41). Charlottesville, VA: AACE.

Quintana, C., Reiser, B. J., Davis, E. A., Krajcik, J., Fretz, E., Golan, R. D., et al. (2004). A scaffolding design framework for software to support science inquiry. *Journal of the Learning Sciences, 13*(3), 337–386.

Rainie, L., & Hitlin, P. (2005). *The internet at school.* Washington, DC: Pew Research Center.

Razel, M., & Eylon, B.-S. (1986). Developing visual language skills: The Agam Program. *Journal of Visual and Verbal Languaging, 6*(1), 49–54.

Redish, E. F. (2003). *Teaching physics with the physics suite.* New York: John Wiley and Sons, Inc.

Redish, E. F., Saul, J. M., & Steinberg, R. N. (1998). Student expectations in introductory Physics. *American Journal of Physics, 66,* 212–224.

Reid, F. (2001). *The stage lighting handbook (stage and costume).* London, UK: A & C Black.

Reiner, M., Slotta, J. D., Chi, M. T. H., & Resnick, L. B. (2000). Naive physics reasoning: A commitment to substance-based conceptions. *Cognition and Instruction, 18*(1), 1–34.

Reiser, B. (2004). Scaffolding complex learning: The mechanisms of structuring and problematizing student work. *Journal of the Learning Sciences, 13*(3), 273–304.

Reiser, B. J., Tabak, I., Sandoval, W. A., Smith, B. K., Steinmuller, F., & Leone, A. J. (2001). BGuILE: Strategic and conceptual scaffolds for scientific inquiry in biology classrooms. In S. M. Carver & D. Klahr (Eds.), *Cognition and instruction: Twenty five years of progress* (pp. 263–305). Mahway, N.J.: Lawrence Erlbaum.

Renninger, K. A., & Shumar, W. (Eds.). (2002a). *Building virtual communities.* Cambridge, UK: Cambridge University Press.

Renninger, K. A., & Shumar, W. (2002b). Community building with and for teachers at the Math Forum. In K. A. Renninger & W. Shumar (Eds.), *Building virtual communities* (pp. 60–95). Cambridge, UK: Cambridge University Press.

Richland, L. E., Linn, M. C., & Bjork, R. A. (2007). Chapter 21: Instruction. In F. T. Durso (Ed.), *Handbook of applied cognition* (2nd ed., pp. 555–583). West Sussex, UK: John Wiley & Sons, Ltd.

Ridgeway, D. (1971). CHEM study—Its background—Its influence—Its revisions. *Canadian Chemical Education, 6,* 5–9.

Rivet, A. E., & Krajcik, J. S. (2004). Achieving standards in urban systemic reform: An example of a sixth grade project-based science curriculum. *Journal of Research in Science Teaching, 41*(7), 669–692.

Rogers, M. P., Abell, S., Lannin, J., Wang, C.-Y., Musikul, K., Barker, D., et al. (2007). Effective professional development in science and mathematics education: Teachers' and facilitators' views. *International Journal of Science and Mathematics Education, 5*(3), 507–532.

Rogoff, B. (1990). *Apprenticeship in thinking: Cognitive development in social context*. New York: Oxford University Press.

Ronen-Fuhrmann, T., & Kali, Y. (2009). Characterizing and instructing design knowledge in the context of educational technology design. In *Proceedings of the 4th Chais conference on instructional technologies research, 2009 (In Hebrew)* (pp. 168–176). Raanana: The Open University.

Roseman, J. E., Kesidou, S., Stern, L., & Caldwell, A. (1999). Heavy books light on learning: AAAS Project 2061 evaluates middle grades science textbooks. *Science Books and Films, 35*(6), 243–247.

Roseman, J. E., Linn, M. C., & Koppal, M. (2008). Characterizing curriculum coherence. In Y. Kali, M. C. Linn & J. E. Roseman (Eds.), *Designing coherent science education* (pp. 13–38). New York: Teachers College Press.

Roth, K. (1991). Reading science texts for conceptual change. In C. M. Santa & D. E. Alverman (Eds.), *Science learning processes and applications* (pp. 48–63). Newark, DE: International Reading Association.

Roth, K. J., Druker, S. L., Garnier, H. E., Lemmens, M., Chen, C., Kawanaka, T., et al. (2006). *Teaching science in five countries: Results from the TIMSS 1999 video study (statistical analysis report NCES 2006–011)*. U.S. Department of Education, National Center for Education Statistics. Washington, DC: U.S. Government Printing Office.

Rozenblit, L., & Keil, F. (2002). The misunderstood limits of folk science: An illusion of explanatory depth. *Cognitive Science, 26*(5), 521–562.

Rubin, A., & Doubler, S. J. (2009). The role of representations in shaping a community of scientific inquiry online. In J. Falk & B. Drayton (Eds.), *Creating and sustaining online professional learning communities* (pp. 153–174). New York: Teachers College Press.

Ruiz-Primo, M. A., Li, M., Tsai, S.-P., & Schneider, J. (2010). Testing one premise of scientific inquiry in science classrooms: Examining students' scientific explanations and student learning. *Journal of Research in Science Teaching, 47*(5), 583–608.

Ruiz-Primo, M. A., & Shavelson, R. J. (1996). Rhetoric and reality in science performance assessments: An update. *Journal of Research in Science Teaching, 33*(10), 1045–1063.

Russell, J., & Kozma, R. (2005). Assessing learning from the use of multimedia chemical visualization software. In J. Gilbert (Ed.), *Visualization in science education* (pp. 299–332). London: Kluwer.

Sadler, P. M. (1992). *The initial knowledge state of high school astronomy students*. Unpublished Doctoral Dissertation, Harvard University, Cambridge, MA.

Sadler, T., Barab, S., & Scott, B. (2007). What do students gain by engaging in socioscientific inquiry. *Research in Science Education, 37*(4), 371–391.

Sadler, T. D., Chambers, F. W., & Zeidler, D. L. (2004). Student conceptualizations of the nature of science in response to a socioscientific issue. *International Journal of Science Education Review, 26*(4), 387–409.

Sampson, V., & Clark, D. B. (2007). Incorporating scientific argumentation into inquiry-based activities with online personally-seeded discussions. *The Science Scope, 30*(6), 43–47.

Sampson, V., & Clark, D. B. (2009). The impact of collaboration on the outcomes of scientific argumentation. *Science Education, 93*(3), 448–484.

Sampson, V. D., & Clark, D. B. (2011). Comparison of more and less successful groups in collaboration. *Research in Science Education, 41*(1), 63–97.

Sandoval, W. A., & Reiser, B. J. (2004). Explanation-driven inquiry: integrating conceptual and epistemic scaffolds for scientific inquiry. *Science Education, 88*(3), 345–372.

Saxe, G. B. (1999). Cognition, development, and cultural practices. *New Directions for Child and Adolescent Development, 83*, 19–35.

Scardamalia, M., & Bereiter, C. (1994). Computer support for knowledge-building communities. *The Journal of the Learning Sciences, 3*(3), 265–283.

Scardamalia, M., & Bereiter, C. (1998). *Web knowledge forum: User guide*. Santa Cruz, CA: Learning in Motion.

Scardamalia, M., & Bereiter, C. (1999). Schools as knowledge-building organizations. In D. Keating & C. Hertzman (Eds.), *Today's children tomorrow's society: The developmental health and wealth of nations* (pp. 274–289). New York: Guildford.

Scardamalia, M., & Bereiter, C. (2006). Knowledge building: Theory, pedagogy, and technology. In K. Sawyer (Ed.), *Cambridge handbook of the learning sciences* (pp. 97–118). New York: Cambridge University Press.

Scardamalia, M., Bereiter, C., Hewitt, J., & Webb, J. (1996). Constructive learning from texts in biology. In K. M. Fischer & M. Kirby (Eds.), *Relations and biology learning: The acquisition and use of knowledge structures in biology* (pp. 44–64). Berlin: Springer-Verlag.

Schank, P., & Kozma, R. (2002). Learning chemistry through the use of a representation-based knowledge building environment. *Journal of Computers in Mathematics and Science Teaching, 21*(3), 253–279.

Schank, R. C. (1982). *Dynamic memory*. Cambridge: Cambridge University Press.

Schank, R. C. (1999). *Dynamic memory revisited* (2nd ed.). Cambridge, MA: Cambridge University Press.

Schaps, E. (2003). Creating a school community. *Creating Caring Schools, 60*(6), 31–33.

Schaps, E., Battistich, V., & Solomon, D. (2004). Community in school as key to student growth: Findings from the child development project. In J. Zins, R. Weissberg, M. Wang & H. Walberg (Eds.), *Building academic success on social and emotional learning: What does the research say?* (pp. 189–205). New York: Teachers College Press.

Schauble, L., & Glaser, R. (Eds.). (1996). *Innovations in learning: New environments for education*. Hillsdale, NJ: Lawrence Erlbaum Associates.

Schmidt, W. H., McKnight, C. C., Houang, R. T., Wang, H., Wiley, D. E., Cogan, L. S., et al. (Eds.). (2001). *Why schools matter: A cross-national comparison of curriculum and learning*. San Francisco, CA: Jossey-Bass.

Schmidt, W. H., McKnight, C. C., & Raizen, S. A. (1996). *A splintered vision: An investigation of U.S. science and mathematics education*: U.S. National Research Center for the Third International Mathematics Science Study, Michigan State University.

Schmidt, W. H., Raizen, S. A., Britton, E. D., Bianchi, L. J., & Wolfe, R. G. (1997). *Many visions, many aims: A cross-national investigation of curricular intentions in school science*. Boston: Kluwer Academic Publishers.

Schneider, R. M., Krajcik, J., & Blumenfeld, P. (2005). Enacting reform-based science materials: The range of teacher enactments in reform classrooms. *Journal of Research in Science Teaching, 42*(3), 283–312.

Schneps, M. H., & Sadler, P. M. (1989). *A private universe*. Cambridge, MA: Harvard-Smithsonian Center for Astrophysics.

Schofield, J. W. (1995). *Computers and classroom culture*. New York: Cambridge University Press.

Schon, D. (1983). *The reflective practitioner: How professionals think in action.* New York: Basic Books.

Seethaler, S., & Linn, M. C. (2004). Genetically modified food in perspective: An inquiry-based curriculum to help middle school students make sense of tradeoffs. *International Journal of Science Education, 26*(14), 1765–1785.

Shakhashiri, B. Z. (1985). *Chemical demonstrations* (Vol. 2). Madison, WI: University of Wisconsin Press.

Shear, L., Bell, P., & Linn, M. (2004). Partnership models: The case of the deformed frogs. In M. C. Linn, E. A. Davis & P. Bell (Eds.), *Internet environments for science education* (pp. 289–314). Mahwah, NJ: Lawrence Erlbaum Associates.

Shen, J., & Linn, M. C. (in press). A Technology-enhanced unit of modeling static electricity: Integrating scientific explanations and everyday observations. *International Journal of Science Education.*

Shepard, L. A. (2000). The role of assessment in a learning culture. *Educational Researcher, 29*(7), 4–14.

Sherin, B., Reiser, B. J., & Edelson, D. C. (2004). Scaffolding analysis: Extending the scaffolding metaphor to learning artifacts. *The Journal of the Learning Sciences, 13*(3), 387–421.

Siegler, R. S. (2000). The rebirth of children's learning. *Child Development, 71*(1), 26–35.

Simon, B., Anderson, R., Hoyer, C., & Su, J. (2004). Preliminary experiences with a tablet PC based system to support active learning in computer science courses. In *Proceedings of the 9th annual SIGCSE conference on innovation and technology in computer science education.* Leeds, United Kingdom: Association for Computing Machinery (ACM).

Sinapuelas, M. (2010). *Performance predictors: A study of introductory chemistry students' circumstances and their influence on students' study strategies and performance.* Unpublished Dissertation Proposal, University of California, Berkeley.

Singer, S. R., Hilton, M. L., & Schweingruber, H. A. (Eds.). (2005). *America's lab report: Investigations in high school science.* Washington, DC: The National Academies Press.

Sisk-Hilton, S. (2009). *Teaching and learning in public: Professional development through shared inquiry.* Columbia, NY: Teachers College Press.

Skamp, K. (1999). Are atoms and molecules too difficult for primary children? *School Science Review, 81*, 87–96.

Skoog, G. (1979). Topic of evolution in secondary school biology textbooks: 1900–1977. *Science Education, 63*(5), 621–640.

Skoog, G. (2005). The emphasis on human evolution in the high school biology textbooks of the 20th century and the current state science standards. *Science and Education, 14*(3–5), 395–422.

Slator, B. M. (2006). *Electric worlds in the classroom: Teaching and learning with role-based computer games.* New York: Teachers College Press.

Slavin, R. E. (1990). *Cooperative learning: Theory, research, and practice.* Englewood Cliffs, NJ: Prentice Hall.

Slotta, J., & Aleahmad, T. (2002). Integrating handheld technology and web-based science activities. In P. Barker & S. Rebelsky (Eds.), *Proceedings of world conference on educational multimedia, hypermedia and telecommunications 2002* (Vol. 1, pp. 25–30). Chesapeake, VA: AACE.

Slotta, J. D. (2004). The web-based inquiry science environment (WISE): Scaffolding knowledge integration in the science classroom. In M. C. Linn, E. A. Davis & P. Bell (Eds.), *Internet environments for science education* (pp. 203–232). Mahwah, NJ: Lawrence Erlbaum Associates.

Slotta, J. D., & Chi, M. T. H. (2006). Helping students understand challenging topics in science through ontology training. *Cognition and Instruction, 24*(2), 261–289.

Slotta, J. D., Chi, M. T. H., & Joram, E. (1995). Assessing the ontological nature of conceptual physics: A contrast of experts and novices. *Cognition and Instruction, 13*(3), 373–400.

Slotta, J. D., & Linn, M. C. (2000). The knowledge integration environment: Helping students use the internet effectively. In M. J. Jacobson & R. B. Kozma (Eds.), *Innovations in science and mathematics education: advanced designs for technologies of learning* (pp. 193–226). Mahwah, NJ: Lawrence Erlbaum Associates.

Slotta, J. D., & Linn, M. C. (2009). *WISE science: Web-based inquiry in the classroom.* New York: Teachers College Press.

Smith, J. P., III, diSessa, A. A., & Roschelle, J. (1993). Misconceptions reconceived: A constructivist analysis of knowlege in transition. *Journal of the Learning Sciences, 3*(2), 115–163.

Snyder, L., Aho, A. V., Linn, M. C., Packer, A., Tucker, A., Ullman, J., et al. (1999). *Be FIT! Being fluent with information technology.* Washington, D.C.: The National Academies Press.

Sokoloff, D. R., & Thornton, R. K. (2004). *Interactive lecture demonstrations in introductory physics.* New York: John Wiley and Sons.

Soloway, E., Guzdial, M., & Hay, K. E. (1994). Learner-centered design: The challenge for HCI in the 21st century. *ACM Interactions, 1*(2), 36–48.

Songer, N., Lee, H. S., & McDonald, S. (2003). Research towards an expanded understanding of inquiry science beyond one idealized standard. *Science Education, 87*(4), 490–516.

Songer, N. B. (1996). Exploring learning opportunities in coordinated network-enhanced classrooms—A case of kids as global scientists. *Journal of the Learning Sciences, 5*(4), 297–327.

Songer, N. B., Lee, H. S., & Kam, R. (2002). Technology-rich inquiry science in urban classrooms: What are the barriers to inquiry pedagogy? *Journal of Research in Science Teaching, 39*(2), 128–150.

Songer, N. B., & Linn, M. C. (1991). How do students' views of science influence knowledge integration? *Journal of Research in Science Teaching, 28*(9), 761–784.

Sorby, S. A. (2009). Educational research in developing 3–D spatial skills for engineering students. *International Journal of Science Education, 31*(3), 459–480.

Spitulnik, M. W., & Linn, M. C. (2007). *Professional development and teachers' curriculum customizations: Supporting science in diverse middle schools* (MODELS Report). University of California, Berkeley.

Sprott, J. C. (1991). Physics to the people. *The Physics Teacher, 29,* 212–213.

Steinkuehler, C. (2008). Massively multiplayer online games as an educational technology: An outline for research. *Educational Technology Magazine: The Magazine for Managers of Change in Education, 48*(1), 10–21.

Stern, J. L., & Kirkpatrick, D. H. (1991). Computer as lab partner project. *Chemunications Newsletter, VI 1*(2), 1, 14–15.

Stern, L., & Roseman, J. (2004). Can middle school science textbooks help students learn important ideas? *Journal of Research in Science Teaching, 41*(6), 538–568.

Stieff, M. (2005). Connected chemistry: A novel modeling environment for the chemistry classroom. *Journal of Chemical Education, 82*(489–493).

Stigler, J. W., Gonzales, P., Kawanaka, T., Knoll, S., & Serrano, A. (1999). *The TIMSS videotape classroom study: Methods and findings from an exploratory research project on eighth-grade mathematics instruction in Germany, Japan, and the United States (NCES 1999–074).* Washington, DC: National Center for Education Statistics.

Stipek, D., Salmon, J. M., Givvin, K. B., Kazemi, E., Saxe, G., & MacGyvers, V. L. (1998). The value (and convergence) of practices suggested by motivation research and promoted by mathematics education reformers. *Journal for Research in Mathematics Education, 29*(4), 465–488.

Strauss, S. (2005). Teaching as a natural cognitive ability: Implications for classroom practice and teacher education. In D. B. Pillemer & S. H. White (Eds.), *Developmental psychology and social change: Research, history, and policy* (pp. 368–388). Cambridge, UK: Cambridge University Press.

Strike, K. A., & Posner, G. J. (1985). A conceptual change view of learning and understanding. In L. H. West & A. L. Pines (Eds.), *Cognitive structure and conceptual change* (pp. 211–231). Orlando, FL: Academic Press.

Supovitz, J. A., Mayer, D. P., & Kahle, J. B. (2000). Promoting inquiry-based instructional practice: The longitudinal impact of professional development in the context of systemic reform. *Educational Policy, 14*(3), 331–356.

Supovitz, J. A., & Turner, H. M. (2000). The effects of professional development on science teaching practices and classroom culture. *Journal of Research in Science Teaching, 37*(9), 963–980.

Suthers, D. D., & Hundhausen, C. D. (2001). Learning by constructing collaborative representations: An empirical comparison of three alternatives. In P. Dillenbourg, A. Eurelings & K. Hakkarainen (Eds.), *European perspectives on computer-supported collaborative learning, procedings of the first European conference on computer-supported collaborative learning* (pp. 577–584). Maastrict, The Netherlands: Universiteit Maastricht.

Svihla, V., Ryoo, K., Sato, E., Swanson, H., & Linn, M. C. (2010). Measuring cumulative learning across disciplines. In *Proceedings of the Ninth International Conference of the Learning Sciences* (pp. 252–259). Chicago, IL: International Society of the Learning Sciences.

Tabak, I. (2004). Synergy: A complement to emerging patterns of distributed scaffolding. *Journal of the Learning Sciences, 13*(3), 305–335.

Tabak, I., & Reiser, B. J. (1997). Complementary roles of software-based scaffolding and teacher-student interactions in inquiry learning. In R. Hall, N. Miyake & N. Enyedy (Eds.), *Proceedings of Computer Support for Collaborative Learning '97* (pp. 289–298). Toronto, Canada.

Tabak, I., & Reiser, B. J. (2008). Software-realized inquiry support for cultivating a disciplinary stance. *Pragmatics & Cognition, 16*(2), 307–355.

Tai, R. H., Liu, C. Q., Maltese, A. V., & Fan, X. (2006). Planning early for careers in science. *Science, 312*(5777), 1143–1144.

Tal, T., Krajcik, J. S., & Blumenfeld, P. (2006). Urban schools teachers enacting project-based science. *Journal of Research in Science Teaching, 43*(7), 722–745.

Tarbuck, E. J., & Lutgens, F. K. (2008). *Earth science* (12th ed.). New Jersey: Prentice Hall.

Tate, E. D. (2009). *Asthma in the community: Designing instruction to help students explore scientific dilemmas that impact their lives.* Unpublished Doctoral Dissertation, University of California, Berkeley.

Taylor, R. (Ed.). (1980). *The computer in the school: Tutor, tool, tutee.* New York: Teachers College Press.

Teasley, S. D. (1997). Talking about reasoning: How important is the peer in peer collaborations? In L. B. Resnick, R. Saljo, C. Pontecorvo & B. Burge (Eds.), *Discourse, tools, and reasoning: Situated cognition and technologically supported environments* (pp. 361–384). Berlin: Springer-Verlag.

Thagard, P. (1992). *Conceptual revolutions.* Princeton, NJ: Princeton University Press.

Thagard, P. (2000). *Coherence in thought and action.* Cambridge, MA: The MIT Press.

The Woodrow Wilson National Fellowship Foundation. (2007). http://www.woodrow. org/teachers/ci/faraday/lect1.html. Retrieved September 10, 2010

Thornton, R. K., & Sokoloff, D. R. (1998). Assessing student learning of Newton's laws: The force and motion conceptual evaluation. *American Journal of Physics, 66*(4), 228–351.

Tinker, R. (2008). Forward. In Y. Kali, J. E. Roseman, & M. C. Linn (Eds.), *Designing coherent science education* (pp. vii–x). New York: Teachers College Press.

Tinker, R., & Staudt, C. (2009). The greenhouse effect @ Concord (pp. 12–13). Concord, MA: Concard Consortium.

Tinker, R., & Xie, Q. (2008). Applying computational science to education: The Molecular Workbench paradigm. *Computing in Science and Engineering, 10*(5), 24–27.

Titterton, N., Lewis, C. M., & Clancy, M. J. (2010). Experiences with lab-centric instruction. *Computer Science Education, 20*(2), 79–102.

Topping, K. J. (2003). Self and peer assessment in school and university: Reliability, validity and utility. In *Optimising new modes of assessment: In search of qualities and standards* (Vol. 1, pp. 55–87), Dordrecht: Kluwer Academic Publishers.

Topping, K. J. (2005). Trends in peer learning. *Educational Psychology: An International Journal of Experimental Educational Psychology, 25*(6), 631–645.

Toulmin, S. (1961). *Foresight and understanding.* Indianapolis, IN: Indiana University Press.

Triona, L. M., & Klahr, D. (2003). Point and click or grab and heft: Comparing the influence of physical and virtual instruction materials on elementary school students' ability to design experiments. *Cognition and Instruction, 21*(2), 149–173.

Tufte, E. R. (2001). *The visual display of quantitative information* (2nd ed.). Chelshire, CT: Graphics Press.

Tversky, B., Morrison, J. B., & Betrancourt, M. (2002). Animation: Can it facilitate? *International Journal of Human-Computer Studies, 57*(4), 247–262.

Tweney, R. D. (1991). Faraday's notebooks: The active organization of creative science. *Physics Education, 26*, 301–306.

Tyson, H. (1997). *Overcoming structural barriers to good textbooks.* Washington, DC: National Education Goals Panel.

Tyson-Bernstein, H., & Woodward, A. (1991). Nineteenth century policies for twenty-first century practice: The textbook reform dilemma. In P. G. Altbach, G. P. Kelly, H. G. Petrie & L. Weis (Eds.), *Textbooks in American society* (pp. 91–104). New York: State University of New York Press.

University of Maryland Physics Education Research Group. (Fall 2002). 'Class discussion: the president-for-life of mistake-avoidance strategies,' available online at: http://www. physics.umd.edu/perg/ILD/ILD_01_Motion_Graphs.pdf.

Van Dijk, L. A., Van Der Berg, G. C., & Van Keulen, H. (2001). Interactive lectures in engineering education. *European Journal of Engineering Education, 26*(1), 15–28.

van Driel, J. H., & Verloop, N. (2002). Experienced teachers' knowledge of teaching and learning of models and modelling in science education *International Journal of Science Education, 24*(12), 1255–1272.

Van Heuvelen, A. (1991). Learning to think like a physicist: A review of research-based instructional strategies. *American Journal of Physics, 59*(10), 891–897.

van Zee, E. H., Iwasyk, M., Kurose, A., Simpson, D., & Wild, J. (2001). Student and teacher questioning during conversations about science. *Journal of Research in Science Teaching, 38*(2), 159–190.

van Zee, E. H., & Minstrell, J. (1997). Reflective discourse: developing shared understandings in a physics classroom. *International Journal of Science Education, 19*(2), 209–228.

VanLehn, K. (2006). The behavior of tutoring systems. *International Journal of Artificial Intelligence in Education, 16*(3), 227–265.

VanLehn, K., Graesser, A. C., Jackson, G. T., Jordan, P., Olney, A., & Rose, C. P. (2007). When are tutorial dialogues more effective than reading? *Cognitive Science, 31*(1), 3–62.

VanLehn, K., Lynch, C., Schulze, K., Shapiro, J. A., Shelby, R., Taylor, L., et al. (2005). The Andes physics tutoring system: Five years of evaluations. In G. McCalla, C. K. Looi, B. Bredeweg & J. Breuker (Eds.), *Artificial intelligence in education* (pp. 678–685). Amsterdam, Netherlands: IOS Press.

Varma, K., & Linn, M. C. (in press). Using interactive technology to support students' understanding of the greenhouse effect and global warming. *Journal of Science Education and Technology.*

Varma, K., Husic, F., & Linn, M. C. (2008). Targeted support for using technology-enhanced science inquiry modules. *Journal of Science Education and Technology, 17*(4), 341–356.

Varma, K., Gerard, L., Liu, O. L., Corliss, S., & Linn, M. C. (2011). *Comparison of two professional development programs on student learning.* Paper to be presented at the 2011 annual meeting of the American Educational Research Association, New Orleans, Louisiana.

Vos, P., & Kuiper, W. (2005). Trends (1995–2000) in the TIMSS mathematics performance assessment in the Netherlands. *Educational Research and Evaluation, 11*(2), 141–154.

Vosniadou, S., (Ed.) (2008). *International handbook of research on conceptual change.* New York, Routledge.

Vygotsky, L. S. (1978). *Mind in society: The development of higher psychological processes.* Cambridge, MA: Harvard University Press.

Watson, M., & Ecken, L. (2003). *Learning to trust: Transforming difficult elementary classrooms through developmental discipline.* San Francisco, CA: Jossey-Bass.

Webb, N. M., & Farivar, S. (1999). Developing productive group interaction in middle-school mathematics. In A. M. O'Donnell, & A. King (Eds.), *Cognitive perspectives on peer learning.* (pp. 117–149). Hillside, NJ: Erlbaum.

Webb, N. M., & Farivar, S. (1994). Promoting helping behavior in cooperative small groups in middle school mathematics. *American Educational Research Journal, 31*, 369–395.

Webb, N. M., & Palincsar, A. M. (1996). Group processes in the classroom. In D. C. Berliner & R. C. Calfee (Eds.), *Handbook of educational psychology* (pp. 841–873). New York: Macmillan Library Reference USA.

Weinberger, A., Stegmann, K., & Fischer, F. (2007b). Knowledge convergence in collaborative learning: concepts and assessment. *Learning and Instruction, 17*(4), 416–426.

Weinberger, A., Clark, D., Häkkinen, P., Tamura, Y., & Fischer, F. (2007a). Argumentative knowledge construction in online learning environments in and across different cultures: A collaboration script perspective. *Research in Comparative and International Education, 2*(1), 68–79.

Weizmann Institute of Science. (2009). MATMON curriculum. Retrieved January 1, 2010, from http://stwww.weizmann.ac.il/menu/groups/index.html

Wells, L. B. (2010). *Designing teacher practices to capitalize on online science assessments.* Unpublished Master's thesis, submitted in partial fulfillment of Master's of Arts degree in Education, University of California, Berkeley.

Wertsch, J. V. (1985). *Vygotsky and the social formation of mind.* Cambridge: Harvard University Press.

White, B. Y., & Frederiksen, J. R. (1990). Causal model progressions as a foundation for intelligent learning environments. *Artificial Intelligence 42*, 99–157.

White, B. Y., & Frederiksen, J. R. (1998). Inquiry, modeling, and metacognition: Making science accessible to all students. *Cognition and Instruction, 16*(1), 3–118.

White, B. Y., & Frederiksen, J. R. (2000). Technological tools and instructional approaches for making scientific inquiry accessible to all. In M. J. Jacobson & R. B. Kozma (Eds.), *Innovations in science and mathematics education* (pp. 321–359). Mahwah, NJ: Lawrence Erlbaum Associates.

White, B. Y., Shimoda, T. A., & Frederiksen, J. R. (1999). Enabling students to construct theories of collaborative inquiry and reflective learning: Computer support for metacognitive development. *The International Journal of Artificial Intelligence in Education, 10*(2), 1–33.

White, R., & Gunstone, R. (1992). *Probing understanding.* New York: The Falmer Press.

Wieman, C. E., Adams, W. K., & Perkins, K. K. (2008). PhET: Simulations that enhance Learning. *Science, 322*(5902), 682–683.

Wilensky, U., & Rand, W. (in press). *An introduction to agent-based modeling: Modeling natural, social and engineered complex systems with NetLogo.* Cambridge, MA: MIT Press.

Williams, M. (2008). Moving technology to the center of instruction: How one experienced teacher incorporates a web-based environment over time. *Journal of Science Education and Technology, 17*(4), 316–333.

Williams, M., Linn, M. C., Ammon, P., & Gearhart, M. (2004). Learning to teach inquiry science in a technology-based environment: A case study. *Journal of Science Education and Technology, 13*(2), 189–206.

Wilson, C., Taylor, J., Kowalski, S., & Carlson, J. (2010). The relative effects of inquiry-based and commonplace science teaching on students' knowledge, reasoning and argumentation: A randomized control trial. *Journal of Research in Science Teaching, 47*(3), 276–301.

Winerip, M. (2010, July 18). A popular principal, wounded by government's good intentions [Electronic version]. *The New York Times.* Retrieved September 10, 2010 from http://www.nytimes.com/2010/07/19/education/19winerip.html.

WISE (1998). wise.berkeley.edu. Retrieved February 10, 2010

Wiser, M., & Carey, S. (1983). When heat and temperature were one. In D. Gentner & A. L. Stevens (Eds.), *Mental models* (pp. 267–298). Hillsdale, NJ: Lawrence Erlbaum Associates.

Xie, Q., & Tinker, R. (2006). Molecular dynamics simulations of chemical reactions for use in education. *Journal of Chemical Education, 83*(1), 77–83.

Yacoubian, H. A., & BouJaoude, S. (2010). The effect of reflective discussions following inquiry-based laboratory activities on students' views of nature of science. *Journal of Research in Science Teaching, 47*(10), 1229–1250.

Yang, E.-M., Andre, T., & Greenbowe, T. J. (2003). Spatial ability and the impact of visualization/animation on learning electrochemistry. *International Journal of Science Education, 25*(3), 329–349.

Yarnall, L., Shechtman, N., & Penuel, W. R. (2006). Using handheld computers to support improved classroom assessment in science: Results from a field trial. *Journal of Science Education and Technology, 15*(2), 142–155.

Yayon, M., Margel, H., & Scherz, Z. (2001). *From elements to complex structure.* Rehovot, Israel: Weizmann Institute of Science.

Yayon, M., & Scherz, Z. (2008). The return of the black box. *Journal of Chemical Education, 85,* 541–543.

Zhang, Z. (2010, March 22). *Promote learning with dynamic visualizations: Drawing and selection.* Paper presented at the annual meeting of the National Association of Research in Science Teaching (NARST), Philadelphia, PA.

Zhang, Z., & Linn, M. C. (2008). Using drawings to support learning from dynamic visualizations. In *International perspectives in the learning sciences: Cre8ting a learning world. Proceedings of the 8th International Conference of the Learning Sciences* (Vol. 3, pp. 161–162). Utrecht, The Netherlands: International Society of the Learning Sciences, Inc.

Zhang, Z., & Linn, M. C. (2010). How can selection and drawing support learning from dynamic visualizations? In K. Gomez, L. Lyons & J. Radinsky (Eds.), *Learning in the disciplines. Proceedings of the 9th International Conference of the Learning Sciences* (Vol. 2, pg. 165–166). Chicago, IL: International Society of the Learning Sciences.

Zilag, Y., Orpaz, N., Ben-Zvi, N., Dory, E., Novick, S., Robinfeld, S., et al. (1980). *Chemistry and electricity.* Jerusalem, Israel: Ministry of Education.

Zohar, A. (2006). The nature and development of teachers' metastrategic knowledge in the context of teaching higher order thinking. *The Journal of Learning Sciences, 15*(3), 331–377.

Zohar, A., & Nemet, F. (2002). Fostering students' knowledge and argumentation skills through dilemmas in human genetics. *Journal of Research in Science Teaching, 39*(1), 35–62.

Zohar, A., & Peled, B. (2008). The effects of explicit teaching of metastrategic knowledge on low- and high-achieving students. *Learning and Instruction, 18*(4), 337–353.

Zucker, A. A. (2008). *Transforming schools with technology: How smart use of digital tools helps achieve six key education goals.* Cambridge, MA: Harvard Education Press.

INDEX